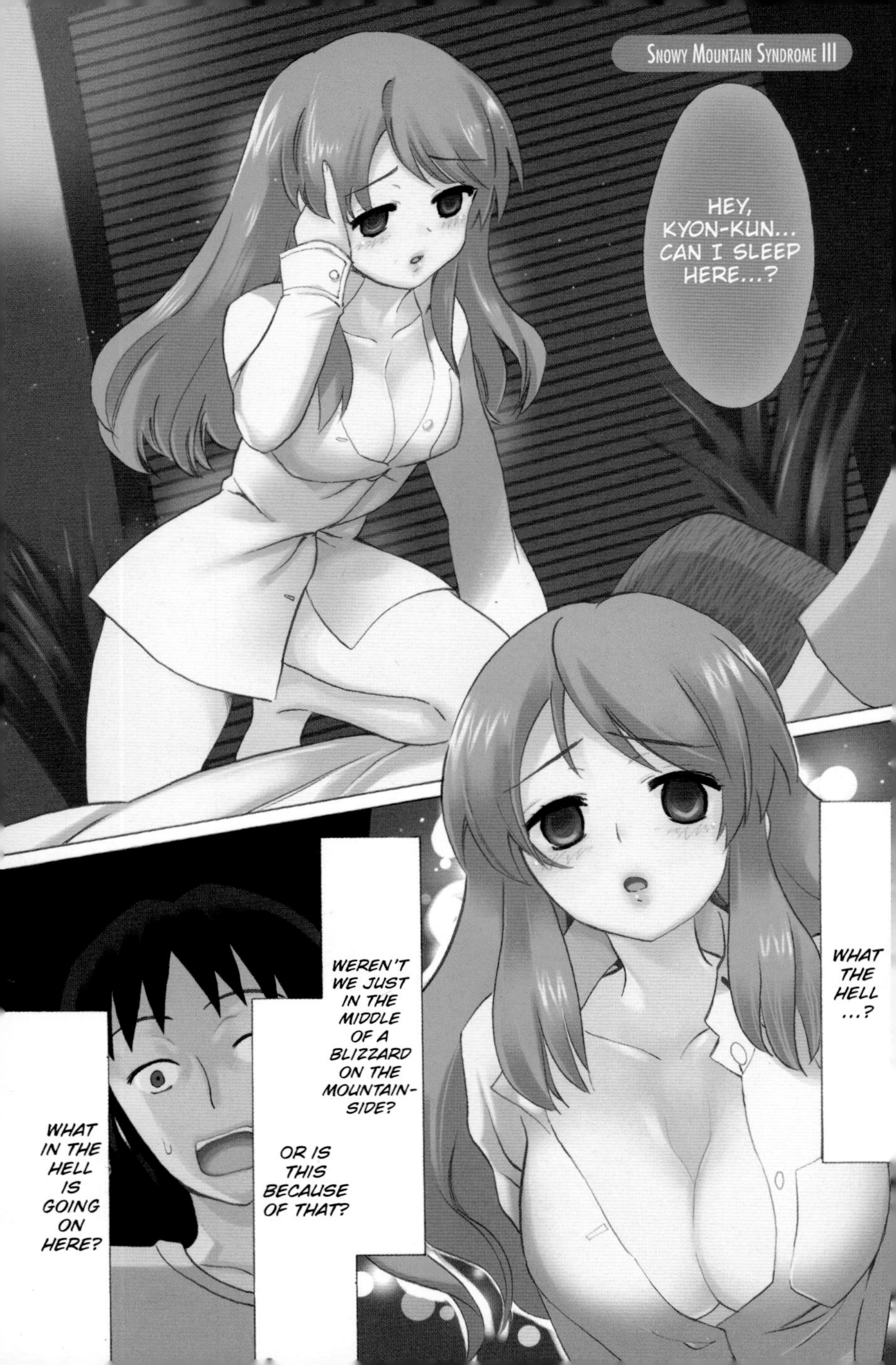
Snowy Mountain Syndrome III
Hey, Kyon-kun... can I sleep here...?
What the hell ...?
Weren't we just in the middle of a blizzard on the mountain-side?
Or is this because of that?
What in the hell is going on here?

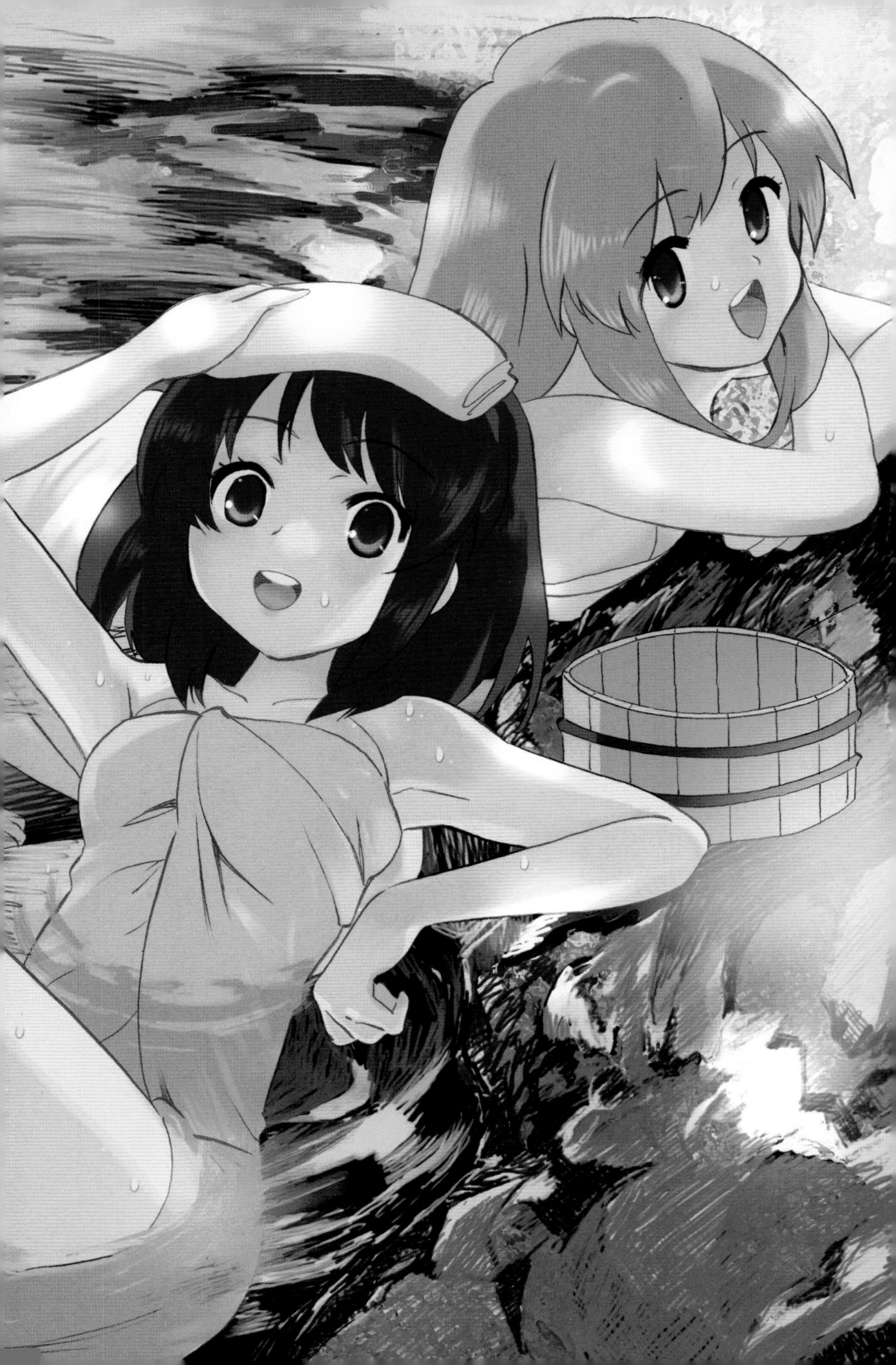

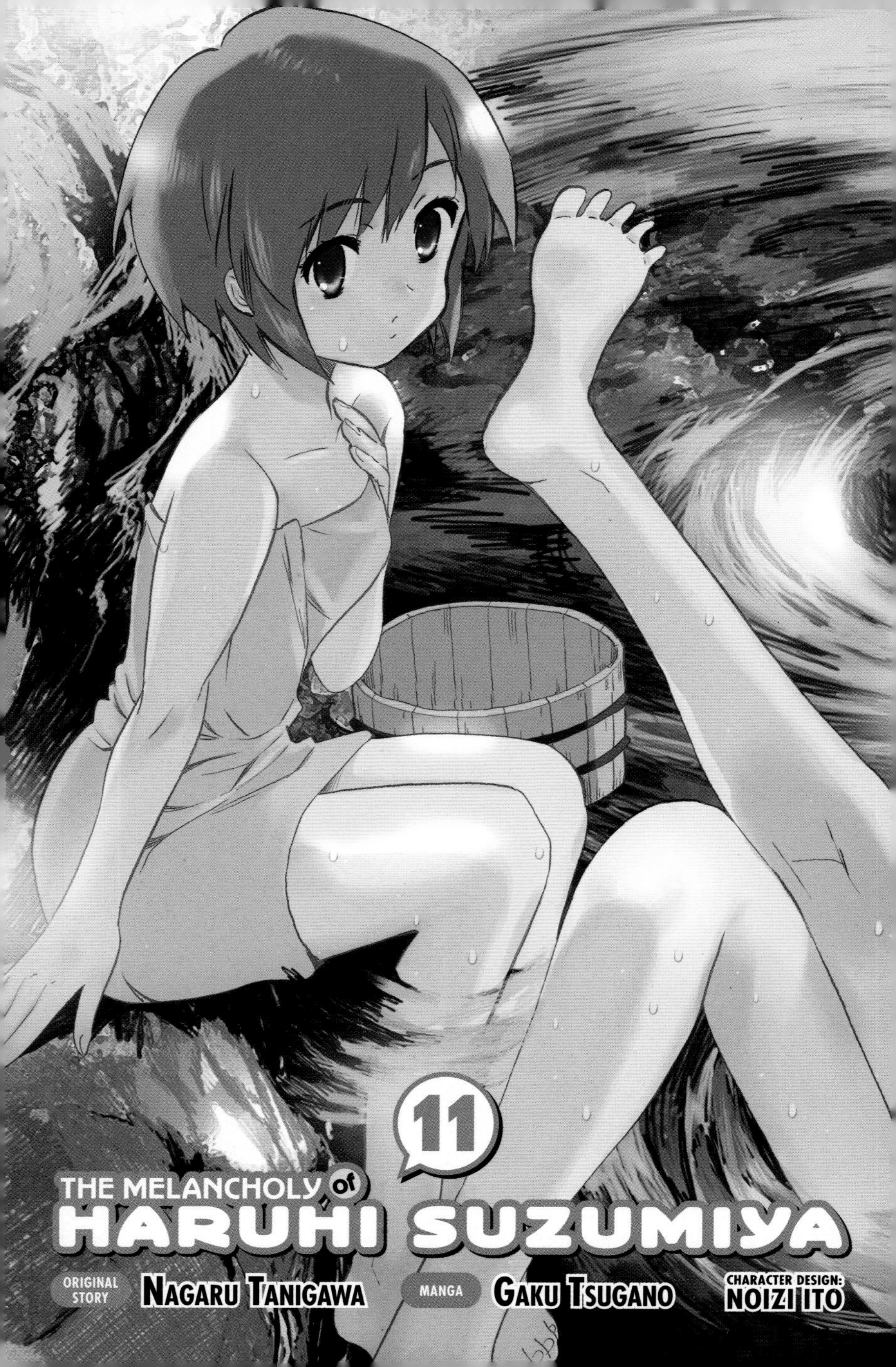
11
THE MELANCHOLY of
HARUHI SUZUMIYA
ORIGINAL STORY
NAGARU TANIGAWA
MANGA
GAKU TSUGANO
CHARACTER DESIGN:
NOIZI ITO

CONTENTS

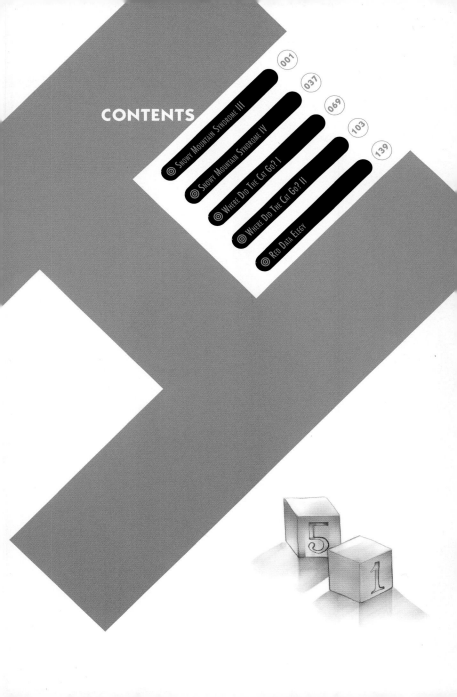

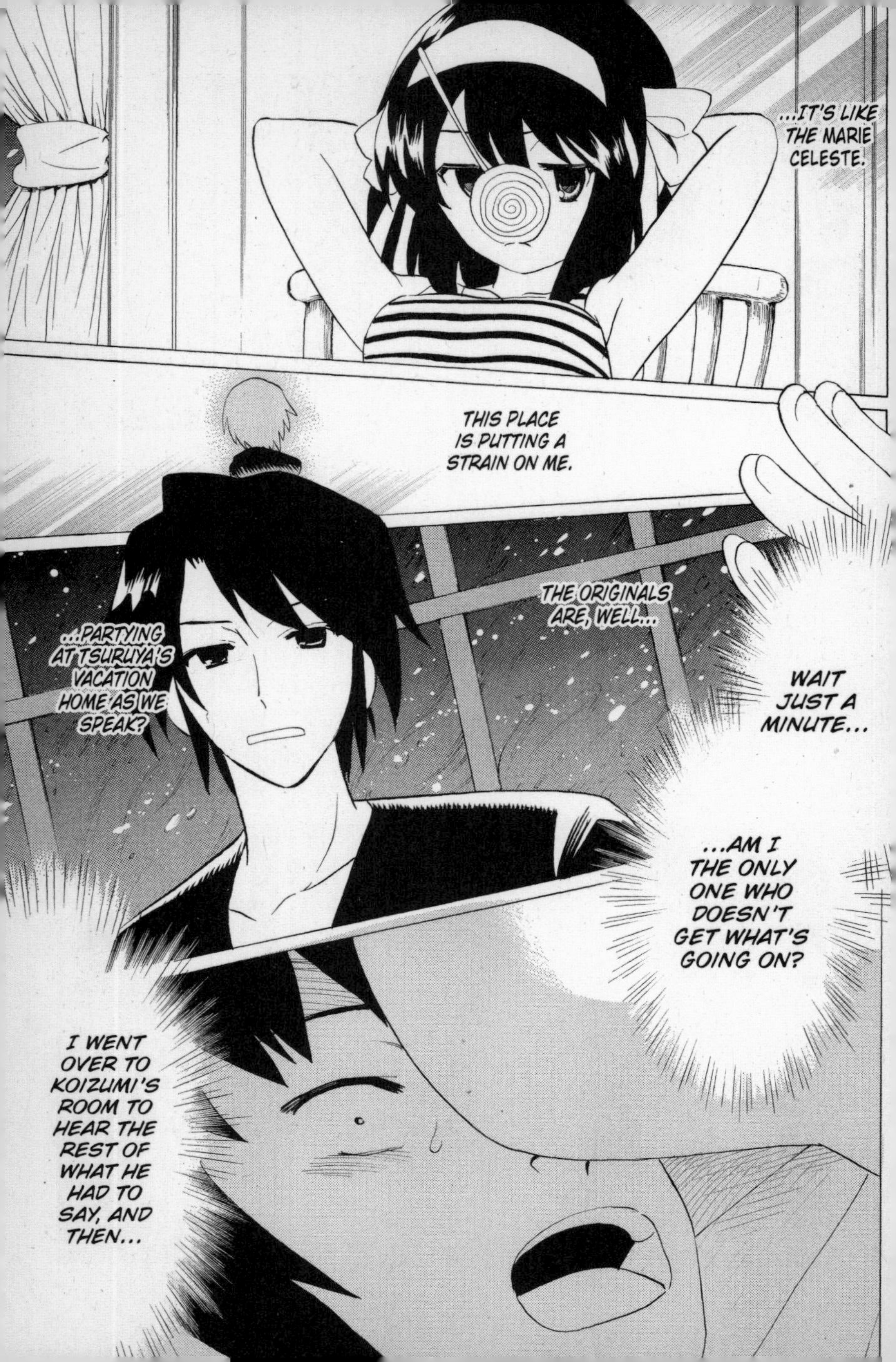
...IT'S LIKE THE MARIE CELESTE.
THIS PLACE IS PUTTING A STRAIN ON ME.
THE ORIGINALS ARE, WELL...
...PARTYING AT TSURUYA'S VACATION HOME AS WE SPEAK?
WAIT JUST A MINUTE...
...AM I THE ONLY ONE WHO DOESN'T GET WHAT'S GOING ON?
I WENT OVER TO KOIZUMI'S ROOM TO HEAR THE REST OF WHAT HE HAD TO SAY, AND THEN...

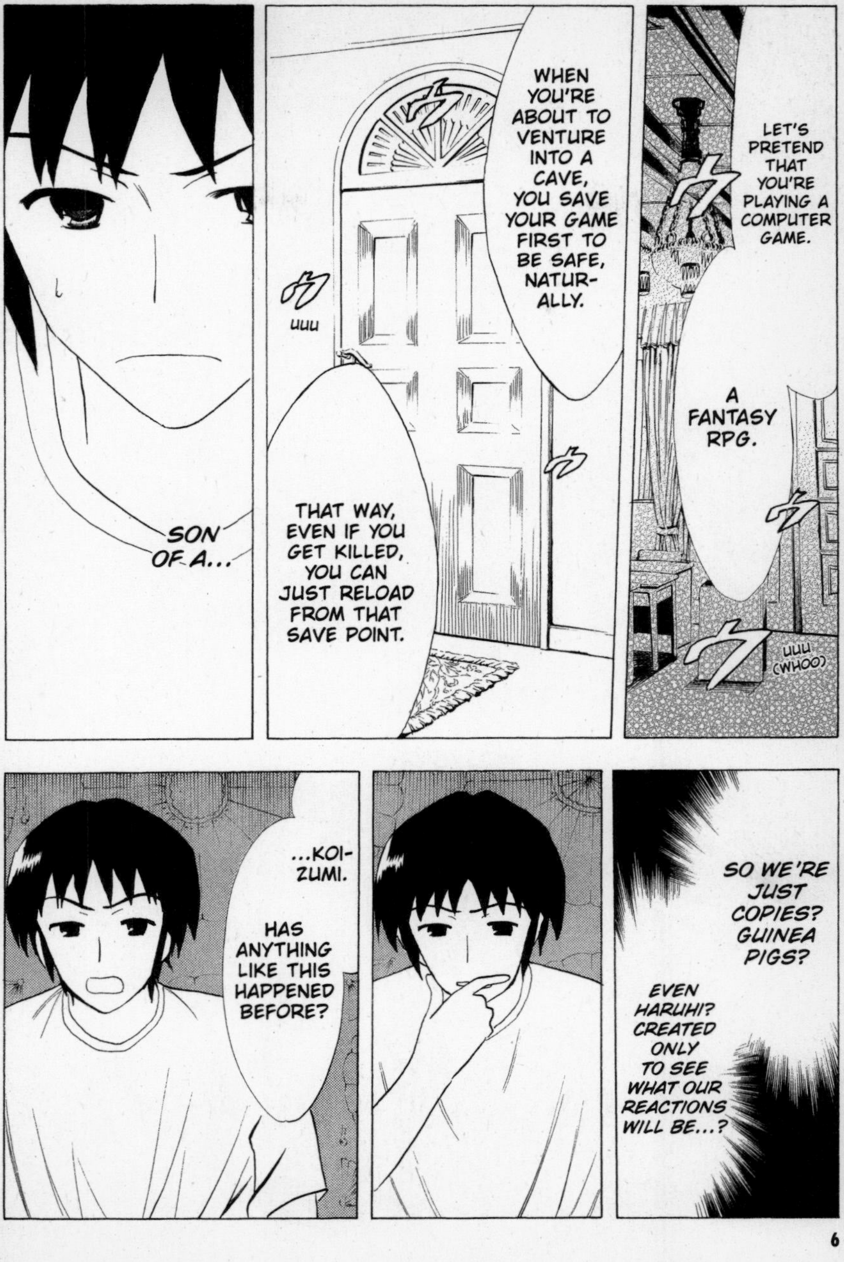
LET'S PRETEND THAT YOU'RE PLAYING A COMPUTER GAME.
A FANTASY RPG.
UUU (WHOO)
WHEN YOU'RE ABOUT TO VENTURE INTO A CAVE, YOU SAVE YOUR GAME FIRST TO BE SAFE, NATURALLY.
UUU
THAT WAY, EVEN IF YOU GET KILLED, YOU CAN JUST RELOAD FROM THAT SAVE POINT.
SON OF A...
SO WE'RE JUST COPIES? GUINEA PIGS?
EVEN HARUHI? CREATED ONLY TO SEE WHAT OUR REACTIONS WILL BE...?
...KOI-ZUMI.
HAS ANYTHING LIKE THIS HAPPENED BEFORE?

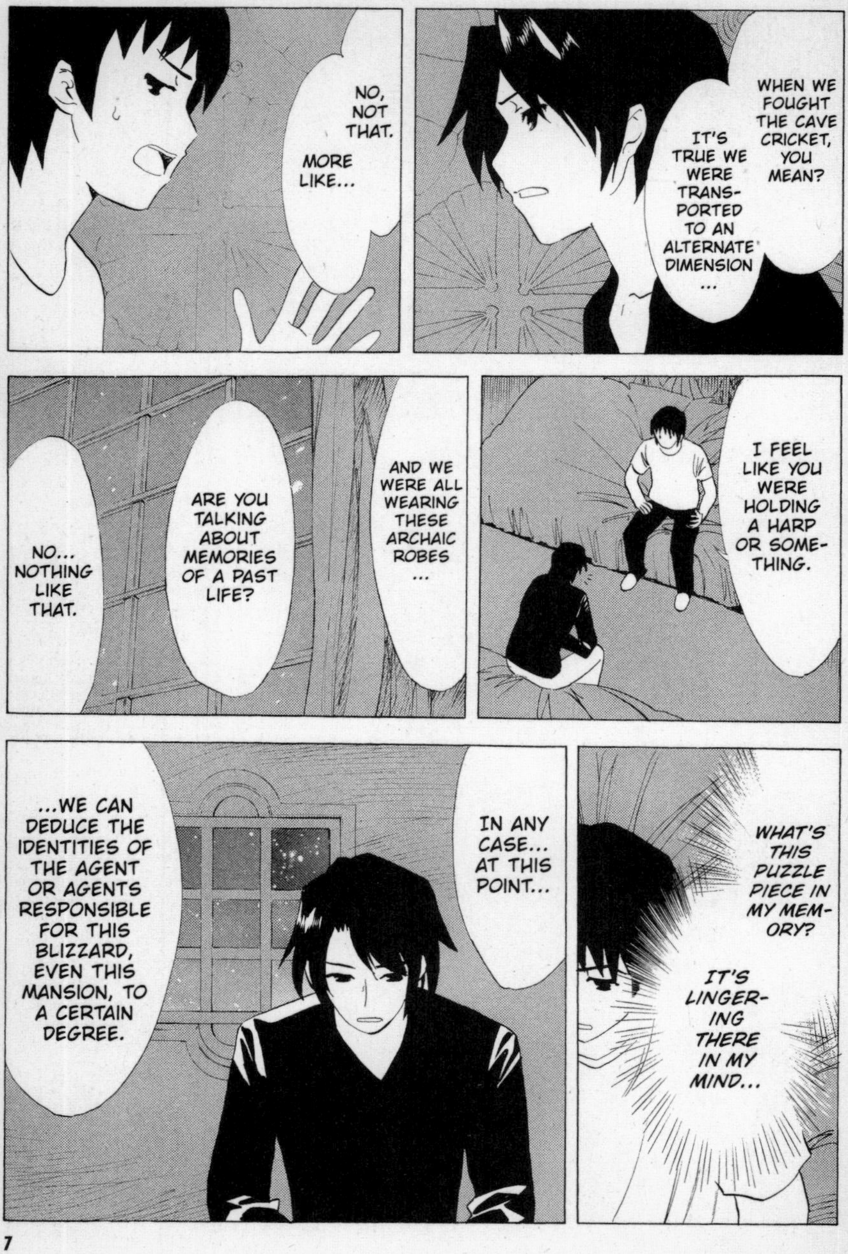
WHEN WE FOUGHT THE CAVE CRICKET, YOU MEAN?
IT'S TRUE WE WERE TRANS-PORTED TO AN ALTERNATE DIMENSION...
NO, NOT THAT.
MORE LIKE...
I FEEL LIKE YOU WERE HOLDING A HARP OR SOME-THING.
AND WE WERE ALL WEARING THESE ARCHAIC ROBES...
ARE YOU TALKING ABOUT MEMORIES OF A PAST LIFE?
NO... NOTHING LIKE THAT.
WHAT'S THIS PUZZLE PIECE IN MY MEM-ORY?
IT'S LINGER-ING THERE IN MY MIND...
IN ANY CASE... AT THIS POINT...
...WE CAN DEDUCE THE IDENTITIES OF THE AGENT OR AGENTS RESPONSIBLE FOR THIS BLIZZARD, EVEN THIS MANSION, TO A CERTAIN DEGREE.

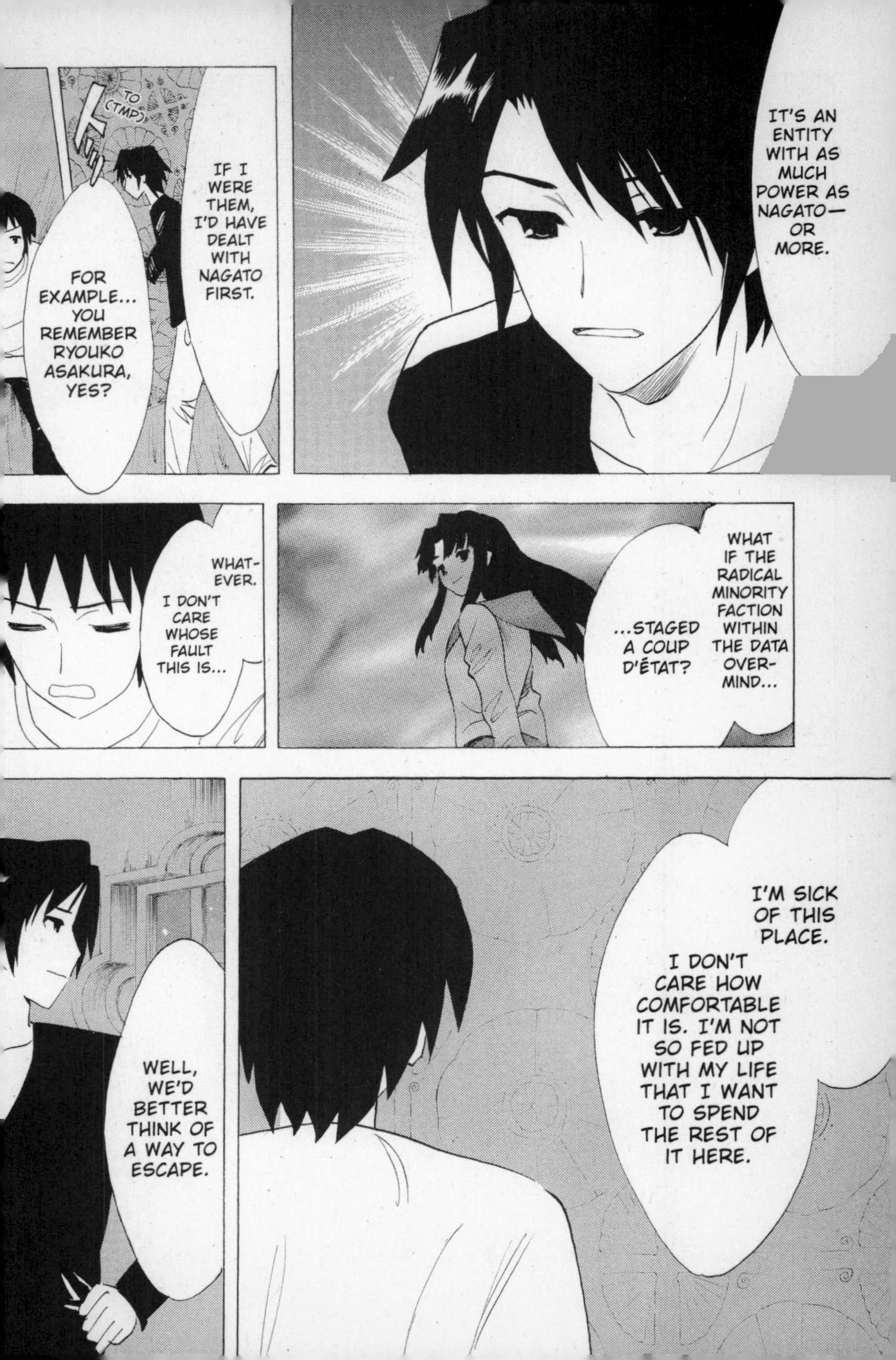
IT'S AN ENTITY WITH AS MUCH POWER AS NAGATO— OR MORE.
TO (TMP)
IF I WERE THEM, I'D HAVE DEALT WITH NAGATO FIRST.
FOR EXAMPLE... YOU REMEMBER RYOUKO ASAKURA, YES?
WHAT IF THE RADICAL MINORITY FACTION WITHIN THE DATA OVER-MIND...
...STAGED A COUP D'ÉTAT?
WHAT-EVER.
I DON'T CARE WHOSE FAULT THIS IS...
I'M SICK OF THIS PLACE.
I DON'T CARE HOW COMFORTABLE IT IS. I'M NOT SO FED UP WITH MY LIFE THAT I WANT TO SPEND THE REST OF IT HERE.
WELL, WE'D BETTER THINK OF A WAY TO ESCAPE.

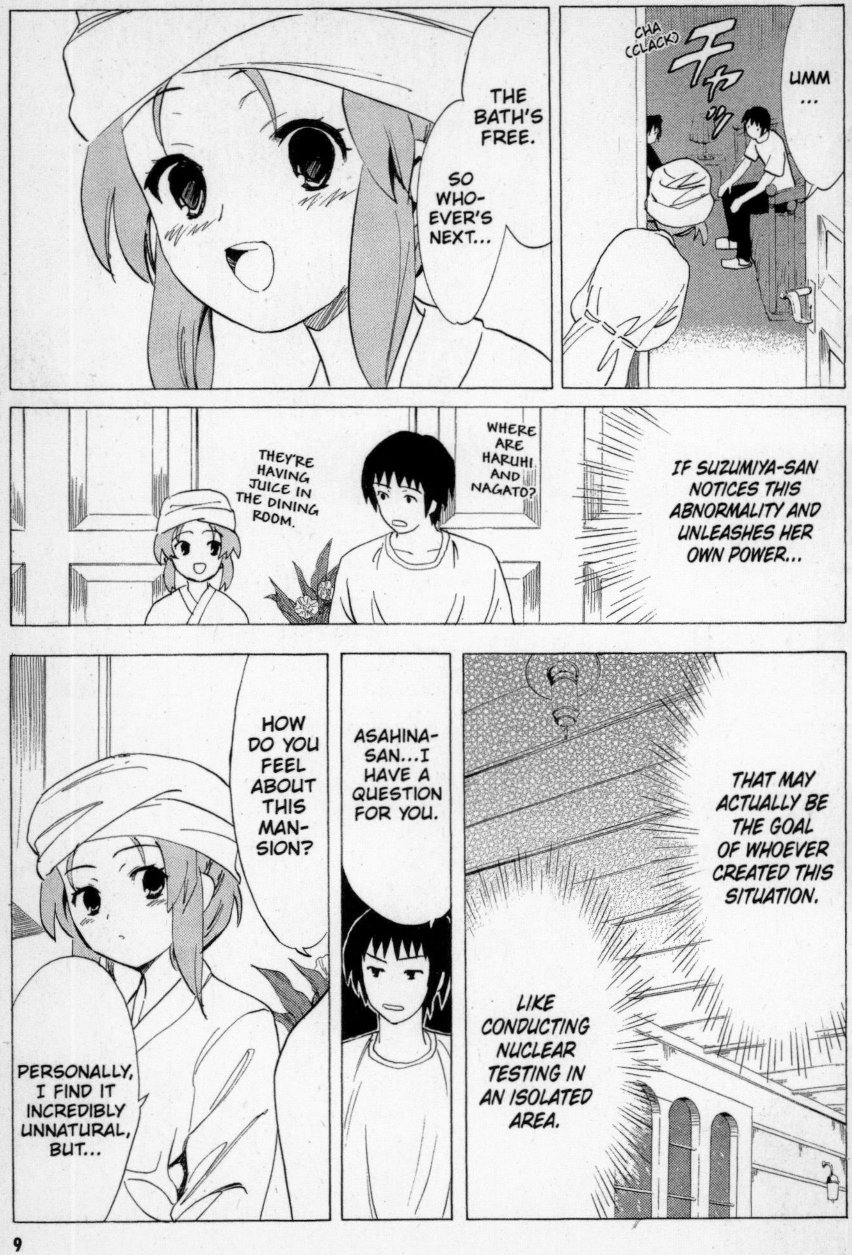
CHA (CLACK)
UMM...
THE BATH'S FREE.
SO WHO-EVER'S NEXT...
IF SUZUMIYA-SAN NOTICES THIS ABNORMALITY AND UNLEASHES HER OWN POWER...
WHERE ARE HARUHI AND NAGATO?
THEY'RE HAVING JUICE IN THE DINING ROOM.
THAT MAY ACTUALLY BE THE GOAL OF WHOEVER CREATED THIS SITUATION.
LIKE CONDUCTING NUCLEAR TESTING IN AN ISOLATED AREA.
ASAHINA-SAN...I HAVE A QUESTION FOR YOU.
HOW DO YOU FEEL ABOUT THIS MAN-SION?
PERSONALLY, I FIND IT INCREDIBLY UNNATURAL, BUT...

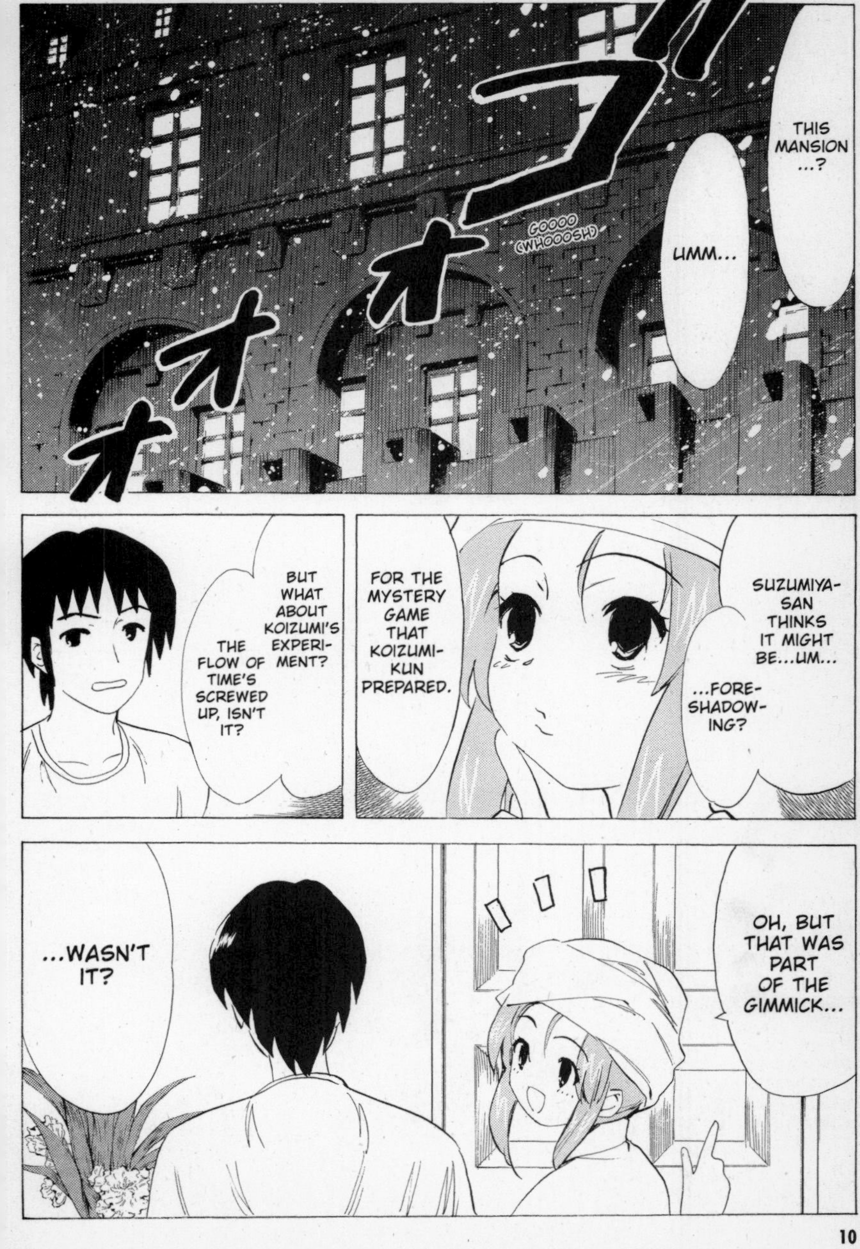
THIS MANSION ...?
UMM...
GOOOO (WHOOOSH)
SUZUMIYA-SAN THINKS IT MIGHT BE...UM...
...FORE-SHADOW-ING?
FOR THE MYSTERY GAME THAT KOIZUMI-KUN PREPARED.
BUT WHAT ABOUT KOIZUMI'S EXPERI-MENT?
THE FLOW OF TIME'S SCREWED UP, ISN'T IT?
OH, BUT THAT WAS PART OF THE GIMMICK...
...WASN'T IT?

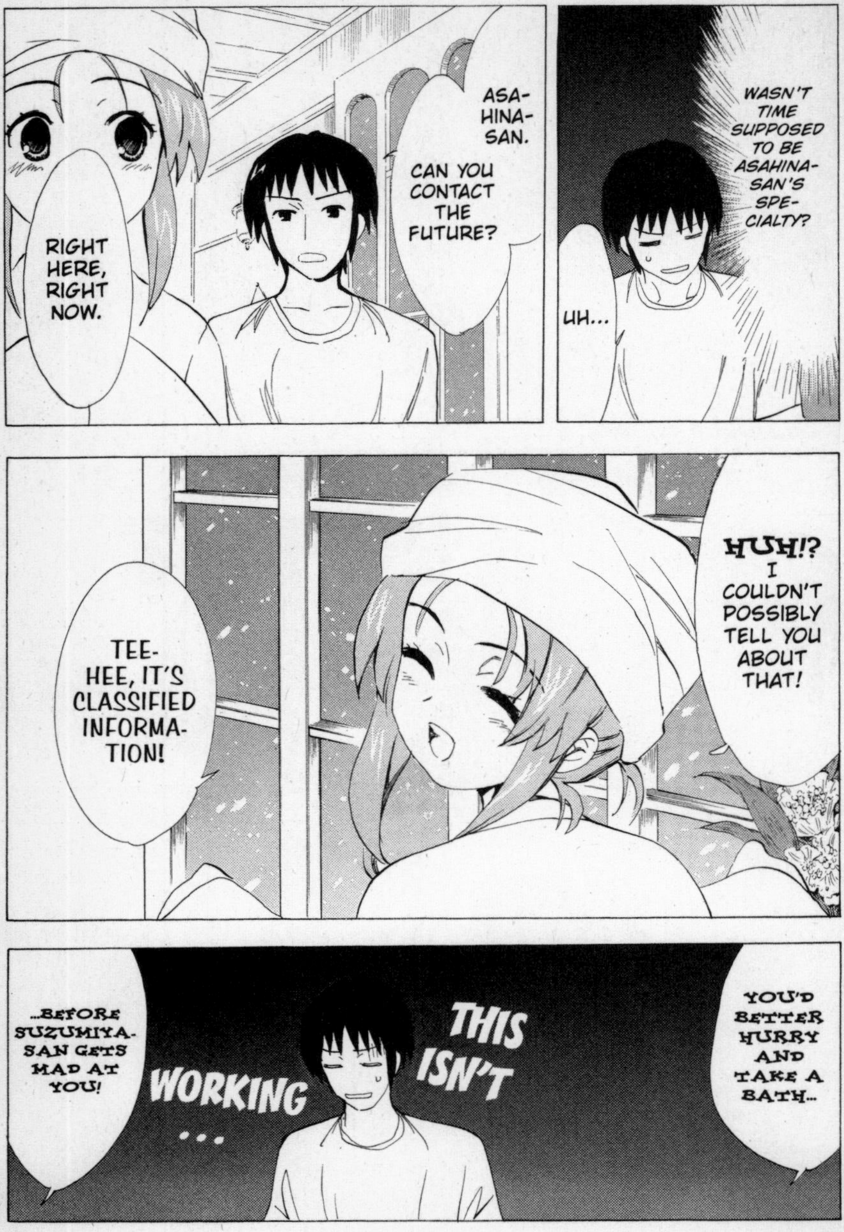
WASN'T TIME SUPPOSED TO BE ASAHINA-SAN'S SPE-CIALTY?
UH...
ASA-HINA-SAN.
CAN YOU CONTACT THE FUTURE?
RIGHT HERE, RIGHT NOW.
HUH!? I COULDN'T POSSIBLY TELL YOU ABOUT THAT!
TEE-HEE, IT'S CLASSIFIED INFORMA-TION!
YOU'D BETTER HURRY AND TAKE A BATH...
THIS ISN'T WORKING...
...BEFORE SUZUMIYA-SAN GETS MAD AT YOU!

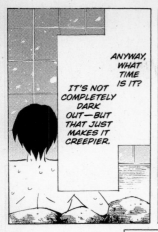

KOOOON (DOOONG)
WHAT AM I GONNA DO...?
ANYWAY, WHAT TIME IS IT?
IT'S NOT COMPLETELY DARK OUT—BUT THAT JUST MAKES IT CREEPIER.
LET'S GO PLAY IN THE REC ROOM!
I HAVEN'T PLAYED MAH-JONGG IN FOREVER.
DOUBLE POINTS FOR THIRTEEN ORPHANS AND FOUR CONCEALED TRIPLETS, OKAY? ♡
EVERYBODY READY?
NAH.
LET'S GET SOME SLEEP FIRST.
I KNOW, RIGHT?
WE CARRIED OUR SKIS AROUND FOR HOURS, AFTER ALL.

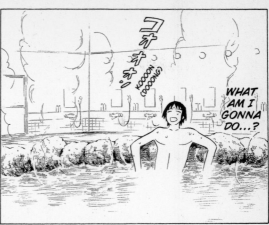

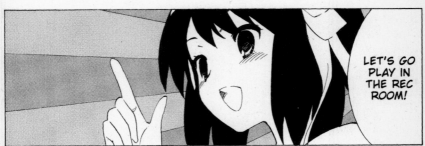

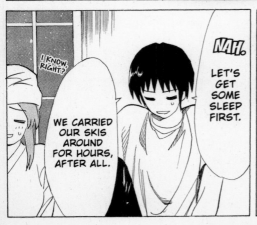

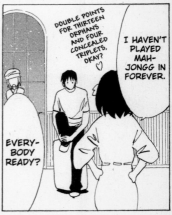

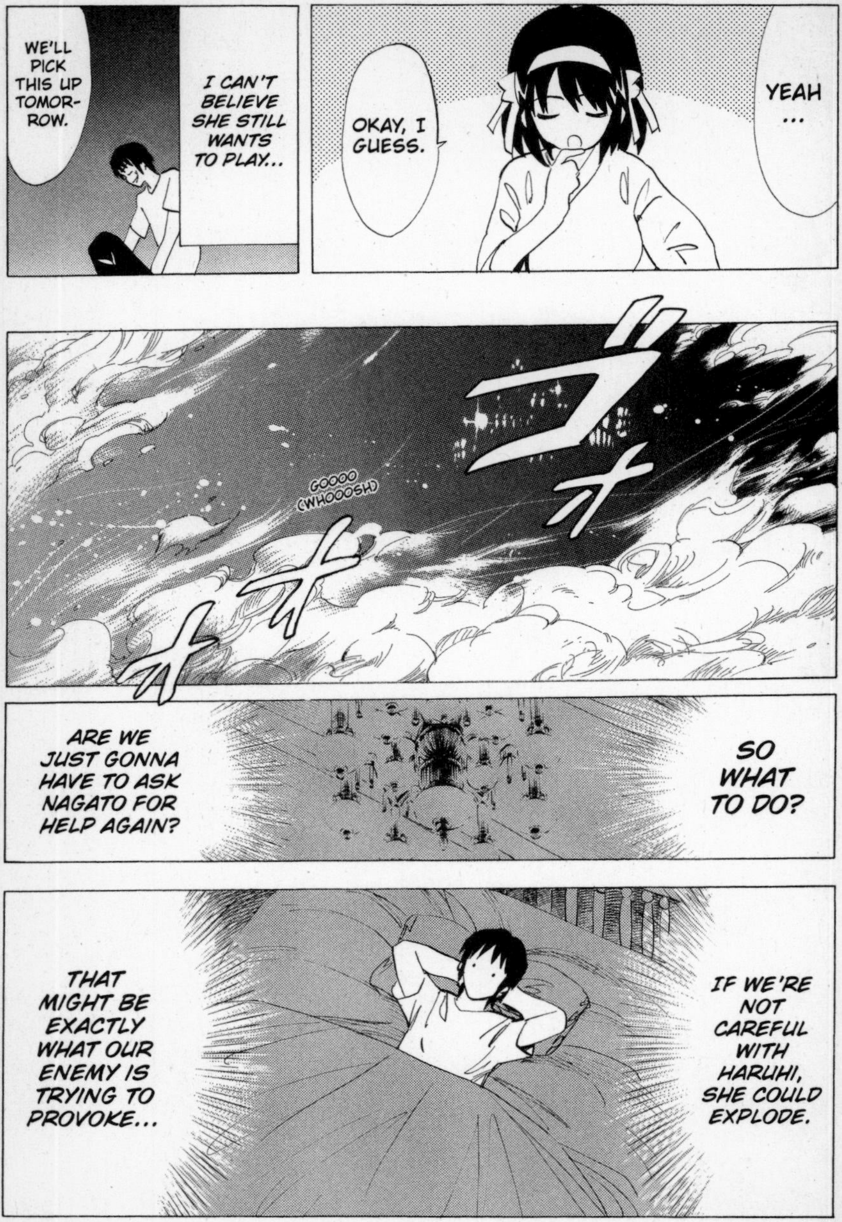
YEAH ...
OKAY, I GUESS.
I CAN'T BELIEVE SHE STILL WANTS TO PLAY...
WE'LL PICK THIS UP TOMORROW.
GOOOO (WHOOOSH)
SO WHAT TO DO?
ARE WE JUST GONNA HAVE TO ASK NAGATO FOR HELP AGAIN?
IF WE'RE NOT CAREFUL WITH HARUHI, SHE COULD EXPLODE.
THAT MIGHT BE EXACTLY WHAT OUR ENEMY IS TRYING TO PROVOKE...

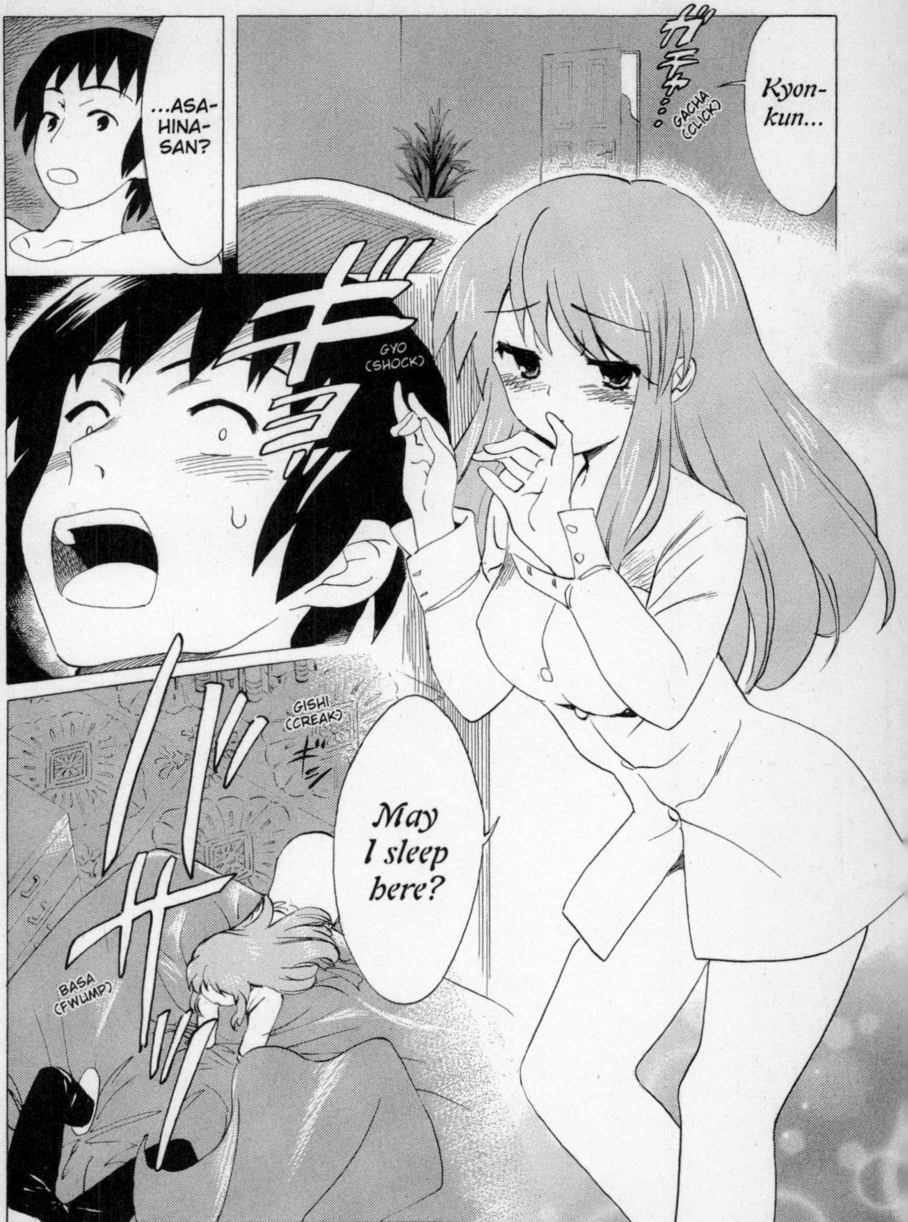
GACHA (CLICK)
Kyon-kun...
...ASA-HINA-SAN?
GYO (SHOCK)
GISHI (CREAK)
May I sleep here?
BASA (FWUMP)

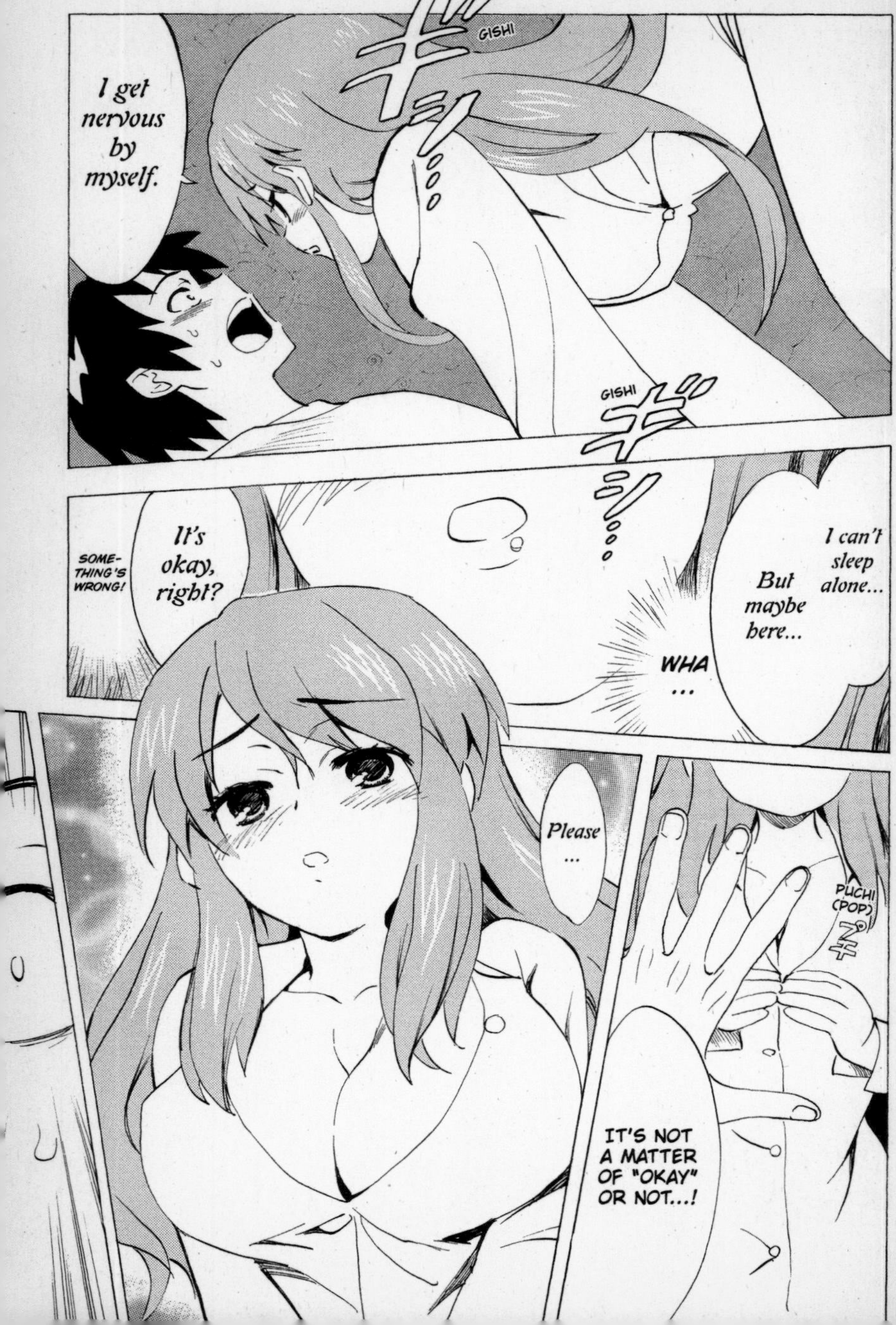
GISHI
I get nervous by myself.
GISHI
I can't sleep alone...
But maybe here...
WHA ...
It's okay, right?
SOME-THING'S WRONG!
PUCHI (POP)
IT'S NOT A MATTER OF "OKAY" OR NOT...!
Please ...

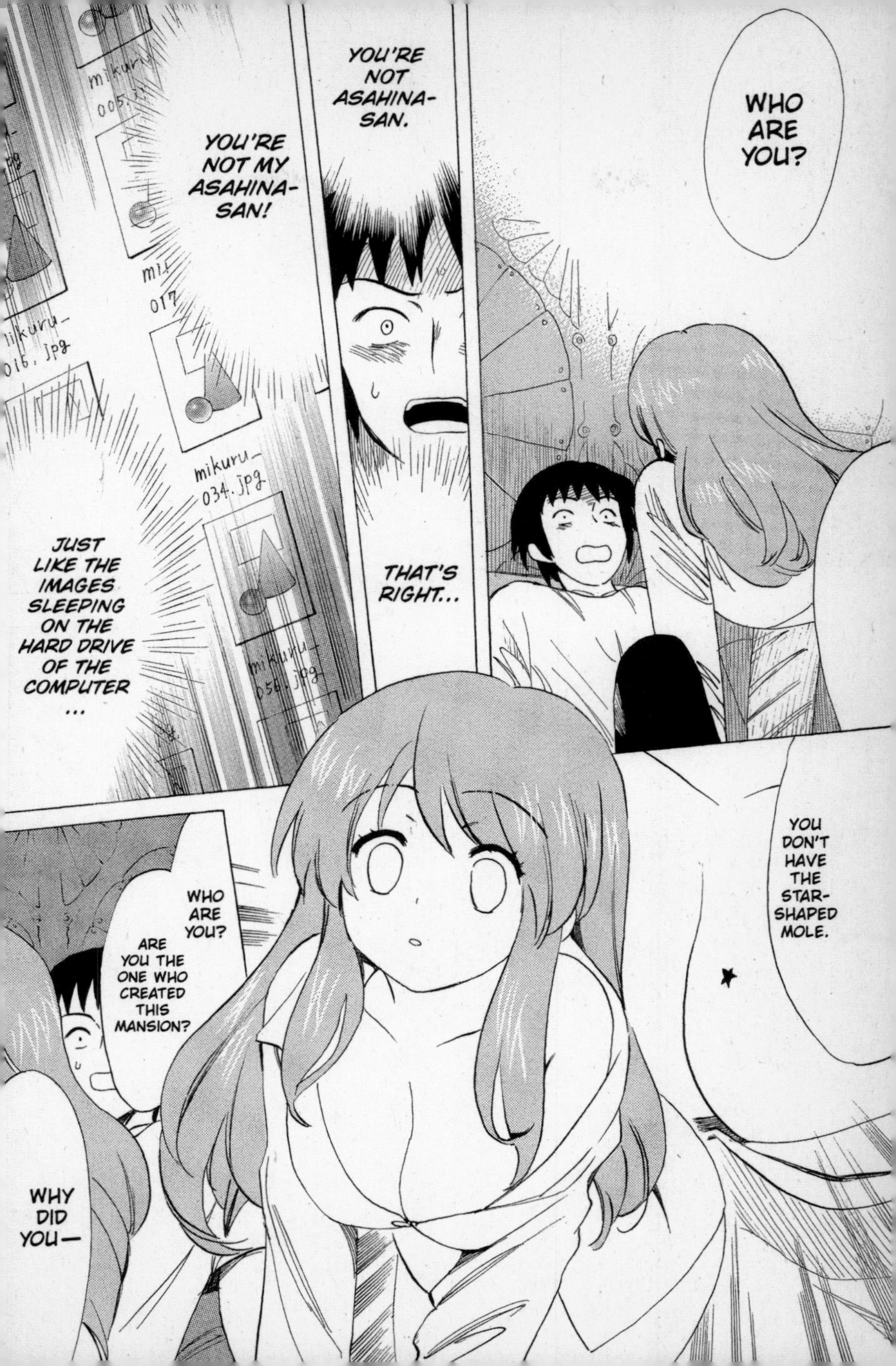
WHO ARE YOU?
YOU'RE NOT ASAHINA-SAN.
THAT'S RIGHT...
YOU'RE NOT MY ASAHINA-SAN!
mikuru-034.jpg
JUST LIKE THE IMAGES SLEEPING ON THE HARD DRIVE OF THE COMPUTER...
YOU DON'T HAVE THE STAR-SHAPED MOLE.
WHO ARE YOU?
ARE YOU THE ONE WHO CREATED THIS MANSION?
WHY DID YOU—

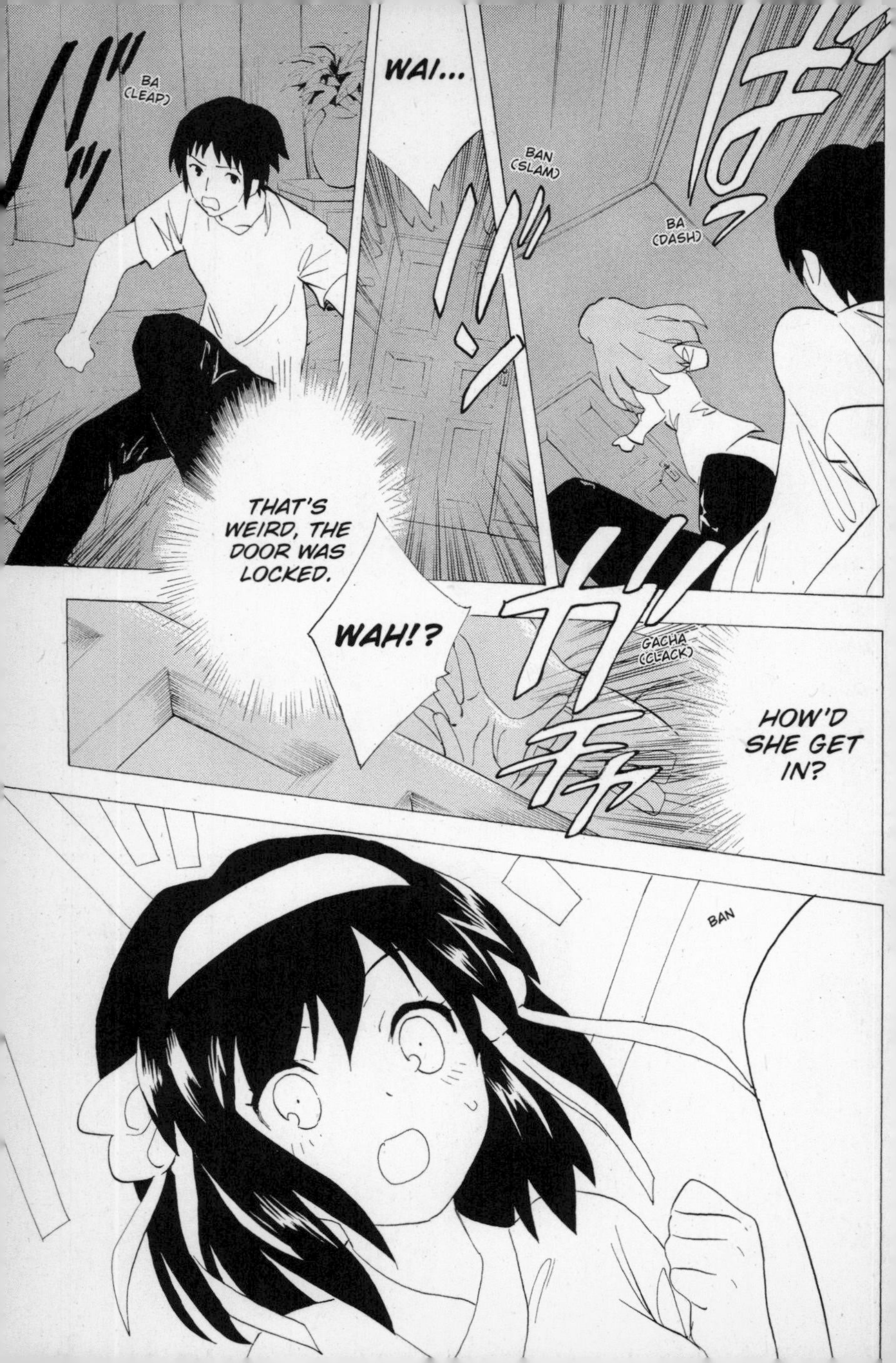
BA (DASH)
BAN (SLAM)
WAI...
BA (LEAP)
THAT'S WEIRD, THE DOOR WAS LOCKED.
HOW'D SHE GET IN?
GACHA (CLACK)
WAH!?
BAN

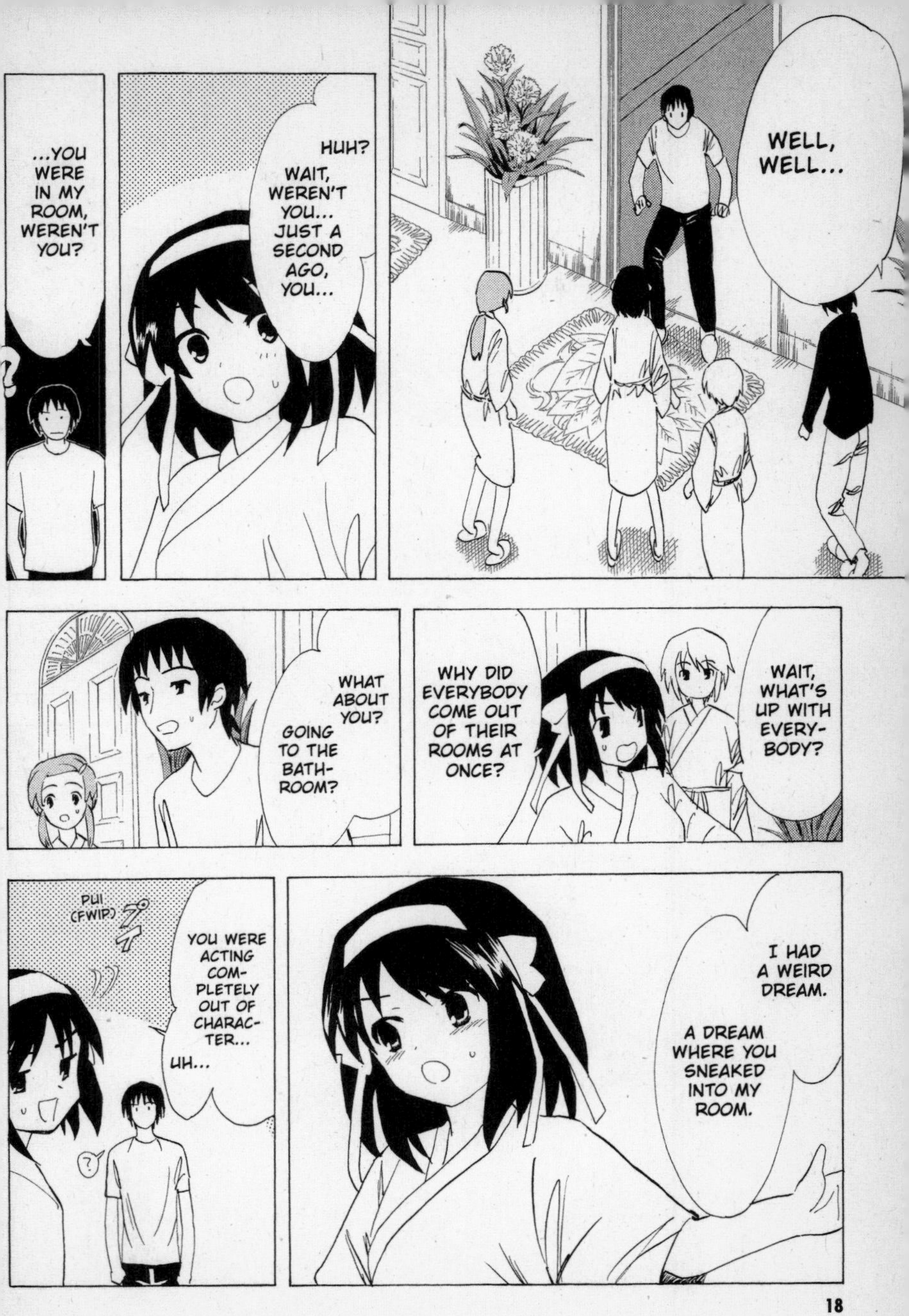
WELL, WELL...
HUH?
WAIT, WEREN'T YOU... JUST A SECOND AGO, YOU...
...YOU WERE IN MY ROOM, WEREN'T YOU?
WAIT, WHAT'S UP WITH EVERY-BODY?
WHY DID EVERYBODY COME OUT OF THEIR ROOMS AT ONCE?
WHAT ABOUT YOU?
GOING TO THE BATH-ROOM?
I HAD A WEIRD DREAM.
A DREAM WHERE YOU SNEAKED INTO MY ROOM.
YOU WERE ACTING COM-PLETELY OUT OF CHARAC-TER...
PUI (FWIP)
UH...

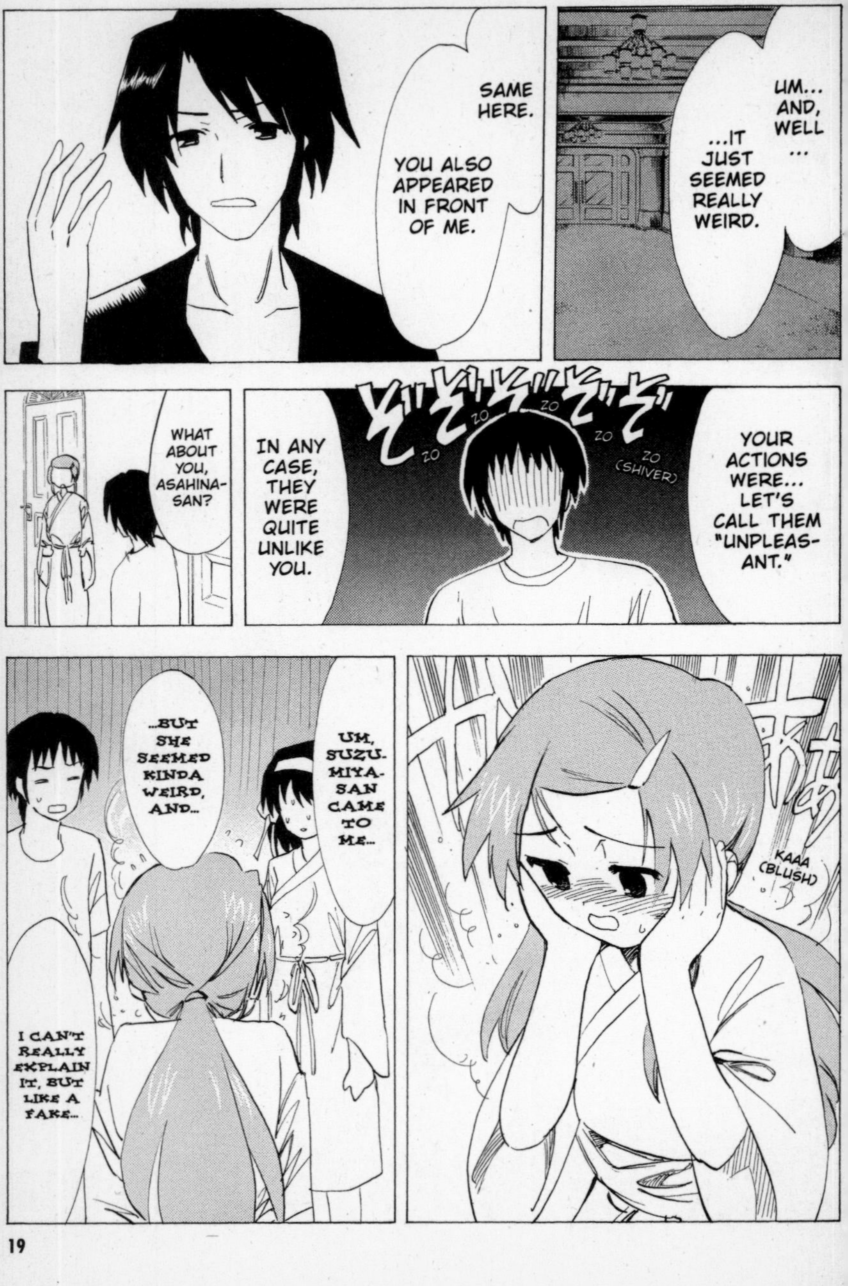
UM... AND, WELL ...
...IT JUST SEEMED REALLY WEIRD.
SAME HERE.
YOU ALSO APPEARED IN FRONT OF ME.
YOUR ACTIONS WERE... LET'S CALL THEM "UNPLEAS-ANT."
ZO ZO ZO ZO ZO (SHIVER)
IN ANY CASE, THEY WERE QUITE UNLIKE YOU.
WHAT ABOUT YOU, ASAHINA-SAN?
KAAA (BLUSH)
UM, SUZU-MIYA-SAN CAME TO ME...
...BUT SHE SEEMED KINDA WEIRD, AND...
I CAN'T REALLY EXPLAIN IT, BUT LIKE A FAKE...

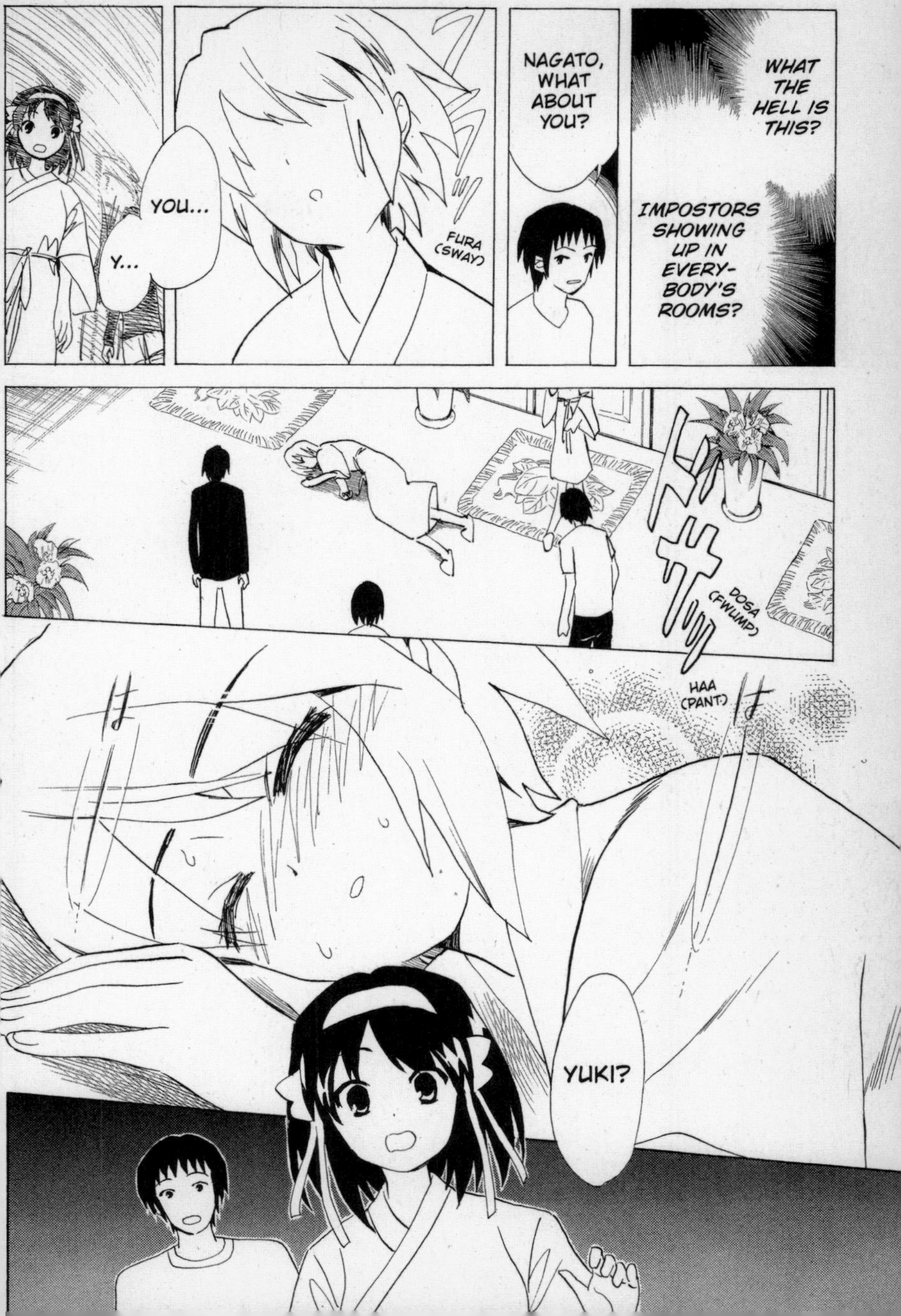
WHAT THE HELL IS THIS?
IMPOSTORS SHOWING UP IN EVERY-BODY'S ROOMS?
NAGATO, WHAT ABOUT YOU?
FURA (SWAY)
YOU...
Y...
DOSA (FWUMP)
HAA (PANT)
YUKI?

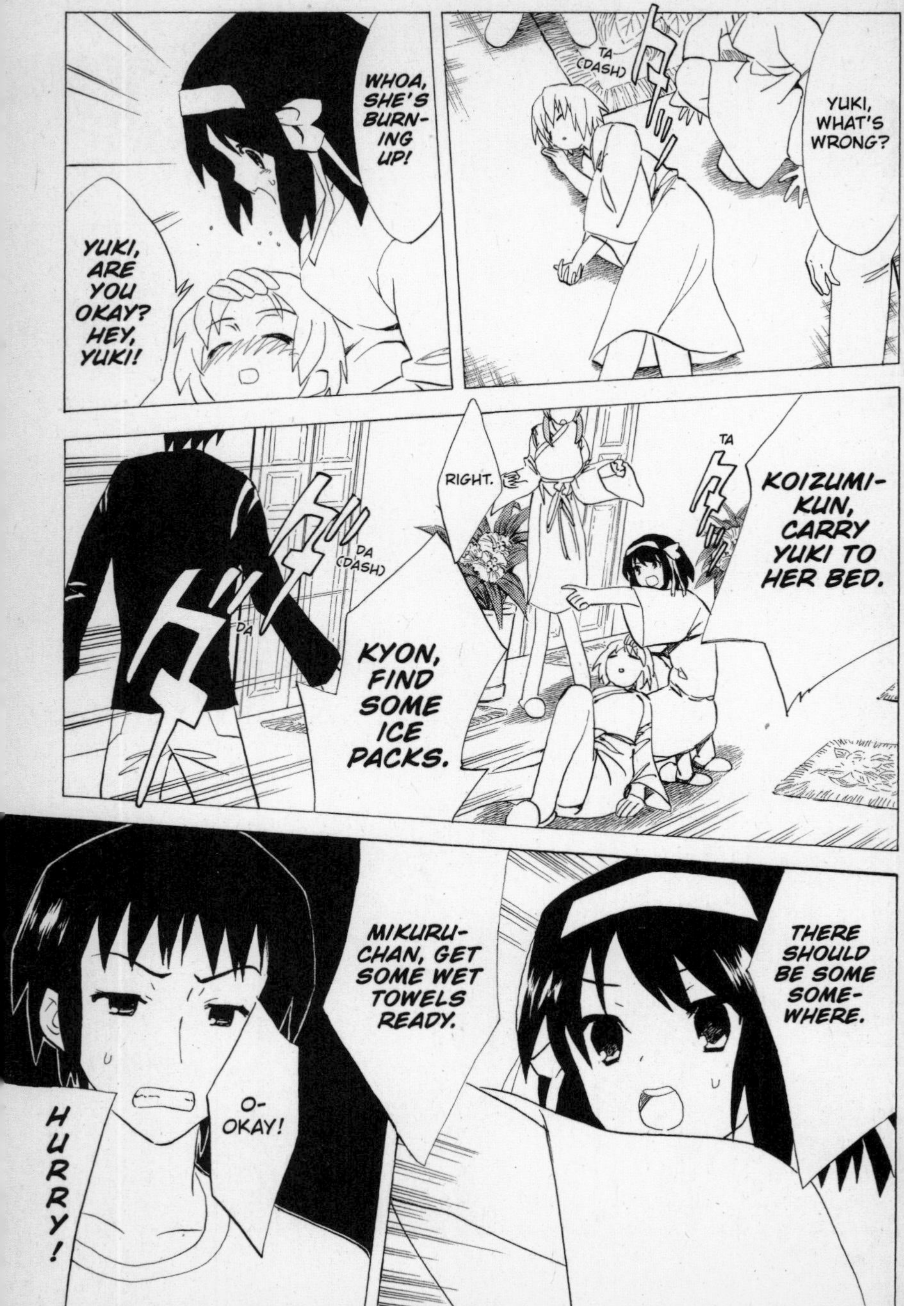
TA (DASH)
YUKI, WHAT'S WRONG?
WHOA, SHE'S BURNING UP!
YUKI, ARE YOU OKAY? HEY, YUKI!
KOIZUMI-KUN, CARRY YUKI TO HER BED.
TA
RIGHT.
KYON, FIND SOME ICE PACKS.
DA (DASH)
DA
THERE SHOULD BE SOME SOMEWHERE.
MIKURU-CHAN, GET SOME WET TOWELS READY.
O-OKAY!
HURRY!

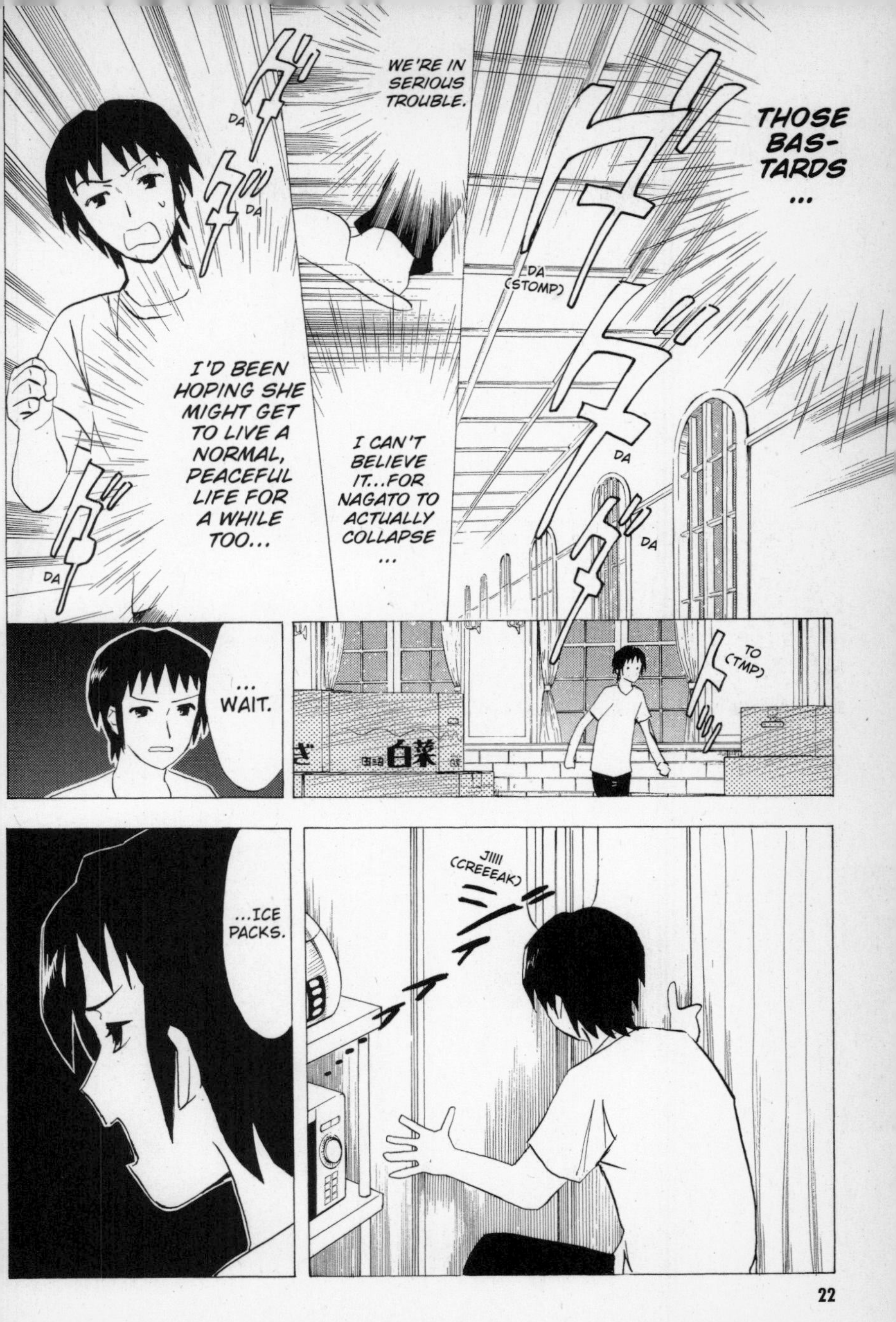
THOSE BASTARDS...
DA (STOMP)
DA
DA
WE'RE IN SERIOUS TROUBLE.
I CAN'T BELIEVE IT...FOR NAGATO TO ACTUALLY COLLAPSE...
DA
DA
I'D BEEN HOPING SHE MIGHT GET TO LIVE A NORMAL, PEACEFUL LIFE FOR A WHILE TOO...
DA
TO (TMP)
白菜
...WAIT.
JIIII (CREEEAK)
...ICE PACKS.

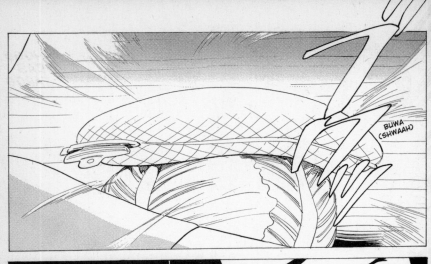

BUWA
(SHWAAH)

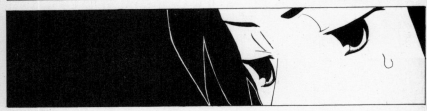

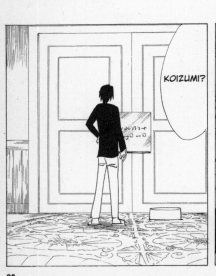

KOIZUMI?

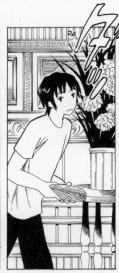

WE CAN'T
STAY
HERE ANY
LONGER...

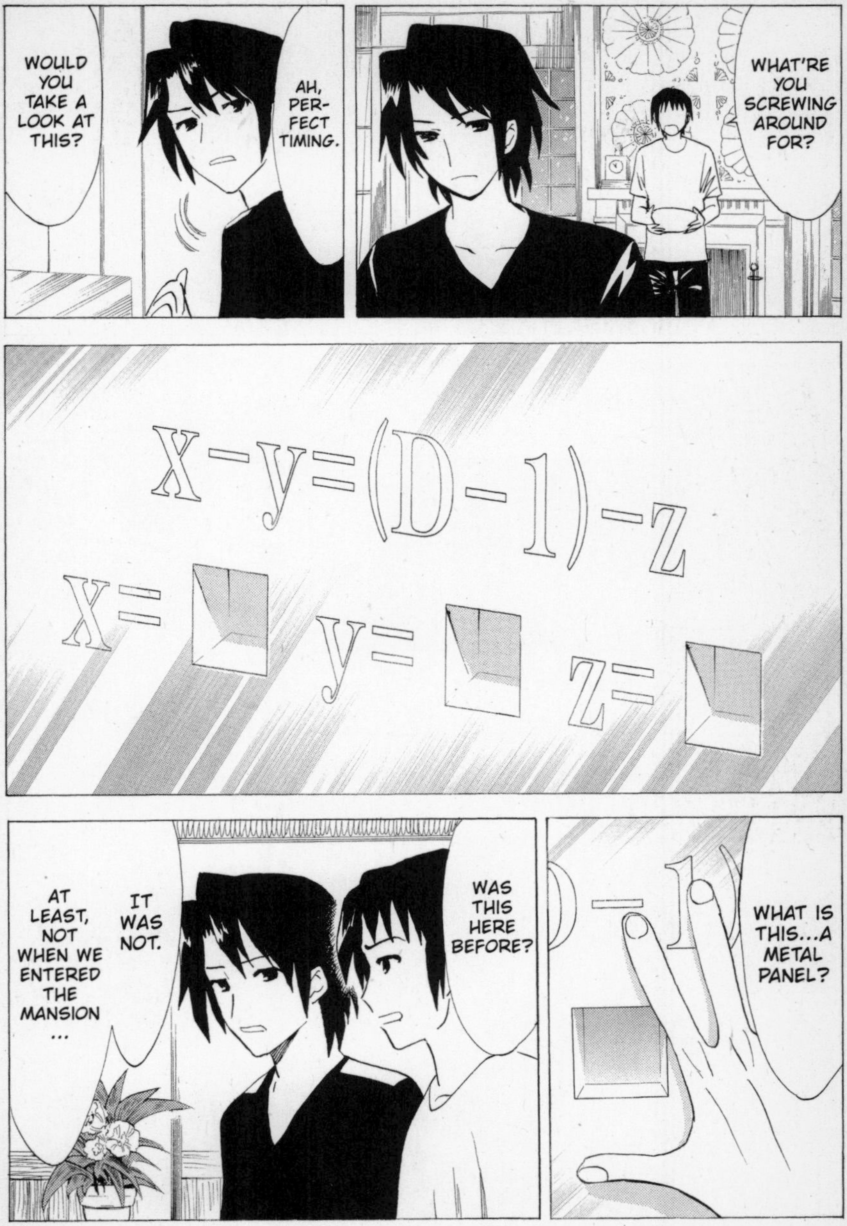
WHAT'RE YOU SCREWING AROUND FOR?
AH, PER-FECT TIMING.
WOULD YOU TAKE A LOOK AT THIS?
X−y=(D−1)−Z
X= y= Z=
WHAT IS THIS...A METAL PANEL?
WAS THIS HERE BEFORE?
IT WAS NOT.
AT LEAST, NOT WHEN WE ENTERED THE MANSION...

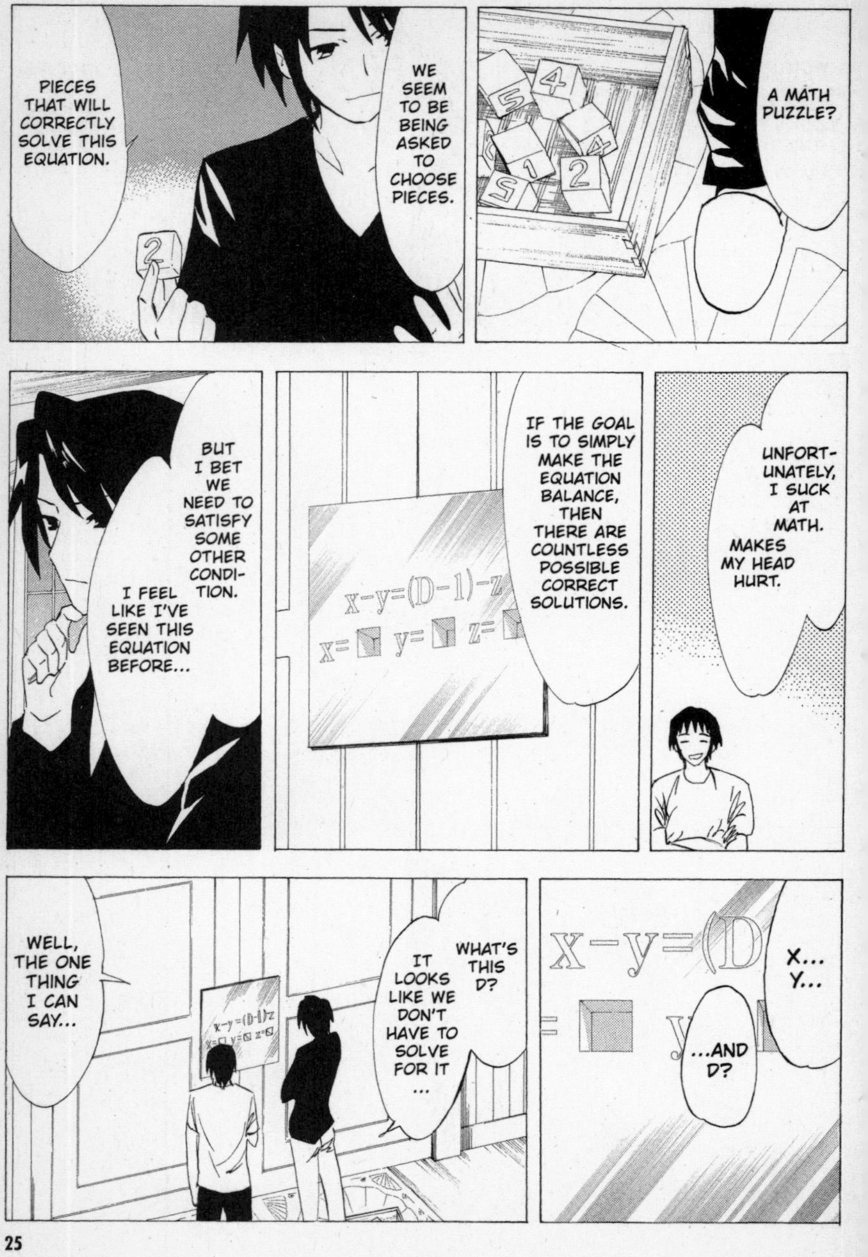
A MATH PUZZLE?
WE SEEM TO BE BEING ASKED TO CHOOSE PIECES.
PIECES THAT WILL CORRECTLY SOLVE THIS EQUATION.
UNFORTUNATELY, I SUCK AT MATH.
MAKES MY HEAD HURT.
IF THE GOAL IS TO SIMPLY MAKE THE EQUATION BALANCE, THEN THERE ARE COUNTLESS POSSIBLE CORRECT SOLUTIONS.
x-y=(D-1)-z
x= y= z=
BUT I BET WE NEED TO SATISFY SOME OTHER CONDITION.
I FEEL LIKE I'VE SEEN THIS EQUATION BEFORE...
X... Y...
...AND D?
WHAT'S THIS D?
IT LOOKS LIKE WE DON'T HAVE TO SOLVE FOR IT...
WELL, THE ONE THING I CAN SAY...

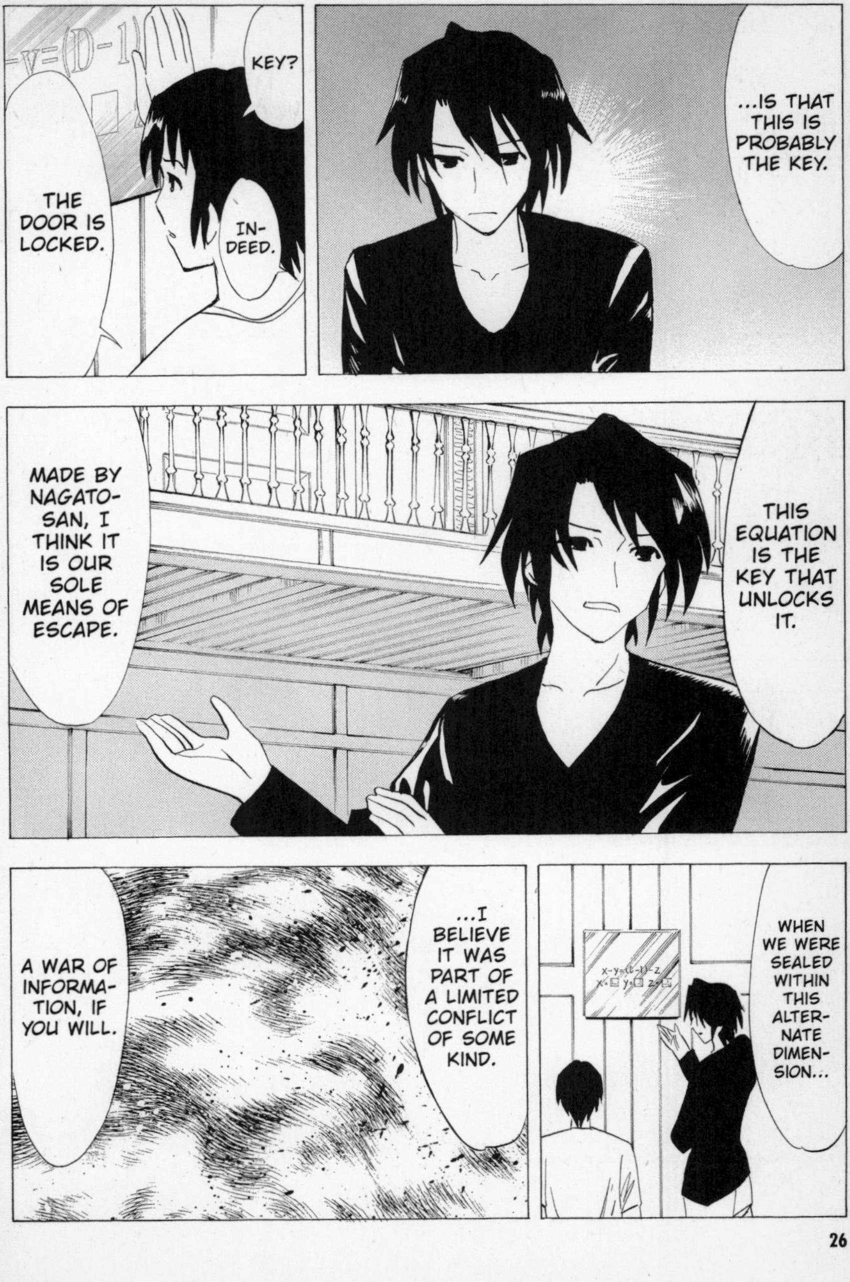
...IS THAT THIS IS PROBABLY THE KEY.
KEY?
IN-DEED.
THE DOOR IS LOCKED.
THIS EQUATION IS THE KEY THAT UNLOCKS IT.
MADE BY NAGATO-SAN, I THINK IT IS OUR SOLE MEANS OF ESCAPE.
WHEN WE WERE SEALED WITHIN THIS ALTERNATE DIMENSION...
...I BELIEVE IT WAS PART OF A LIMITED CONFLICT OF SOME KIND.
A WAR OF INFORMATION, IF YOU WILL.

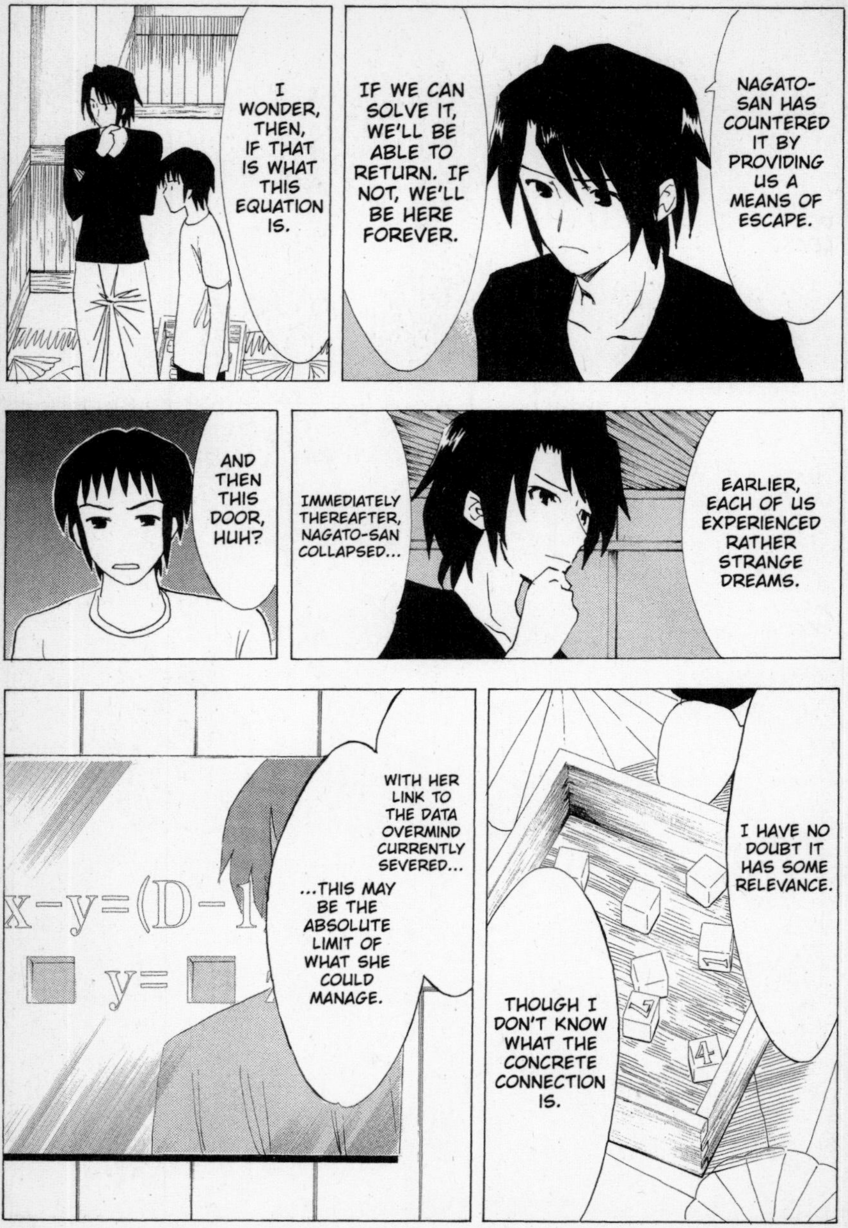
NAGATO-SAN HAS COUNTERED IT BY PROVIDING US A MEANS OF ESCAPE.
IF WE CAN SOLVE IT, WE'LL BE ABLE TO RETURN. IF NOT, WE'LL BE HERE FOREVER.
I WONDER, THEN, IF THAT IS WHAT THIS EQUATION IS.
EARLIER, EACH OF US EXPERIENCED RATHER STRANGE DREAMS.
IMMEDIATELY THEREAFTER, NAGATO-SAN COLLAPSED...
AND THEN THIS DOOR, HUH?
I HAVE NO DOUBT IT HAS SOME RELEVANCE.
THOUGH I DON'T KNOW WHAT THE CONCRETE CONNECTION IS.
WITH HER LINK TO THE DATA OVERMIND CURRENTLY SEVERED...
...THIS MAY BE THE ABSOLUTE LIMIT OF WHAT SHE COULD MANAGE.
x-y=(D-1
y=

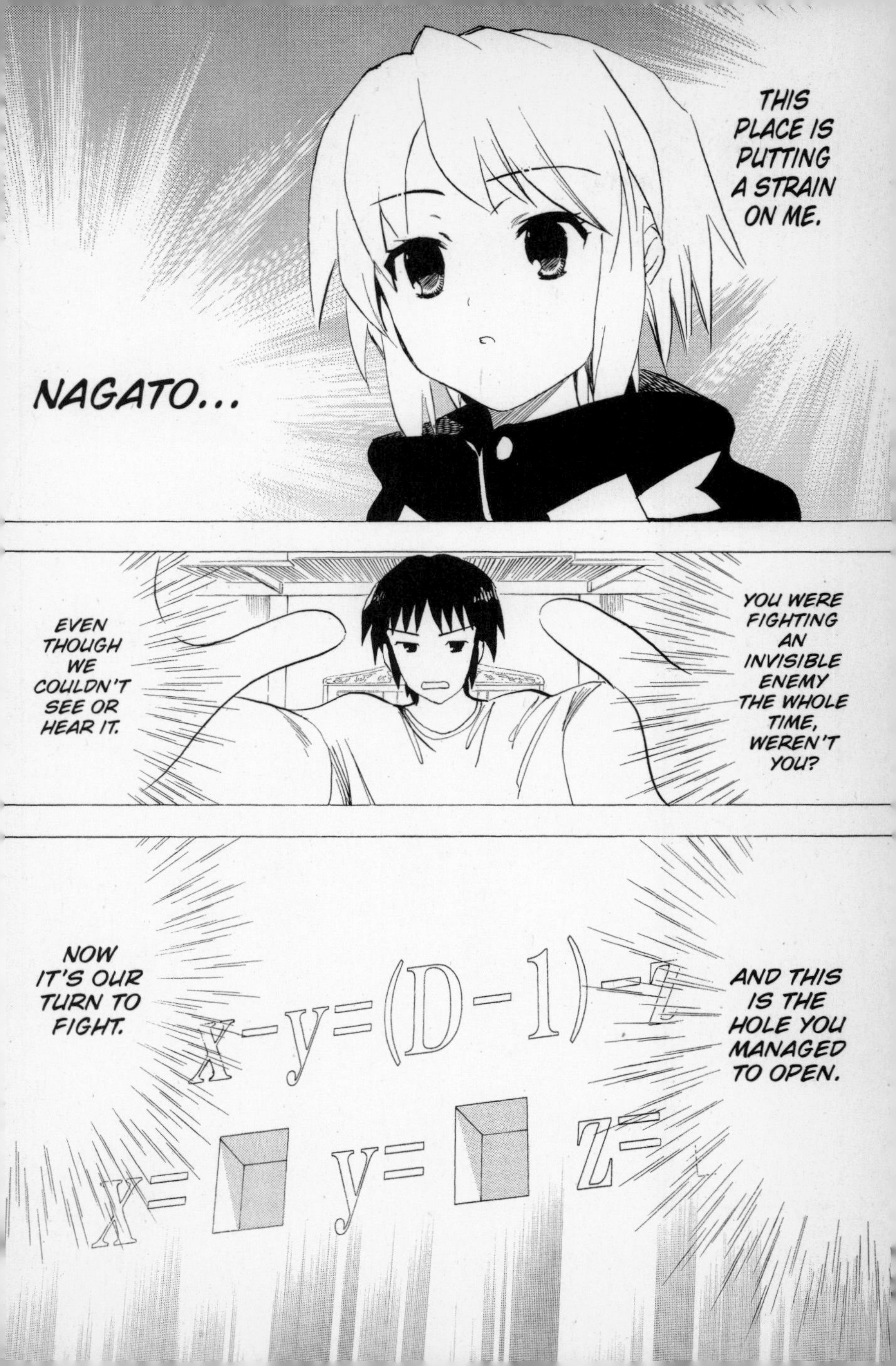
THIS PLACE IS PUTTING A STRAIN ON ME.
NAGATO...
YOU WERE FIGHTING AN INVISIBLE ENEMY THE WHOLE TIME, WEREN'T YOU?
EVEN THOUGH WE COULDN'T SEE OR HEAR IT.
AND THIS IS THE HOLE YOU MANAGED TO OPEN.
NOW IT'S OUR TURN TO FIGHT.
x-y=(D-1)-z
x= y= z=

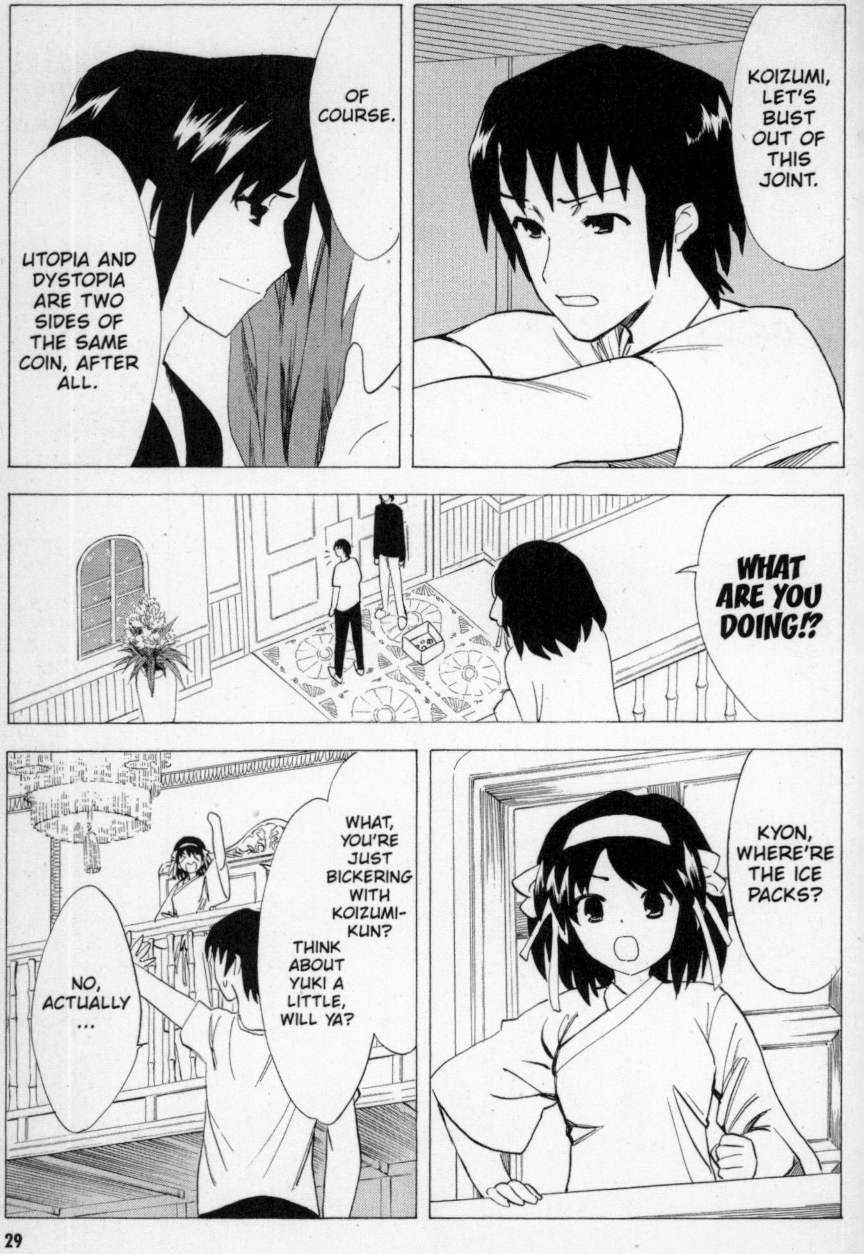
KOIZUMI, LET'S BUST OUT OF THIS JOINT.
OF COURSE.
UTOPIA AND DYSTOPIA ARE TWO SIDES OF THE SAME COIN, AFTER ALL.
WHAT ARE YOU DOING!?
KYON, WHERE'RE THE ICE PACKS?
WHAT, YOU'RE JUST BICKERING WITH KOIZUMI-KUN?
THINK ABOUT YUKI A LITTLE, WILL YA?
NO, ACTUALLY ...

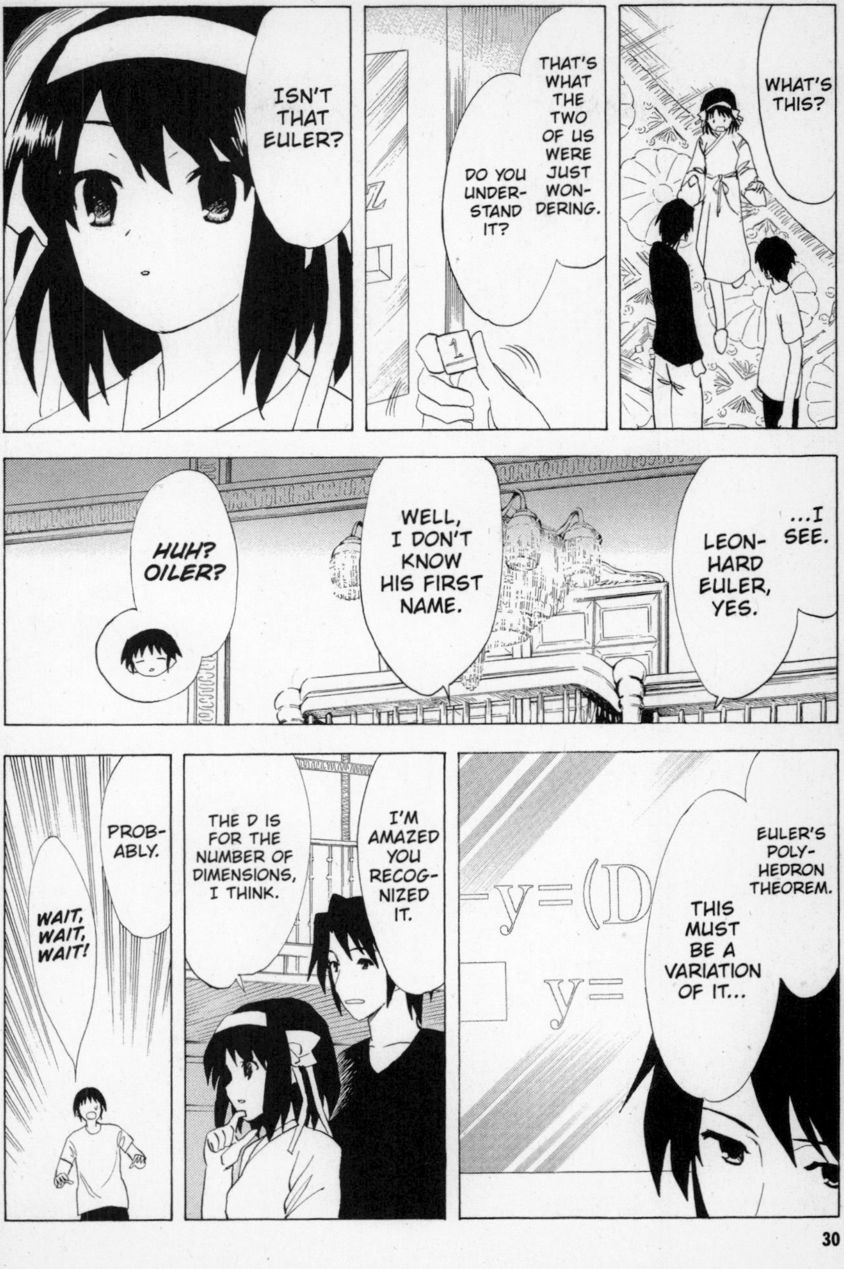
WHAT'S THIS?
THAT'S WHAT THE TWO OF US WERE JUST WONDERING.
DO YOU UNDERSTAND IT?
ISN'T THAT EULER?
...I SEE.
LEONHARD EULER, YES.
WELL, I DON'T KNOW HIS FIRST NAME.
HUH? OILER?
EULER'S POLYHEDRON THEOREM.
THIS MUST BE A VARIATION OF IT...
y=(D
y=
I'M AMAZED YOU RECOGNIZED IT.
THE D IS FOR THE NUMBER OF DIMENSIONS, I THINK.
PROBABLY.
WAIT, WAIT, WAIT!

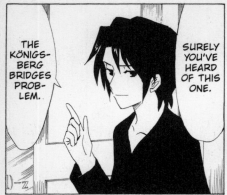

EULER? WHAT?
THE WHAT-NOW THEOREM?
SURELY YOU'VE HEARD OF THIS ONE.
THE KÖNIGSBERG BRIDGES PROBLEM.
KÖ...?
THERE ARE TWO ISLANDS IN A RIVER...
...AND SEVEN BRIDGES CONNECTING THEM TO EACH OTHER AND TO THE MAINLAND...
YOU HAVE TO CROSS ALL THE BRIDGES ONLY ONCE, RIGHT?
YOSHIZAKI-SENSEI WAS RAMBLING ON ABOUT IT IN MATH CLASS.
IT'S IMPOSSIBLE, RIGHT?
EXCELLENT ANSWER.

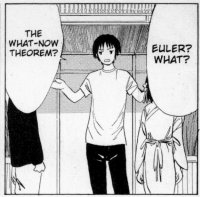

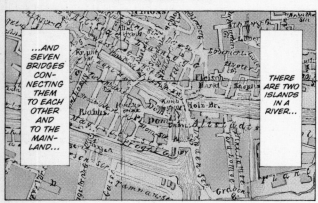

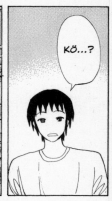

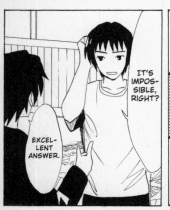

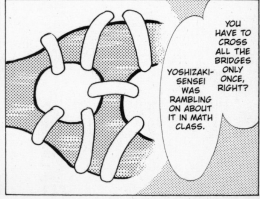

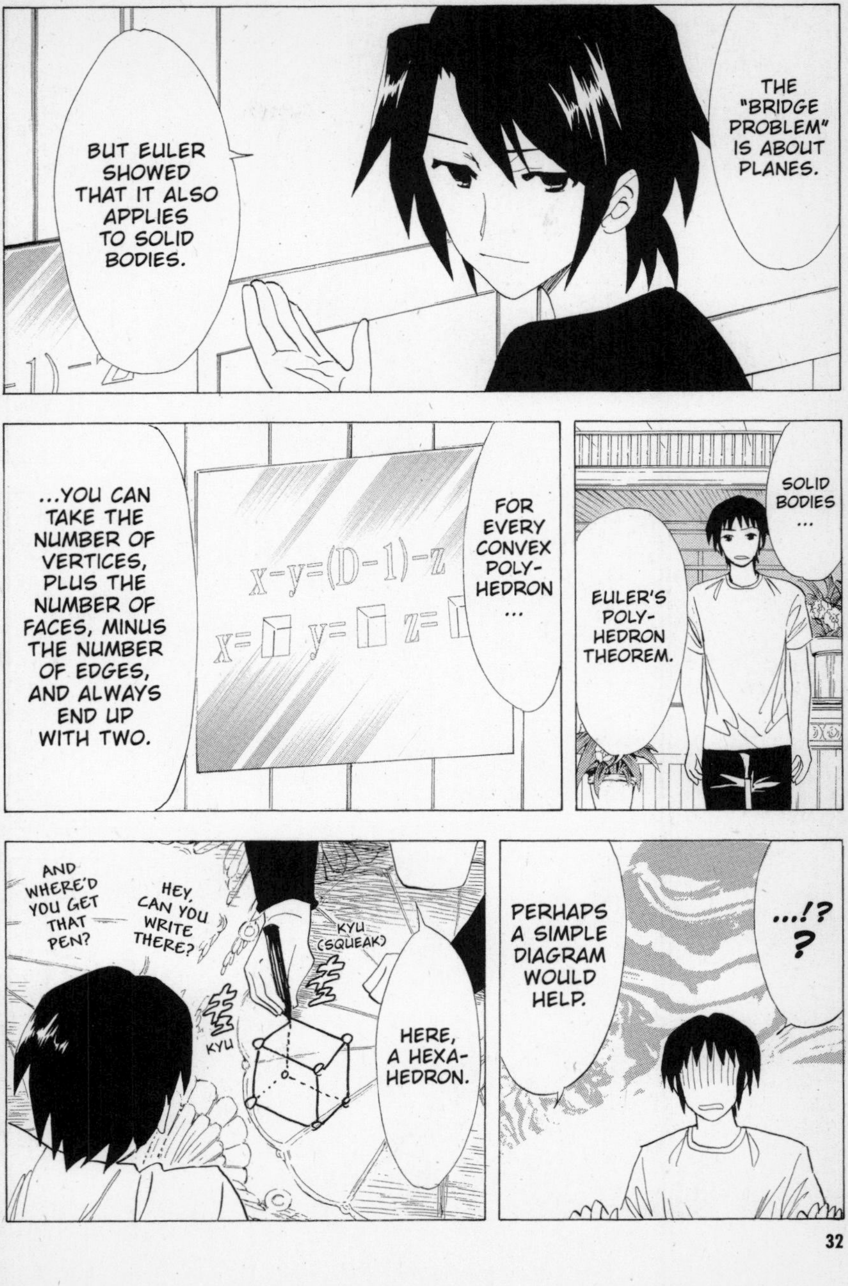
THE "BRIDGE PROBLEM" IS ABOUT PLANES.
BUT EULER SHOWED THAT IT ALSO APPLIES TO SOLID BODIES.
SOLID BODIES ...
EULER'S POLY-HEDRON THEOREM.
FOR EVERY CONVEX POLY-HEDRON ...
x-y=(D-1)-z
...YOU CAN TAKE THE NUMBER OF VERTICES, PLUS THE NUMBER OF FACES, MINUS THE NUMBER OF EDGES, AND ALWAYS END UP WITH TWO.
...!? ?
PERHAPS A SIMPLE DIAGRAM WOULD HELP.
HERE, A HEXA-HEDRON.
KYU (SQUEAK)
KYU
HEY, CAN YOU WRITE THERE?
AND WHERE'D YOU GET THAT PEN?

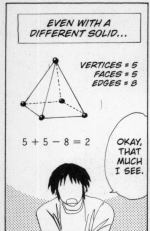

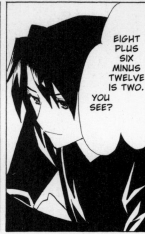

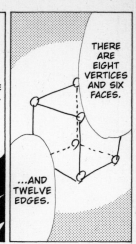

THERE ARE EIGHT VERTICES AND SIX FACES.
...AND TWELVE EDGES.
EIGHT PLUS SIX MINUS TWELVE IS TWO.
YOU SEE?
EVEN WITH A DIFFERENT SOLID...
VERTICES = 5
FACES = 5
EDGES = 8
5 + 5 − 8 = 2
OKAY, THAT MUCH I SEE.
SO WHY DID HARUHI MENTION THE NUMBER OF DIMENSIONS?
THAT IS ALSO QUITE SIMPLE.
THIS THEOREM ALSO APPLIES TO TWO-DIMENSIONAL PLANES.
I DEMONSTRATED SOLIDS JUST NOW...
SO THIS TIME LET'S TRY A FIVE-POINTED STAR.
SURE, WHATEVER.
YOU REALLY SEEM TO BE ENJOYING THIS.

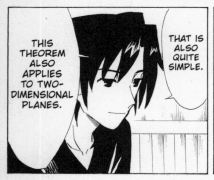

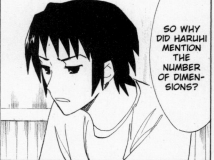

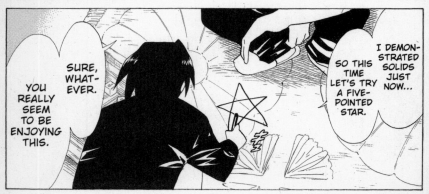

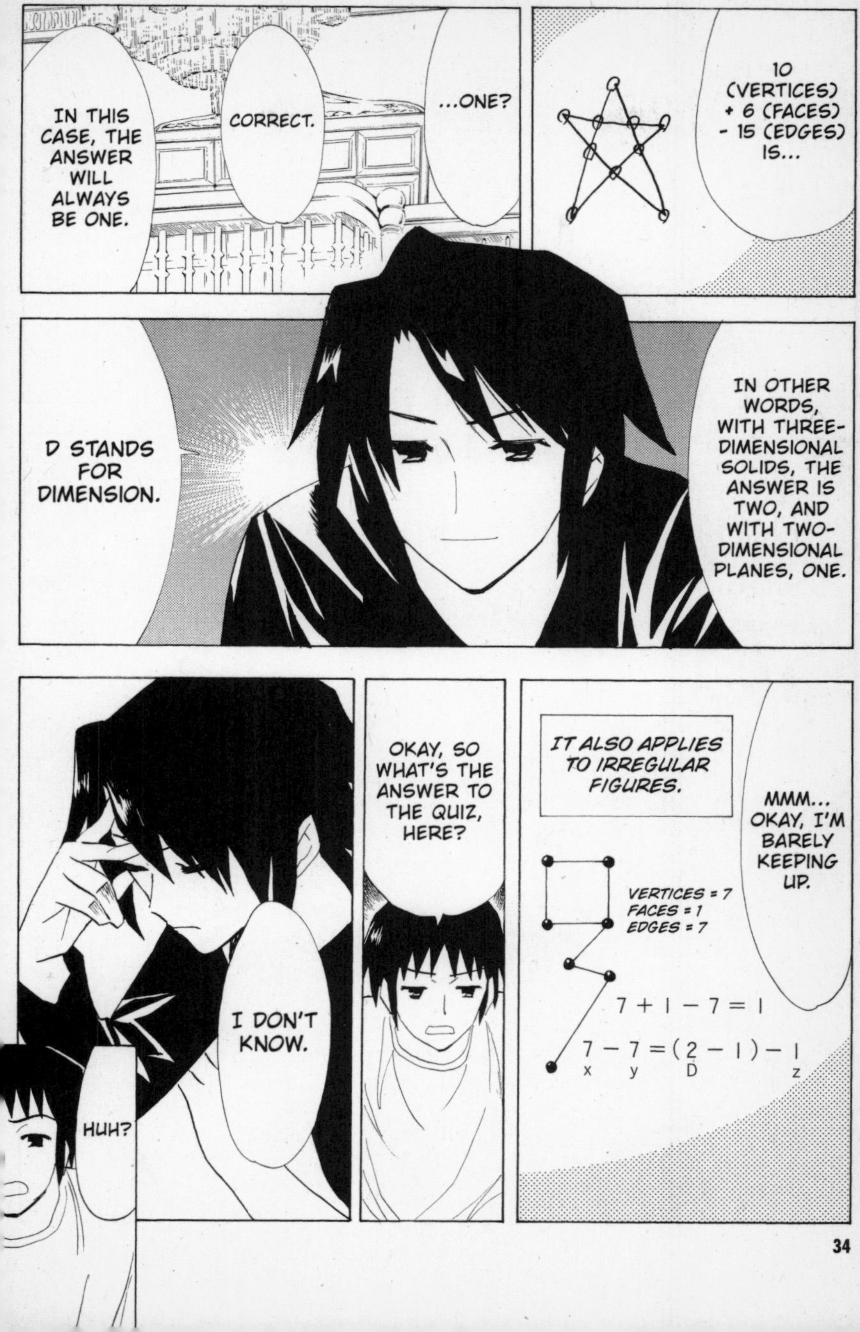
10 (VERTICES) + 6 (FACES) - 15 (EDGES) IS...
...ONE?
CORRECT.
IN THIS CASE, THE ANSWER WILL ALWAYS BE ONE.
IN OTHER WORDS, WITH THREE-DIMENSIONAL SOLIDS, THE ANSWER IS TWO, AND WITH TWO-DIMENSIONAL PLANES, ONE.
D STANDS FOR DIMENSION.
MMM... OKAY, I'M BARELY KEEPING UP.
IT ALSO APPLIES TO IRREGULAR FIGURES.
VERTICES = 7
FACES = 1
EDGES = 7
7 + 1 − 7 = 1
7 − 7 = (2 − 1) − 1
x y D z
OKAY, SO WHAT'S THE ANSWER TO THE QUIZ, HERE?
I DON'T KNOW.
HUH?

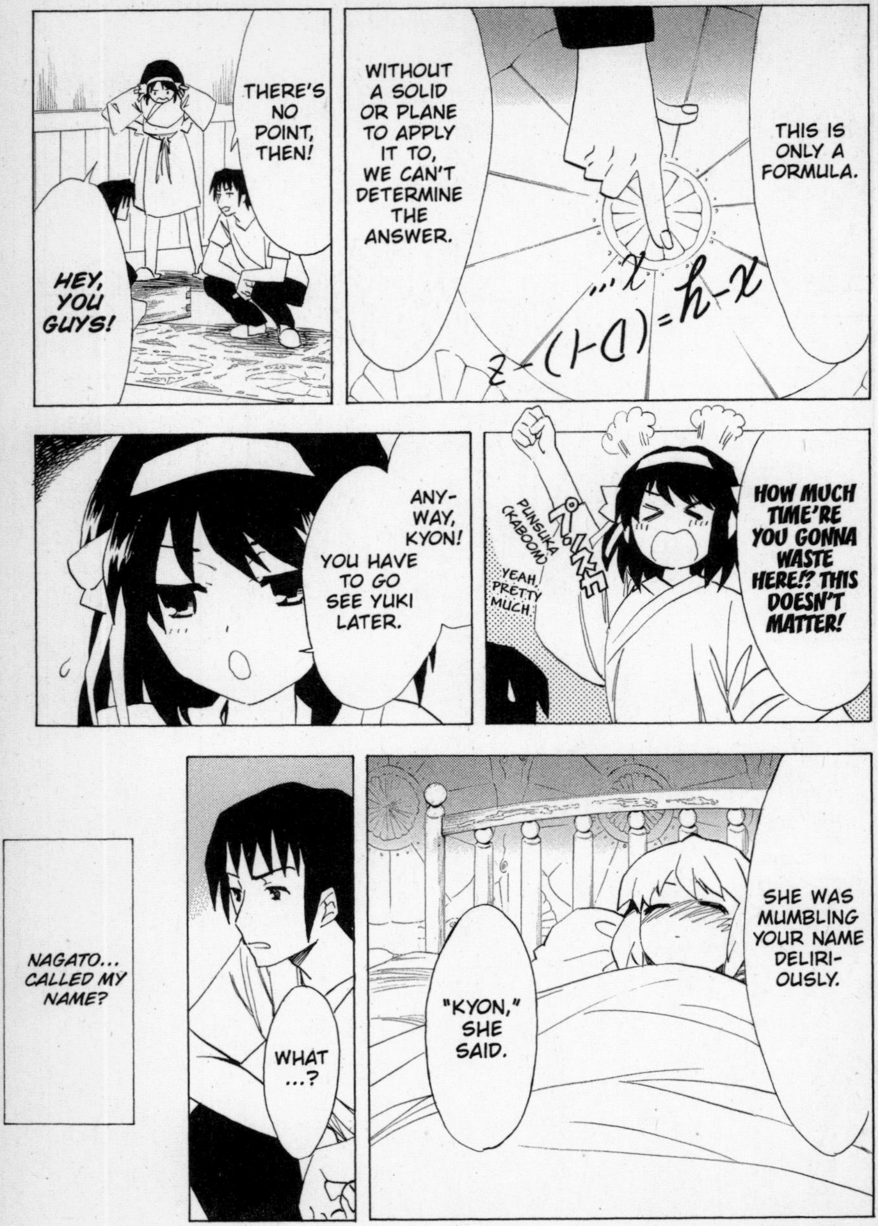
THIS IS ONLY A FORMULA.
WITHOUT A SOLID OR PLANE TO APPLY IT TO, WE CAN'T DETERMINE THE ANSWER.
THERE'S NO POINT, THEN!
HEY, YOU GUYS!
HOW MUCH TIME'RE YOU GONNA WASTE HERE!? THIS DOESN'T MATTER!
PUNSUKA (KABOOM)
YEAH, PRETTY MUCH.
ANY-WAY, KYON! YOU HAVE TO GO SEE YUKI LATER.
SHE WAS MUMBLING YOUR NAME DELIRI-OUSLY.
"KYON," SHE SAID.
WHAT ...?
NAGATO... CALLED MY NAME?

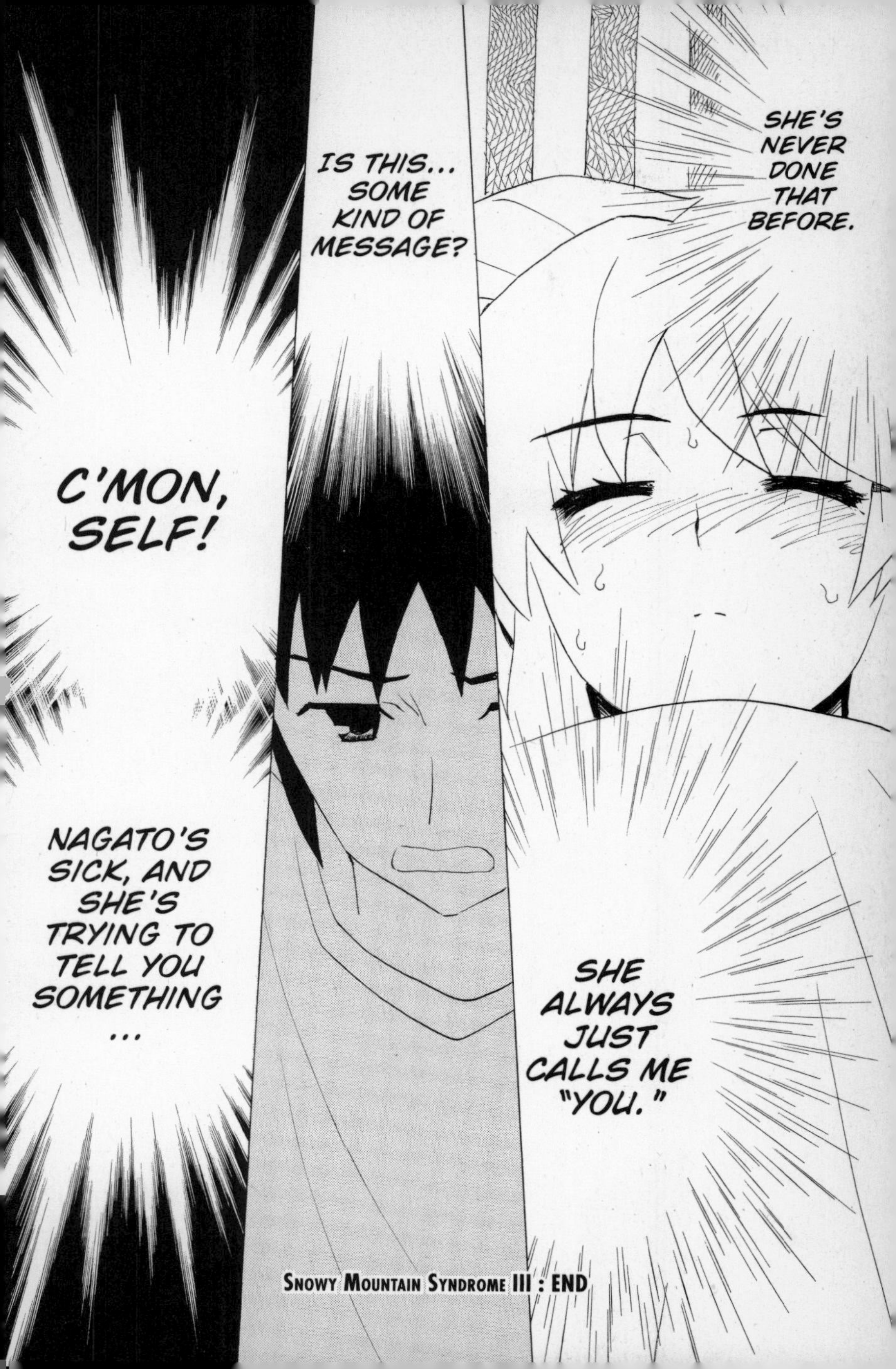
SHE'S NEVER DONE THAT BEFORE.
SHE ALWAYS JUST CALLS ME "YOU."
IS THIS... SOME KIND OF MESSAGE?
C'MON, SELF!
NAGATO'S SICK, AND SHE'S TRYING TO TELL YOU SOMETHING...
SNOWY MOUNTAIN SYNDROME III : END

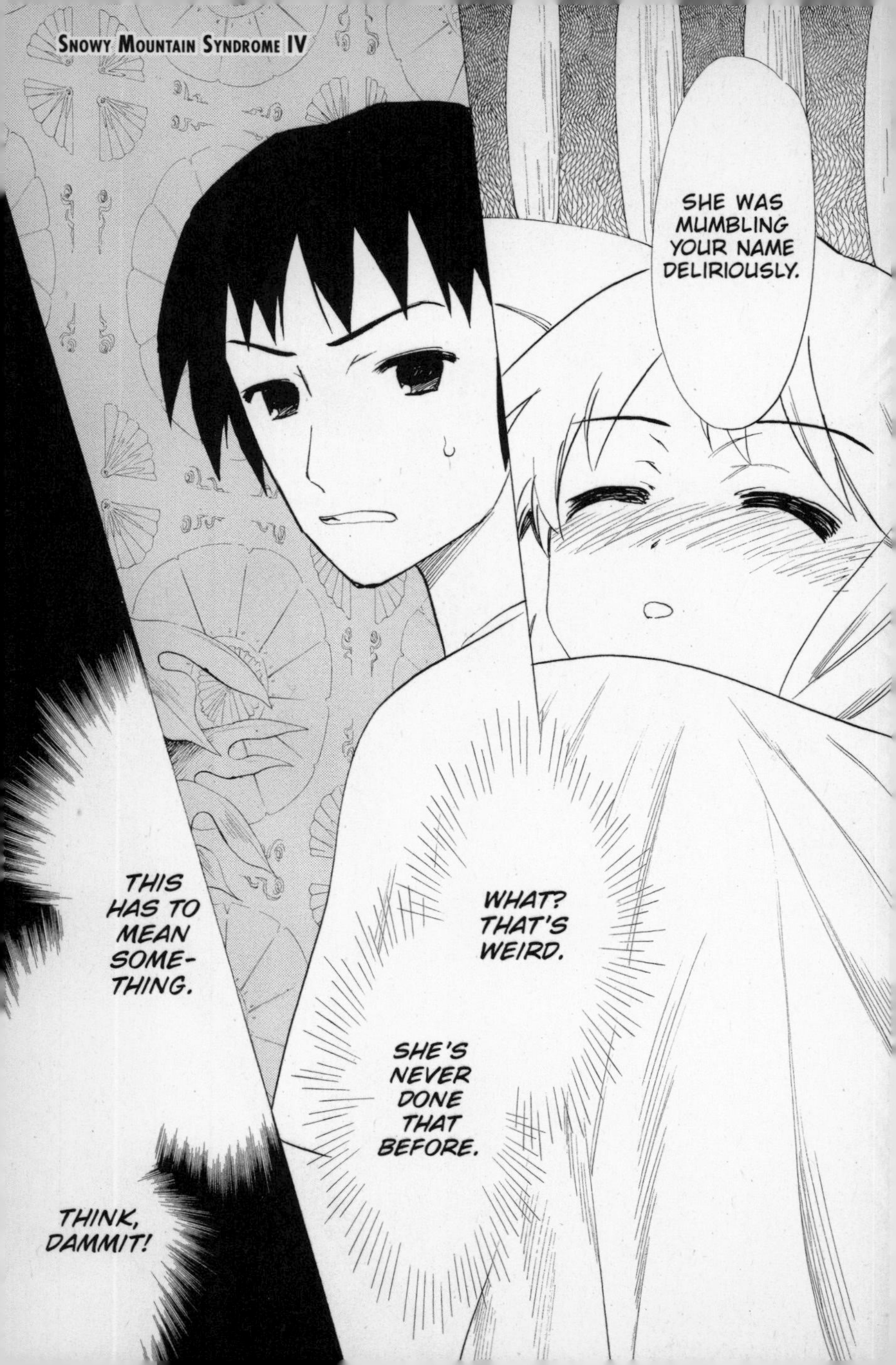
SHE WAS MUMBLING YOUR NAME DELIRIOUSLY.
WHAT? THAT'S WEIRD.
THIS HAS TO MEAN SOME-THING.
SHE'S NEVER DONE THAT BEFORE.
THINK, DAMMIT!

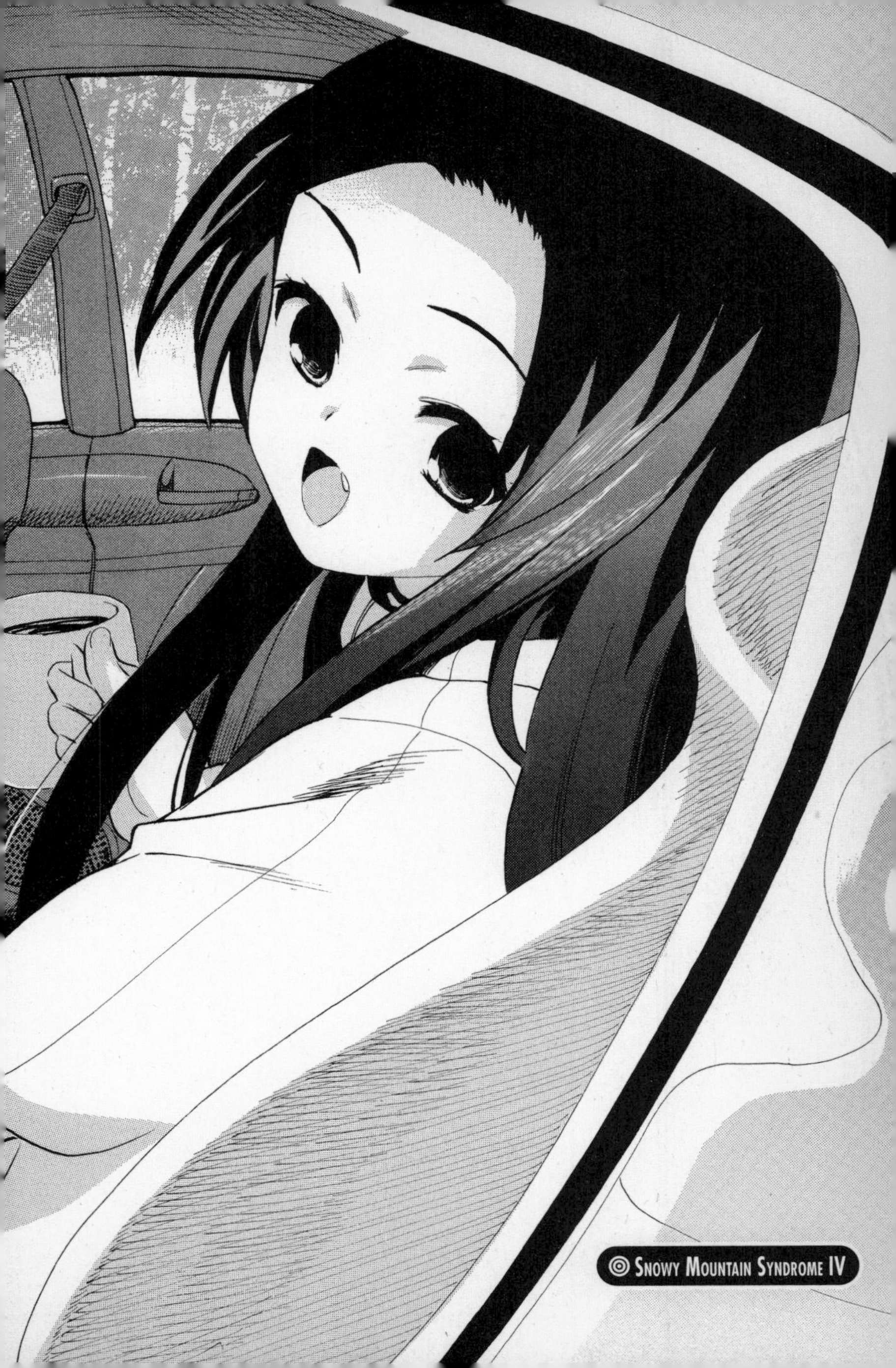
◎ SNOWY MOUNTAIN SYNDROME IV

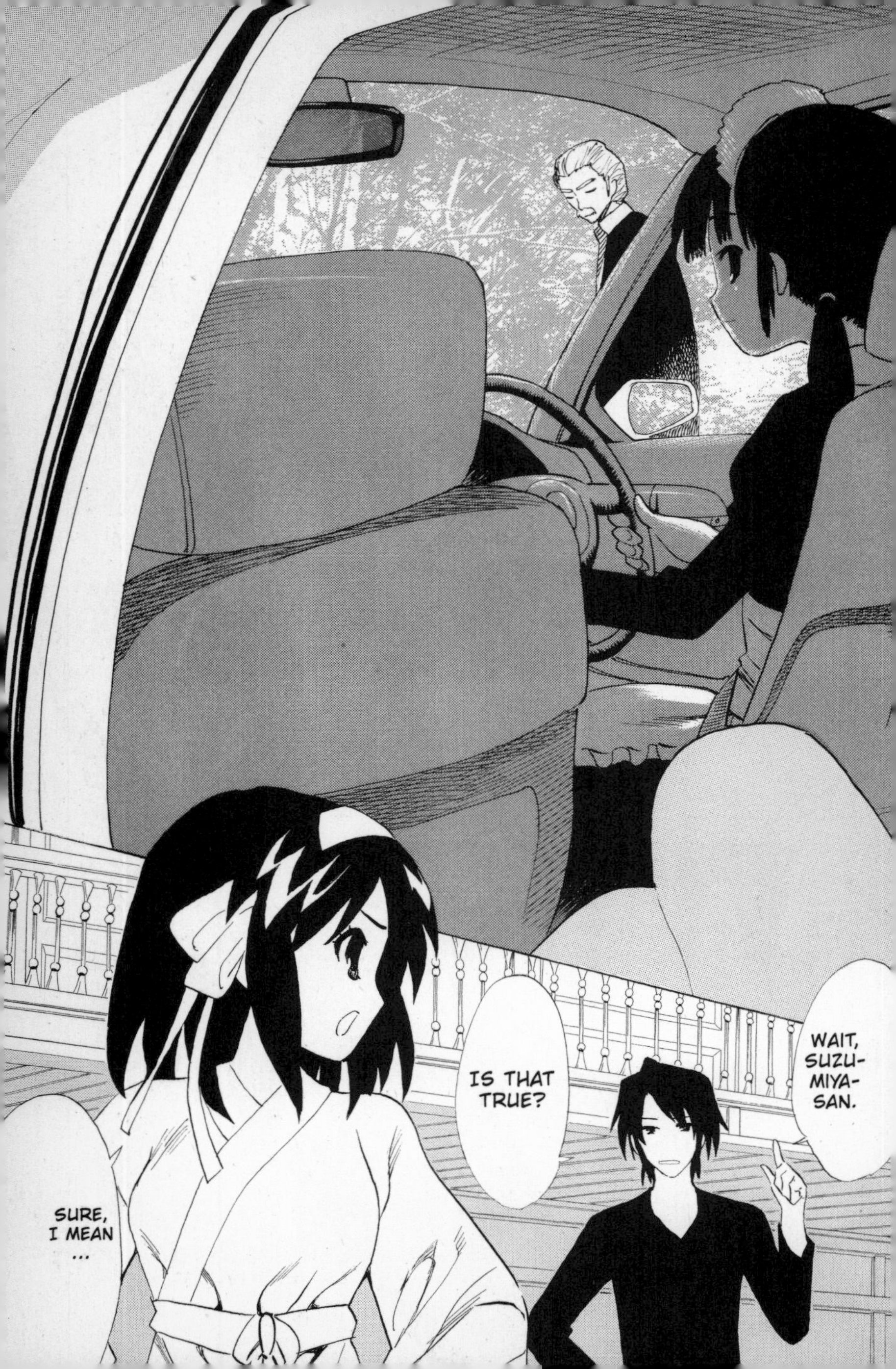
WAIT, SUZU-MIYA-SAN.
IS THAT TRUE?
SURE, I MEAN ...

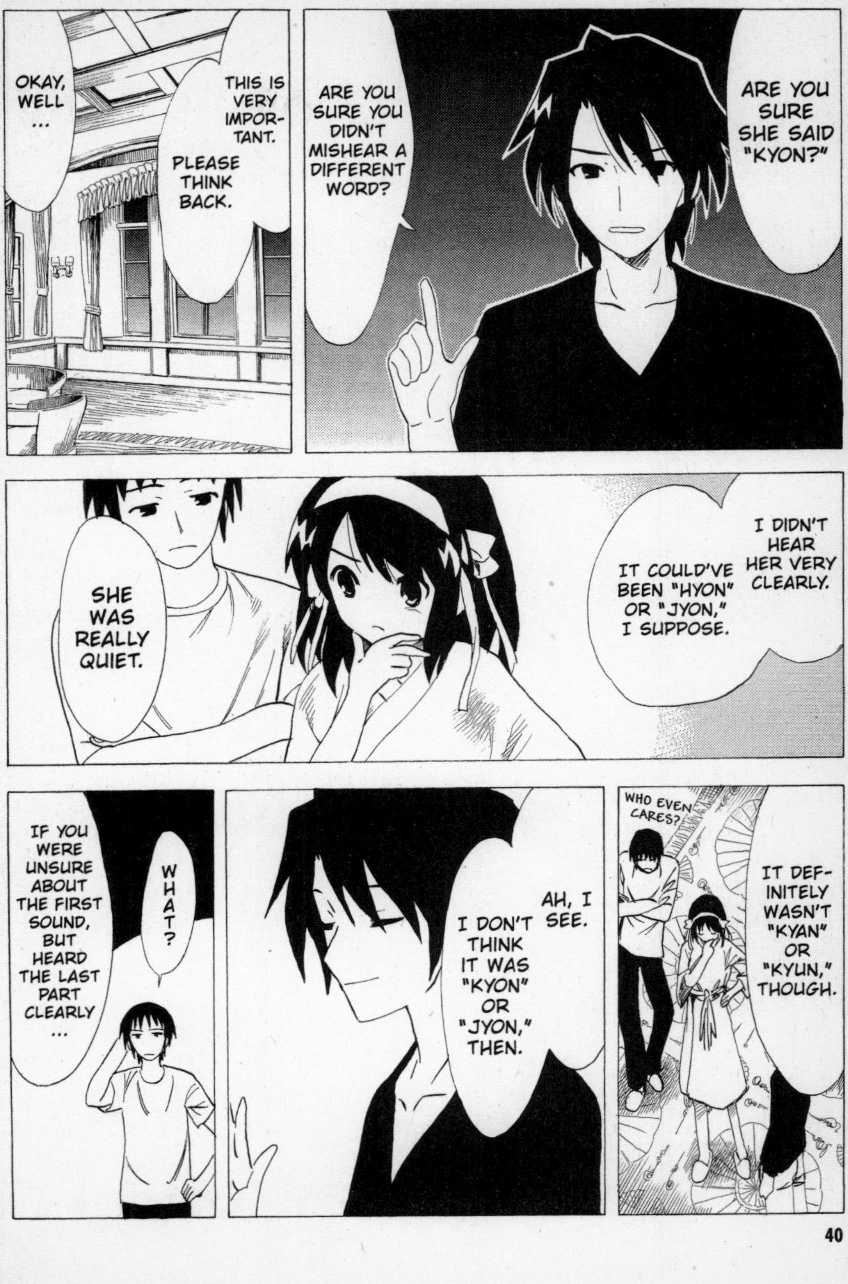
ARE YOU SURE SHE SAID "KYON?"
ARE YOU SURE YOU DIDN'T MISHEAR A DIFFERENT WORD?
THIS IS VERY IMPORTANT.
PLEASE THINK BACK.
OKAY, WELL ...
I DIDN'T HEAR HER VERY CLEARLY.
IT COULD'VE BEEN "HYON" OR "JYON," I SUPPOSE.
SHE WAS REALLY QUIET.
IT DEFINITELY WASN'T "KYAN" OR "KYUN," THOUGH.
WHO EVEN CARES?
AH, I SEE.
I DON'T THINK IT WAS "KYON" OR "JYON," THEN.
WHAT?
IF YOU WERE UNSURE ABOUT THE FIRST SOUND, BUT HEARD THE LAST PART CLEARLY ...

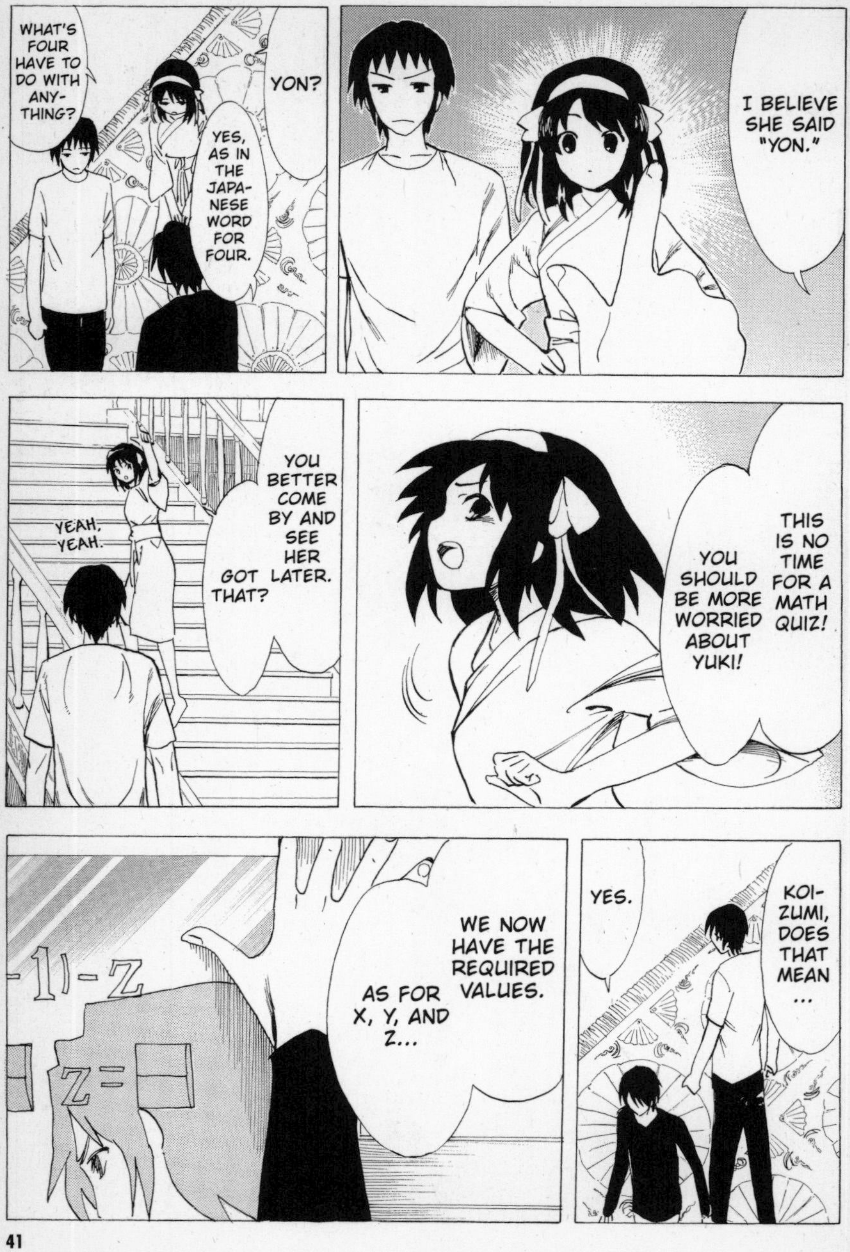
I BELIEVE SHE SAID "YON."
YON?
WHAT'S FOUR HAVE TO DO WITH ANY-THING?
YES, AS IN THE JAPA-NESE WORD FOR FOUR.
THIS IS NO TIME FOR A MATH QUIZ!
YOU SHOULD BE MORE WORRIED ABOUT YUKI!
YOU BETTER COME BY AND SEE HER LATER.
GOT THAT?
YEAH, YEAH.
KOI-ZUMI, DOES THAT MEAN ...
YES.
WE NOW HAVE THE REQUIRED VALUES.
AS FOR X, Y, AND Z...

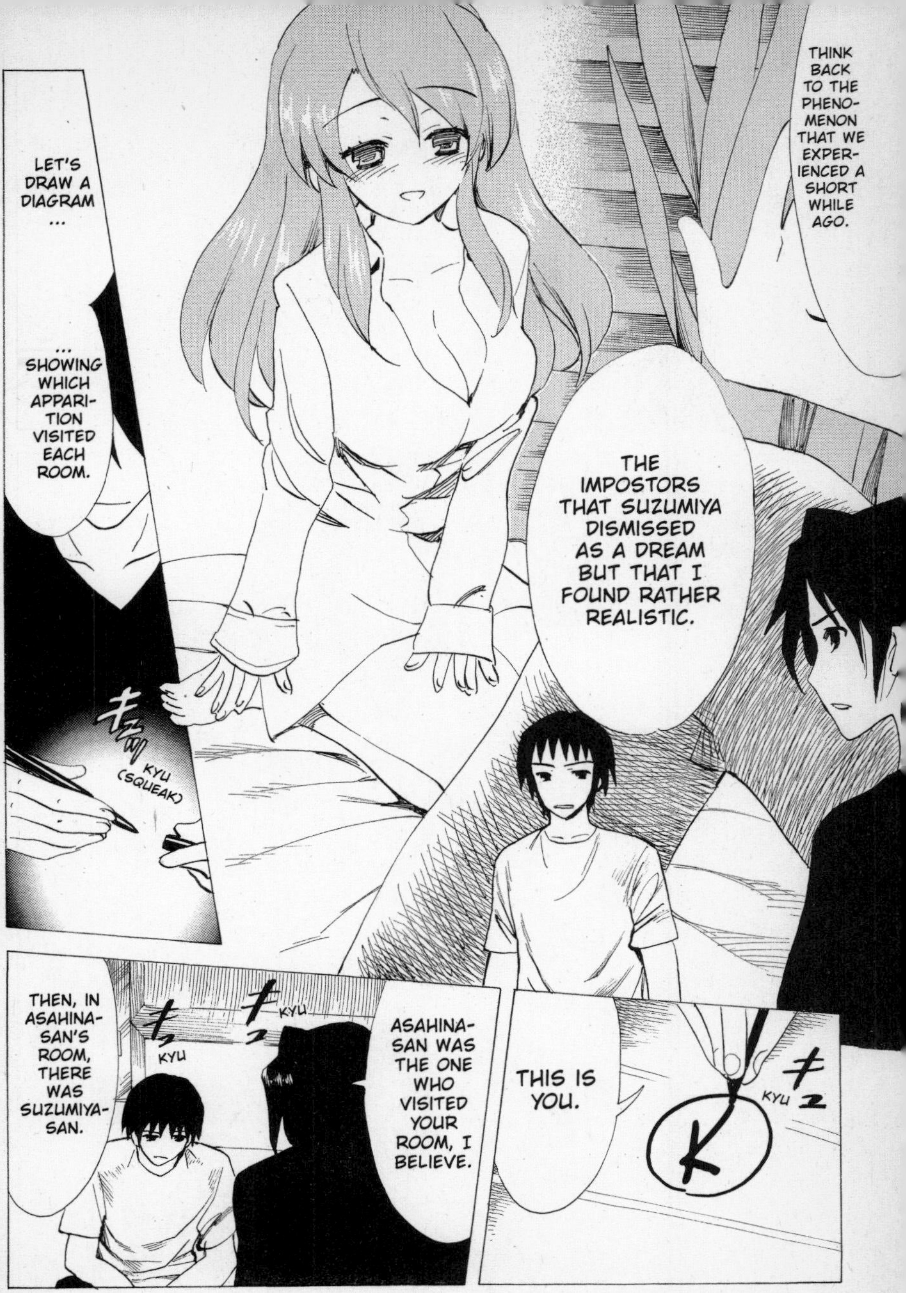
THINK BACK TO THE PHENOMENON THAT WE EXPERIENCED A SHORT WHILE AGO.
THE IMPOSTORS THAT SUZUMIYA DISMISSED AS A DREAM BUT THAT I FOUND RATHER REALISTIC.
LET'S DRAW A DIAGRAM ...
... SHOWING WHICH APPARITION VISITED EACH ROOM.
KYU (SQUEAK)
THIS IS YOU.
KYU
ASAHINA-SAN WAS THE ONE WHO VISITED YOUR ROOM, I BELIEVE.
THEN, IN ASAHINA-SAN'S ROOM, THERE WAS SUZUMIYA-SAN.
KYU
KYU

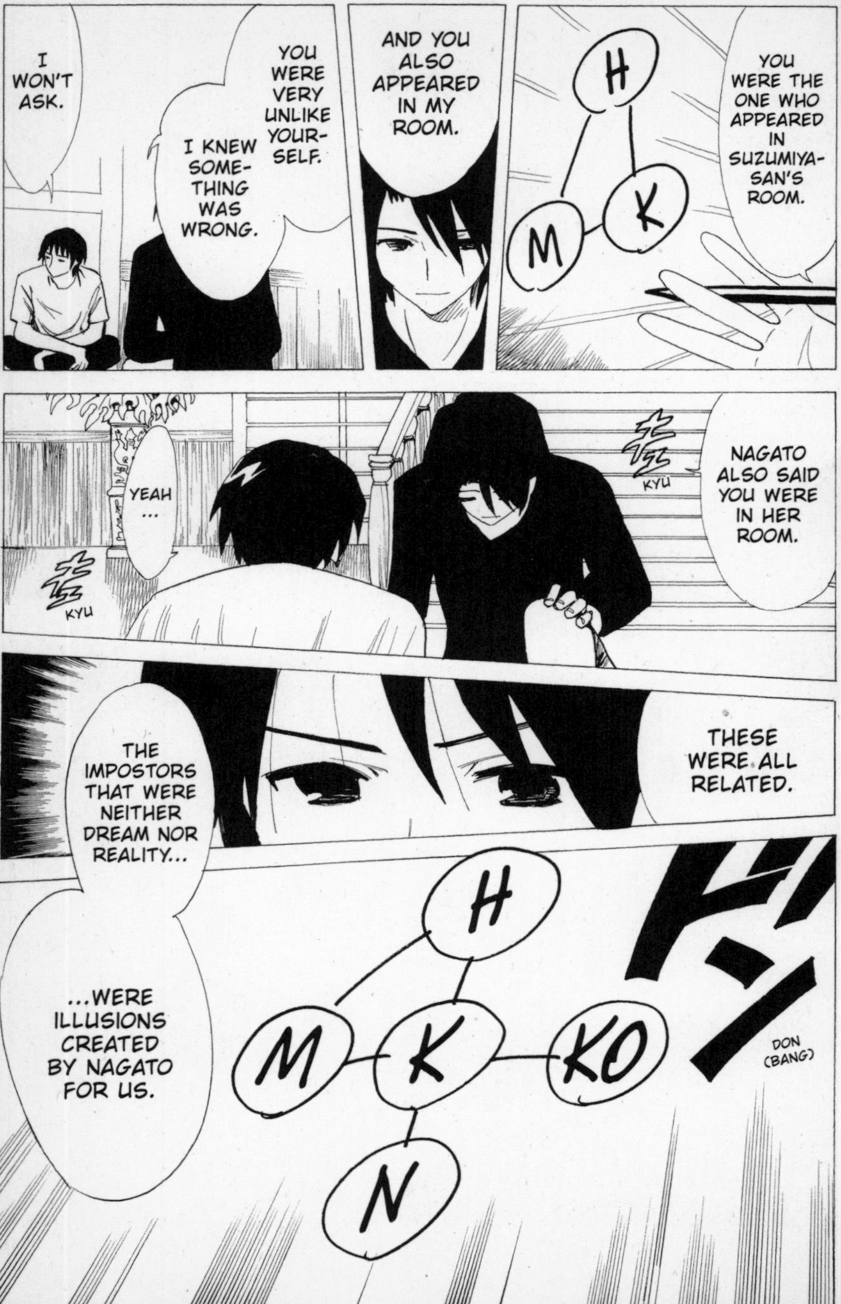
YOU WERE THE ONE WHO APPEARED IN SUZUMIYA-SAN'S ROOM.
H
K
M
AND YOU ALSO APPEARED IN MY ROOM.
YOU WERE VERY UNLIKE YOUR-SELF.
I KNEW SOME-THING WAS WRONG.
I WON'T ASK.
NAGATO ALSO SAID YOU WERE IN HER ROOM.
KYU
YEAH ...
KYU
THESE WERE ALL RELATED.
THE IMPOSTORS THAT WERE NEITHER DREAM NOR REALITY...
DON (BANG)
H
KO
K
M
N
...WERE ILLUSIONS CREATED BY NAGATO FOR US.

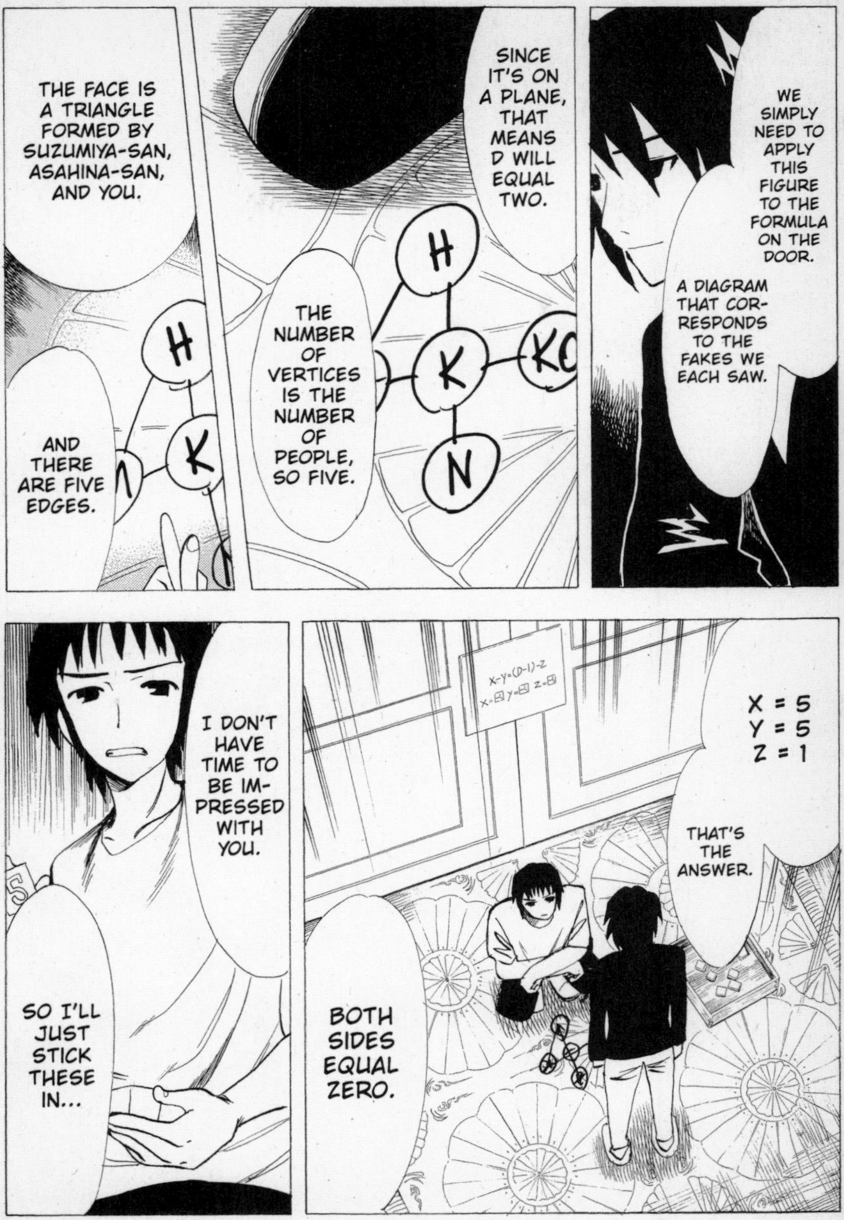
WE SIMPLY NEED TO APPLY THIS FIGURE TO THE FORMULA ON THE DOOR.
A DIAGRAM THAT CORRESPONDS TO THE FAKES WE EACH SAW.
SINCE IT'S ON A PLANE, THAT MEANS D WILL EQUAL TWO.
H
K
KO
N
THE NUMBER OF VERTICES IS THE NUMBER OF PEOPLE, SO FIVE.
THE FACE IS A TRIANGLE FORMED BY SUZUMIYA-SAN, ASAHINA-SAN, AND YOU.
H
K
AND THERE ARE FIVE EDGES.
X = 5
Y = 5
Z = 1
THAT'S THE ANSWER.
BOTH SIDES EQUAL ZERO.
I DON'T HAVE TIME TO BE IMPRESSED WITH YOU.
SO I'LL JUST STICK THESE IN...

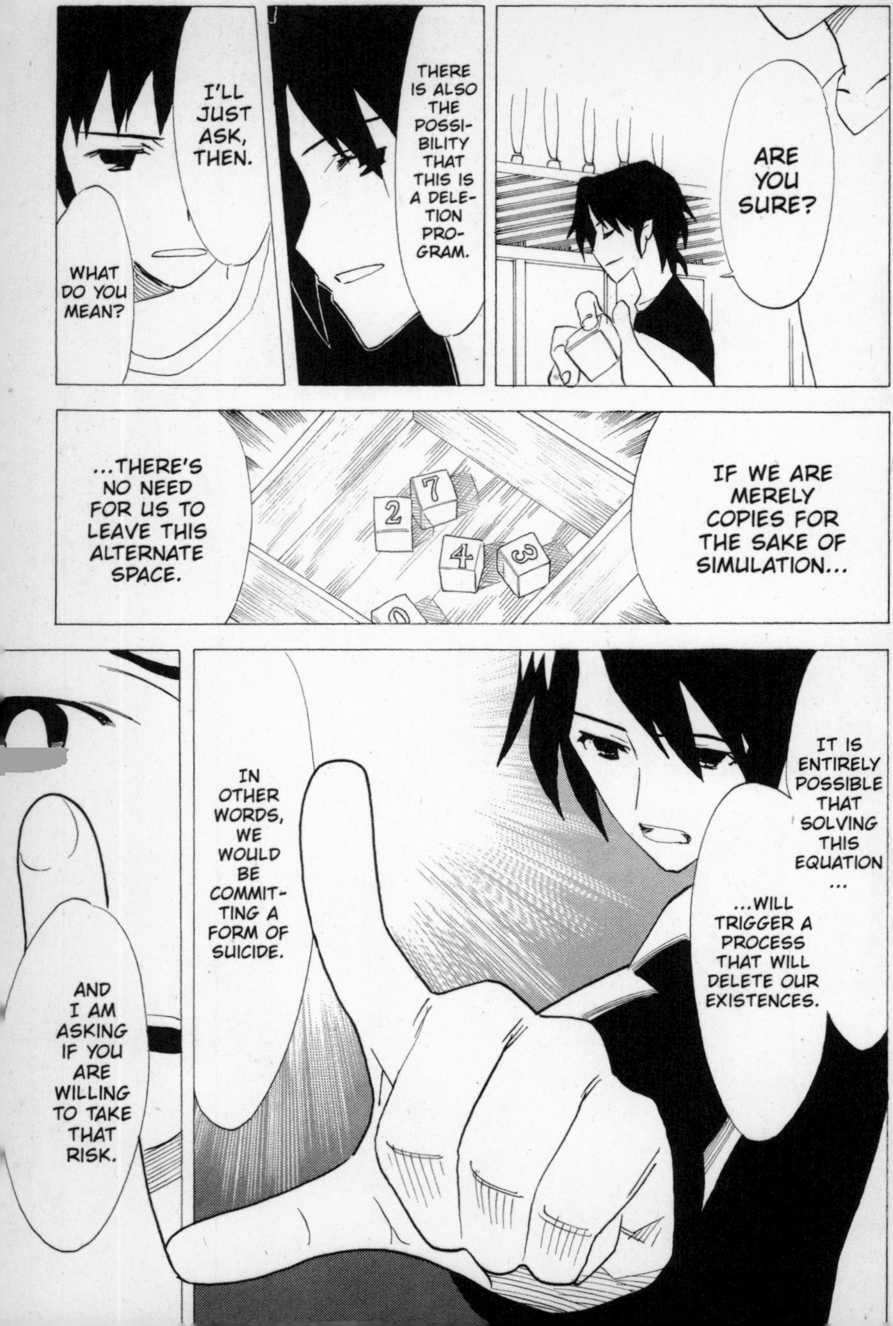
ARE YOU SURE?
THERE IS ALSO THE POSSIBILITY THAT THIS IS A DELETION PROGRAM.
I'LL JUST ASK, THEN.
WHAT DO YOU MEAN?
IF WE ARE MERELY COPIES FOR THE SAKE OF SIMULATION...
...THERE'S NO NEED FOR US TO LEAVE THIS ALTERNATE SPACE.
IT IS ENTIRELY POSSIBLE THAT SOLVING THIS EQUATION...
...WILL TRIGGER A PROCESS THAT WILL DELETE OUR EXISTENCES.
IN OTHER WORDS, WE WOULD BE COMMITTING A FORM OF SUICIDE.
AND I AM ASKING IF YOU ARE WILLING TO TAKE THAT RISK.

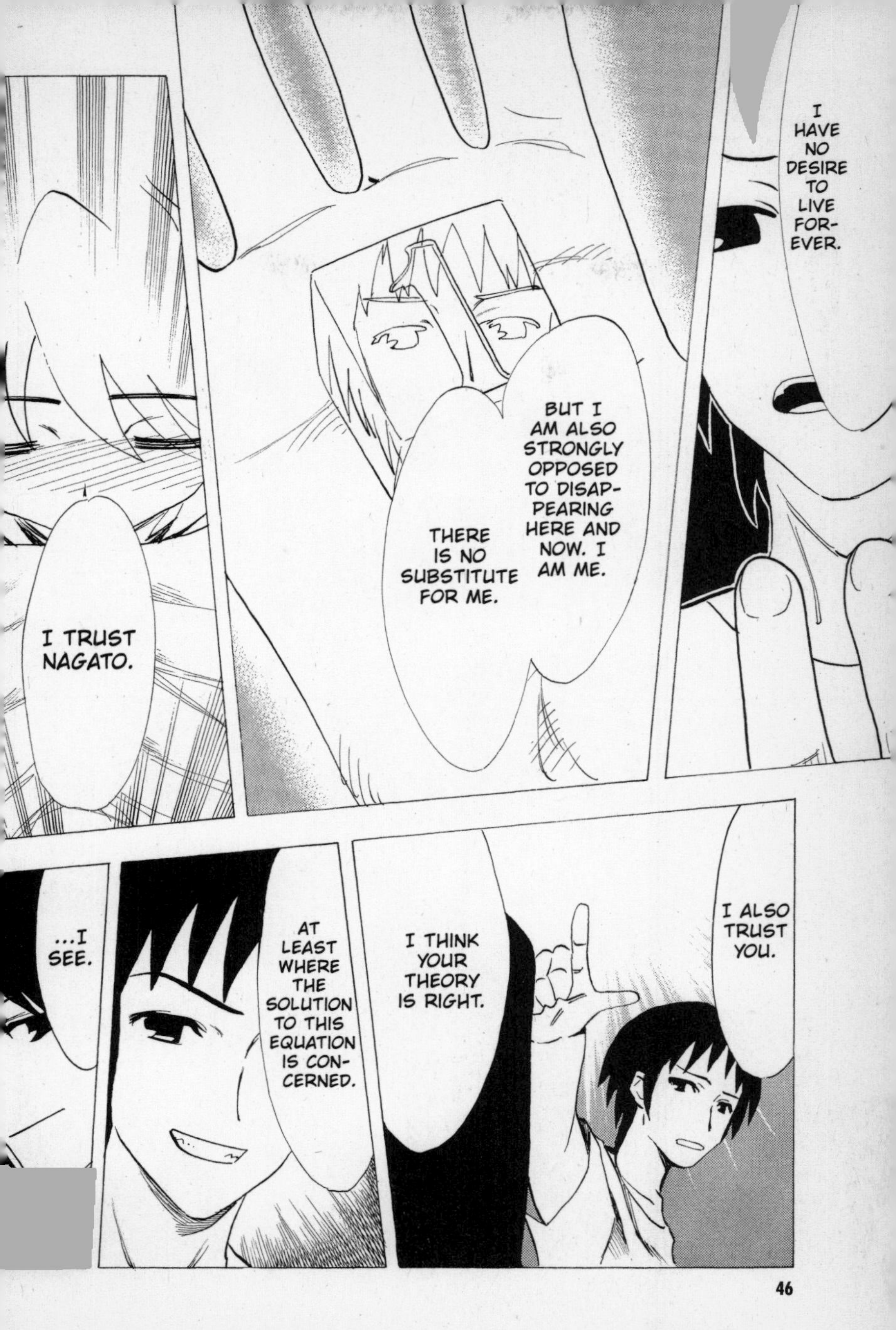
I HAVE NO DESIRE TO LIVE FOREVER.
BUT I AM ALSO STRONGLY OPPOSED TO DISAPPEARING HERE AND NOW. I AM ME.
THERE IS NO SUBSTITUTE FOR ME.
I TRUST NAGATO.
I ALSO TRUST YOU.
I THINK YOUR THEORY IS RIGHT.
AT LEAST WHERE THE SOLUTION TO THIS EQUATION IS CONCERNED.
...I SEE.

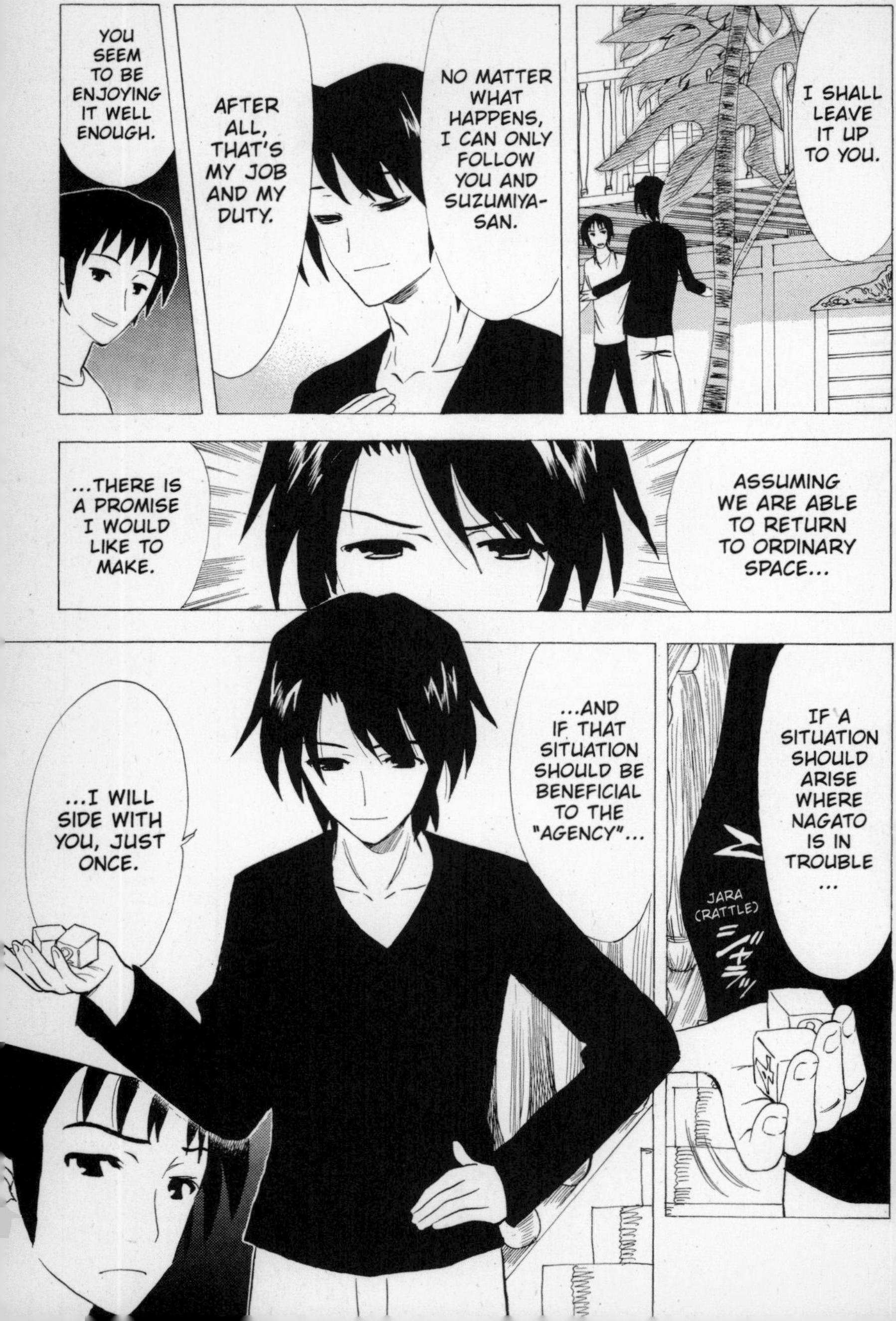
I SHALL LEAVE IT UP TO YOU.
NO MATTER WHAT HAPPENS, I CAN ONLY FOLLOW YOU AND SUZUMIYA-SAN.
AFTER ALL, THAT'S MY JOB AND MY DUTY.
YOU SEEM TO BE ENJOYING IT WELL ENOUGH.
ASSUMING WE ARE ABLE TO RETURN TO ORDINARY SPACE...
...THERE IS A PROMISE I WOULD LIKE TO MAKE.
IF A SITUATION SHOULD ARISE WHERE NAGATO IS IN TROUBLE ...
JARA (RATTLE)
...AND IF THAT SITUATION SHOULD BE BENEFICIAL TO THE "AGENCY"...
...I WILL SIDE WITH YOU, JUST ONCE.

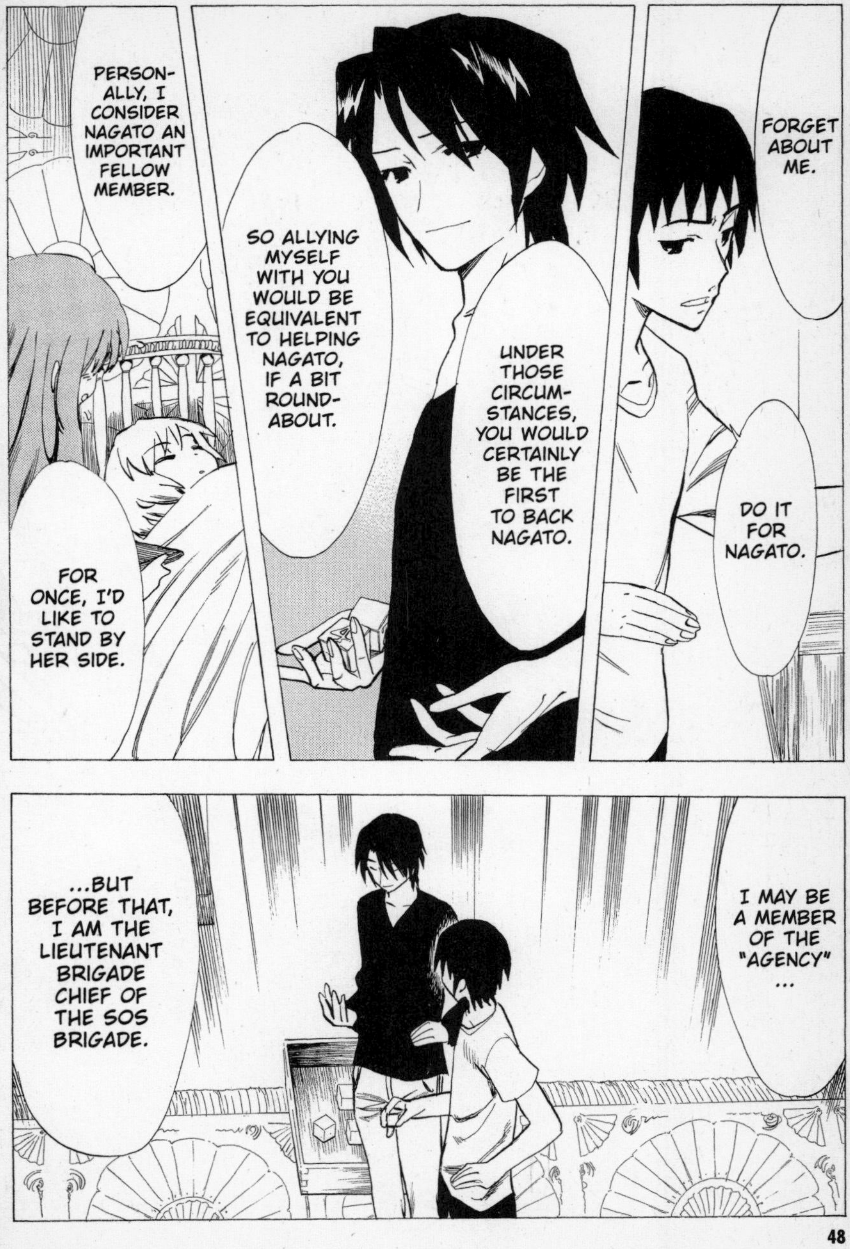
FORGET ABOUT ME.
DO IT FOR NAGATO.
UNDER THOSE CIRCUM-STANCES, YOU WOULD CERTAINLY BE THE FIRST TO BACK NAGATO.
SO ALLYING MYSELF WITH YOU WOULD BE EQUIVALENT TO HELPING NAGATO, IF A BIT ROUND-ABOUT.
PERSON-ALLY, I CONSIDER NAGATO AN IMPORTANT FELLOW MEMBER.
FOR ONCE, I'D LIKE TO STAND BY HER SIDE.
I MAY BE A MEMBER OF THE "AGENCY" ...
...BUT BEFORE THAT, I AM THE LIEUTENANT BRIGADE CHIEF OF THE SOS BRIGADE.

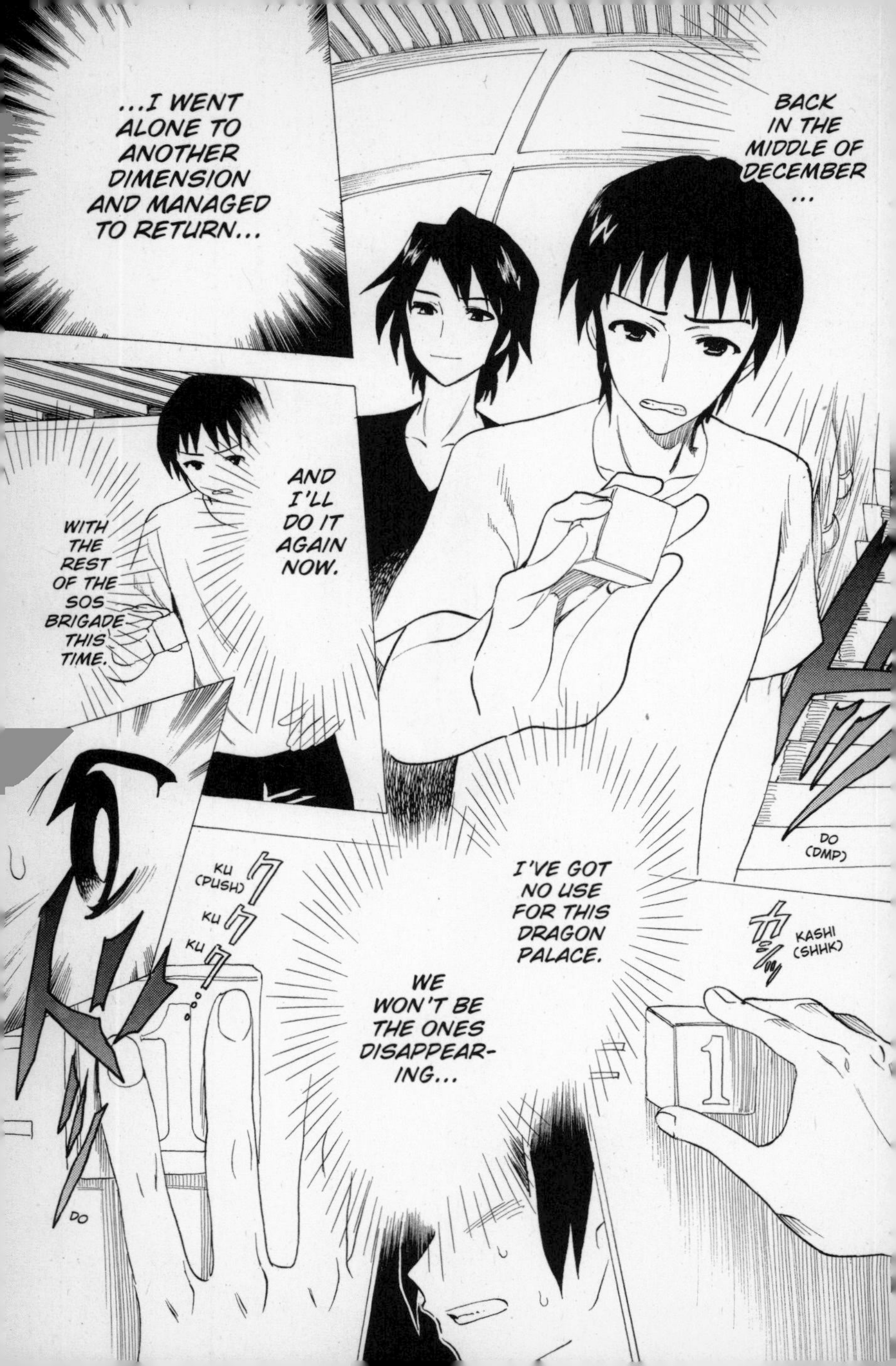
BACK IN THE MIDDLE OF DECEMBER...
...I WENT ALONE TO ANOTHER DIMENSION AND MANAGED TO RETURN...
AND I'LL DO IT AGAIN NOW.
WITH THE REST OF THE SOS BRIGADE THIS TIME.
DO (DMP)
KASHI (SHHK)
I'VE GOT NO USE FOR THIS DRAGON PALACE.
WE WON'T BE THE ONES DISAPPEAR-ING...
KU (PUSH)
KU
KU
DO

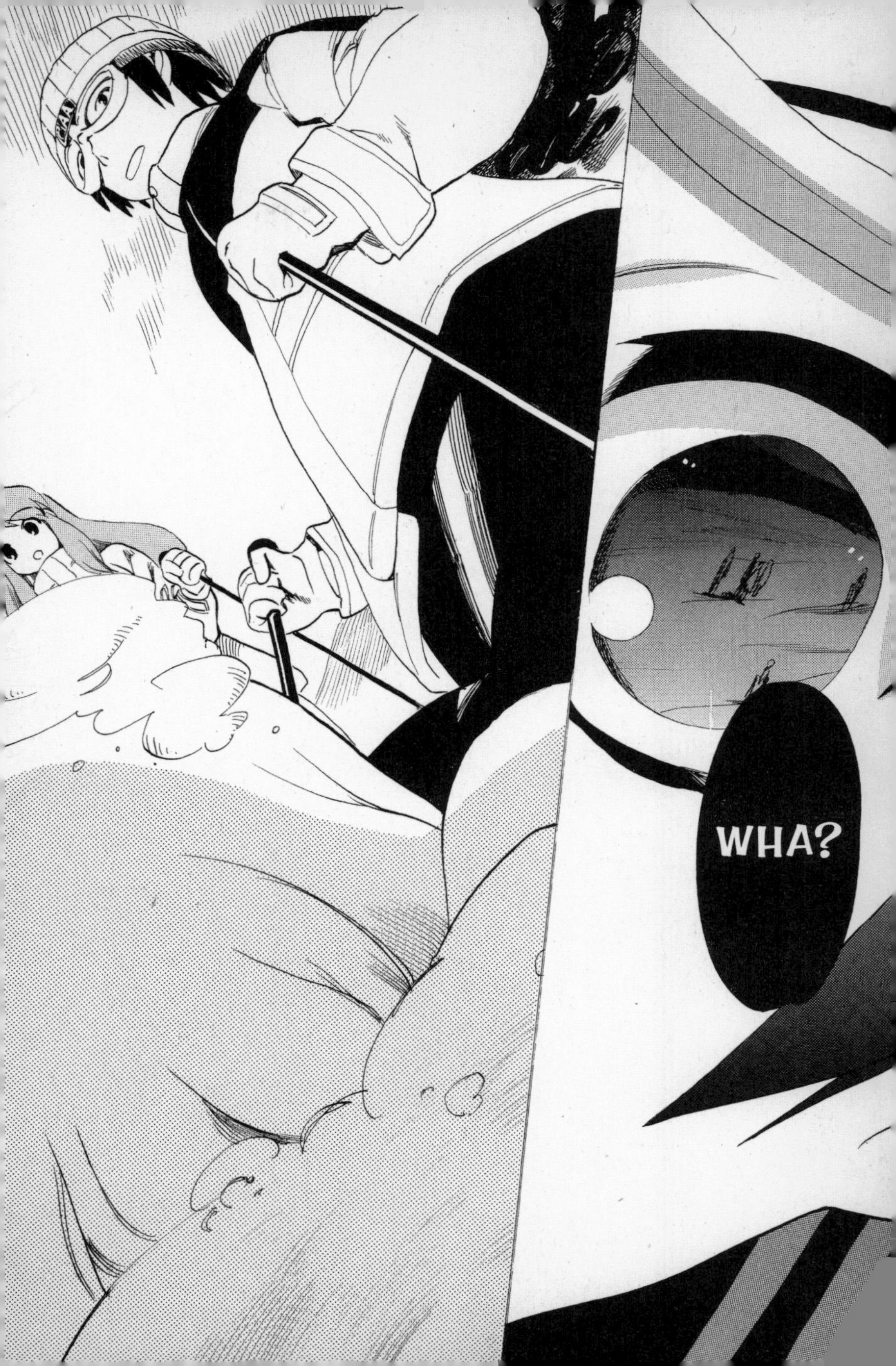
WHA?

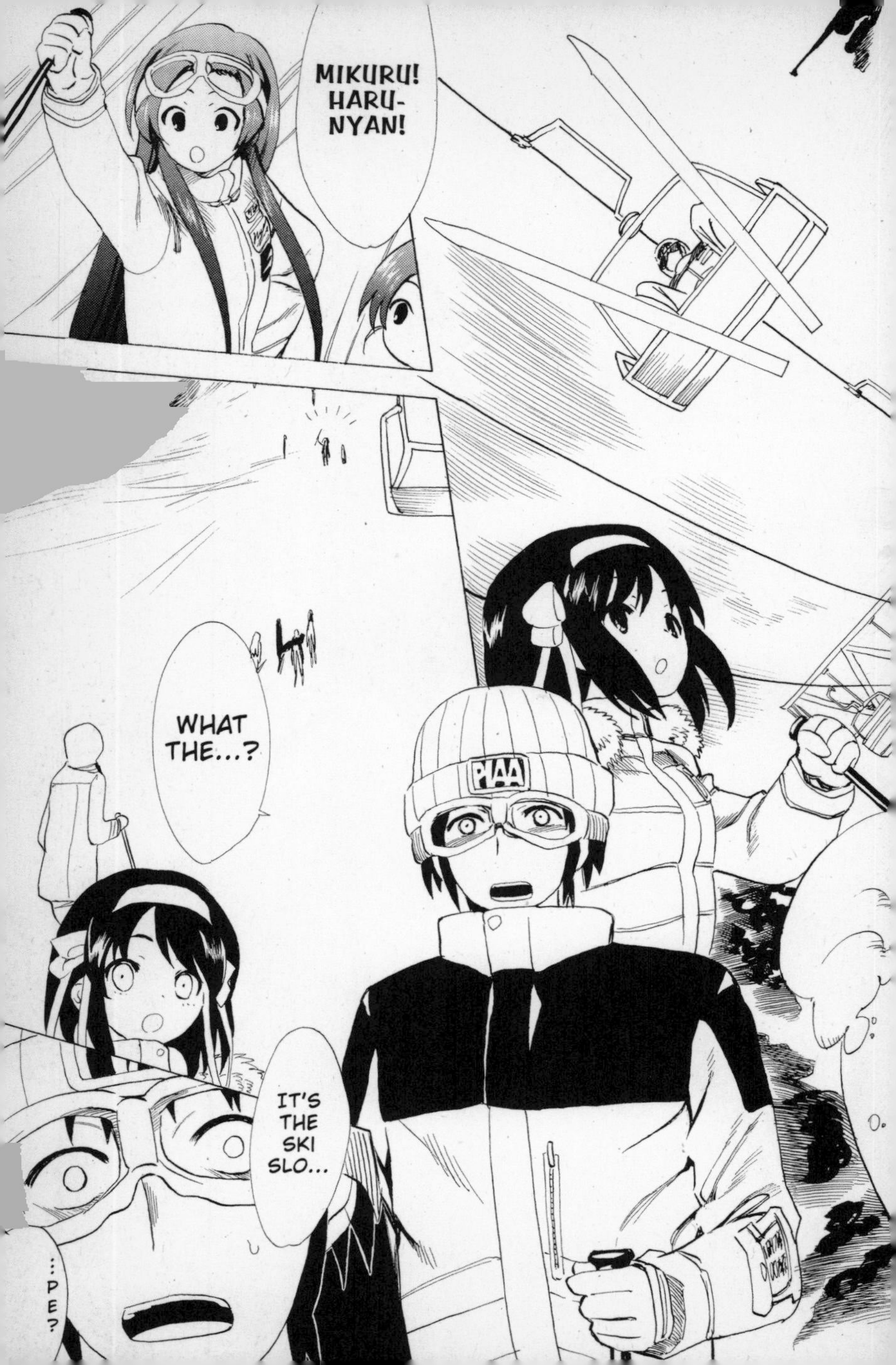
MIKURU! HARU-NYAN!
WHAT THE...?
IT'S THE SKI SLO...
...PE?

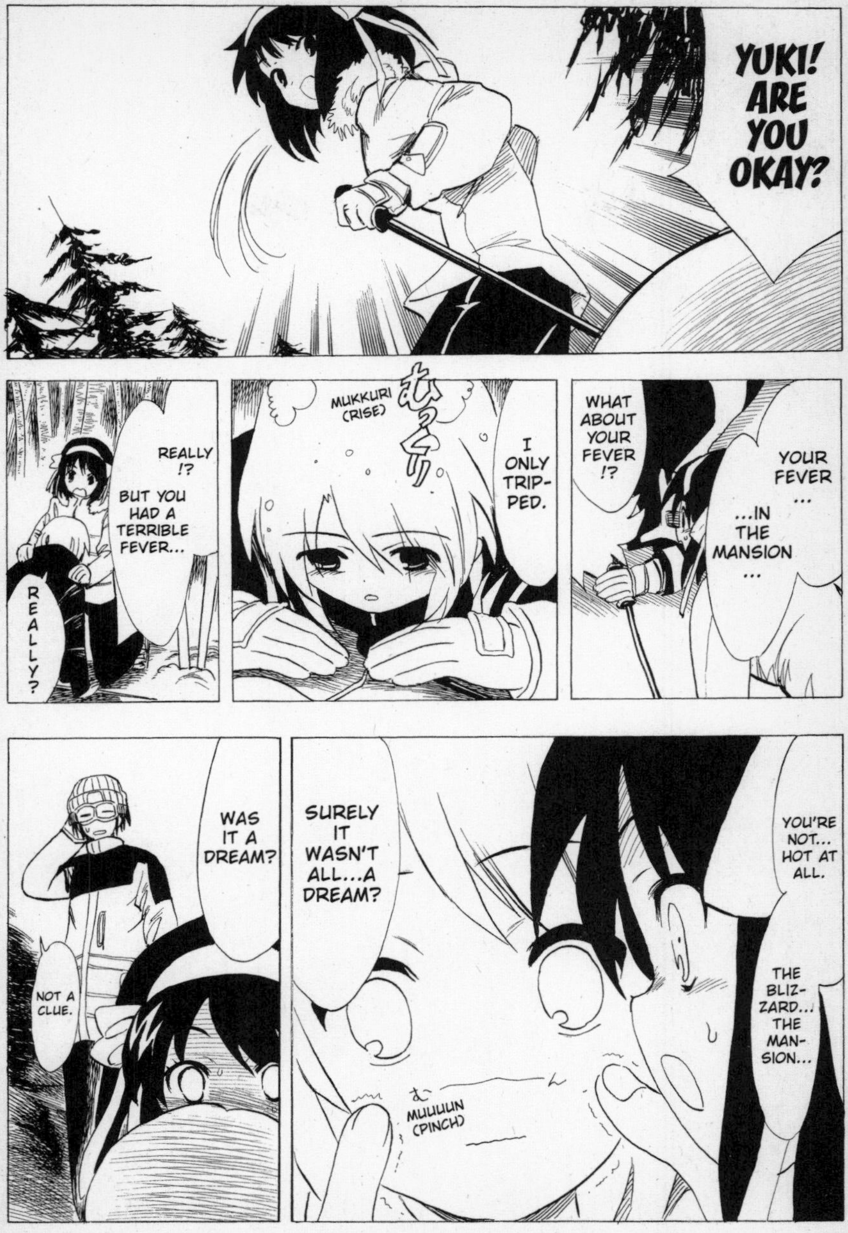
YUKI! ARE YOU OKAY?
WHAT ABOUT YOUR FEVER !?
YOUR FEVER ...
...IN THE MANSION ...
むっくり
MUKKURI (RISE)
I ONLY TRIP-PED.
REALLY !?
BUT YOU HAD A TERRIBLE FEVER...
REALLY?
YOU'RE NOT... HOT AT ALL.
SURELY IT WASN'T ALL...A DREAM?
THE BLIZ-ZARD... THE MAN-SION...
む
MUUUUN (PINCH)
WAS IT A DREAM?
NOT A CLUE.

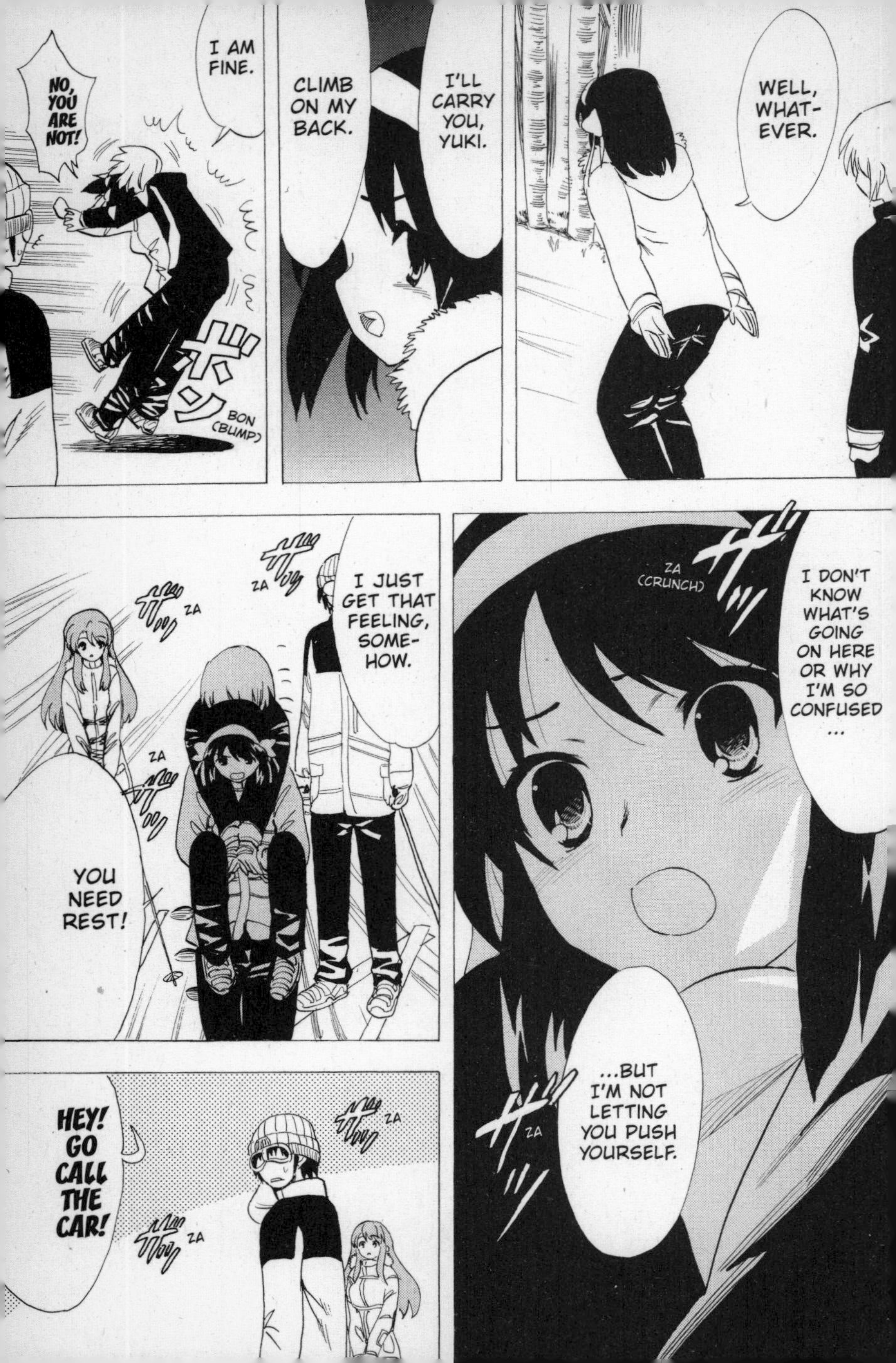

WELL, WHAT-EVER.
I'LL CARRY YOU, YUKI.
CLIMB ON MY BACK.
I AM FINE.
NO, YOU ARE NOT!
BON (BUMP)
ZA (CRUNCH)
I DON'T KNOW WHAT'S GOING ON HERE OR WHY I'M SO CONFUSED ...
...BUT I'M NOT LETTING YOU PUSH YOURSELF.
ZA
I JUST GET THAT FEELING, SOME-HOW.
ZA
ZA
ZA
YOU NEED REST!
ZA
HEY! GO CALL THE CAR!
ZA

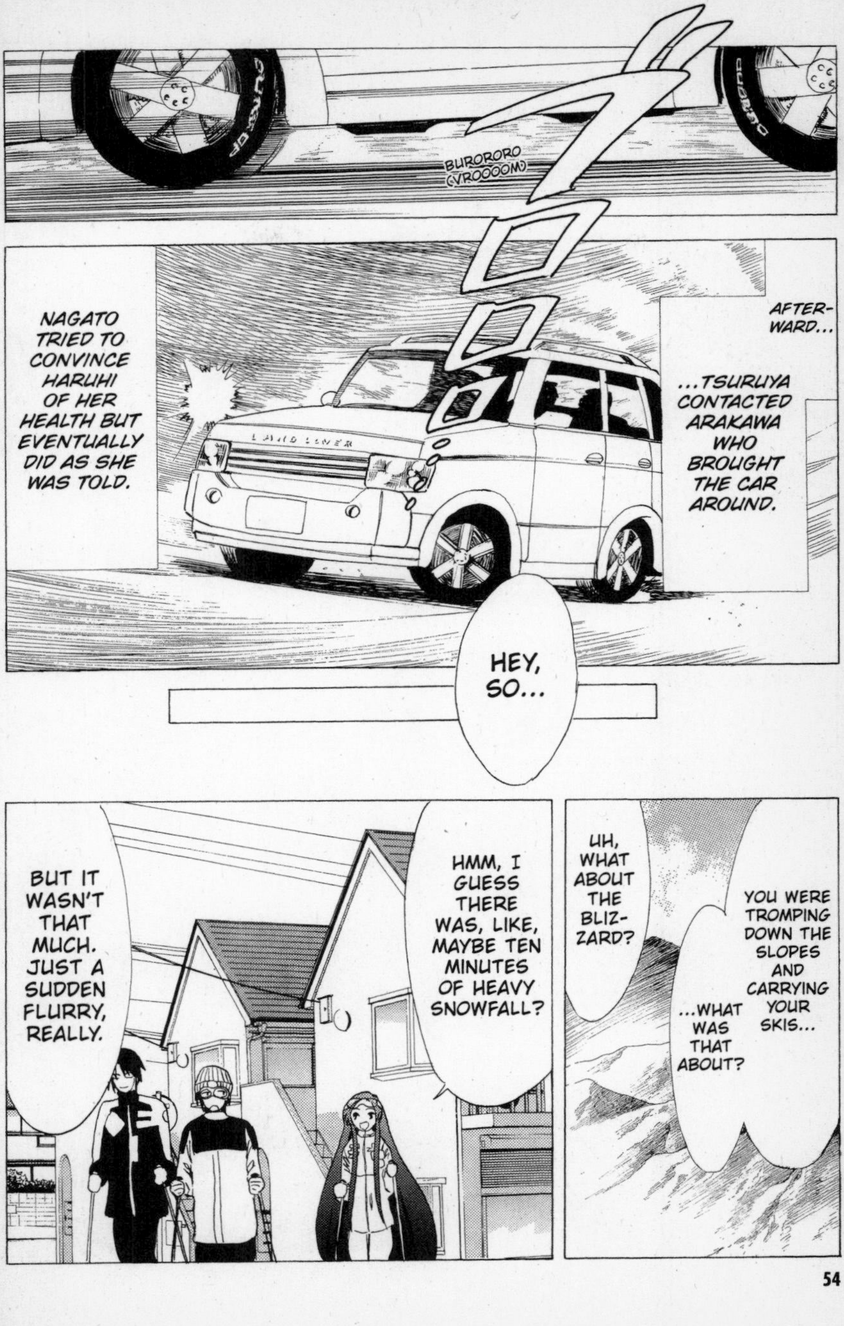

BURORORO (VROOOOM)
AFTERWARD...
...TSURUYA CONTACTED ARAKAWA WHO BROUGHT THE CAR AROUND.
NAGATO TRIED TO CONVINCE HARUHI OF HER HEALTH BUT EVENTUALLY DID AS SHE WAS TOLD.
HEY, SO...
YOU WERE TROMPING DOWN THE SLOPES AND CARRYING YOUR SKIS...
...WHAT WAS THAT ABOUT?
UH, WHAT ABOUT THE BLIZZARD?
HMM, I GUESS THERE WAS, LIKE, MAYBE TEN MINUTES OF HEAVY SNOWFALL?
BUT IT WASN'T THAT MUCH. JUST A SUDDEN FLURRY, REALLY.

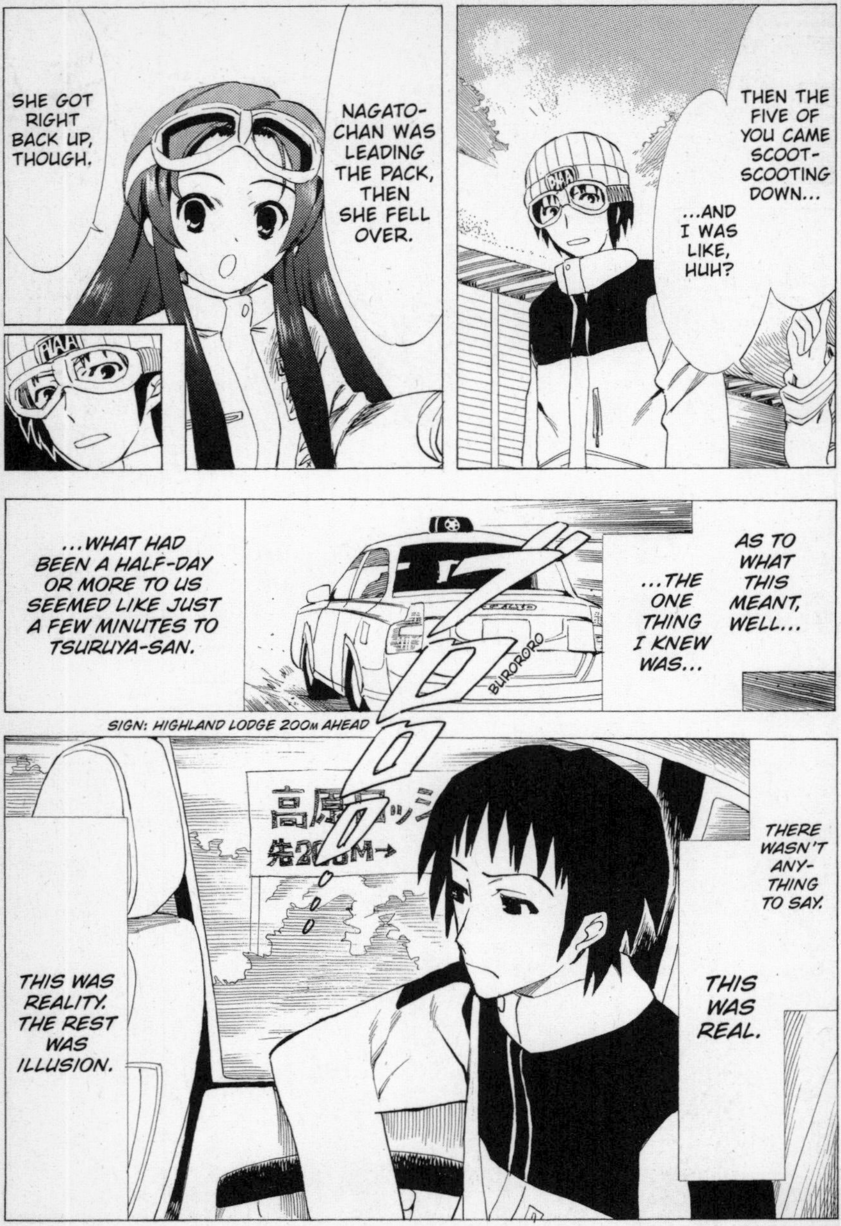

THEN THE FIVE OF YOU CAME SCOOT-SCOOTING DOWN...
...AND I WAS LIKE, HUH?
NAGATO-CHAN WAS LEADING THE PACK, THEN SHE FELL OVER.
SHE GOT RIGHT BACK UP, THOUGH.
AS TO WHAT THIS MEANT, WELL...
...THE ONE THING I KNEW WAS...
BURORORO
...WHAT HAD BEEN A HALF-DAY OR MORE TO US SEEMED LIKE JUST A FEW MINUTES TO TSURUYA-SAN.
SIGN: HIGHLAND LODGE 200m AHEAD
THERE WASN'T ANYTHING TO SAY.
THIS WAS REAL.
THIS WAS REALITY. THE REST WAS ILLUSION.

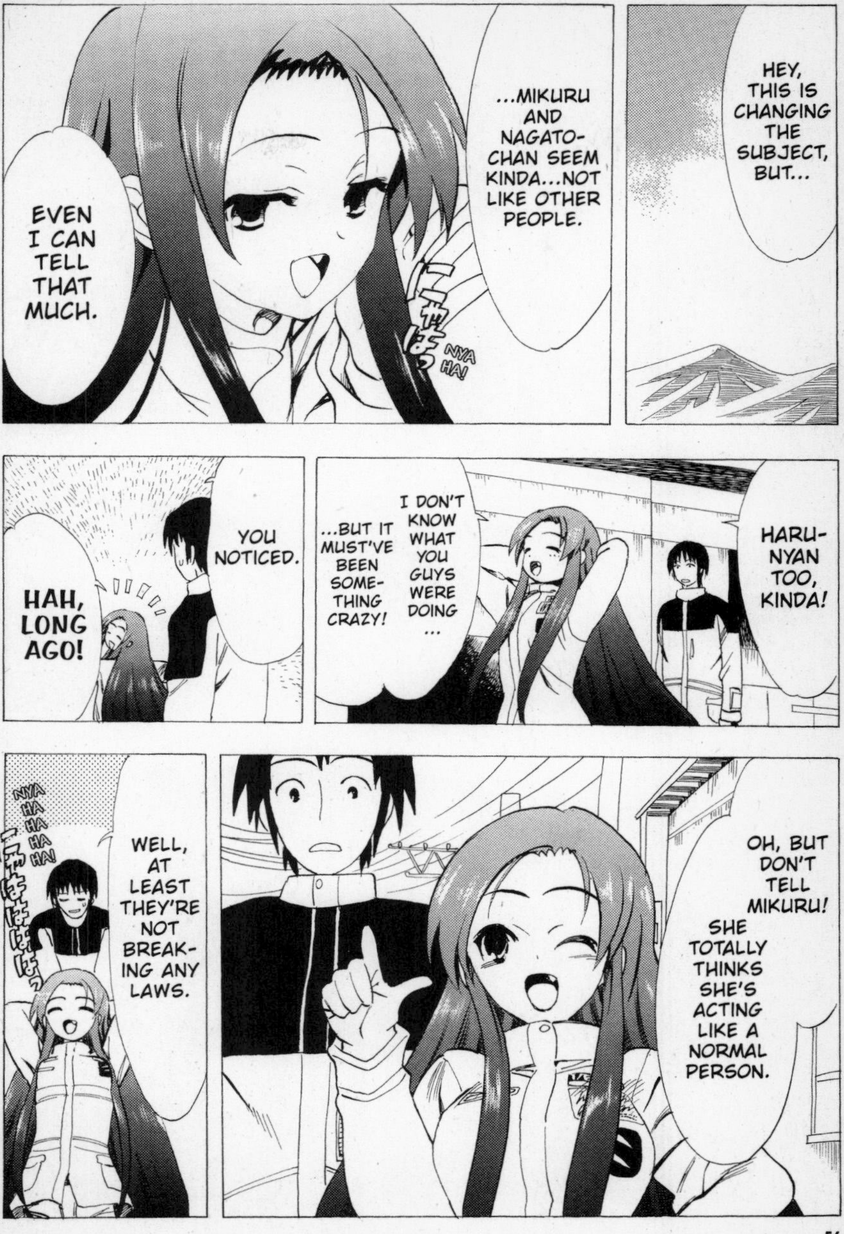
HEY, THIS IS CHANGING THE SUBJECT, BUT...
...MIKURU AND NAGATO-CHAN SEEM KINDA...NOT LIKE OTHER PEOPLE.
NYA HA!
EVEN I CAN TELL THAT MUCH.
HARU-NYAN TOO, KINDA!
I DON'T KNOW WHAT YOU GUYS WERE DOING...
...BUT IT MUST'VE BEEN SOME-THING CRAZY!
YOU NOTICED.
HAH, LONG AGO!
OH, BUT DON'T TELL MIKURU!
SHE TOTALLY THINKS SHE'S ACTING LIKE A NORMAL PERSON.
WELL, AT LEAST THEY'RE NOT BREAK-ING ANY LAWS.
NYA HA HA HA HA!

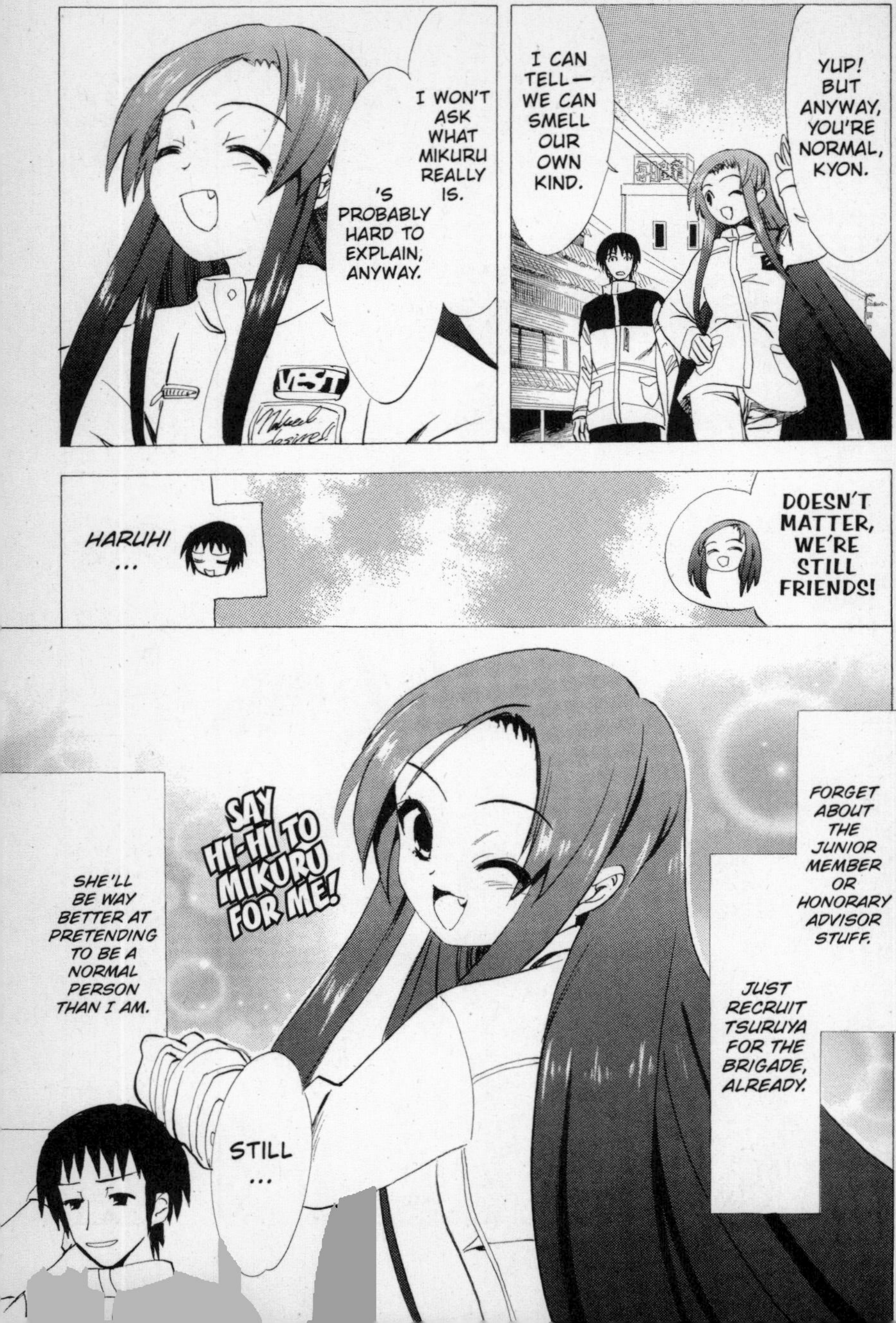
YUP! BUT ANYWAY, YOU'RE NORMAL, KYON.
I CAN TELL— WE CAN SMELL OUR OWN KIND.
I WON'T ASK WHAT MIKURU REALLY IS.
'S PROBABLY HARD TO EXPLAIN, ANYWAY.
DOESN'T MATTER, WE'RE STILL FRIENDS!
HARUHI ...
FORGET ABOUT THE JUNIOR MEMBER OR HONORARY ADVISOR STUFF.
JUST RECRUIT TSURUYA FOR THE BRIGADE, ALREADY.
SAY HI-HI TO MIKURU FOR ME!
SHE'LL BE WAY BETTER AT PRETENDING TO BE A NORMAL PERSON THAN I AM.
STILL ...

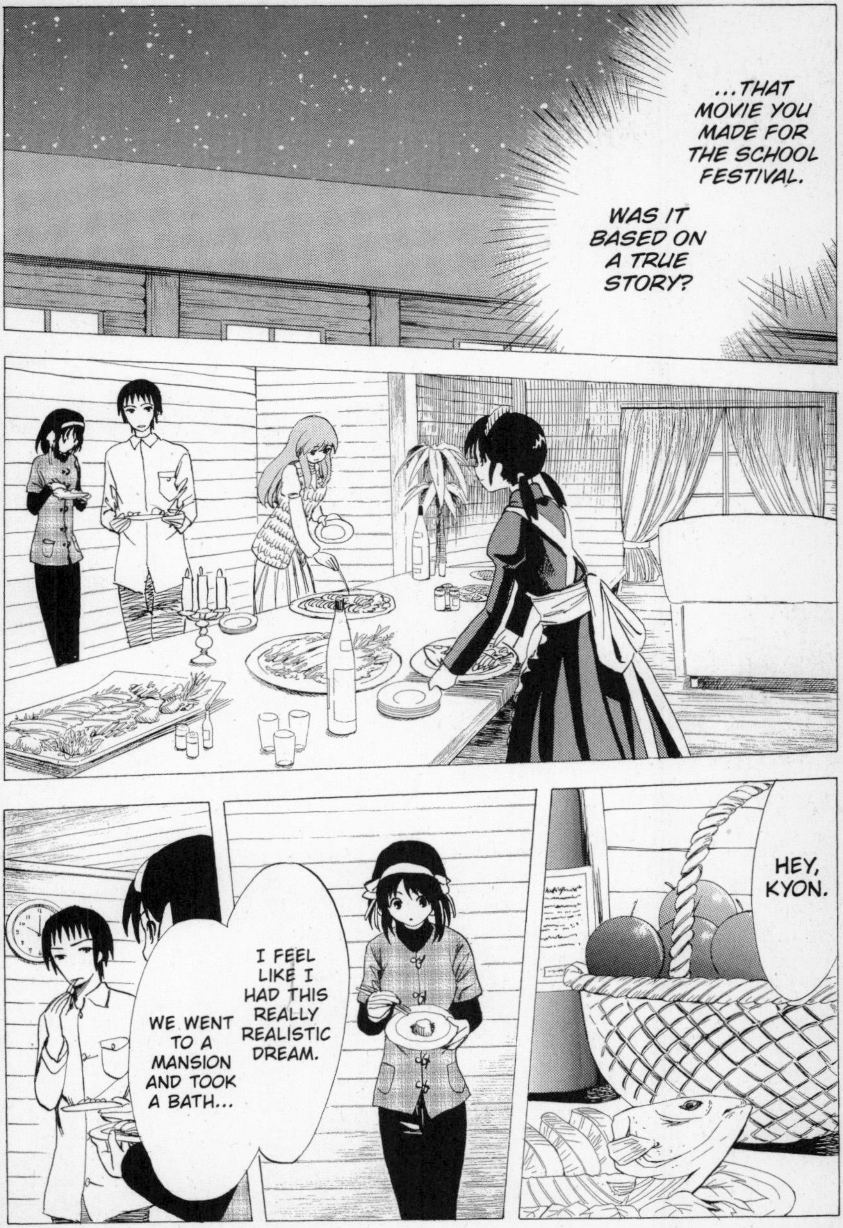
...THAT MOVIE YOU MADE FOR THE SCHOOL FESTIVAL.
WAS IT BASED ON A TRUE STORY?
HEY, KYON.
I FEEL LIKE I HAD THIS REALLY REALISTIC DREAM.
WE WENT TO A MANSION AND TOOK A BATH...

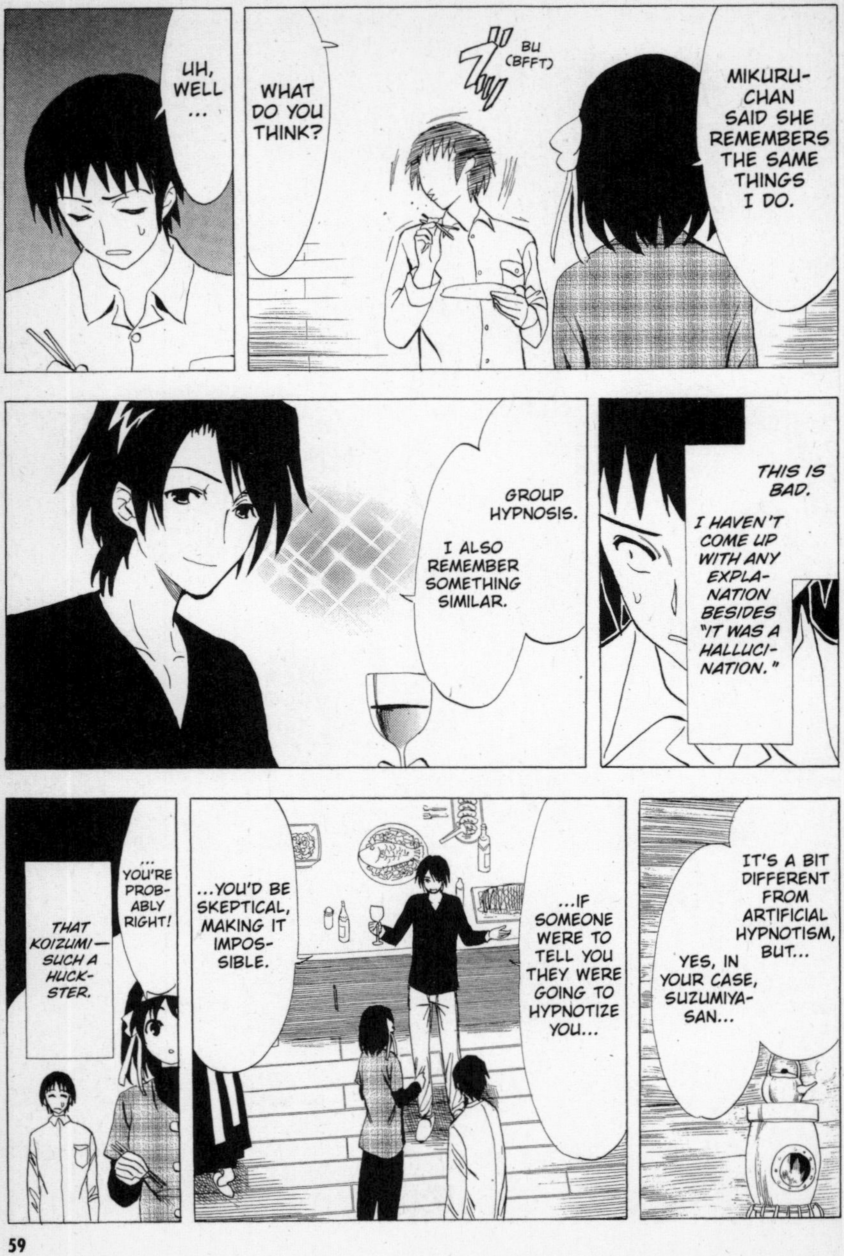
MIKURU-CHAN SAID SHE REMEMBERS THE SAME THINGS I DO.
BU (BFFT)
WHAT DO YOU THINK?
UH, WELL ...
THIS IS BAD.
I HAVEN'T COME UP WITH ANY EXPLANATION BESIDES "IT WAS A HALLUCINATION."
GROUP HYPNOSIS.
I ALSO REMEMBER SOMETHING SIMILAR.
IT'S A BIT DIFFERENT FROM ARTIFICIAL HYPNOTISM, BUT...
YES, IN YOUR CASE, SUZUMIYA-SAN...
...IF SOMEONE WERE TO TELL YOU THEY WERE GOING TO HYPNOTIZE YOU...
...YOU'D BE SKEPTICAL, MAKING IT IMPOSSIBLE.
... YOU'RE PROBABLY RIGHT!
THAT KOIZUMI—SUCH A HUCKSTER.

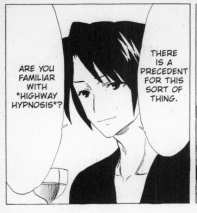

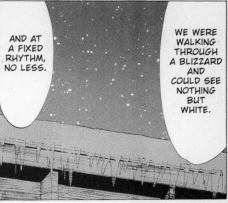

WE WERE WALKING THROUGH A BLIZZARD AND COULD SEE NOTHING BUT WHITE.
AND AT A FIXED RHYTHM, NO LESS.
THERE IS A PRECEDENT FOR THIS SORT OF THING.
ARE YOU FAMILIAR WITH "HIGHWAY HYPNOSIS"?
IF YOU DRIVE ALONG A STRAIGHT HIGHWAY FOR EXTENDED PERIODS OF TIME...
...THE EVENLY SPACED LIGHTS CAN PLACE THE DRIVER IN A STATE OF HYPNOSIS ...
...AND LULL HIM TO SLEEP.
LIKE WHAT HAP-PENED TO US.
RIDING IN A MOVING TRAIN CAR MAKES YOU SLEEPY.
WE PAT BABIES ON THEIR BACKS WHEN WE WANT THEM TO SLEEP.
THERE ARE MANY EXAMPLES OF THIS.

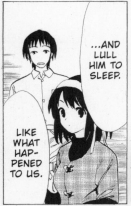

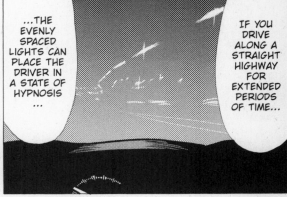

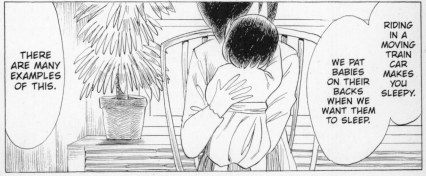

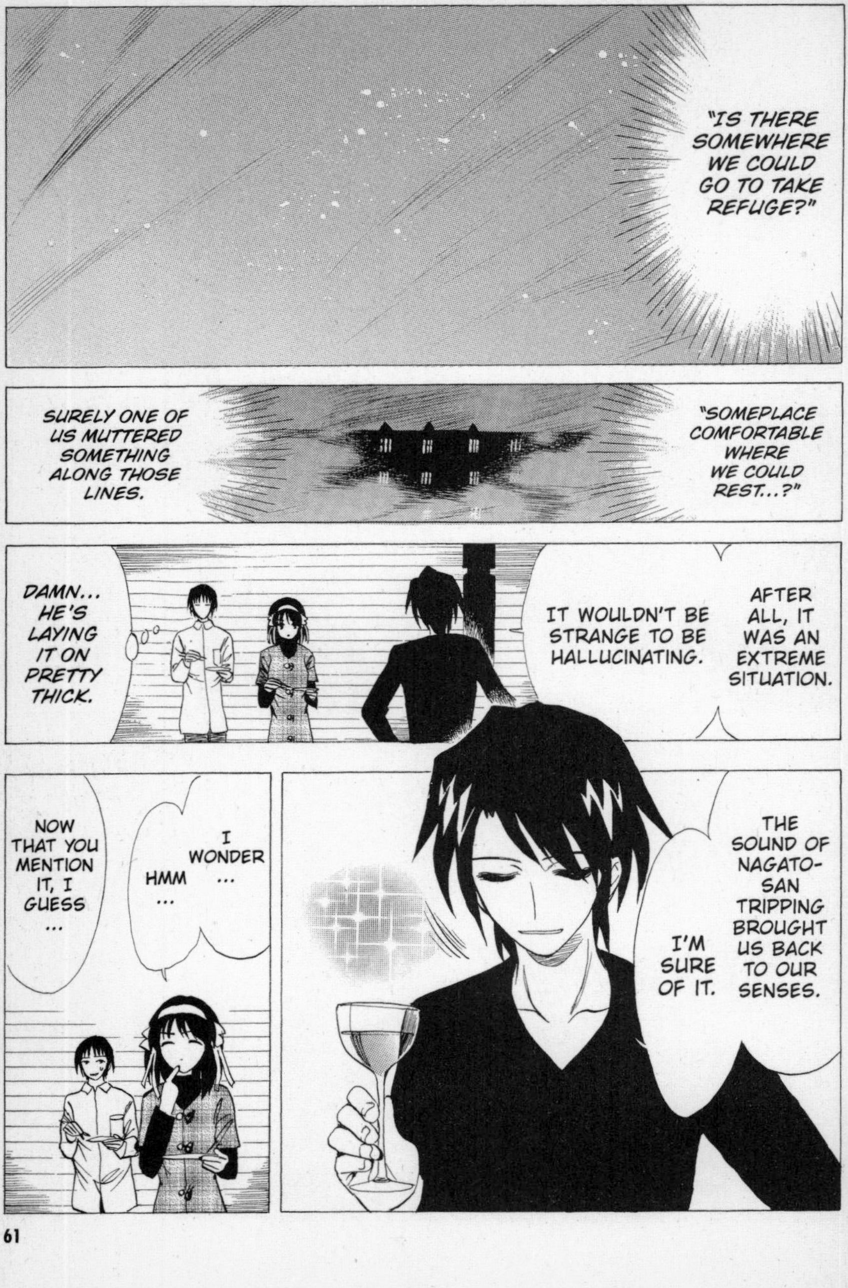
"IS THERE SOMEWHERE WE COULD GO TO TAKE REFUGE?"
"SOMEPLACE COMFORTABLE WHERE WE COULD REST...?"
SURELY ONE OF US MUTTERED SOMETHING ALONG THOSE LINES.
AFTER ALL, IT WAS AN EXTREME SITUATION.
IT WOULDN'T BE STRANGE TO BE HALLUCINATING.
DAMN... HE'S LAYING IT ON PRETTY THICK.
THE SOUND OF NAGATO-SAN TRIPPING BROUGHT US BACK TO OUR SENSES.
I'M SURE OF IT.
I WONDER...
HMM...
NOW THAT YOU MENTION IT, I GUESS...

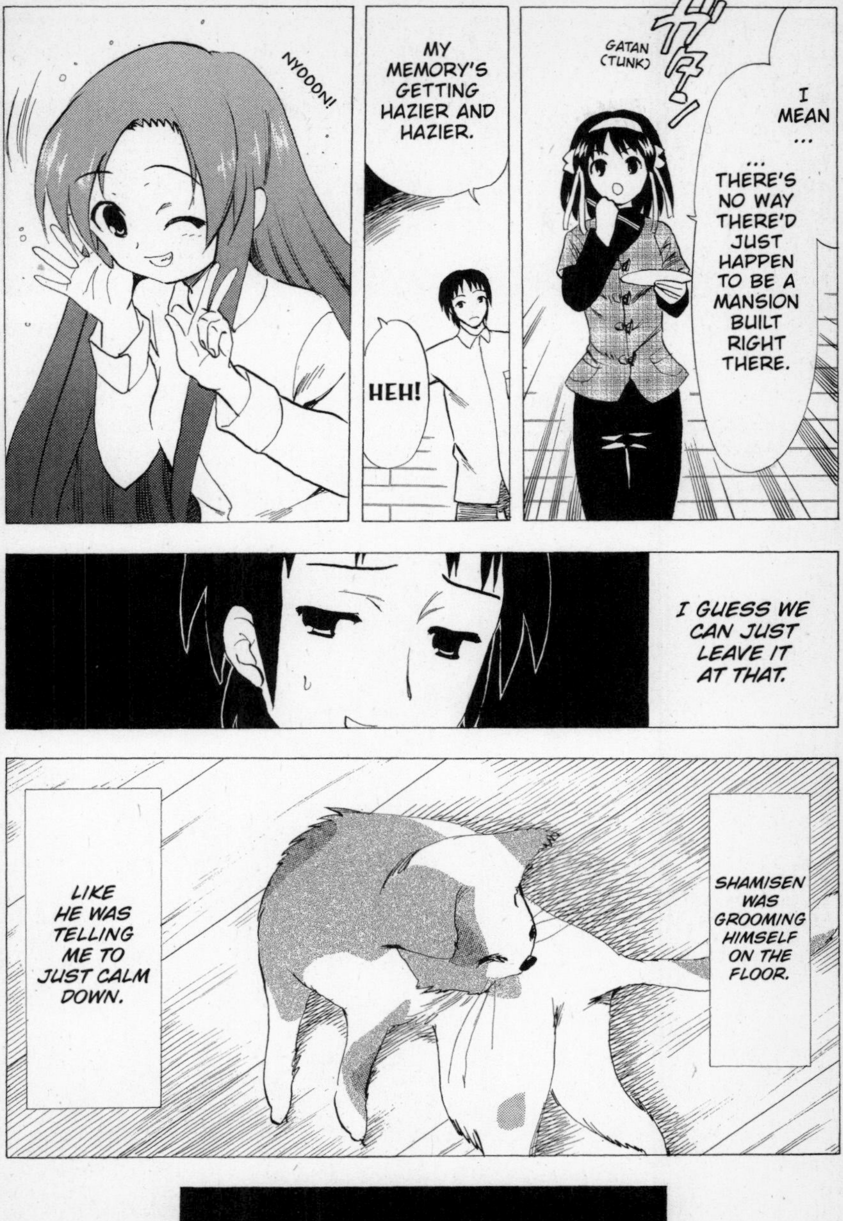
GATAN (TUNK)
I MEAN ...
... THERE'S NO WAY THERE'D JUST HAPPEN TO BE A MANSION BUILT RIGHT THERE.
MY MEMORY'S GETTING HAZIER AND HAZIER.
HEH!
NYOOON!
I GUESS WE CAN JUST LEAVE IT AT THAT.
SHAMISEN WAS GROOMING HIMSELF ON THE FLOOR.
LIKE HE WAS TELLING ME TO JUST CALM DOWN.

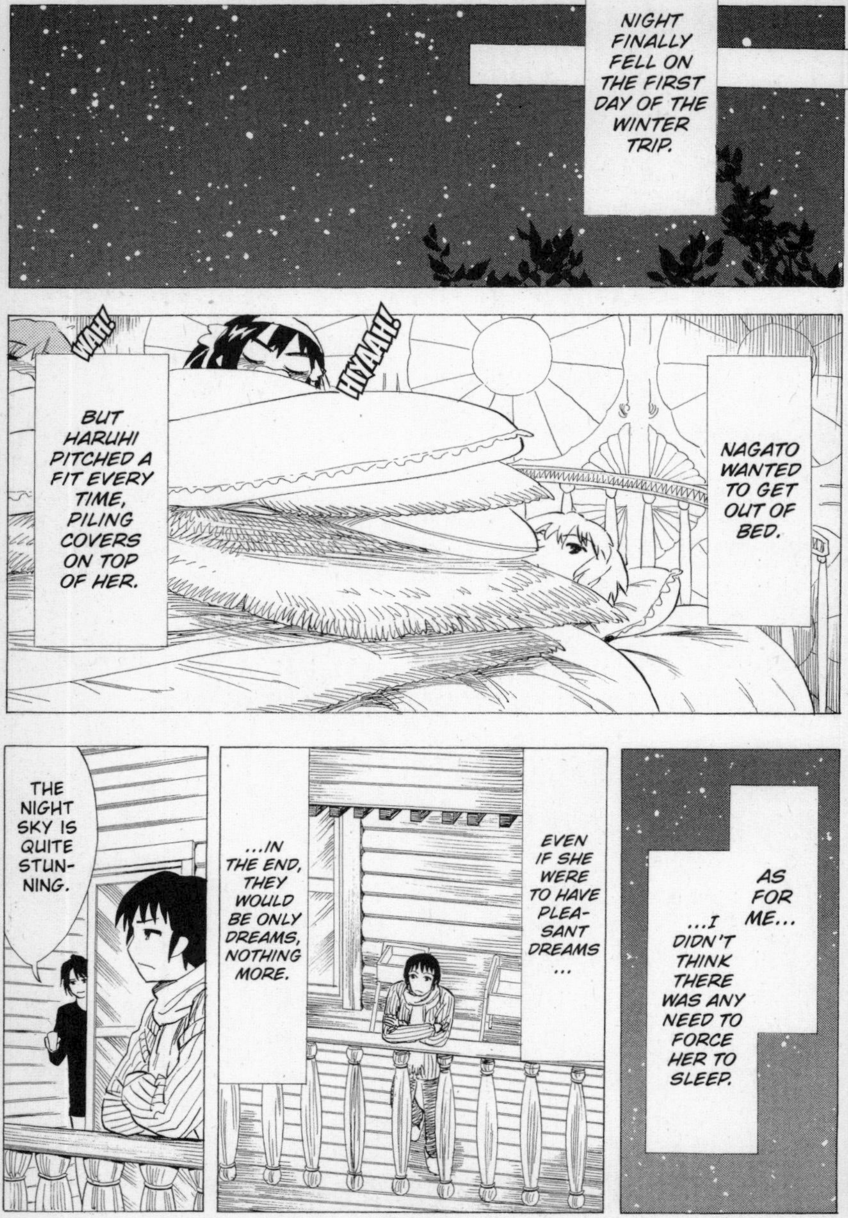
NIGHT FINALLY FELL ON THE FIRST DAY OF THE WINTER TRIP.
NAGATO WANTED TO GET OUT OF BED.
HYAAAH!
WAH!
BUT HARUHI PITCHED A FIT EVERY TIME, PILING COVERS ON TOP OF HER.
AS FOR ME...
...I DIDN'T THINK THERE WAS ANY NEED TO FORCE HER TO SLEEP.
EVEN IF SHE WERE TO HAVE PLEASANT DREAMS...
...IN THE END, THEY WOULD BE ONLY DREAMS, NOTHING MORE.
THE NIGHT SKY IS QUITE STUNNING.

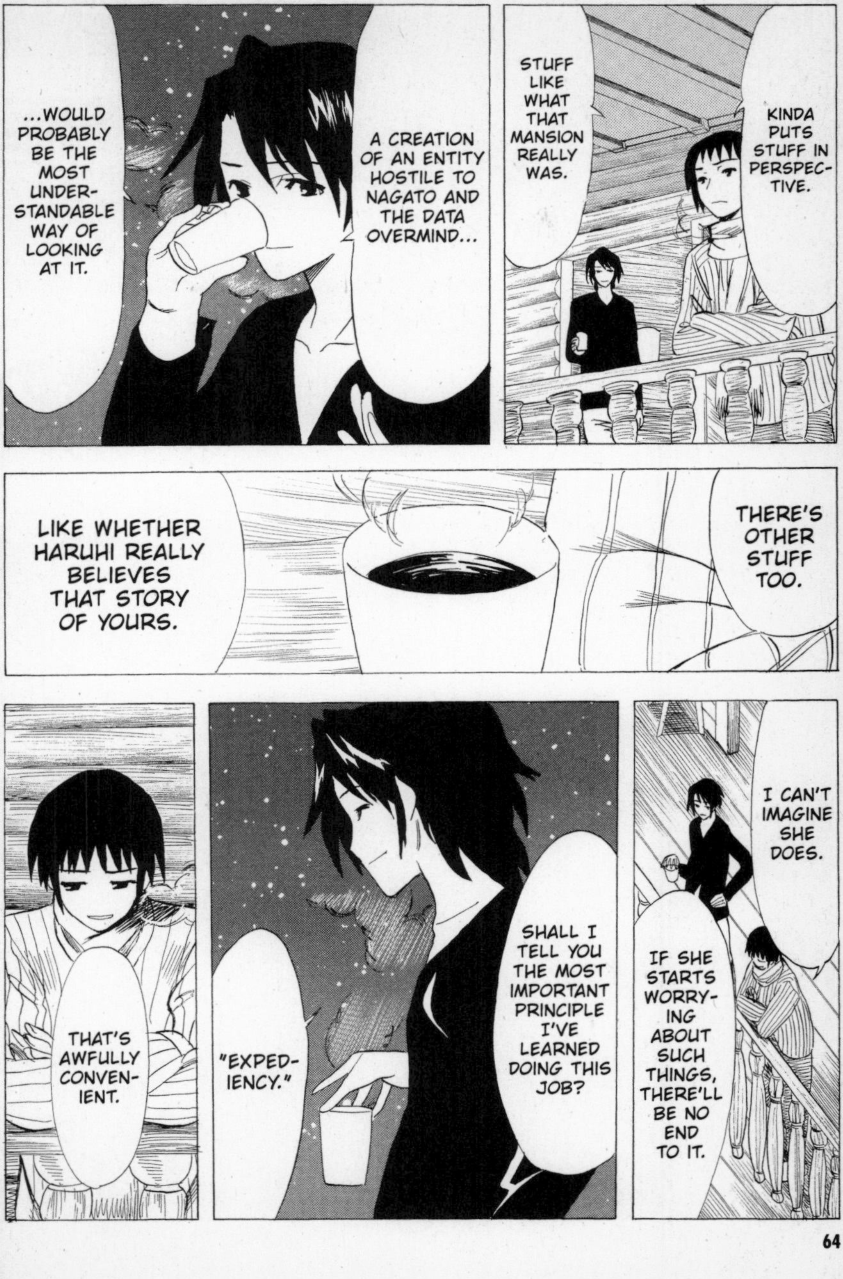
KINDA PUTS STUFF IN PERSPEC-TIVE.
STUFF LIKE WHAT THAT MANSION REALLY WAS.
A CREATION OF AN ENTITY HOSTILE TO NAGATO AND THE DATA OVERMIND...
...WOULD PROBABLY BE THE MOST UNDER-STANDABLE WAY OF LOOKING AT IT.
THERE'S OTHER STUFF TOO.
LIKE WHETHER HARUHI REALLY BELIEVES THAT STORY OF YOURS.
I CAN'T IMAGINE SHE DOES.
IF SHE STARTS WORRY-ING ABOUT SUCH THINGS, THERE'LL BE NO END TO IT.
SHALL I TELL YOU THE MOST IMPORTANT PRINCIPLE I'VE LEARNED DOING THIS JOB?
"EXPED-IENCY."
THAT'S AWFULLY CONVEN-IENT.

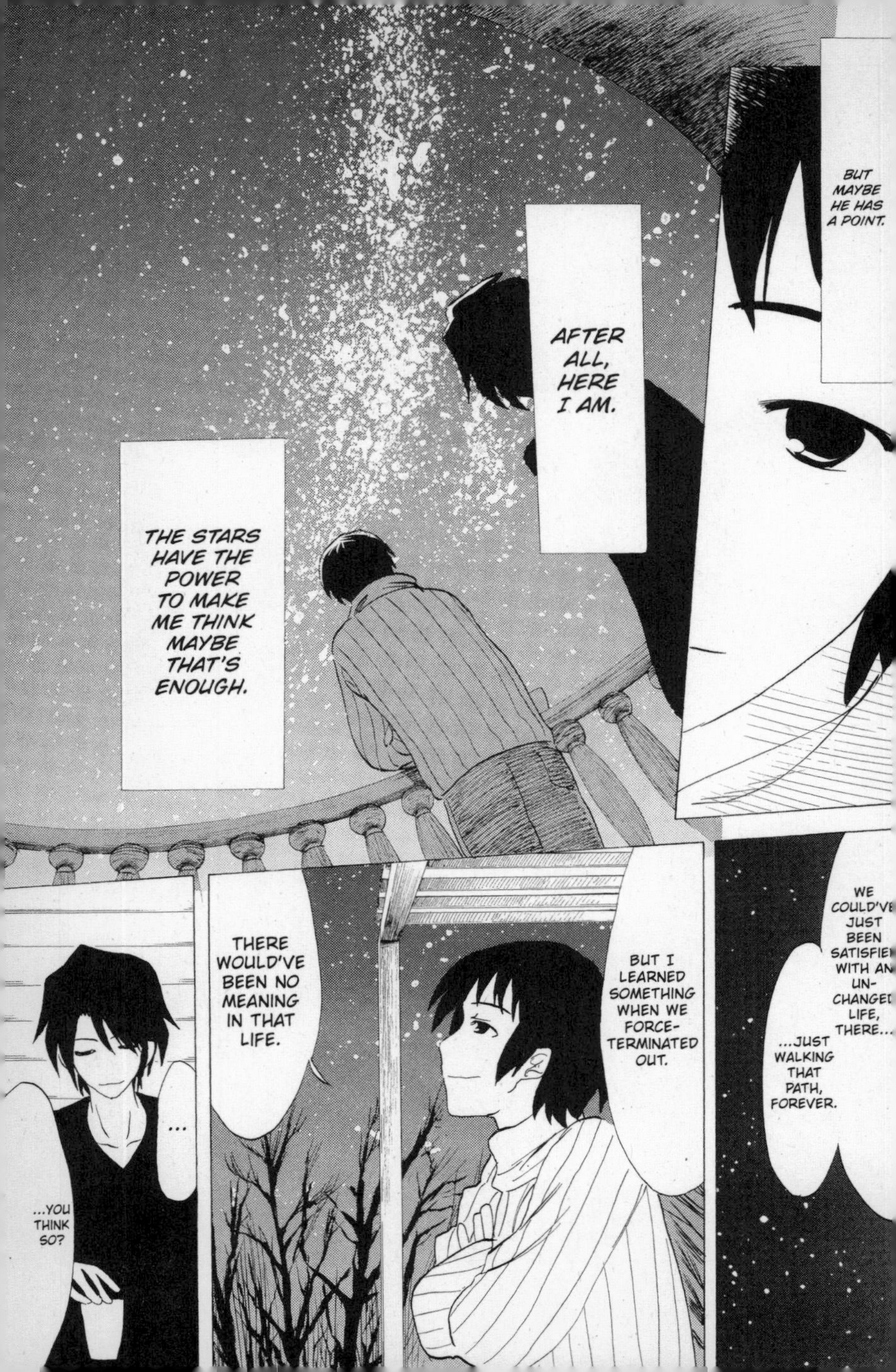
BUT MAYBE HE HAS A POINT.
AFTER ALL, HERE I AM.
THE STARS HAVE THE POWER TO MAKE ME THINK MAYBE THAT'S ENOUGH.
WE COULD'VE JUST BEEN SATISFIE WITH AN UN- CHANGED LIFE, THERE...
...JUST WALKING THAT PATH, FOREVER.
BUT I LEARNED SOMETHING WHEN WE FORCE-TERMINATED OUT.
THERE WOULD'VE BEEN NO MEANING IN THAT LIFE.
...
...YOU THINK SO?

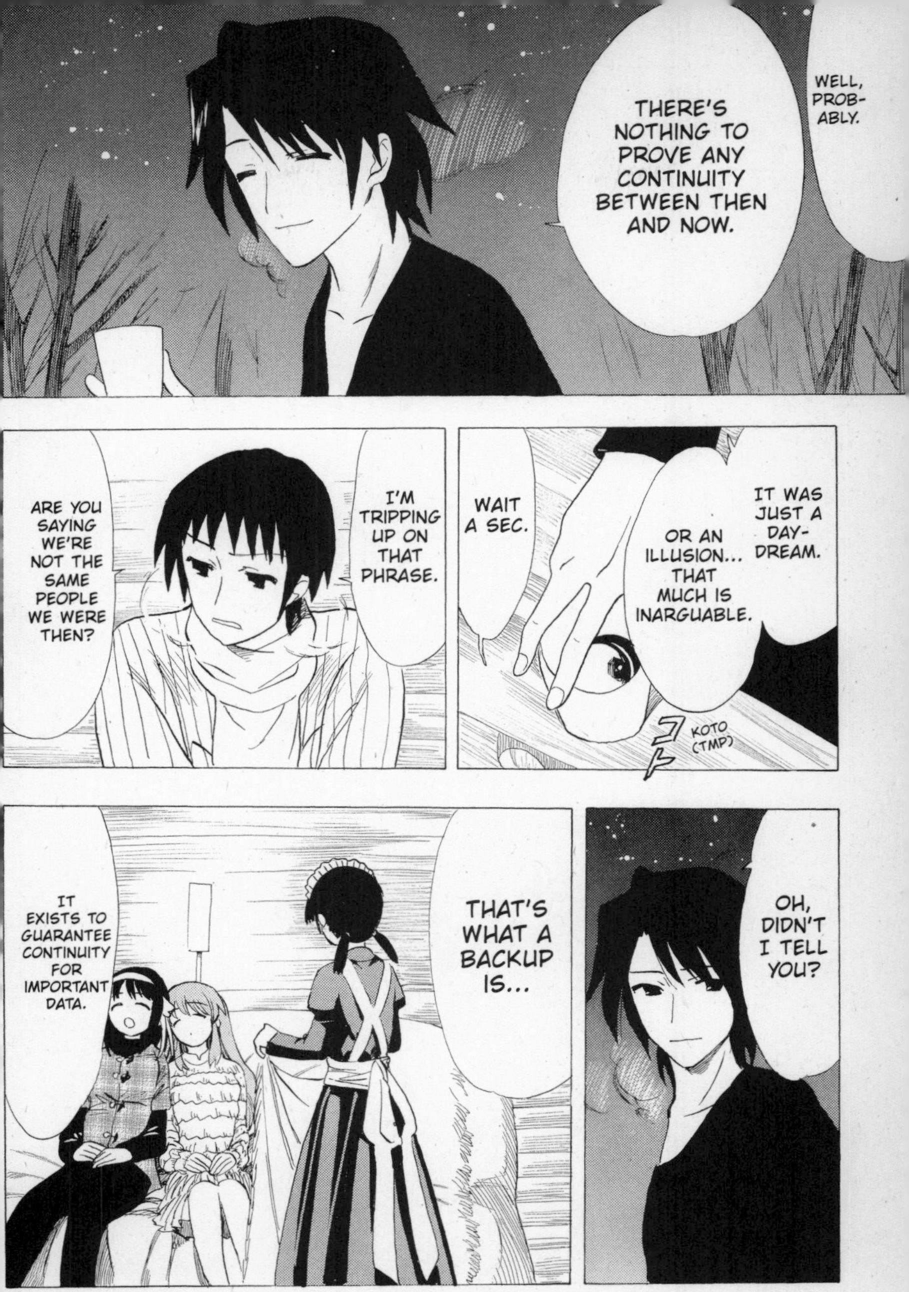

WELL, PROB-ABLY.
THERE'S NOTHING TO PROVE ANY CONTINUITY BETWEEN THEN AND NOW.
IT WAS JUST A DAY-DREAM.
OR AN ILLUSION... THAT MUCH IS INARGUABLE.
WAIT A SEC.
KOTO (TMP)
I'M TRIPPING UP ON THAT PHRASE.
ARE YOU SAYING WE'RE NOT THE SAME PEOPLE WE WERE THEN?
OH, DIDN'T I TELL YOU?
THAT'S WHAT A BACKUP IS...
IT EXISTS TO GUARANTEE CONTINUITY FOR IMPORTANT DATA.

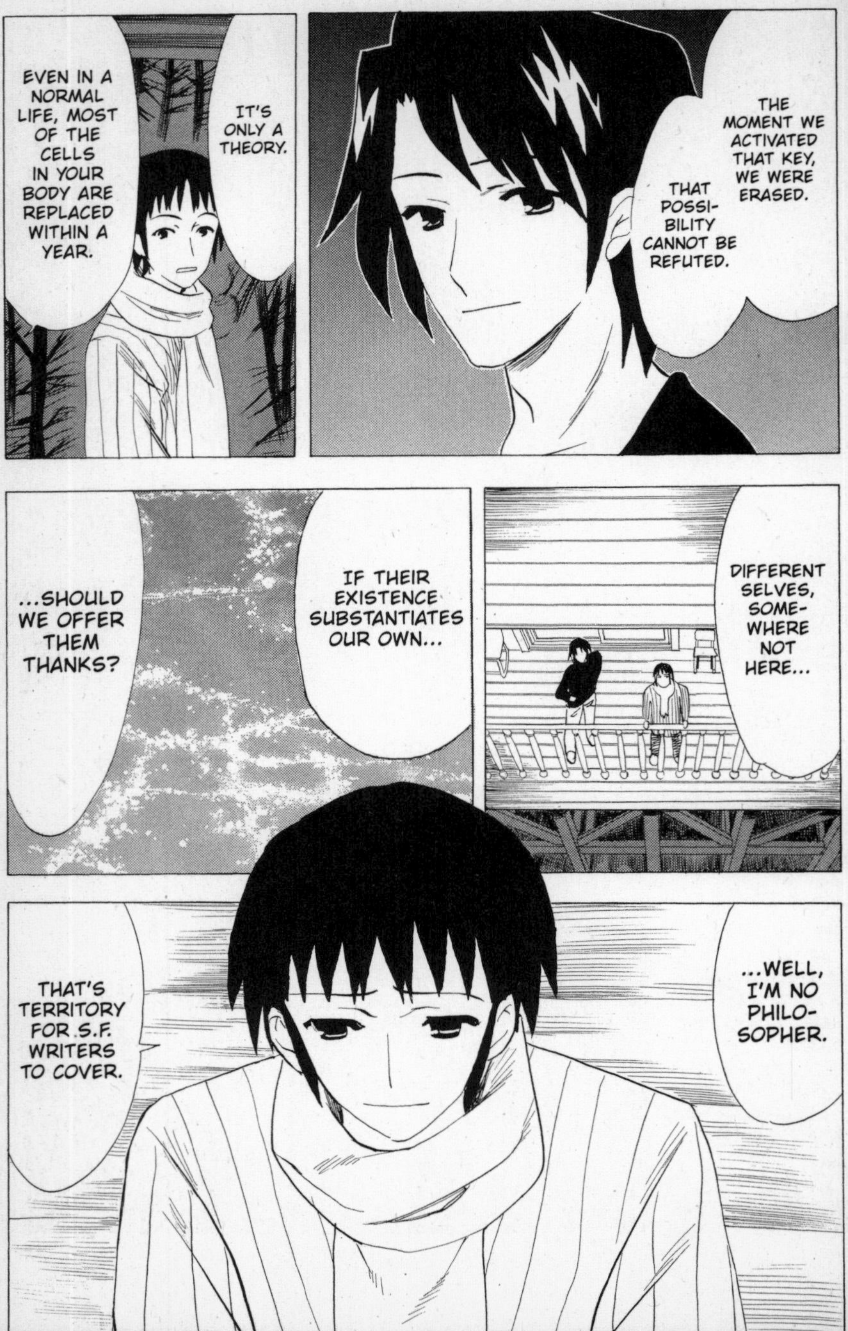
THE MOMENT WE ACTIVATED THAT KEY, WE WERE ERASED.
THAT POSSIBILITY CANNOT BE REFUTED.
IT'S ONLY A THEORY.
EVEN IN A NORMAL LIFE, MOST OF THE CELLS IN YOUR BODY ARE REPLACED WITHIN A YEAR.
DIFFERENT SELVES, SOMEWHERE NOT HERE...
IF THEIR EXISTENCE SUBSTANTIATES OUR OWN...
...SHOULD WE OFFER THEM THANKS?
...WELL, I'M NO PHILOSOPHER.
THAT'S TERRITORY FOR S.F. WRITERS TO COVER.

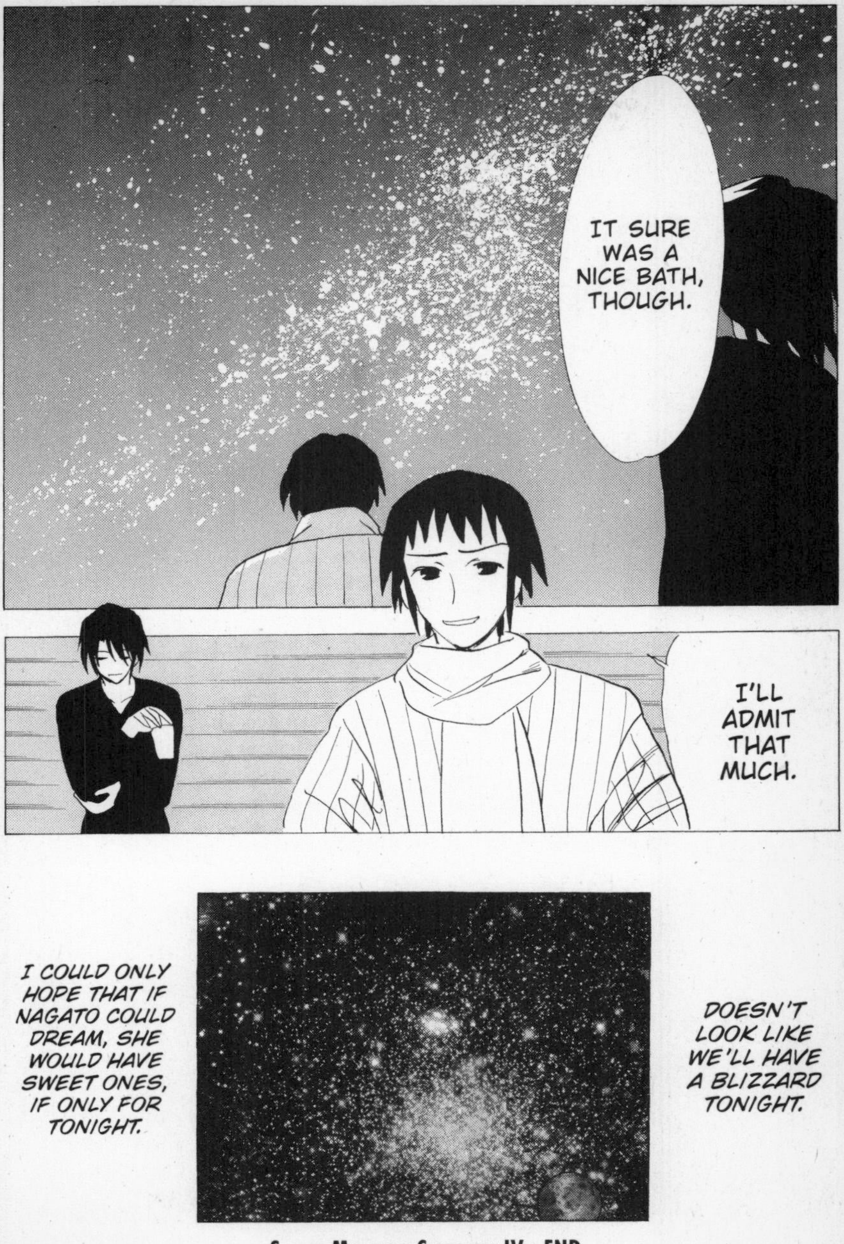
IT SURE WAS A NICE BATH, THOUGH.
I'LL ADMIT THAT MUCH.
DOESN'T LOOK LIKE WE'LL HAVE A BLIZZARD TONIGHT.
I COULD ONLY HOPE THAT IF NAGATO COULD DREAM, SHE WOULD HAVE SWEET ONES, IF ONLY FOR TONIGHT.

Snowy Mountain Syndrome IV : END

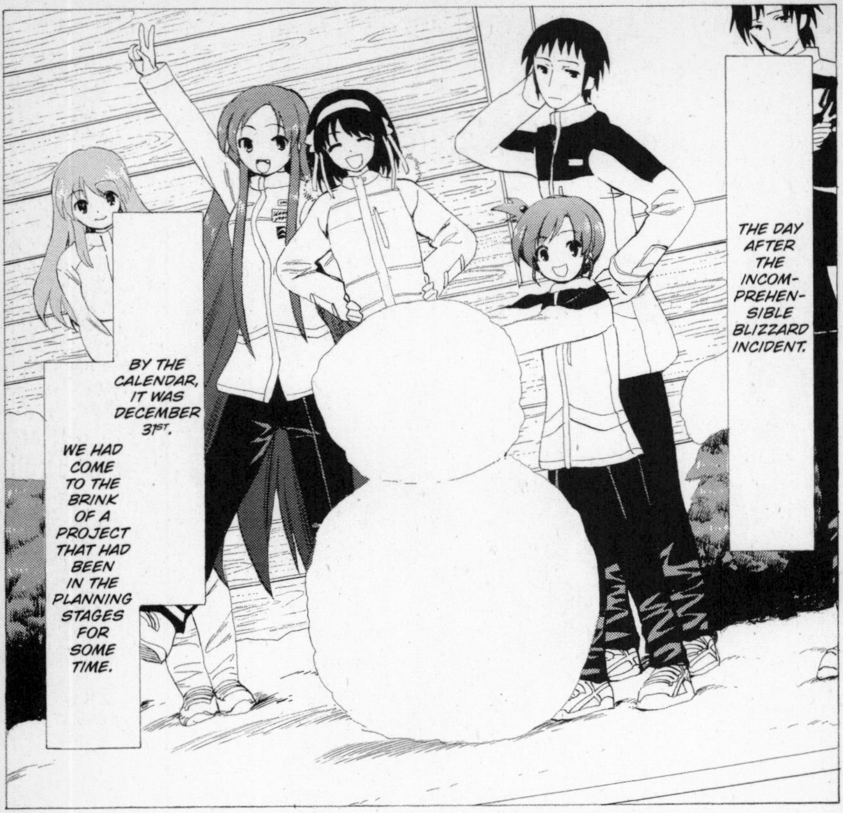
THE DAY AFTER THE INCOMPREHENSIBLE BLIZZARD INCIDENT.
BY THE CALENDAR, IT WAS DECEMBER 31ST.
WE HAD COME TO THE BRINK OF A PROJECT THAT HAD BEEN IN THE PLANNING STAGES FOR SOME TIME.

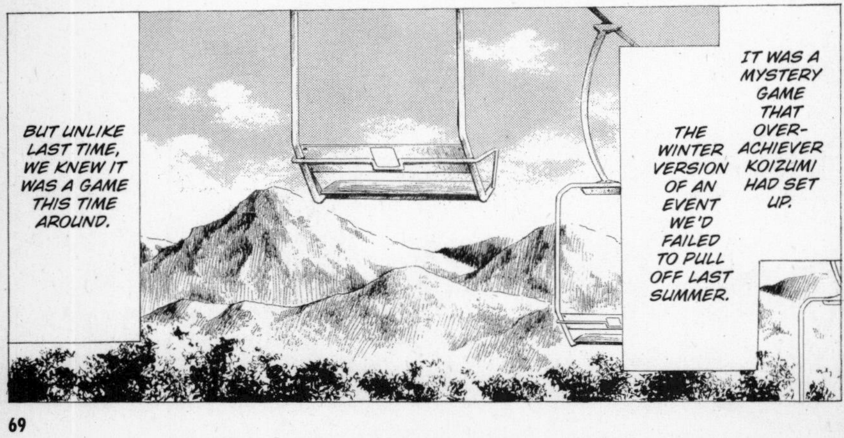
IT WAS A MYSTERY GAME THAT OVER-ACHIEVER KOIZUMI HAD SET UP.
THE WINTER VERSION OF AN EVENT WE'D FAILED TO PULL OFF LAST SUMMER.
BUT UNLIKE LAST TIME, WE KNEW IT WAS A GAME THIS TIME AROUND.

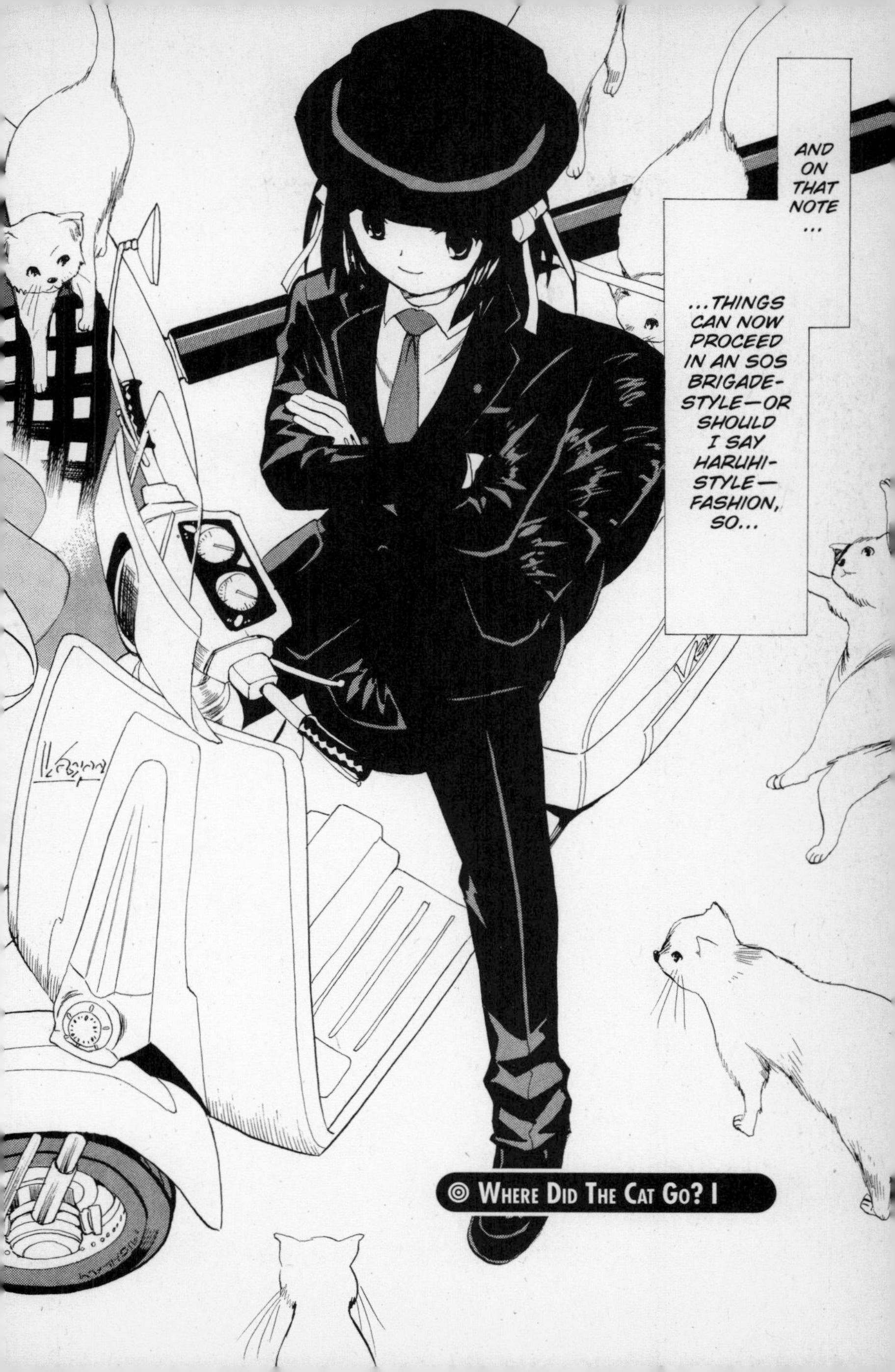
AND ON THAT NOTE ...
...THINGS CAN NOW PROCEED IN AN SOS BRIGADE-STYLE—OR SHOULD I SAY HARUHI-STYLE—FASHION, SO...
◎ WHERE DID THE CAT GO? I

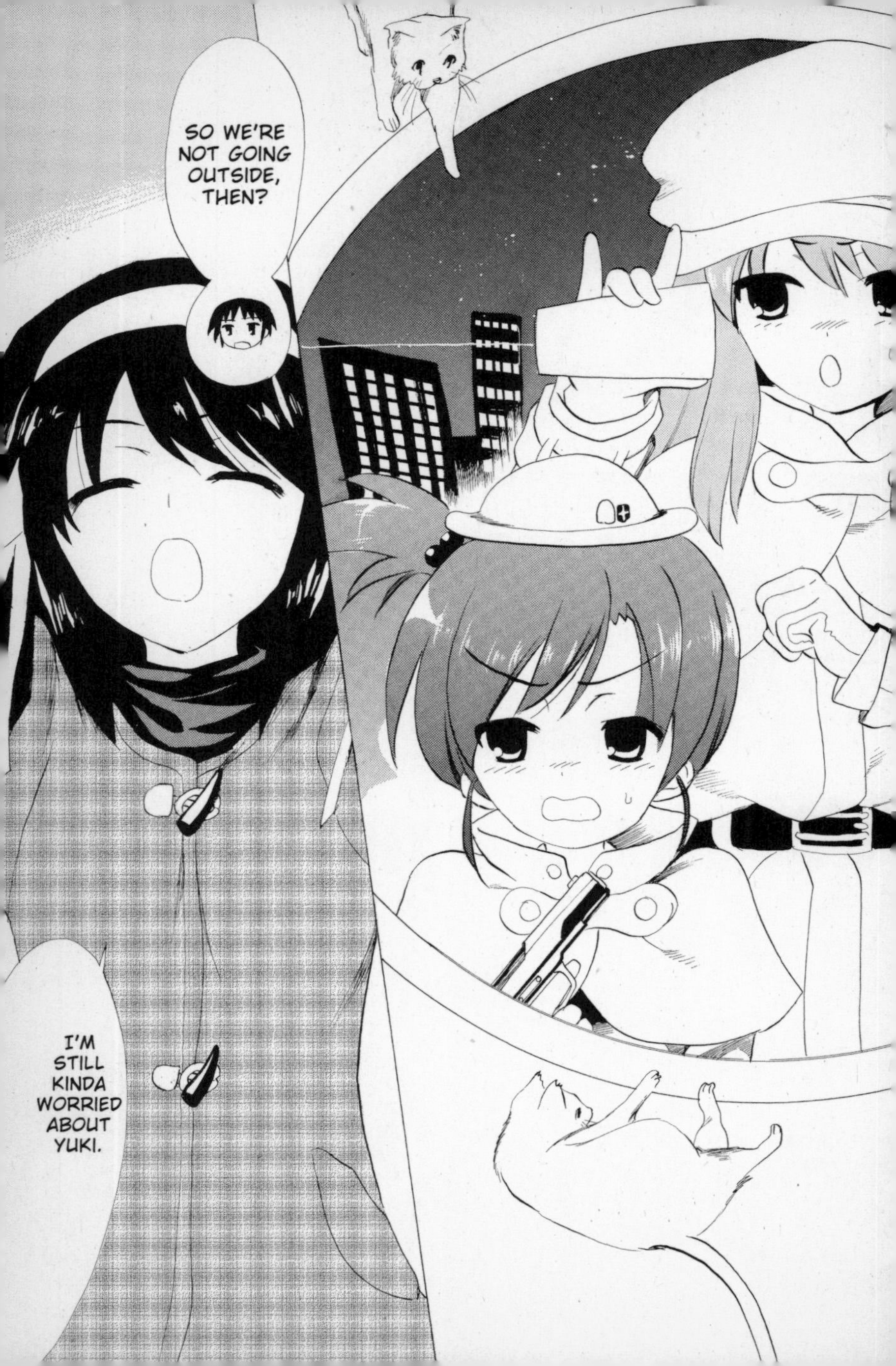
SO WE'RE NOT GOING OUTSIDE, THEN?
I'M STILL KINDA WORRIED ABOUT YUKI.

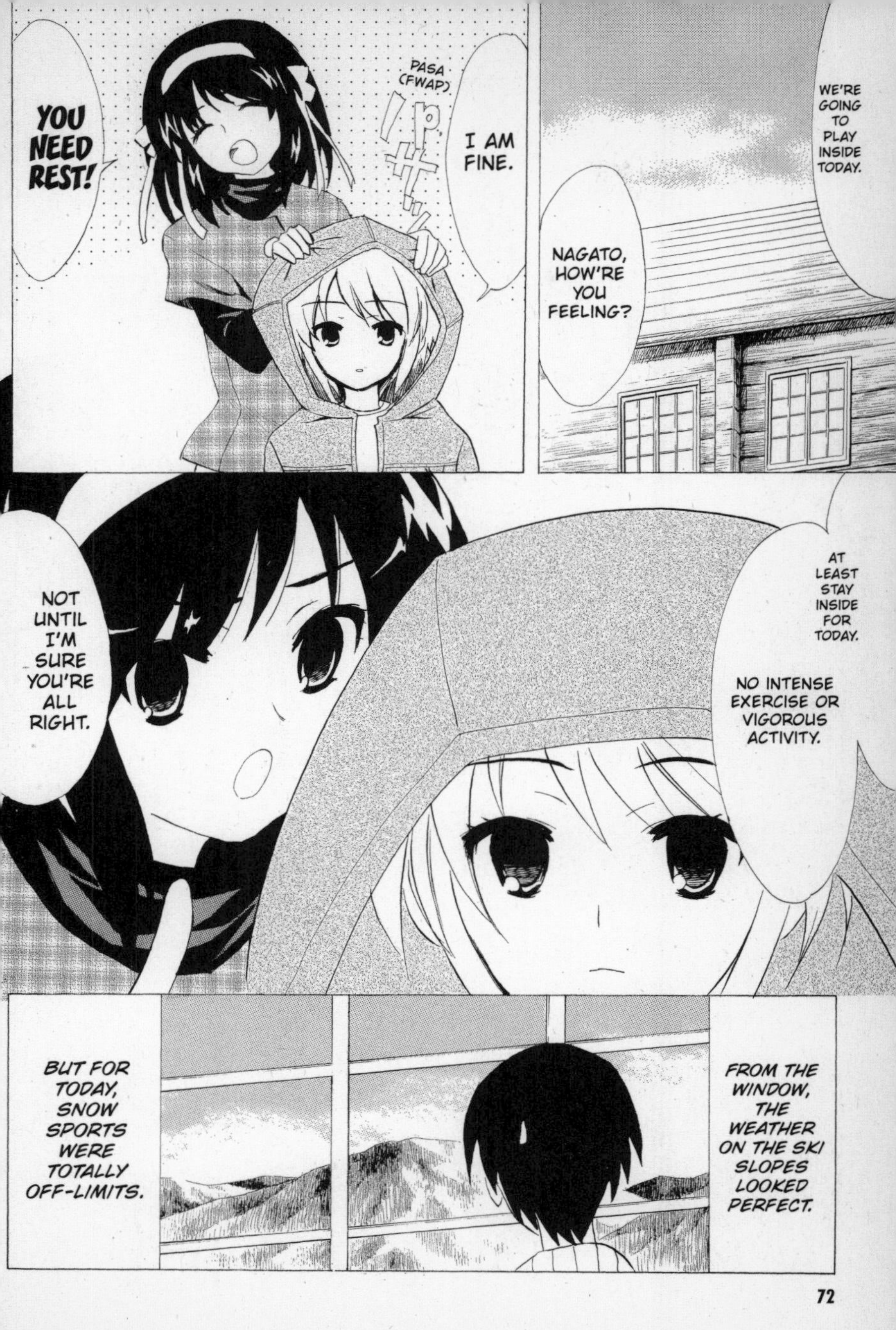
WE'RE GOING TO PLAY INSIDE TODAY.
NAGATO, HOW'RE YOU FEELING?
I AM FINE.
PASA (FWAP)
YOU NEED REST!
AT LEAST STAY INSIDE FOR TODAY.
NO INTENSE EXERCISE OR VIGOROUS ACTIVITY.
NOT UNTIL I'M SURE YOU'RE ALL RIGHT.
FROM THE WINDOW, THE WEATHER ON THE SKI SLOPES LOOKED PERFECT.
BUT FOR TODAY, SNOW SPORTS WERE TOTALLY OFF-LIMITS.

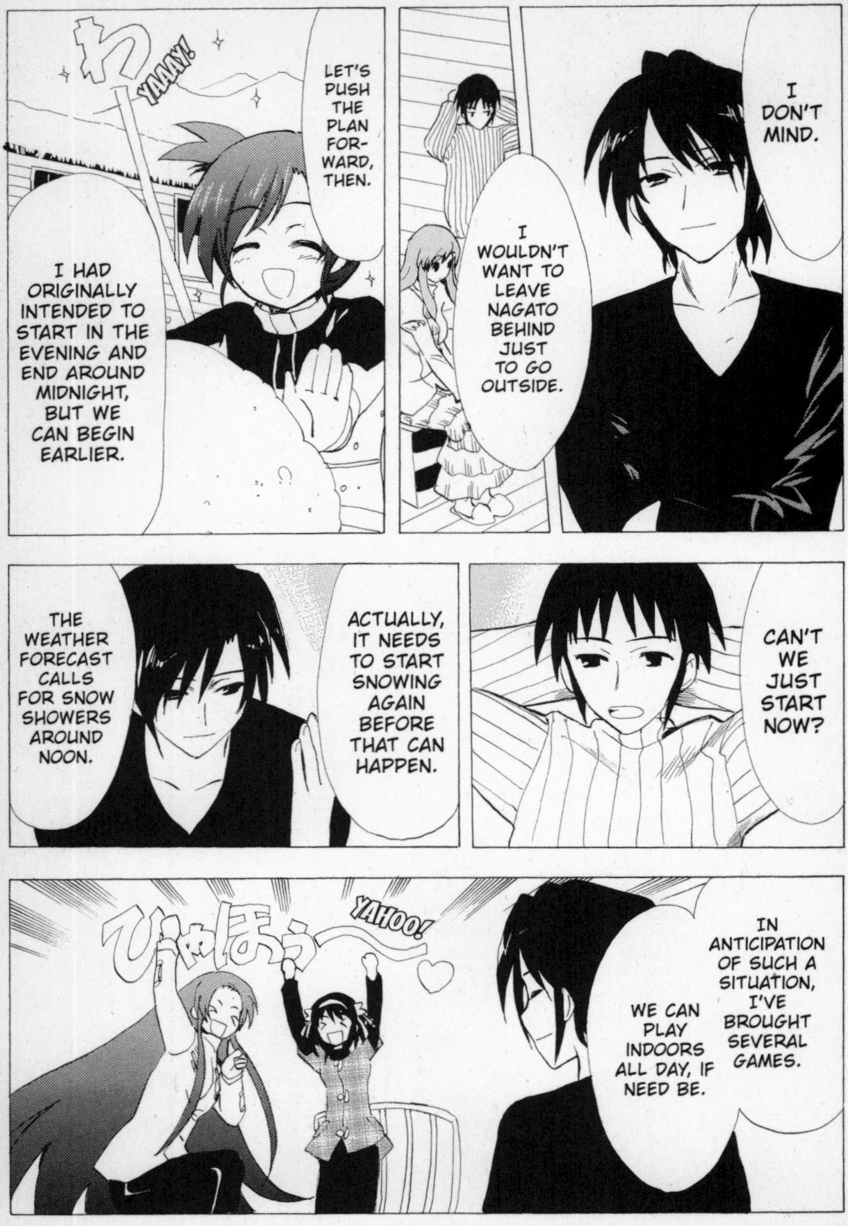
I DON'T MIND.
I WOULDN'T WANT TO LEAVE NAGATO BEHIND JUST TO GO OUTSIDE.
LET'S PUSH THE PLAN FOR-WARD, THEN.
わ
YAAAY!
I HAD ORIGINALLY INTENDED TO START IN THE EVENING AND END AROUND MIDNIGHT, BUT WE CAN BEGIN EARLIER.
CAN'T WE JUST START NOW?
ACTUALLY, IT NEEDS TO START SNOWING AGAIN BEFORE THAT CAN HAPPEN.
THE WEATHER FORECAST CALLS FOR SNOW SHOWERS AROUND NOON.
IN ANTICIPATION OF SUCH A SITUATION, I'VE BROUGHT SEVERAL GAMES.
WE CAN PLAY INDOORS ALL DAY, IF NEED BE.
YAHOO!
ひゃほぉう〜

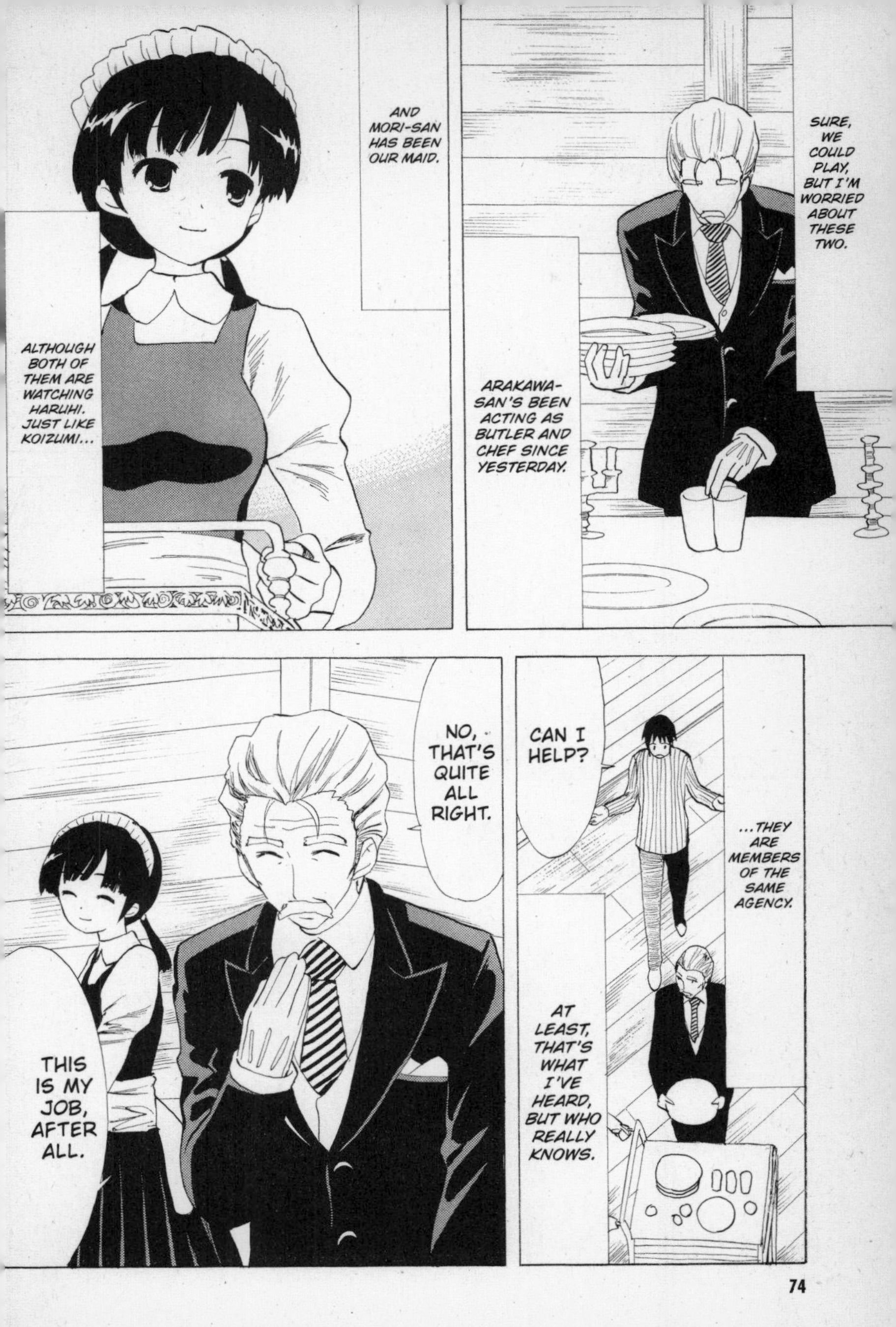
SURE, WE COULD PLAY, BUT I'M WORRIED ABOUT THESE TWO.
ARAKAWA-SAN'S BEEN ACTING AS BUTLER AND CHEF SINCE YESTERDAY.
AND MORI-SAN HAS BEEN OUR MAID.
ALTHOUGH BOTH OF THEM ARE WATCHING HARUHI. JUST LIKE KOIZUMI...
CAN I HELP?
...THEY ARE MEMBERS OF THE SAME AGENCY.
AT LEAST, THAT'S WHAT I'VE HEARD, BUT WHO REALLY KNOWS.
NO, THAT'S QUITE ALL RIGHT.
THIS IS MY JOB, AFTER ALL.

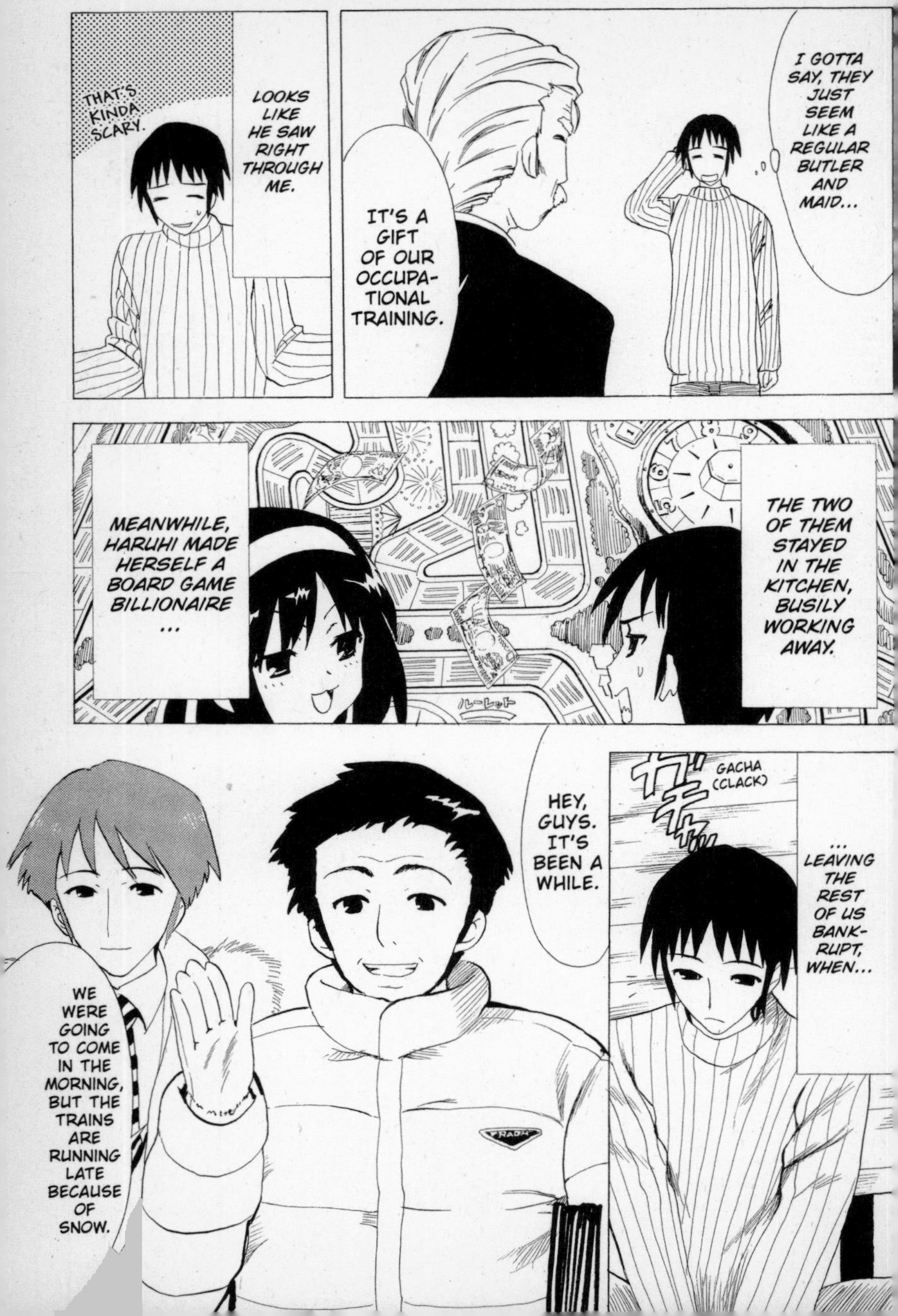
I GOTTA SAY, THEY JUST SEEM LIKE A REGULAR BUTLER AND MAID...
IT'S A GIFT OF OUR OCCUPATIONAL TRAINING.
LOOKS LIKE HE SAW RIGHT THROUGH ME.
THAT'S KINDA SCARY.
THE TWO OF THEM STAYED IN THE KITCHEN, BUSILY WORKING AWAY.
MEANWHILE, HARUHI MADE HERSELF A BOARD GAME BILLIONAIRE...
...LEAVING THE REST OF US BANKRUPT, WHEN...
GACHA (CLACK)
HEY, GUYS. IT'S BEEN A WHILE.
WE WERE GOING TO COME IN THE MORNING, BUT THE TRAINS ARE RUNNING LATE BECAUSE OF SNOW.

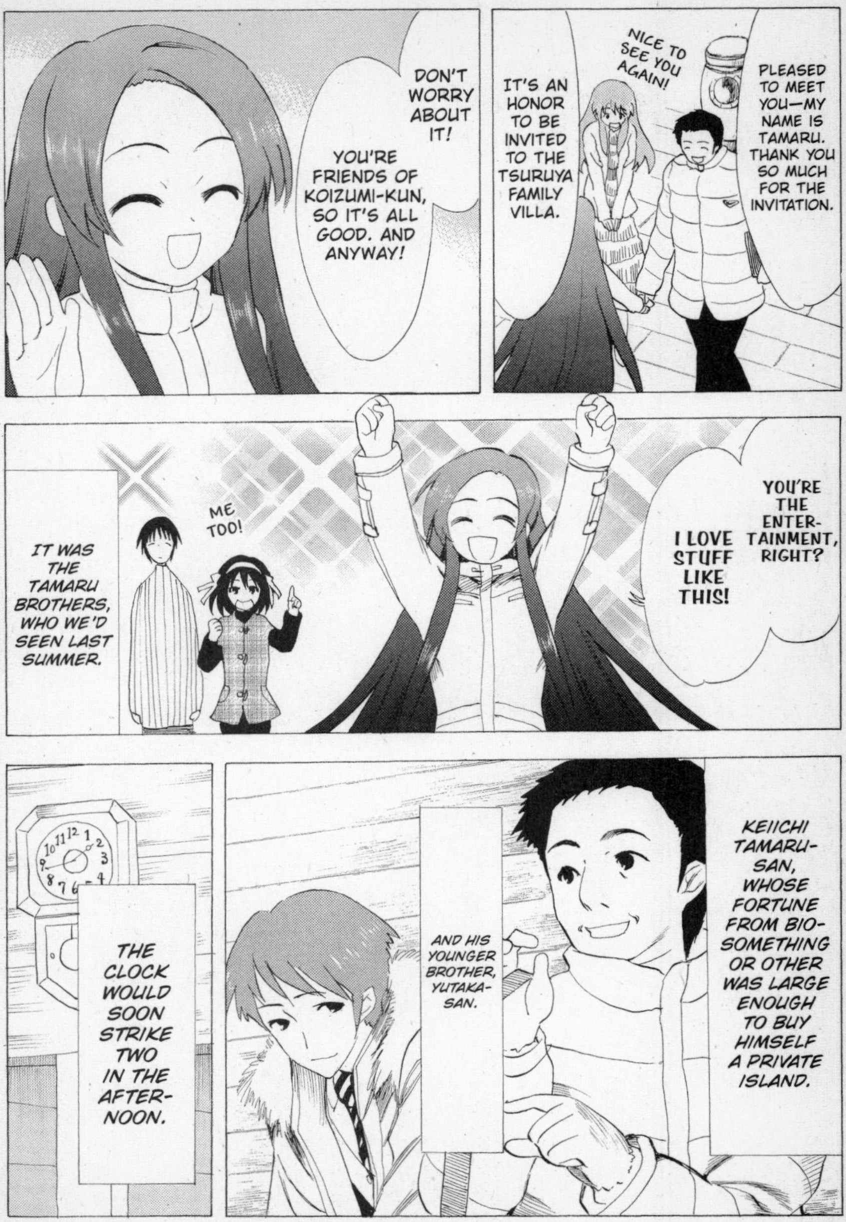
PLEASED TO MEET YOU—MY NAME IS TAMARU. THANK YOU SO MUCH FOR THE INVITATION.
NICE TO SEE YOU AGAIN!
IT'S AN HONOR TO BE INVITED TO THE TSURUYA FAMILY VILLA.
DON'T WORRY ABOUT IT!
YOU'RE FRIENDS OF KOIZUMI-KUN, SO IT'S ALL GOOD. AND ANYWAY!
YOU'RE THE ENTERTAINMENT, RIGHT?
I LOVE STUFF LIKE THIS!
ME TOO!
IT WAS THE TAMARU BROTHERS, WHO WE'D SEEN LAST SUMMER.
KEIICHI TAMARU-SAN, WHOSE FORTUNE FROM BIO-SOMETHING OR OTHER WAS LARGE ENOUGH TO BUY HIMSELF A PRIVATE ISLAND.
AND HIS YOUNGER BROTHER, YUTAKA-SAN.
THE CLOCK WOULD SOON STRIKE TWO IN THE AFTERNOON.

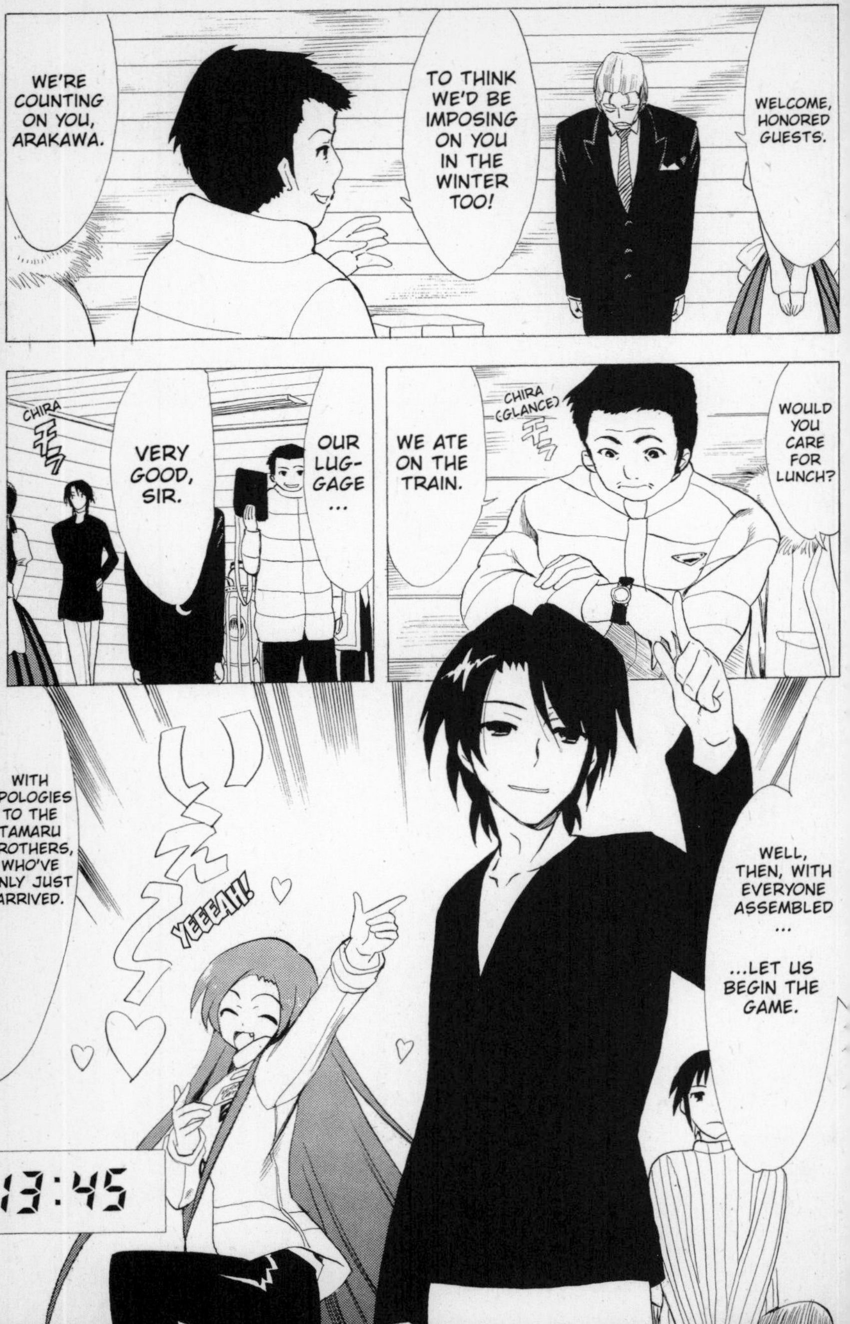
WELCOME, HONORED GUESTS.
TO THINK WE'D BE IMPOSING ON YOU IN THE WINTER TOO!
WE'RE COUNTING ON YOU, ARAKAWA.
WOULD YOU CARE FOR LUNCH?
CHIRA (GLANCE)
WE ATE ON THE TRAIN.
OUR LUG-GAGE...
VERY GOOD, SIR.
CHIRA
WELL, THEN, WITH EVERYONE ASSEMBLED...
...LET US BEGIN THE GAME.
YEEEAH!
WITH APOLOGIES TO THE TAMARU BROTHERS, WHO'VE ONLY JUST ARRIVED.
13:45

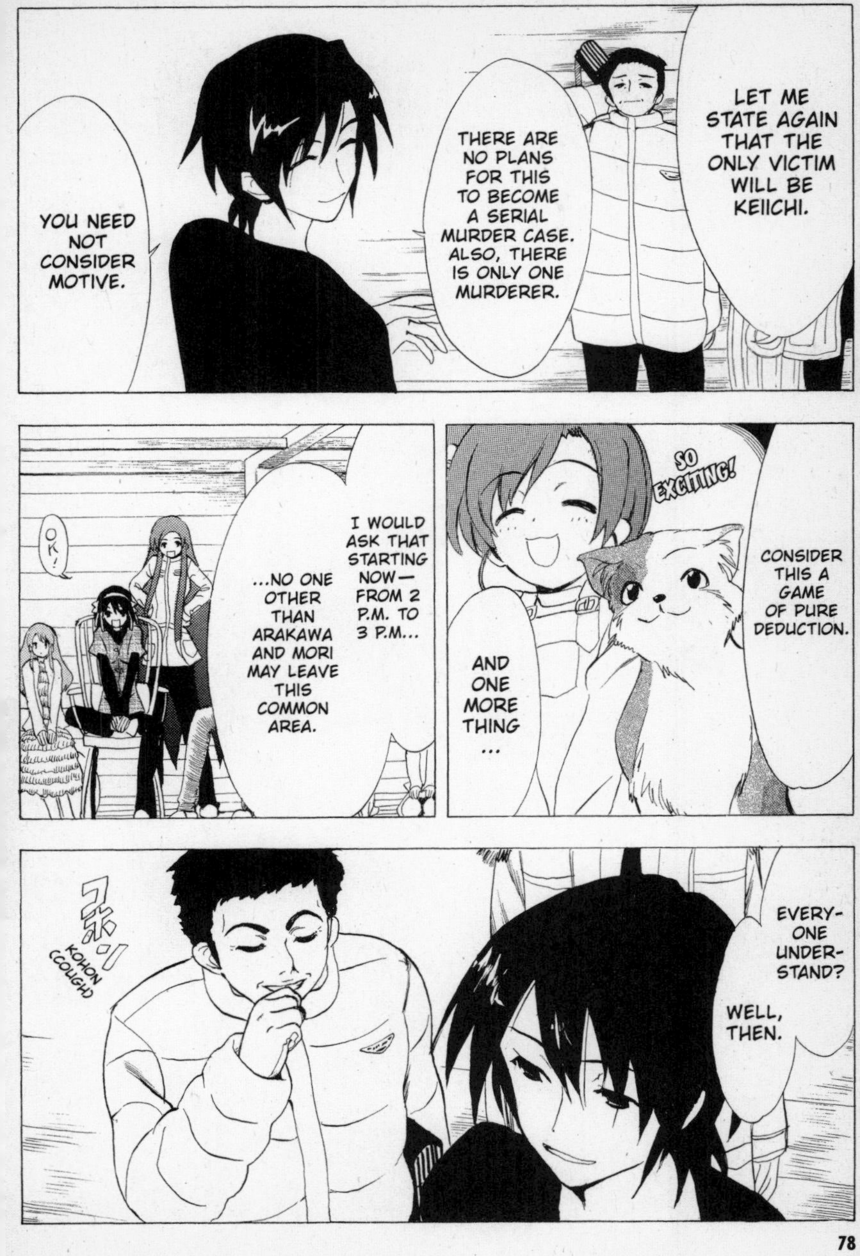
LET ME STATE AGAIN THAT THE ONLY VICTIM WILL BE KEIICHI.
THERE ARE NO PLANS FOR THIS TO BECOME A SERIAL MURDER CASE. ALSO, THERE IS ONLY ONE MURDERER.
YOU NEED NOT CONSIDER MOTIVE.
CONSIDER THIS A GAME OF PURE DEDUCTION.
SO EXCITING!
AND ONE MORE THING ...
I WOULD ASK THAT STARTING NOW— FROM 2 P.M. TO 3 P.M...
...NO ONE OTHER THAN ARAKAWA AND MORI MAY LEAVE THIS COMMON AREA.
OK!
EVERY-ONE UNDER-STAND?
WELL, THEN.
KOHON (COUGH)

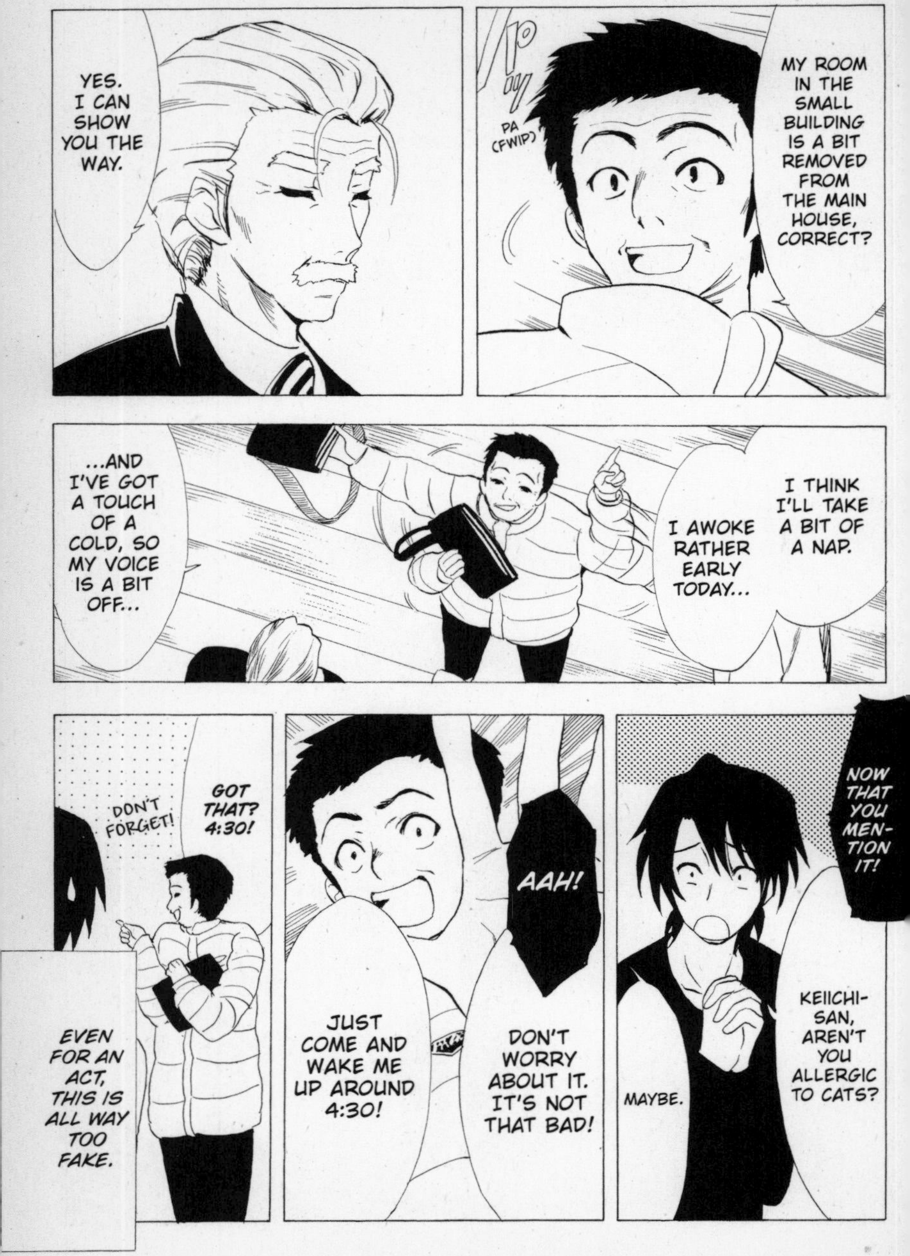
MY ROOM IN THE SMALL BUILDING IS A BIT REMOVED FROM THE MAIN HOUSE, CORRECT?
PA (FWIP)
YES. I CAN SHOW YOU THE WAY.
I THINK I'LL TAKE A BIT OF A NAP.
I AWOKE RATHER EARLY TODAY...
...AND I'VE GOT A TOUCH OF A COLD, SO MY VOICE IS A BIT OFF...
NOW THAT YOU MEN-TION IT!
KEIICHI-SAN, AREN'T YOU ALLERGIC TO CATS?
MAYBE.
AAH!
DON'T WORRY ABOUT IT. IT'S NOT THAT BAD!
JUST COME AND WAKE ME UP AROUND 4:30!
GOT THAT? 4:30!
DON'T FORGET!
EVEN FOR AN ACT, THIS IS ALL WAY TOO FAKE.

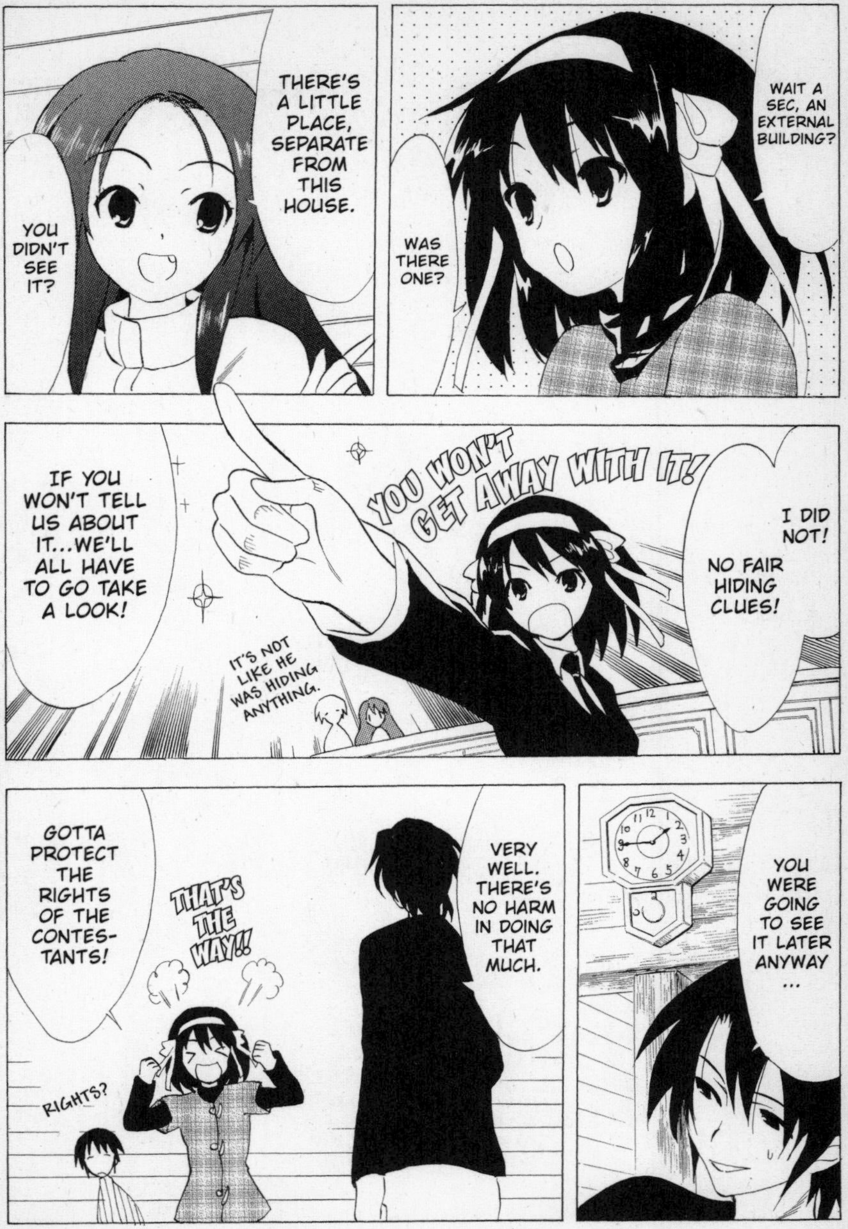
WAIT A SEC, AN EXTERNAL BUILDING?
WAS THERE ONE?
THERE'S A LITTLE PLACE, SEPARATE FROM THIS HOUSE.
YOU DIDN'T SEE IT?
I DID NOT!
NO FAIR HIDING CLUES!
YOU WON'T GET AWAY WITH IT!
IT'S NOT LIKE HE WAS HIDING ANYTHING.
IF YOU WON'T TELL US ABOUT IT...WE'LL ALL HAVE TO GO TAKE A LOOK!
YOU WERE GOING TO SEE IT LATER ANYWAY ...
VERY WELL. THERE'S NO HARM IN DOING THAT MUCH.
THAT'S THE WAY!!
GOTTA PROTECT THE RIGHTS OF THE CONTESTANTS!
RIGHTS?

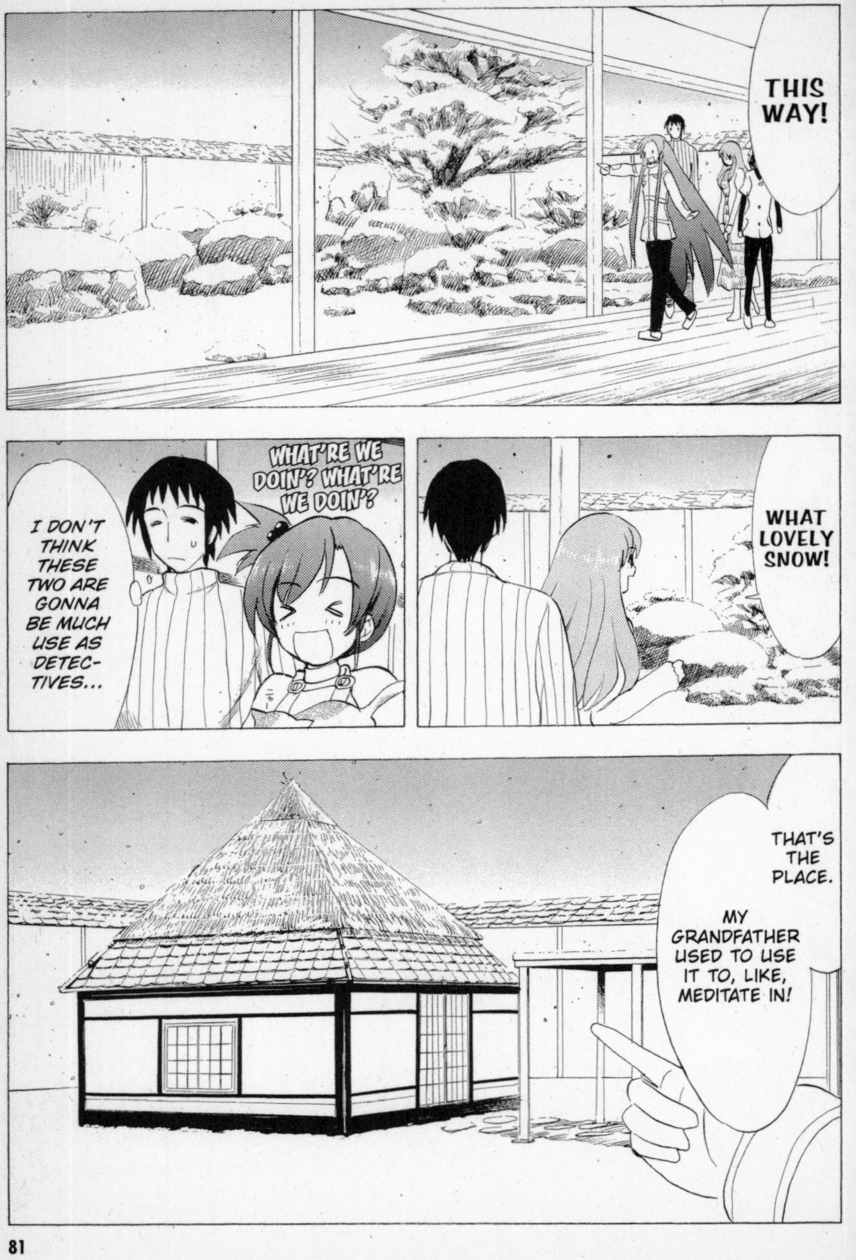
THIS WAY!
WHAT LOVELY SNOW!
WHAT'RE WE DOIN'? WHAT'RE WE DOIN'?
I DON'T THINK THESE TWO ARE GONNA BE MUCH USE AS DETEC-TIVES...
THAT'S THE PLACE.
MY GRANDFATHER USED TO USE IT TO, LIKE, MEDITATE IN!

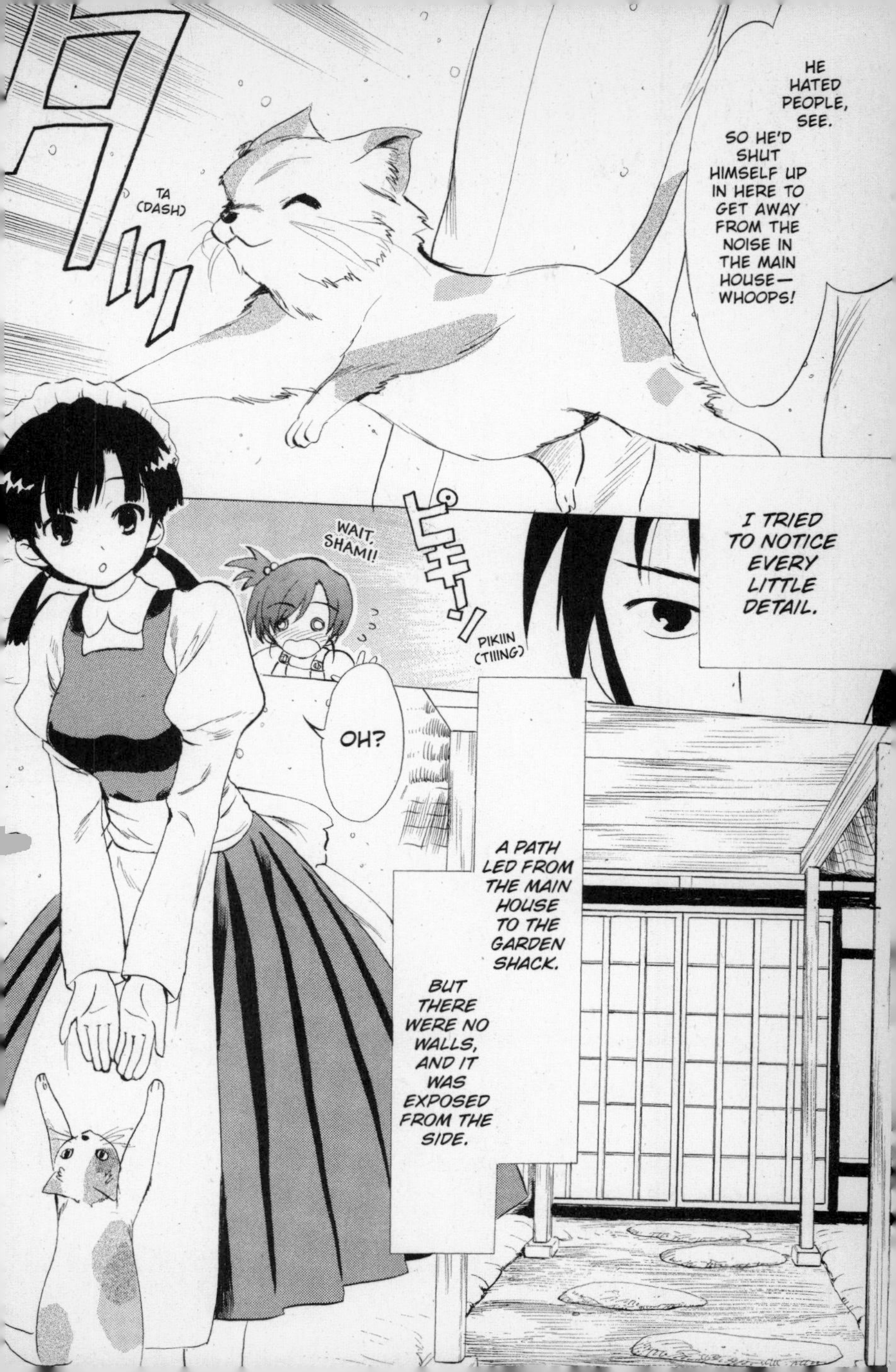
HE HATED PEOPLE, SEE.
SO HE'D SHUT HIMSELF UP IN HERE TO GET AWAY FROM THE NOISE IN THE MAIN HOUSE—WHOOPS!
TA (DASH)
I TRIED TO NOTICE EVERY LITTLE DETAIL.
PIKIIN (TIIING)
WAIT, SHAMI!
A PATH LED FROM THE MAIN HOUSE TO THE GARDEN SHACK.
BUT THERE WERE NO WALLS, AND IT WAS EXPOSED FROM THE SIDE.
OH?

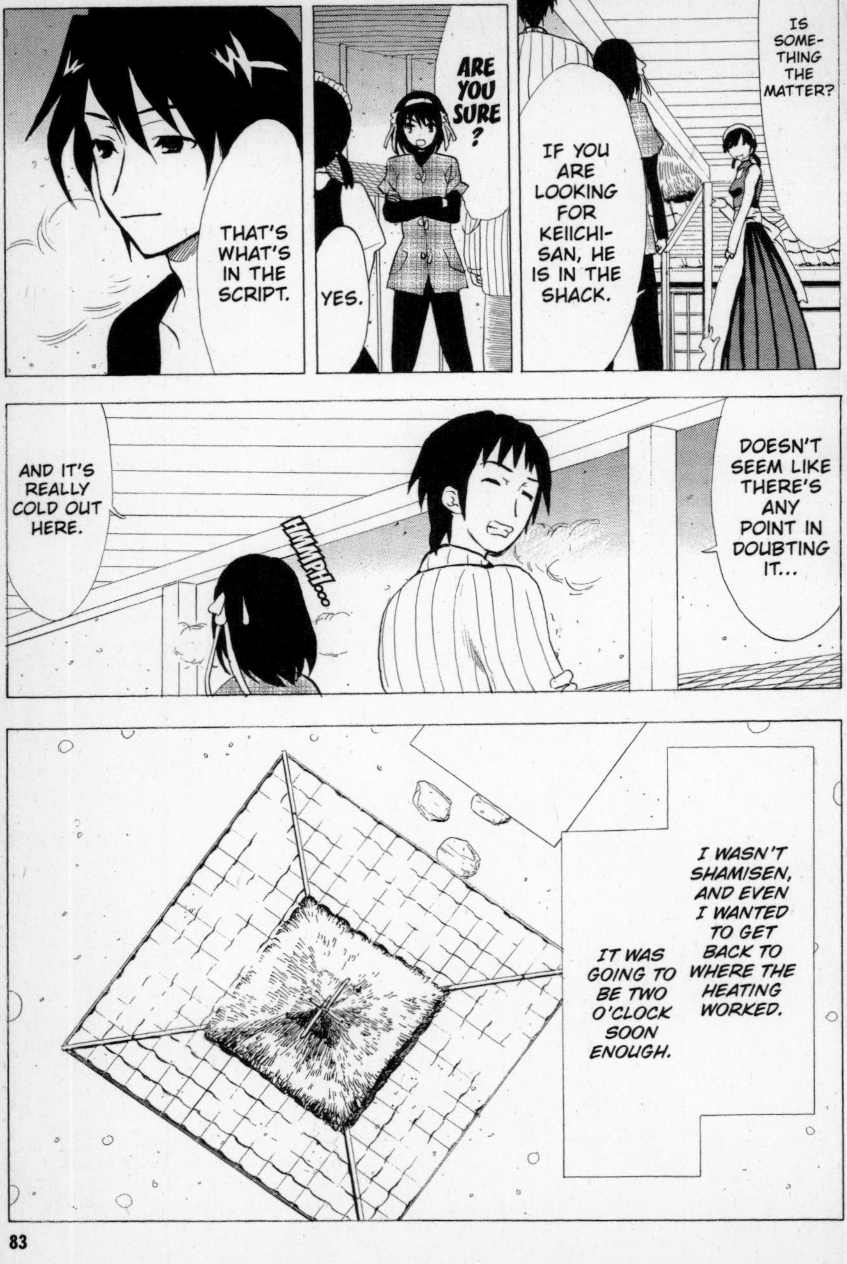
IS SOMETHING THE MATTER?
IF YOU ARE LOOKING FOR KEIICHI-SAN, HE IS IN THE SHACK.
ARE YOU SURE?
YES.
THAT'S WHAT'S IN THE SCRIPT.
DOESN'T SEEM LIKE THERE'S ANY POINT IN DOUBTING IT...
HMMPH...
AND IT'S REALLY COLD OUT HERE.
I WASN'T SHAMISEN, AND EVEN I WANTED TO GET BACK TO WHERE THE HEATING WORKED.
IT WAS GOING TO BE TWO O'CLOCK SOON ENOUGH.

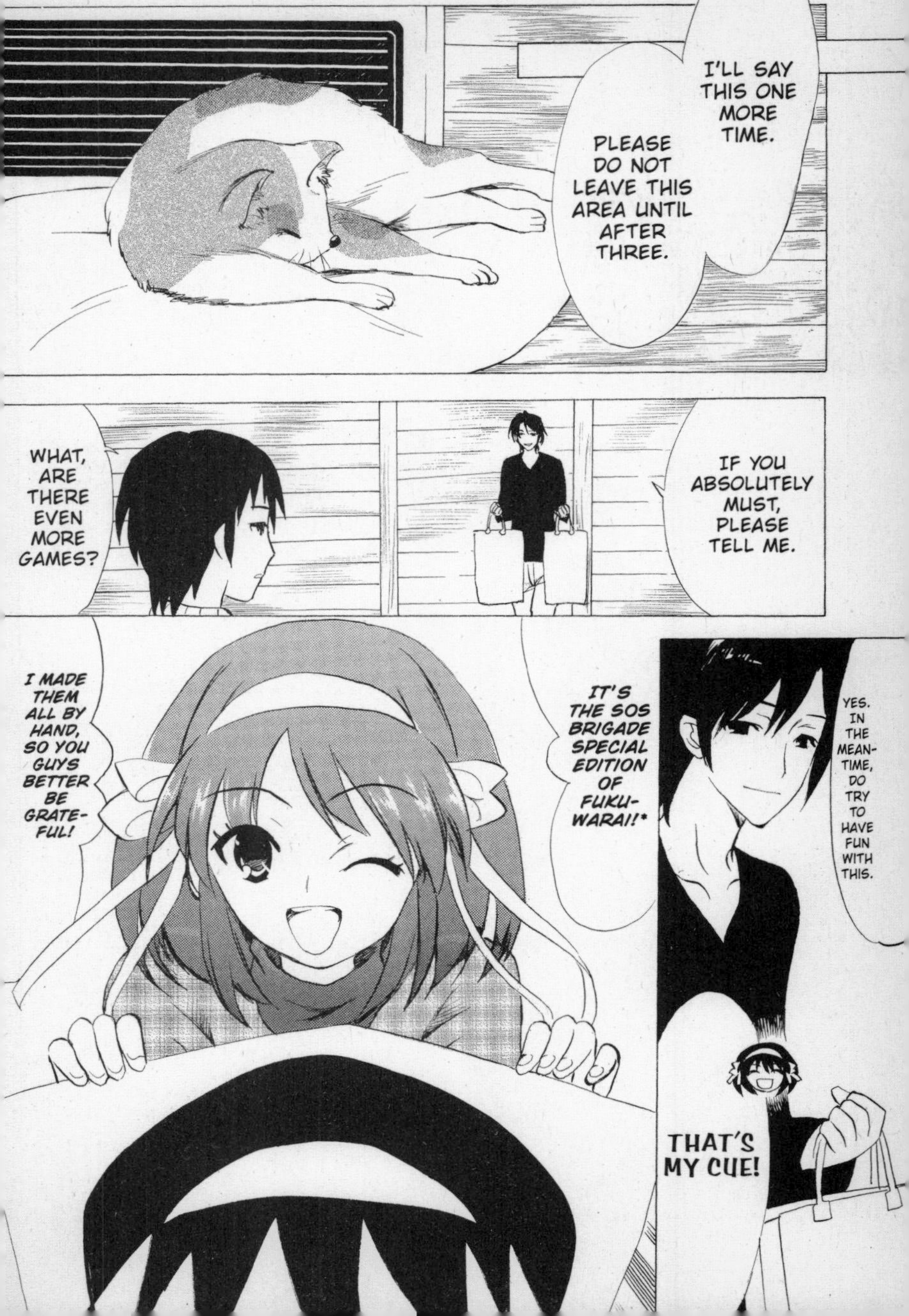
I'LL SAY THIS ONE MORE TIME.
PLEASE DO NOT LEAVE THIS AREA UNTIL AFTER THREE.
IF YOU ABSOLUTELY MUST, PLEASE TELL ME.
WHAT, ARE THERE EVEN MORE GAMES?
YES. IN THE MEANTIME, DO TRY TO HAVE FUN WITH THIS.
THAT'S MY CUE!
IT'S THE SOS BRIGADE SPECIAL EDITION OF FUKUWARAI!*
I MADE THEM ALL BY HAND, SO YOU GUYS BETTER BE GRATEFUL!

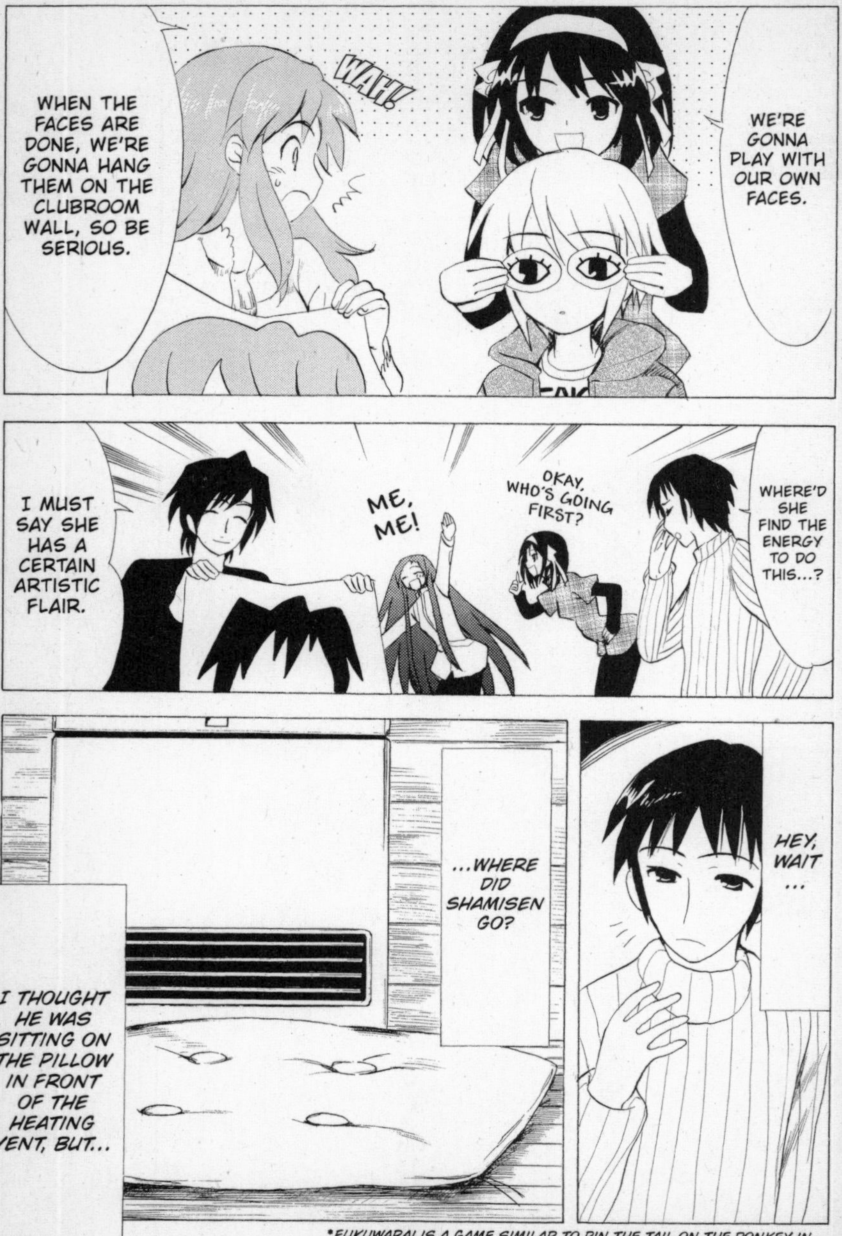
WE'RE GONNA PLAY WITH OUR OWN FACES.
WAH!
WHEN THE FACES ARE DONE, WE'RE GONNA HANG THEM ON THE CLUBROOM WALL, SO BE SERIOUS.
WHERE'D SHE FIND THE ENERGY TO DO THIS...?
OKAY, WHO'S GOING FIRST?
ME, ME!
I MUST SAY SHE HAS A CERTAIN ARTISTIC FLAIR.
HEY, WAIT ...
...WHERE DID SHAMISEN GO?
I THOUGHT HE WAS SITTING ON THE PILLOW IN FRONT OF THE HEATING VENT, BUT...

*FUKUWARAI IS A GAME SIMILAR TO PIN THE TAIL ON THE DONKEY IN WHICH PLAYERS BLINDLY PLACE FACIAL FEATURES ON A BLANK FACE.

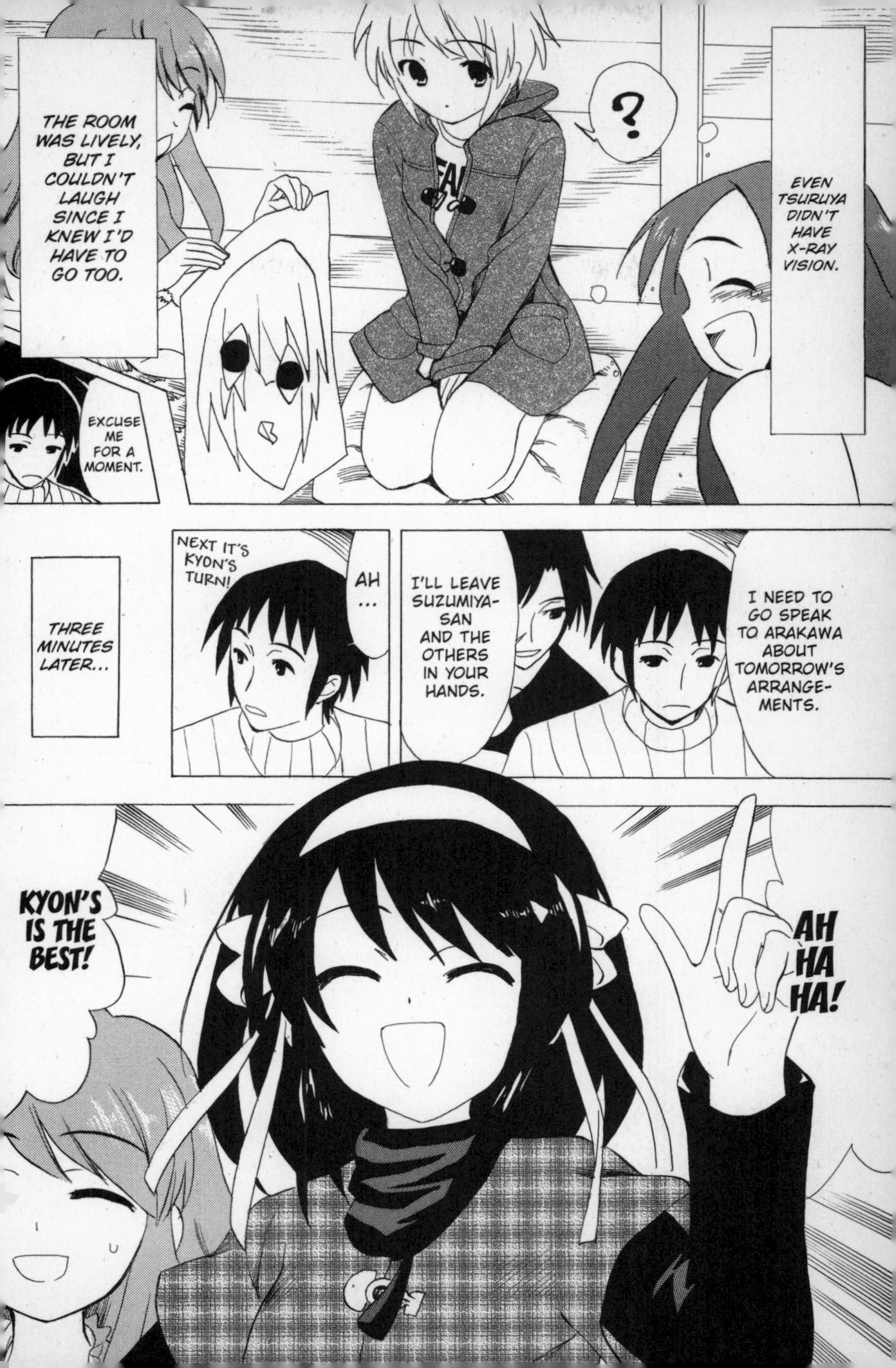
EVEN TSURUYA DIDN'T HAVE X-RAY VISION.
?
THE ROOM WAS LIVELY, BUT I COULDN'T LAUGH SINCE I KNEW I'D HAVE TO GO TOO.
EXCUSE ME FOR A MOMENT.
I NEED TO GO SPEAK TO ARAKAWA ABOUT TOMORROW'S ARRANGEMENTS.
I'LL LEAVE SUZUMIYA-SAN AND THE OTHERS IN YOUR HANDS.
AH...
NEXT IT'S KYON'S TURN!
THREE MINUTES LATER...
AH HA HA!
KYON'S IS THE BEST!

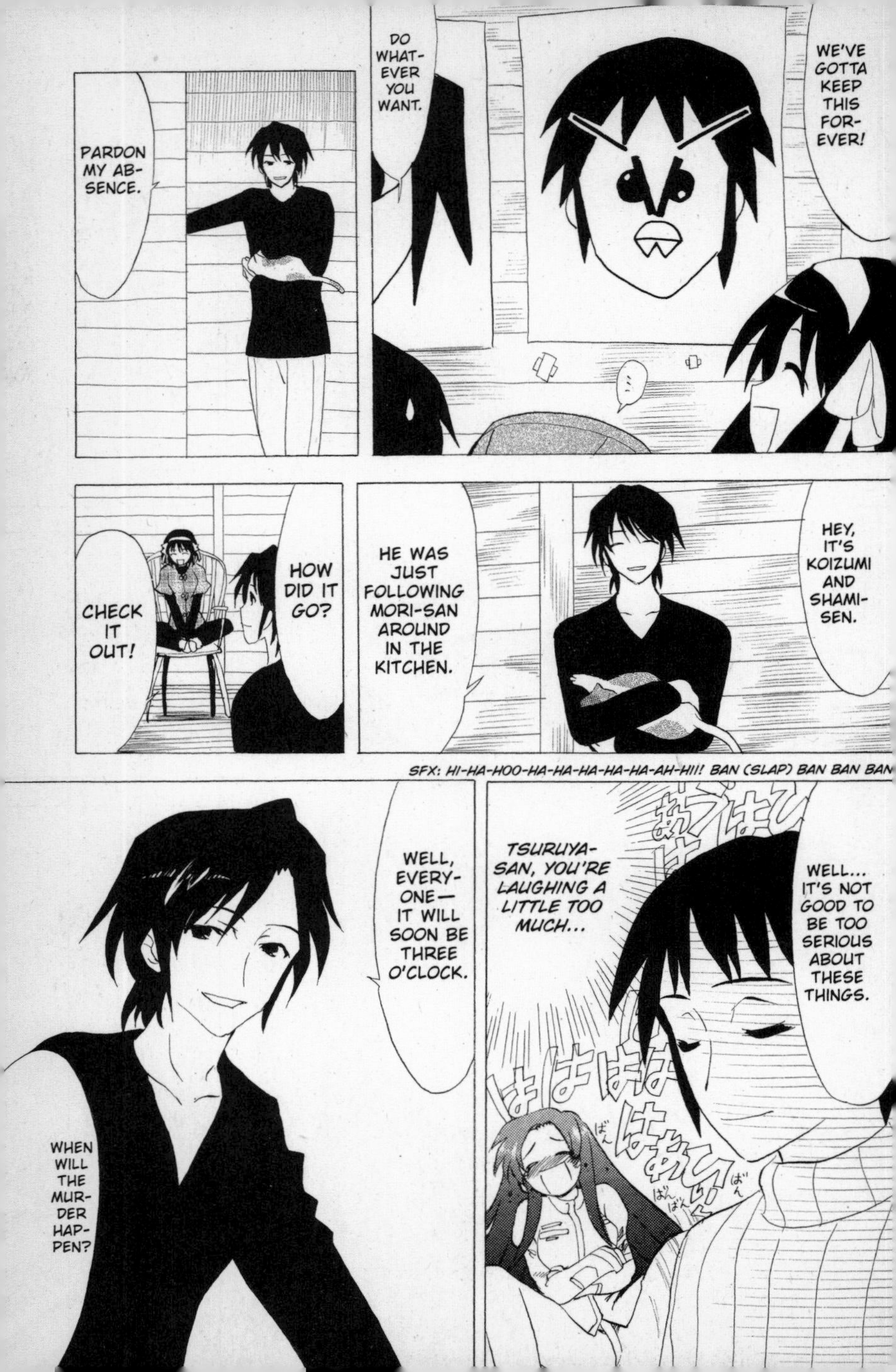
WE'VE GOTTA KEEP THIS FOREVER!
DO WHATEVER YOU WANT.
PARDON MY ABSENCE.
HEY, IT'S KOIZUMI AND SHAMISEN.
HE WAS JUST FOLLOWING MORI-SAN AROUND IN THE KITCHEN.
HOW DID IT GO?
CHECK IT OUT!
SFX: HI-HA-HOO-HA-HA-HA-HA-HA-AH-HII! BAN (SLAP) BAN BAN BAN
WELL... IT'S NOT GOOD TO BE TOO SERIOUS ABOUT THESE THINGS.
TSURUYA-SAN, YOU'RE LAUGHING A LITTLE TOO MUCH...
WELL, EVERYONE— IT WILL SOON BE THREE O'CLOCK.
WHEN WILL THE MURDER HAPPEN?

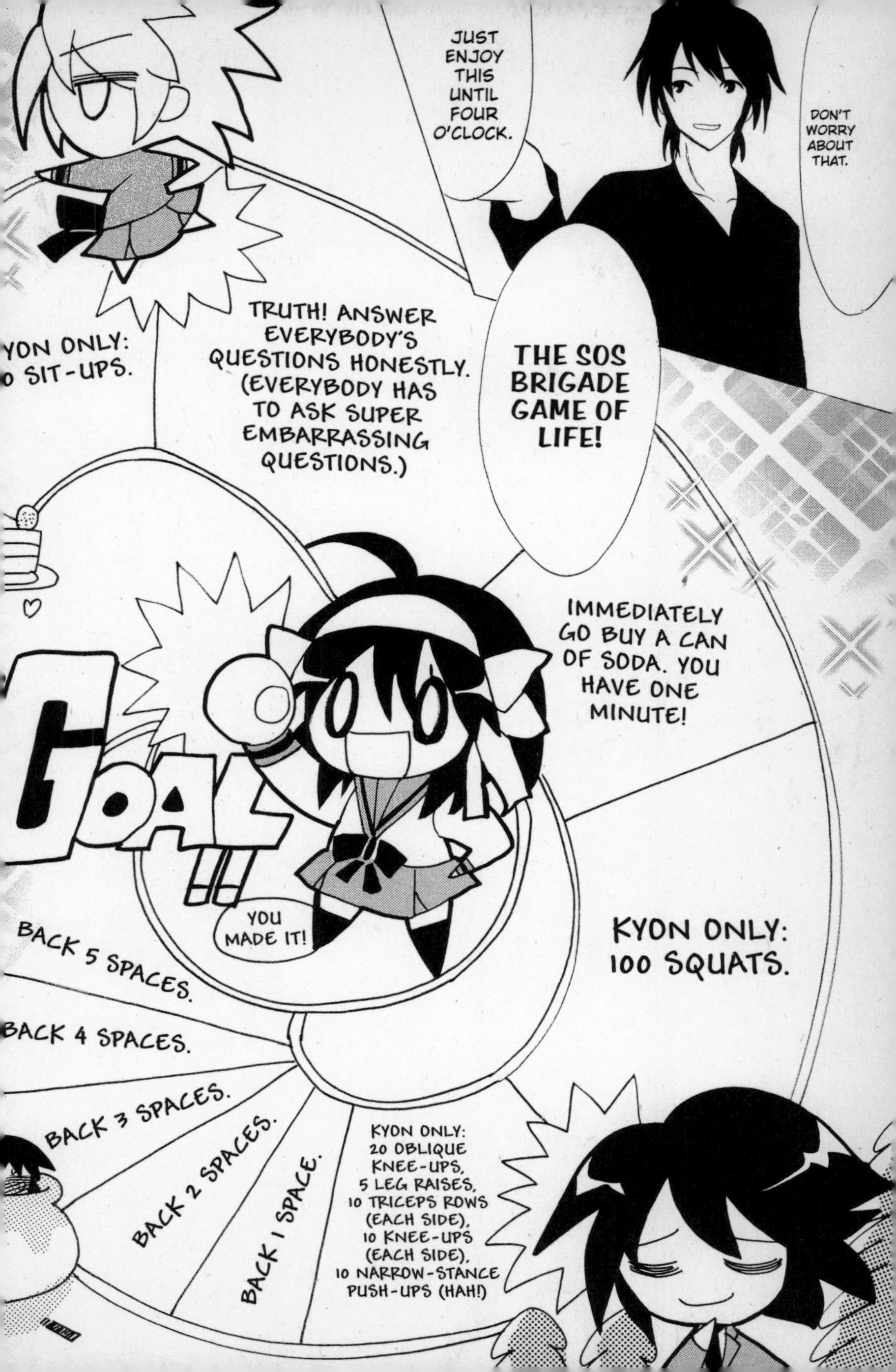

DON'T WORRY ABOUT THAT.
JUST ENJOY THIS UNTIL FOUR O'CLOCK.
THE SOS BRIGADE GAME OF LIFE!
TRUTH! ANSWER EVERYBODY'S QUESTIONS HONESTLY. (EVERYBODY HAS TO ASK SUPER EMBARRASSING QUESTIONS.)
YON ONLY: 0 SIT-UPS.
IMMEDIATELY GO BUY A CAN OF SODA. YOU HAVE ONE MINUTE!
GOAL!!
YOU MADE IT!
KYON ONLY: 100 SQUATS.
KYON ONLY: 20 OBLIQUE KNEE-UPS, 5 LEG RAISES, 10 TRICEPS ROWS (EACH SIDE), 10 KNEE-UPS (EACH SIDE), 10 NARROW-STANCE PUSH-UPS (HAH!)
BACK 1 SPACE.
BACK 2 SPACES.
BACK 3 SPACES.
BACK 4 SPACES.
BACK 5 SPACES.

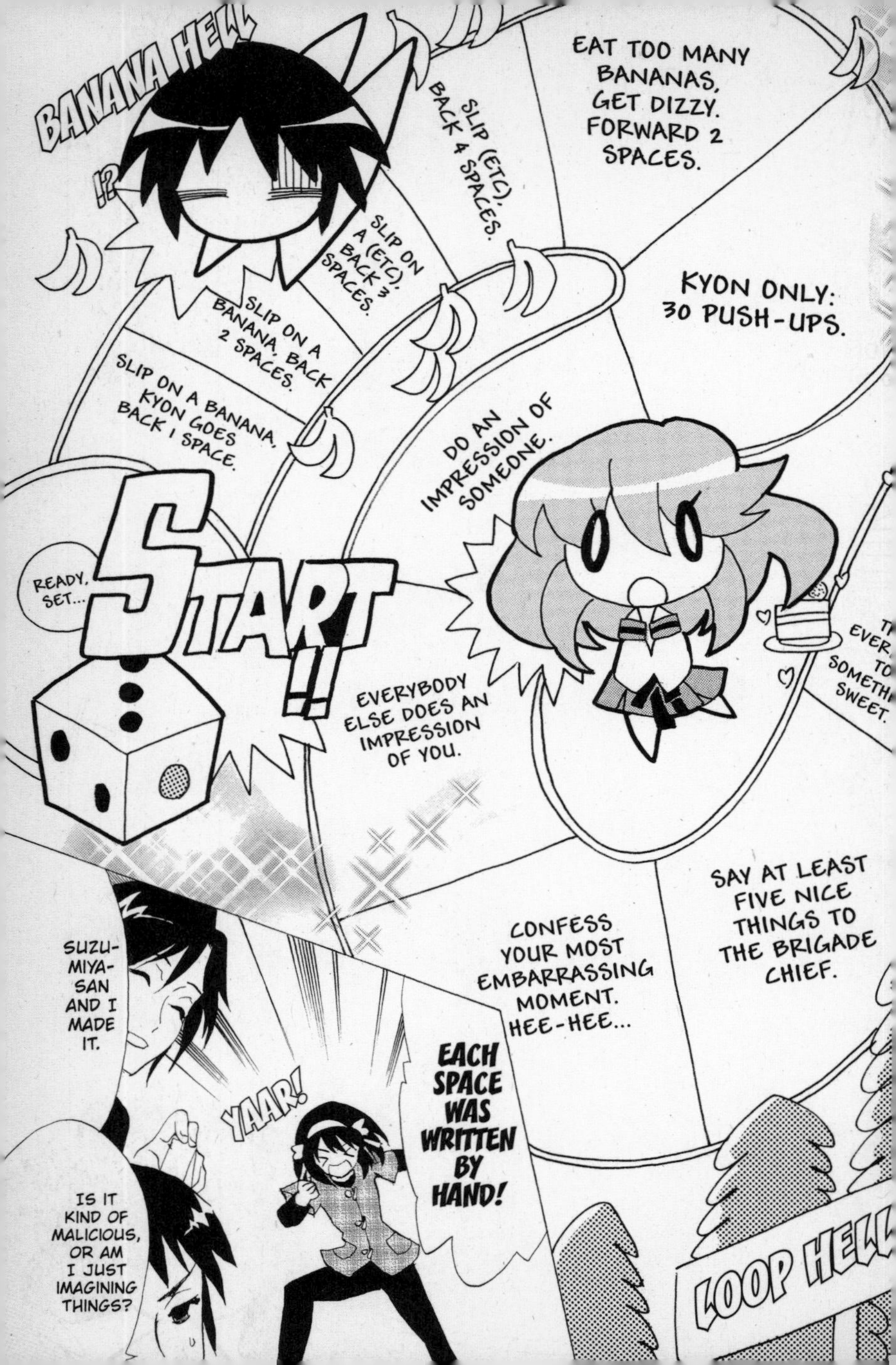

EAT TOO MANY BANANAS, GET DIZZY. FORWARD 2 SPACES.
SLIP (ETC), BACK 4 SPACES.
BANANA HELL
!?
KYON ONLY: 30 PUSH-UPS.
SLIP ON A (ETC), BACK 3 SPACES.
SLIP ON A BANANA, BACK 2 SPACES.
SLIP ON A BANANA, KYON GOES BACK 1 SPACE.
DO AN IMPRESSION OF SOMEONE.
START!!
READY, SET...
EVERYBODY ELSE DOES AN IMPRESSION OF YOU.
SAY AT LEAST FIVE NICE THINGS TO THE BRIGADE CHIEF.
CONFESS YOUR MOST EMBARRASSING MOMENT. HEE-HEE...
LOOP HELL
EACH SPACE WAS WRITTEN BY HAND!
YAAR!
SUZUMIYA-SAN AND I MADE IT.
IS IT KIND OF MALICIOUS, OR AM I JUST IMAGINING THINGS?

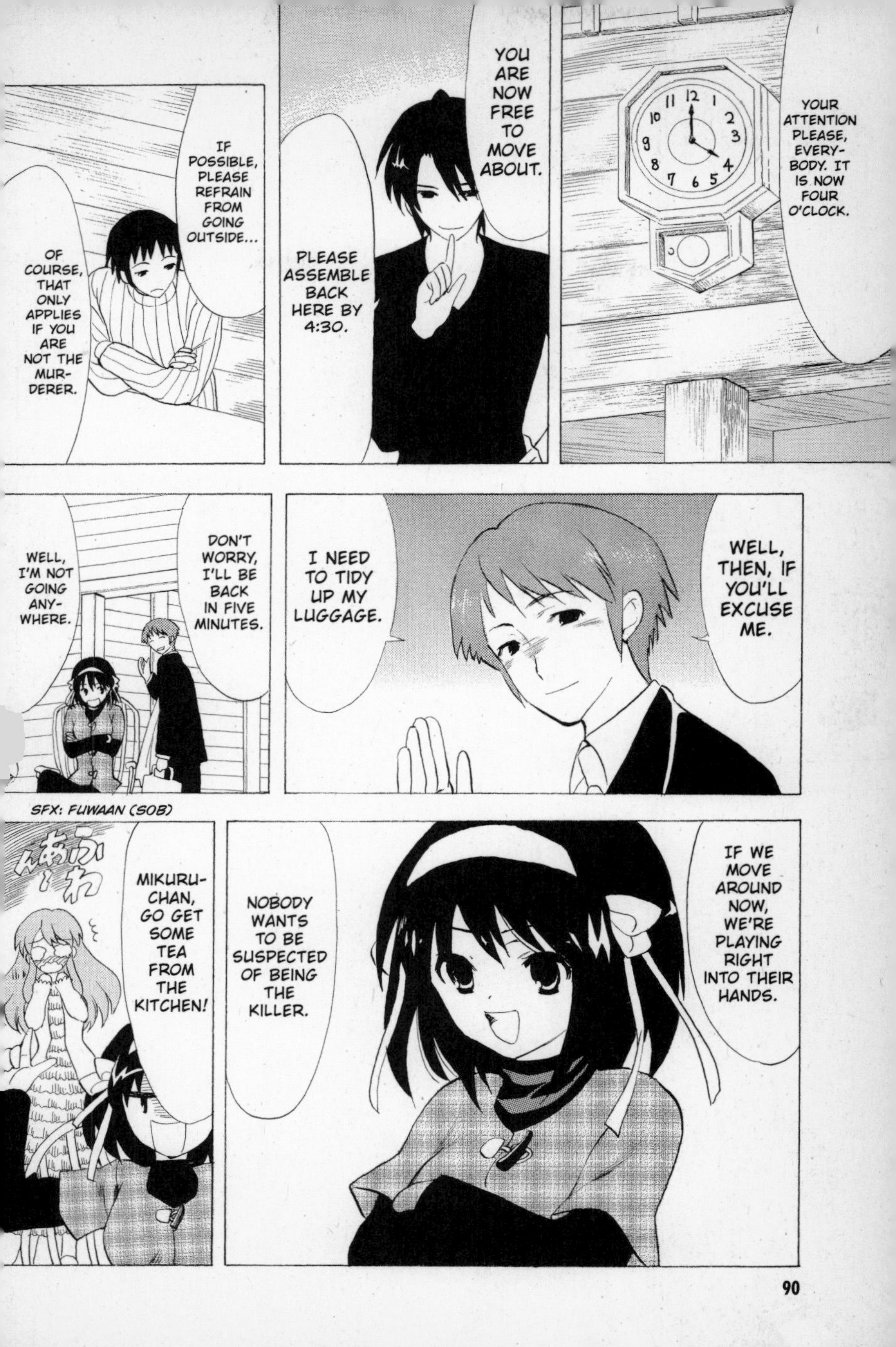
YOUR ATTENTION PLEASE, EVERY-BODY. IT IS NOW FOUR O'CLOCK.
YOU ARE NOW FREE TO MOVE ABOUT.
PLEASE ASSEMBLE BACK HERE BY 4:30.
IF POSSIBLE, PLEASE REFRAIN FROM GOING OUTSIDE...
OF COURSE, THAT ONLY APPLIES IF YOU ARE NOT THE MUR-DERER.
WELL, THEN, IF YOU'LL EXCUSE ME.
I NEED TO TIDY UP MY LUGGAGE.
DON'T WORRY, I'LL BE BACK IN FIVE MINUTES.
WELL, I'M NOT GOING ANY-WHERE.
SFX: FUWAAN (SOB)
IF WE MOVE AROUND NOW, WE'RE PLAYING RIGHT INTO THEIR HANDS.
NOBODY WANTS TO BE SUSPECTED OF BEING THE KILLER.
MIKURU-CHAN, GO GET SOME TEA FROM THE KITCHEN!

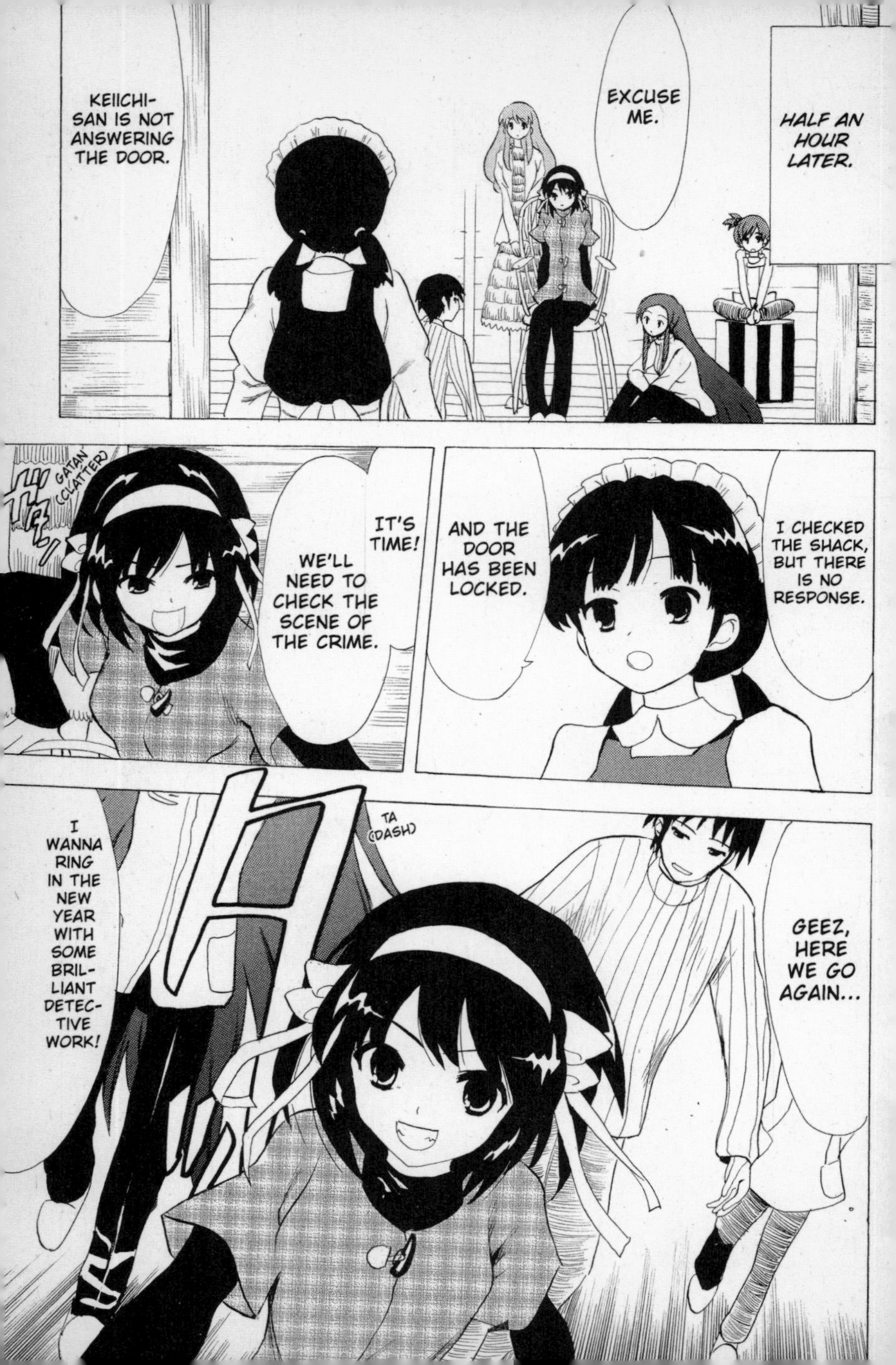
HALF AN HOUR LATER.
EXCUSE ME.
KEIICHI-SAN IS NOT ANSWERING THE DOOR.
I CHECKED THE SHACK, BUT THERE IS NO RESPONSE.
AND THE DOOR HAS BEEN LOCKED.
GATAN (CLATTER)
IT'S TIME!
WE'LL NEED TO CHECK THE SCENE OF THE CRIME.
GEEZ, HERE WE GO AGAIN...
TA (DASH)
I WANNA RING IN THE NEW YEAR WITH SOME BRIL-LIANT DETEC-TIVE WORK!

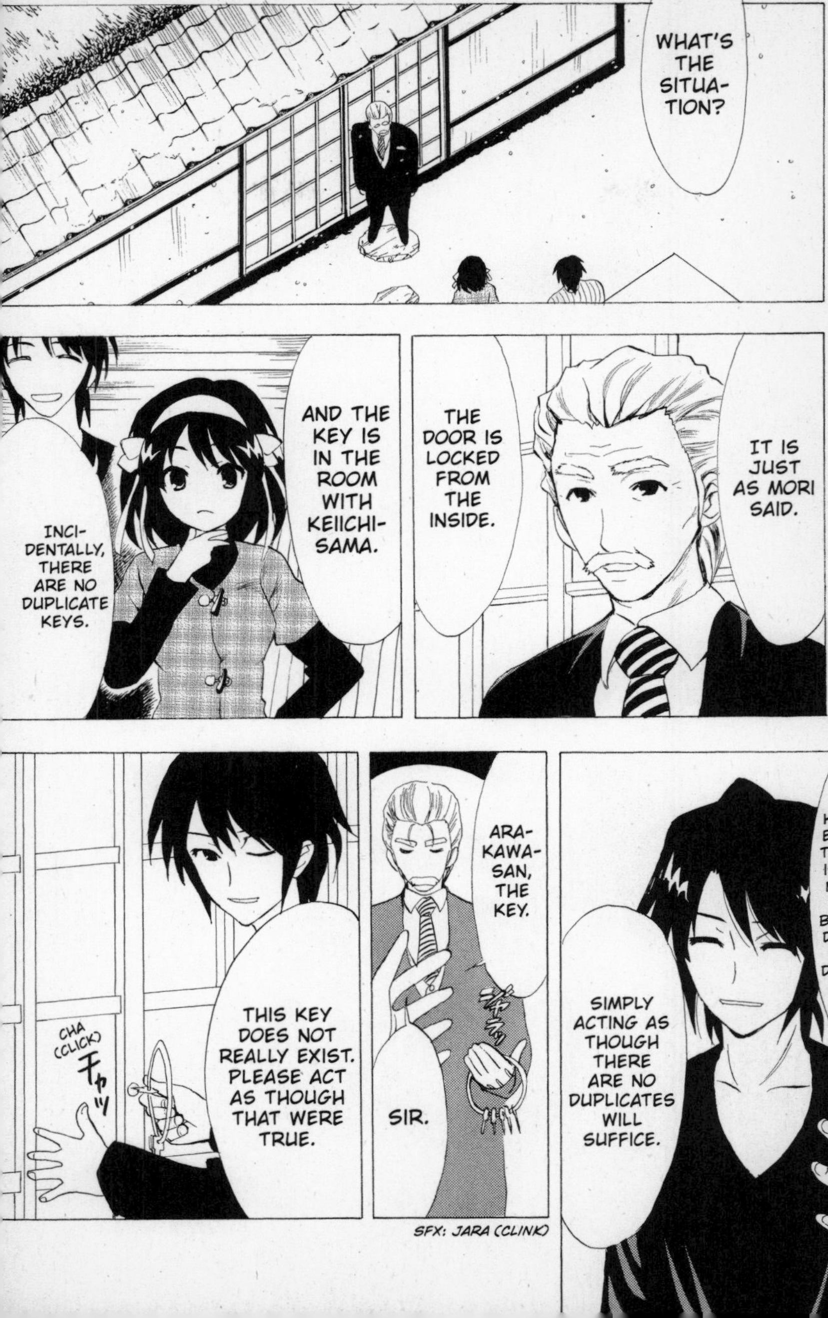
WHAT'S THE SITUATION?
IT IS JUST AS MORI SAID.
THE DOOR IS LOCKED FROM THE INSIDE.
AND THE KEY IS IN THE ROOM WITH KEIICHI-SAMA.
INCIDENTALLY, THERE ARE NO DUPLICATE KEYS.
HOWEVER, THERE IS NO NEED TO BREAK DOWN THE DOOR.
SIMPLY ACTING AS THOUGH THERE ARE NO DUPLICATES WILL SUFFICE.
ARAKAWA-SAN, THE KEY.
SIR.
THIS KEY DOES NOT REALLY EXIST. PLEASE ACT AS THOUGH THAT WERE TRUE.
CHA (CLICK)
チャッ
SFX: JARA (CLINK)

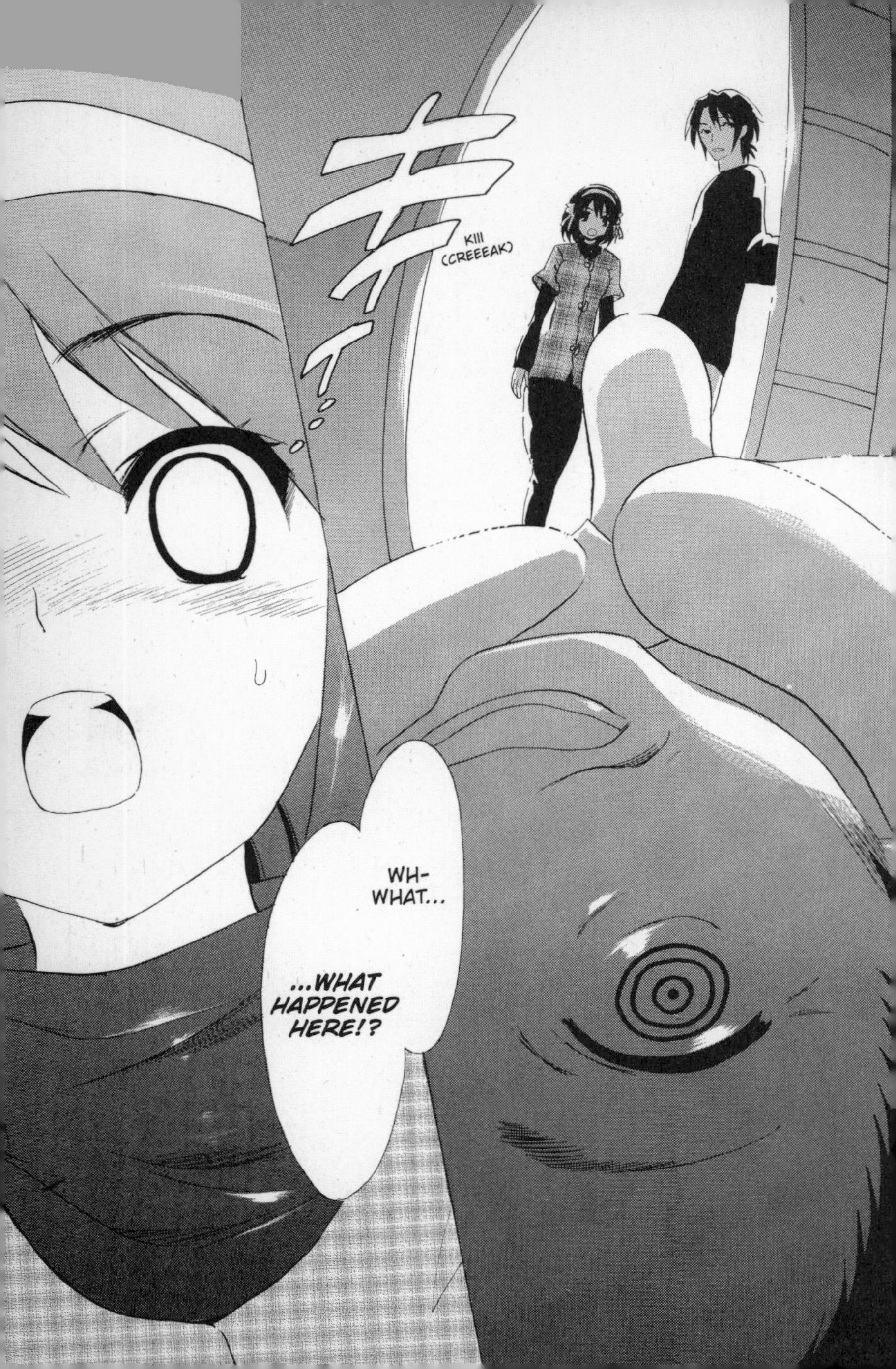
キイィ…
KIII (CREEEAK)
WH- WHAT... ...WHAT HAPPENED HERE!?

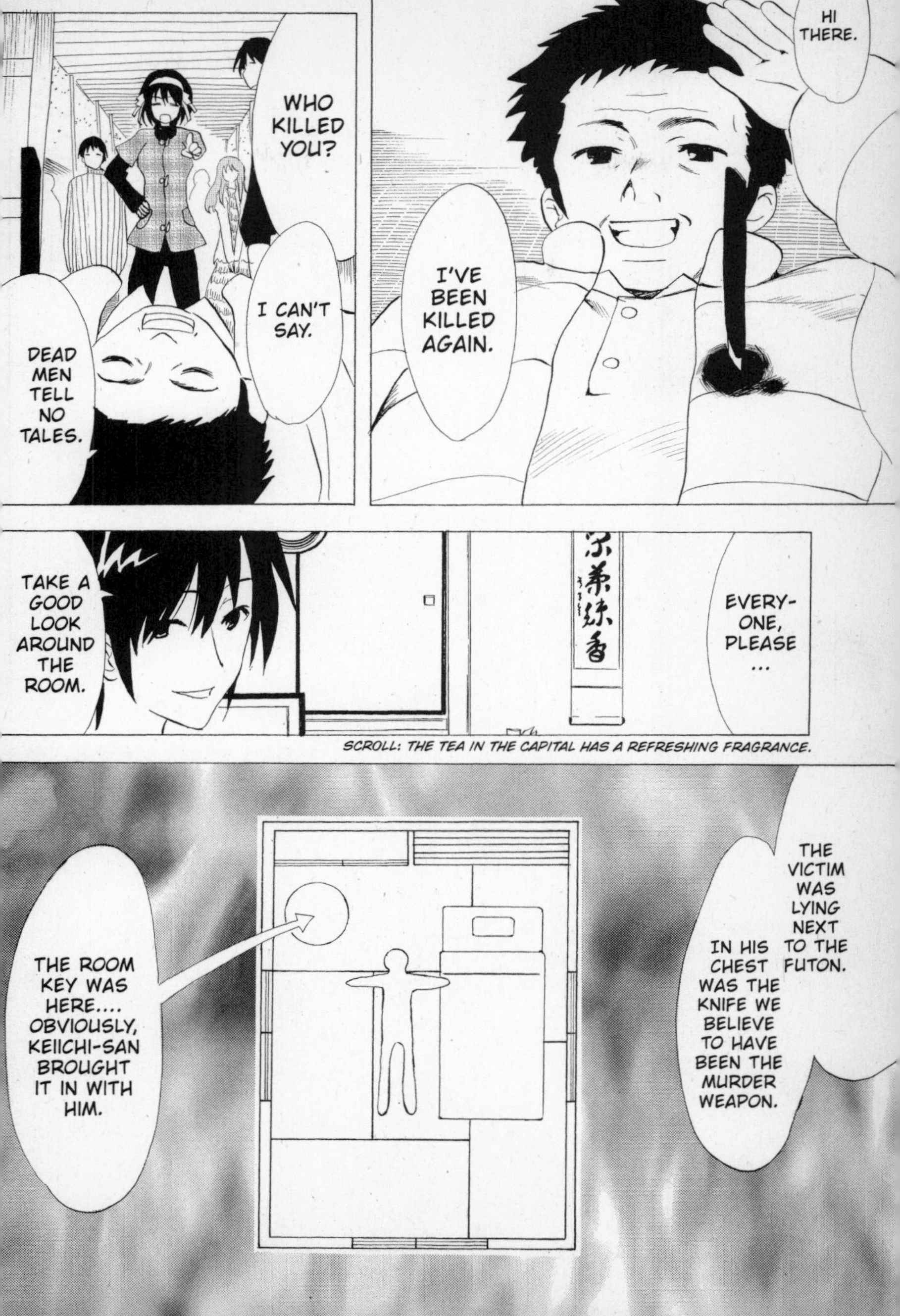
HI THERE.
I'VE BEEN KILLED AGAIN.
WHO KILLED YOU?
I CAN'T SAY.
DEAD MEN TELL NO TALES.
EVERY-ONE, PLEASE ...
TAKE A GOOD LOOK AROUND THE ROOM.
SCROLL: THE TEA IN THE CAPITAL HAS A REFRESHING FRAGRANCE.
THE VICTIM WAS LYING NEXT TO THE FUTON.
IN HIS CHEST WAS THE KNIFE WE BELIEVE TO HAVE BEEN THE MURDER WEAPON.
THE ROOM KEY WAS HERE.... OBVIOUSLY, KEIICHI-SAN BROUGHT IT IN WITH HIM.

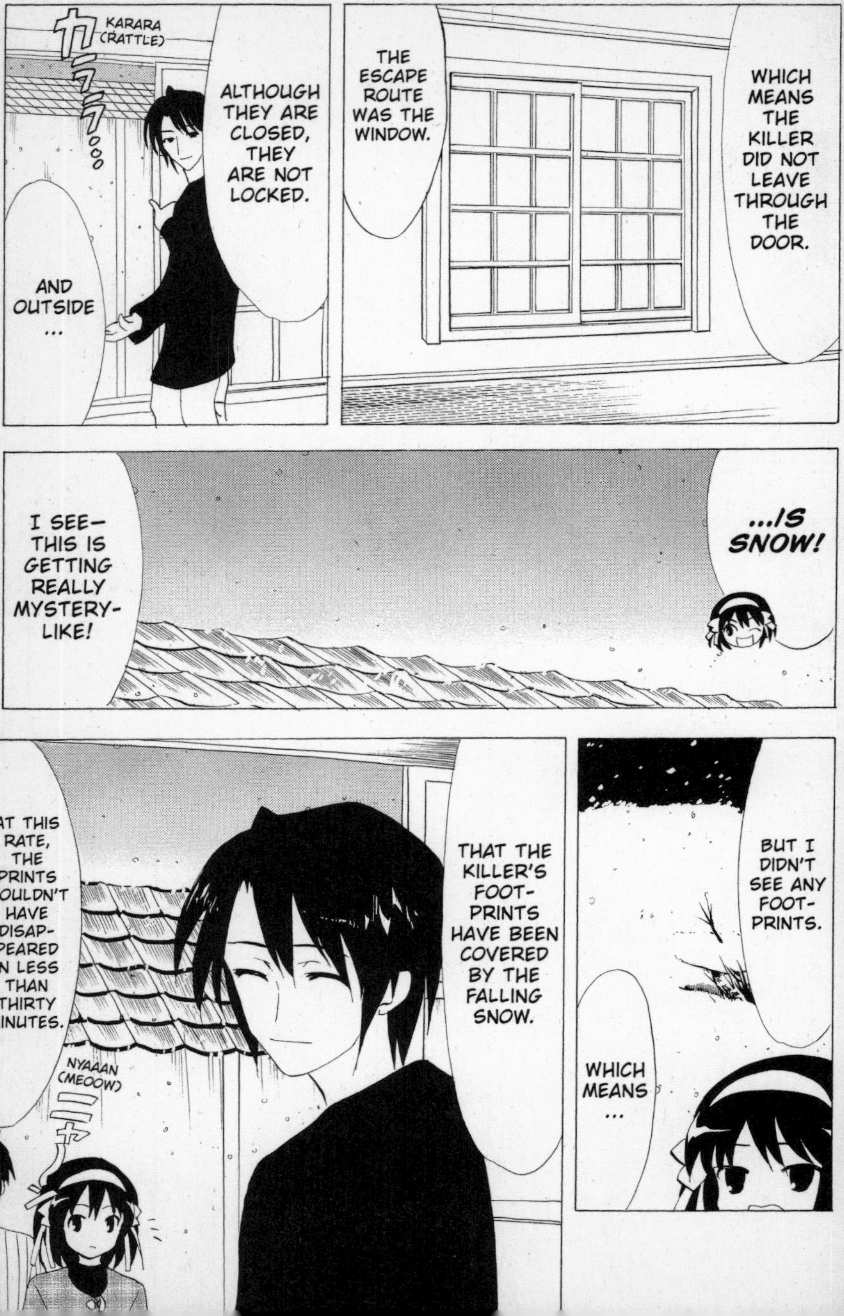
WHICH MEANS THE KILLER DID NOT LEAVE THROUGH THE DOOR.
THE ESCAPE ROUTE WAS THE WINDOW.
KARARA (RATTLE)
ALTHOUGH THEY ARE CLOSED, THEY ARE NOT LOCKED.
AND OUTSIDE ...
...IS SNOW!
I SEE— THIS IS GETTING REALLY MYSTERY-LIKE!
BUT I DIDN'T SEE ANY FOOT-PRINTS.
WHICH MEANS ...
THAT THE KILLER'S FOOT-PRINTS HAVE BEEN COVERED BY THE FALLING SNOW.
AT THIS RATE, THE PRINTS WOULDN'T HAVE DISAP-PEARED IN LESS THAN THIRTY MINUTES.
NYAAAN (MEOOW)

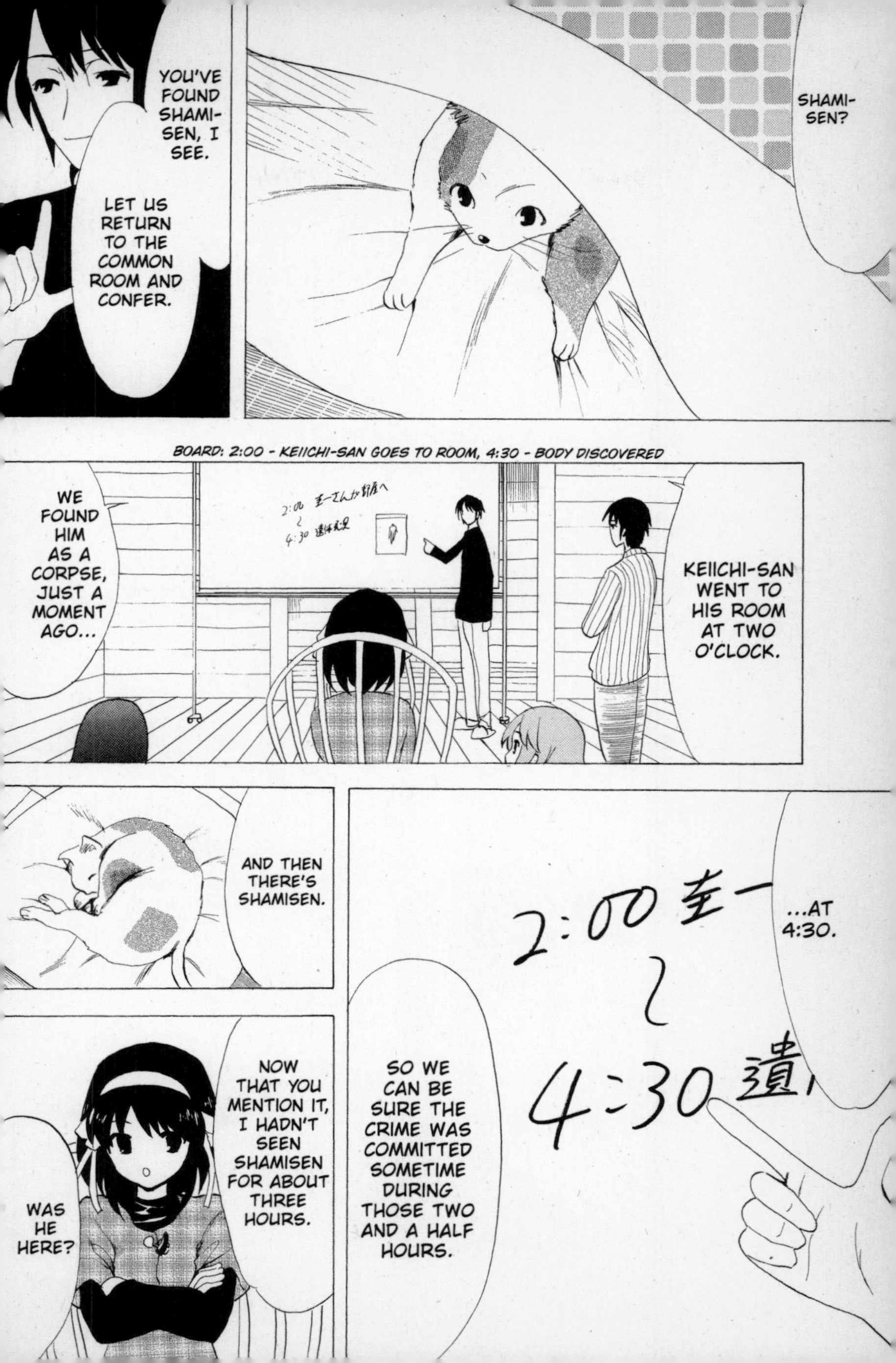
SHAMI-SEN?
YOU'VE FOUND SHAMI-SEN, I SEE.
LET US RETURN TO THE COMMON ROOM AND CONFER.
BOARD: 2:00 - KEIICHI-SAN GOES TO ROOM, 4:30 - BODY DISCOVERED
KEIICHI-SAN WENT TO HIS ROOM AT TWO O'CLOCK.
WE FOUND HIM AS A CORPSE, JUST A MOMENT AGO...
...AT 4:30.
SO WE CAN BE SURE THE CRIME WAS COMMITTED SOMETIME DURING THOSE TWO AND A HALF HOURS.
AND THEN THERE'S SHAMISEN.
NOW THAT YOU MENTION IT, I HADN'T SEEN SHAMISEN FOR ABOUT THREE HOURS.
WAS HE HERE?

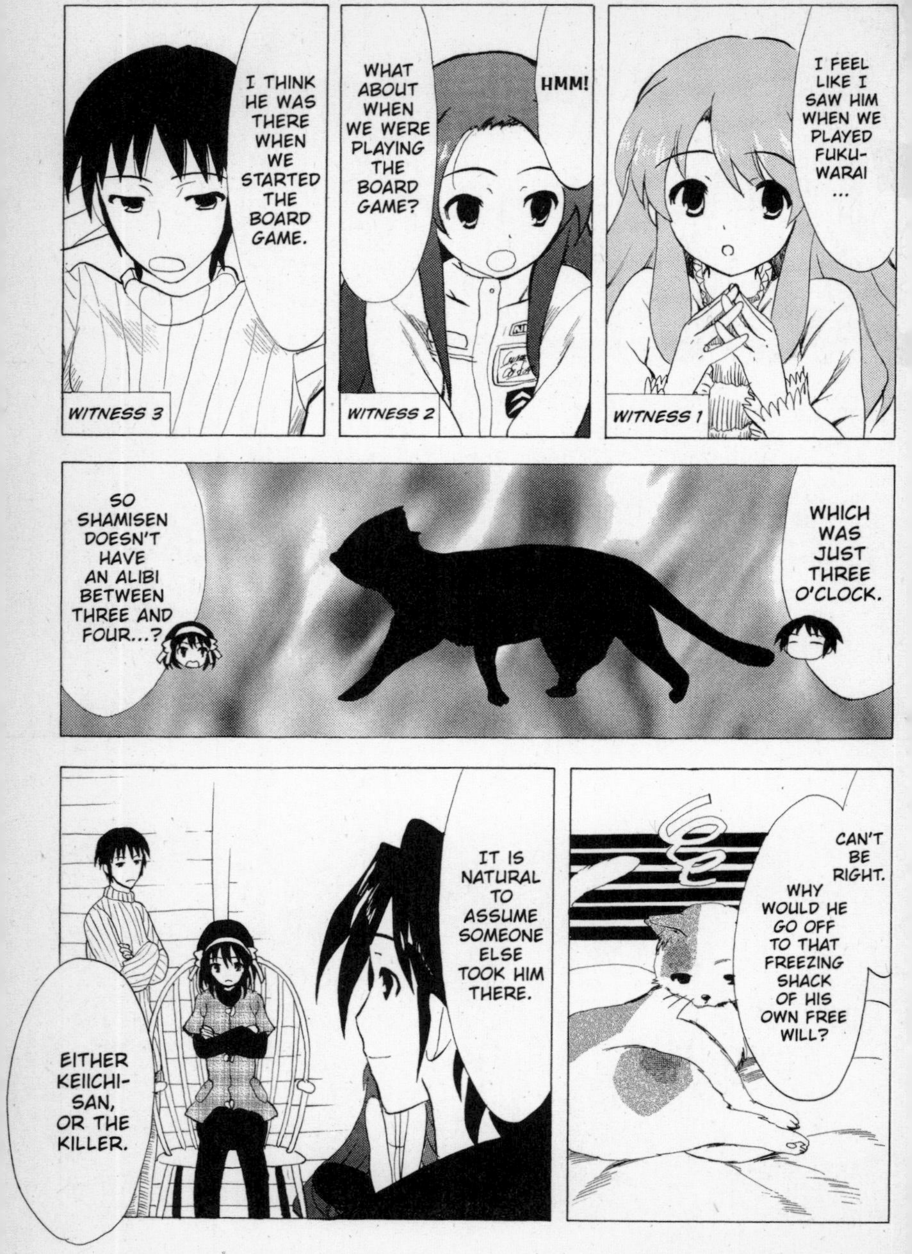
I FEEL LIKE I SAW HIM WHEN WE PLAYED FUKU-WARAI ...
WITNESS 1
HMM!
WHAT ABOUT WHEN WE WERE PLAYING THE BOARD GAME?
WITNESS 2
I THINK HE WAS THERE WHEN WE STARTED THE BOARD GAME.
WITNESS 3
WHICH WAS JUST THREE O'CLOCK.
SO SHAMISEN DOESN'T HAVE AN ALIBI BETWEEN THREE AND FOUR...?
CAN'T BE RIGHT. WHY WOULD HE GO OFF TO THAT FREEZING SHACK OF HIS OWN FREE WILL?
IT IS NATURAL TO ASSUME SOMEONE ELSE TOOK HIM THERE.
EITHER KEIICHI-SAN, OR THE KILLER.

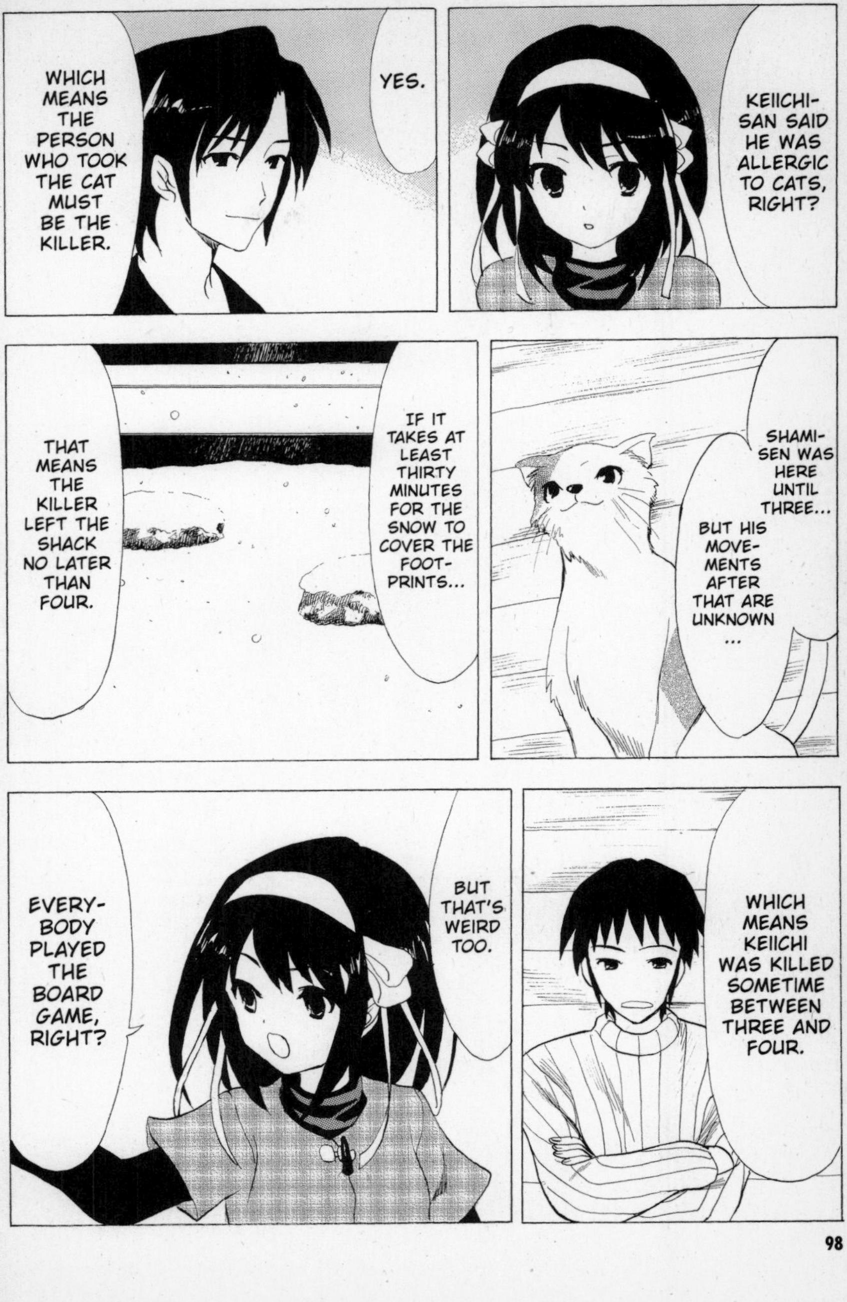
KEIICHI-SAN SAID HE WAS ALLERGIC TO CATS, RIGHT?
YES.
WHICH MEANS THE PERSON WHO TOOK THE CAT MUST BE THE KILLER.
SHAMISEN WAS HERE UNTIL THREE...
BUT HIS MOVEMENTS AFTER THAT ARE UNKNOWN...
IF IT TAKES AT LEAST THIRTY MINUTES FOR THE SNOW TO COVER THE FOOTPRINTS...
THAT MEANS THE KILLER LEFT THE SHACK NO LATER THAN FOUR.
WHICH MEANS KEIICHI WAS KILLED SOMETIME BETWEEN THREE AND FOUR.
BUT THAT'S WEIRD TOO.
EVERYBODY PLAYED THE BOARD GAME, RIGHT?

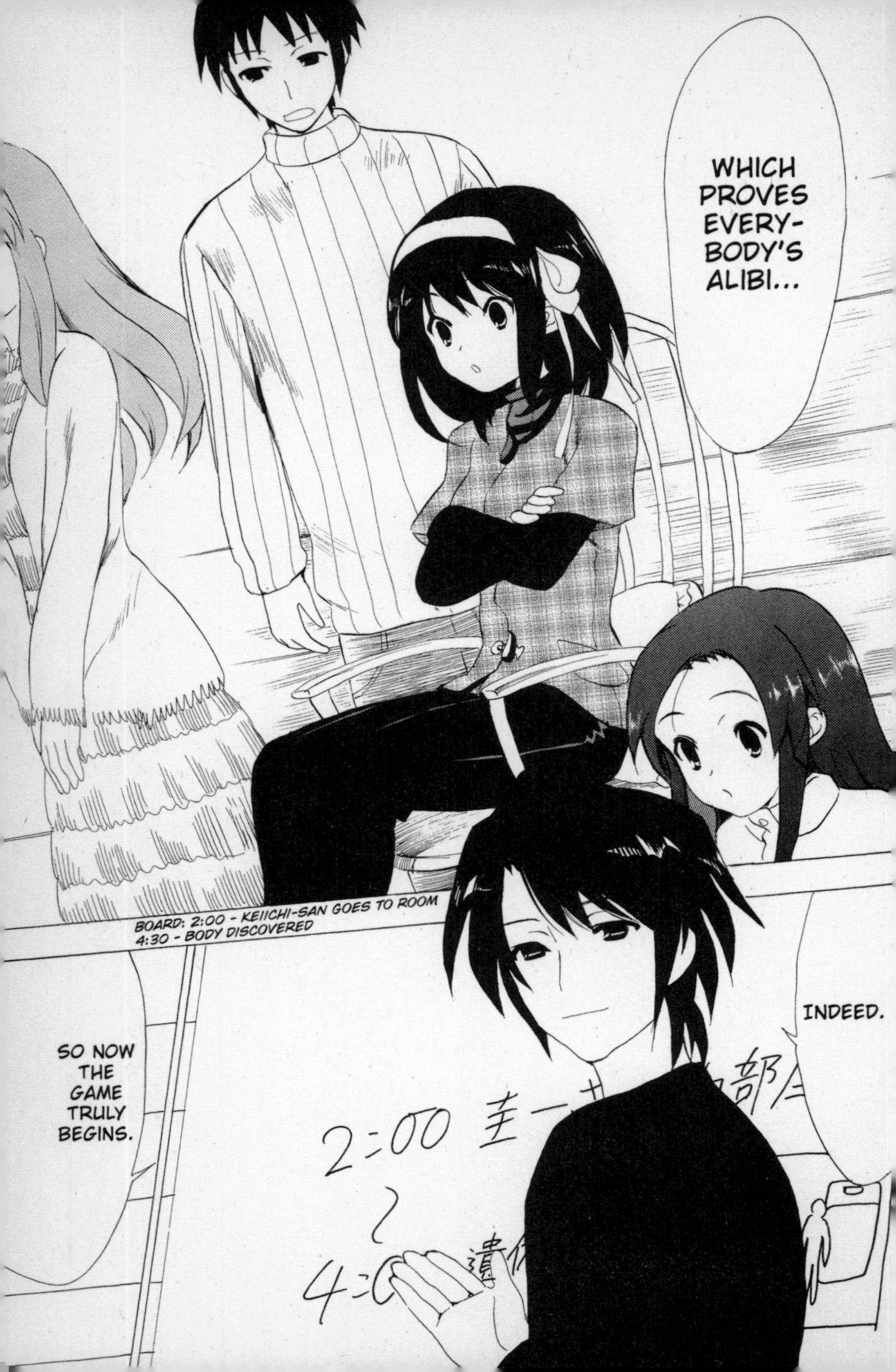
WHICH PROVES EVERY-BODY'S ALIBI...
INDEED.
BOARD: 2:00 - KEIICHI-SAN GOES TO ROOM
4:30 - BODY DISCOVERED
SO NOW THE GAME TRULY BEGINS.

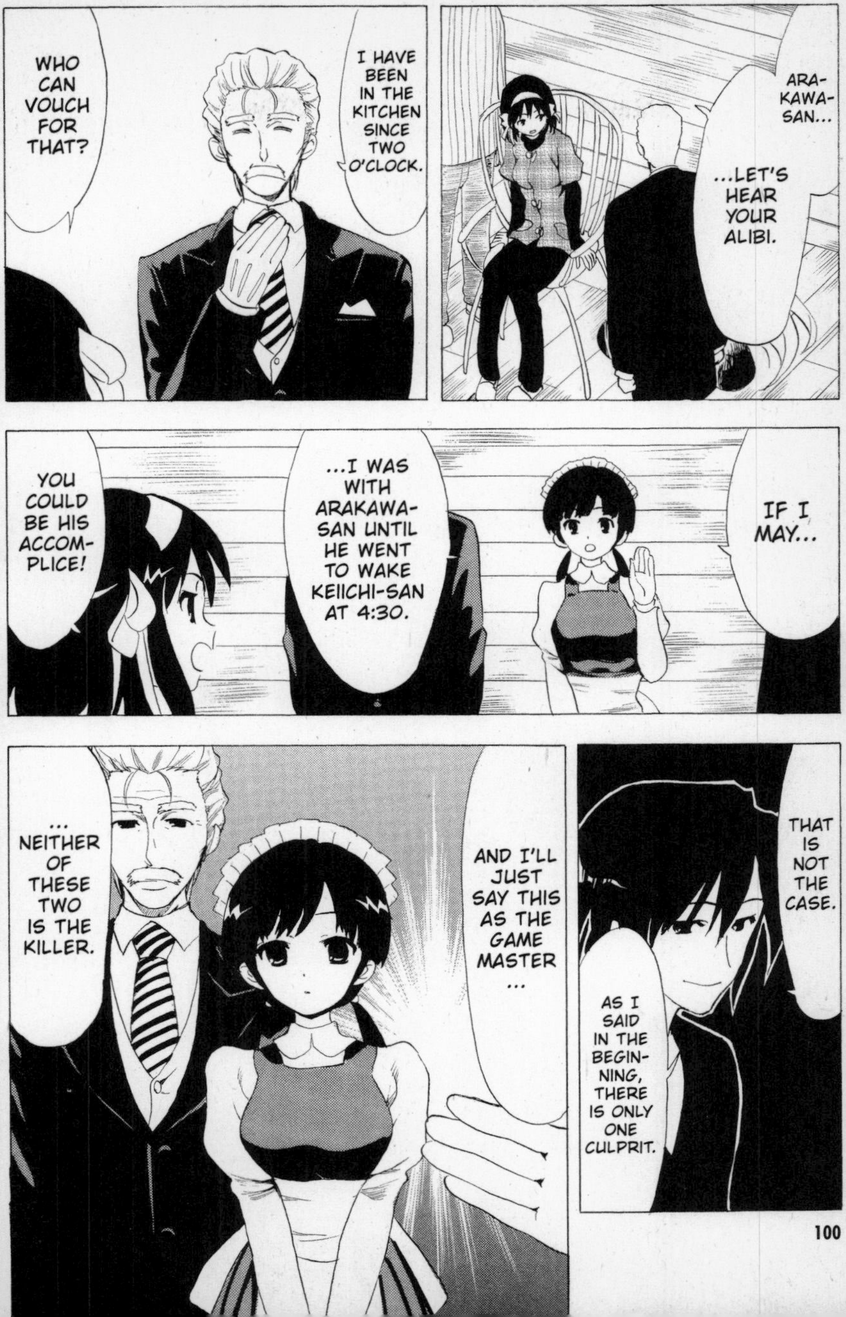
ARAKAWA-SAN...
...LET'S HEAR YOUR ALIBI.
I HAVE BEEN IN THE KITCHEN SINCE TWO O'CLOCK.
WHO CAN VOUCH FOR THAT?
IF I MAY...
...I WAS WITH ARAKAWA-SAN UNTIL HE WENT TO WAKE KEIICHI-SAN AT 4:30.
YOU COULD BE HIS ACCOMPLICE!
THAT IS NOT THE CASE.
AS I SAID IN THE BEGINNING, THERE IS ONLY ONE CULPRIT.
AND I'LL JUST SAY THIS AS THE GAME MASTER...
...NEITHER OF THESE TWO IS THE KILLER.

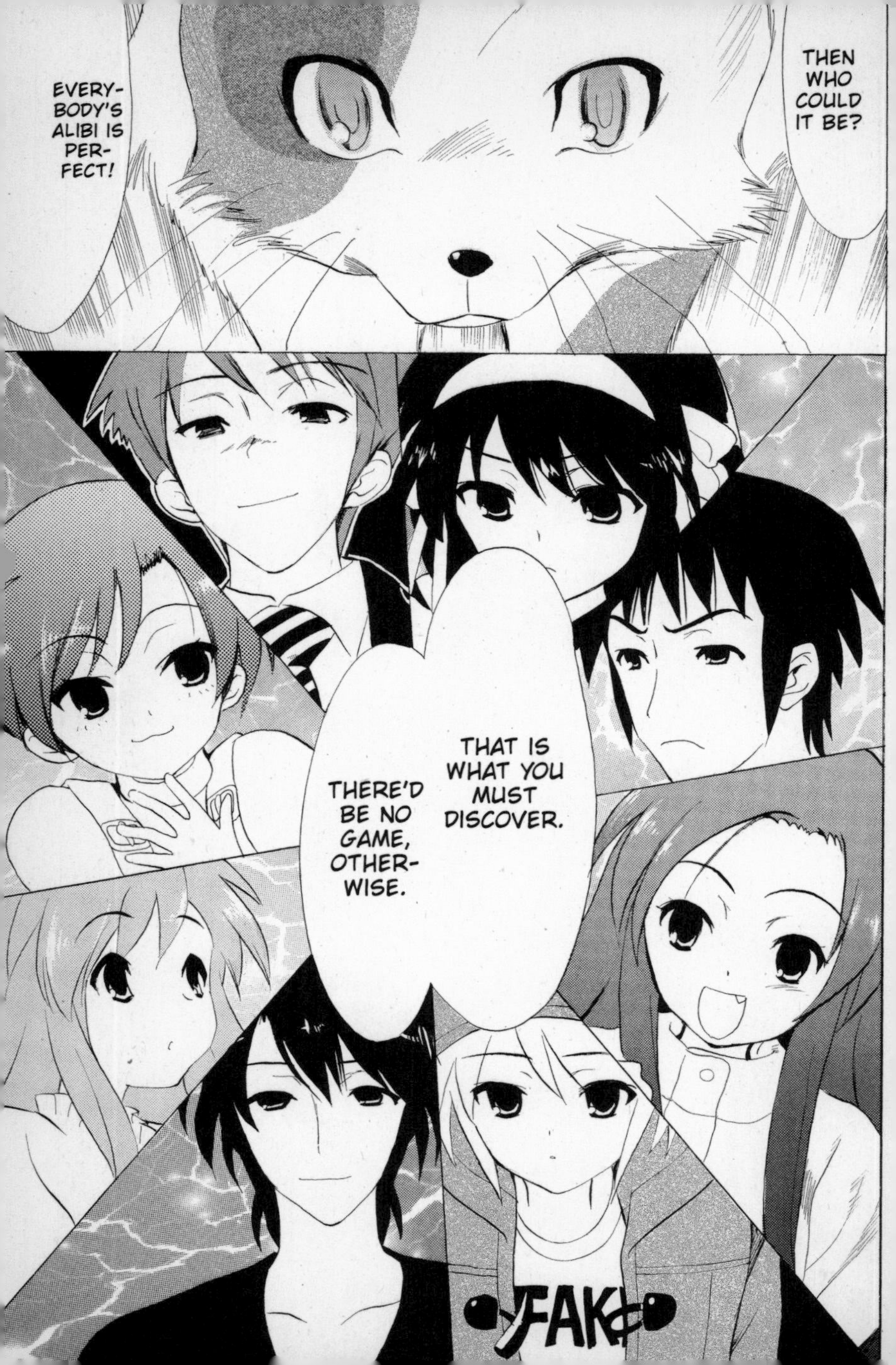
THEN WHO COULD IT BE?
EVERY-BODY'S ALIBI IS PER-FECT!
THAT IS WHAT YOU MUST DISCOVER.
THERE'D BE NO GAME, OTHER-WISE.

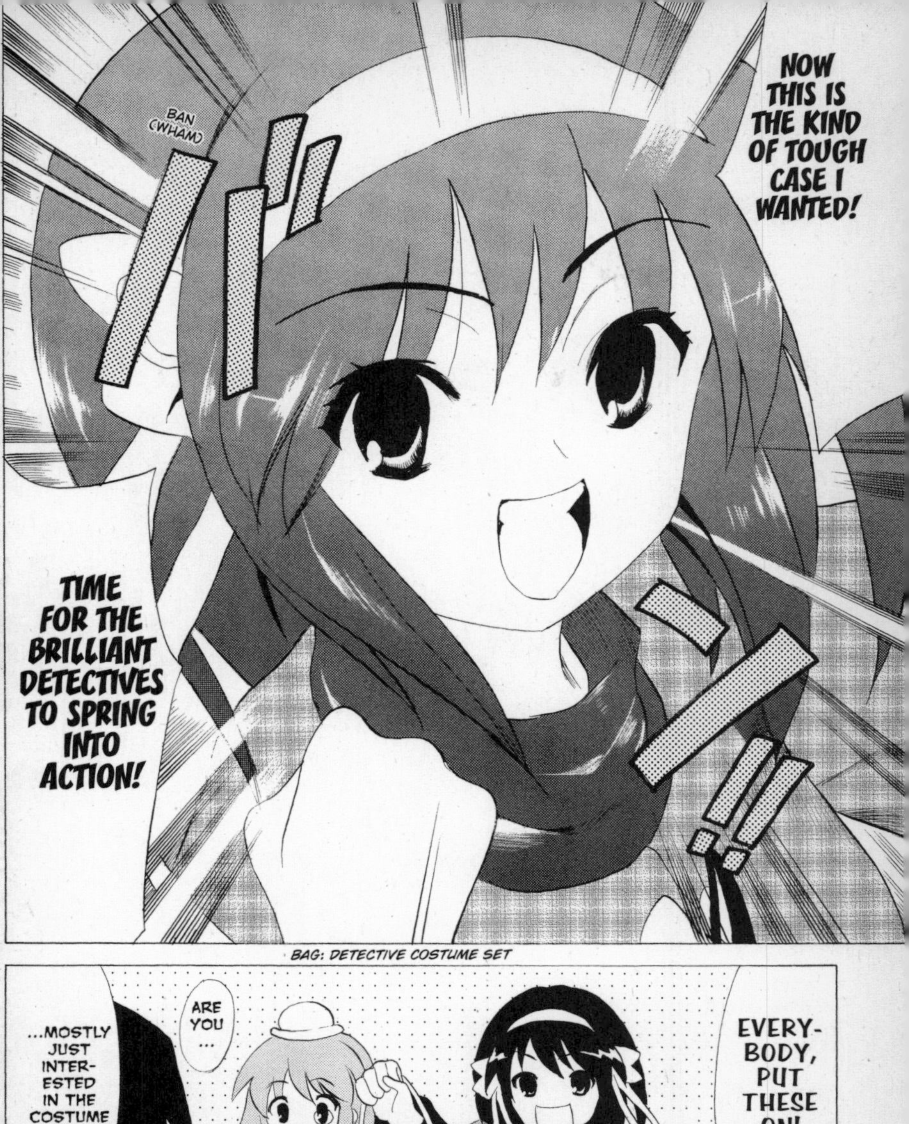
NOW THIS IS THE KIND OF TOUGH CASE I WANTED!
BAN (WHAM)
TIME FOR THE BRILLIANT DETECTIVES TO SPRING INTO ACTION!

BAG: DETECTIVE COSTUME SET

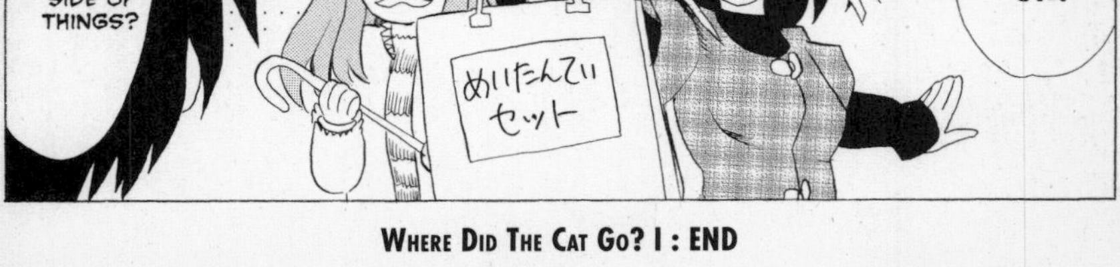
EVERY-BODY, PUT THESE ON!
めいたんてい セット
ARE YOU ...
...MOSTLY JUST INTER-ESTED IN THE COSTUME SIDE OF THINGS?

WHERE DID THE CAT GO? I : END

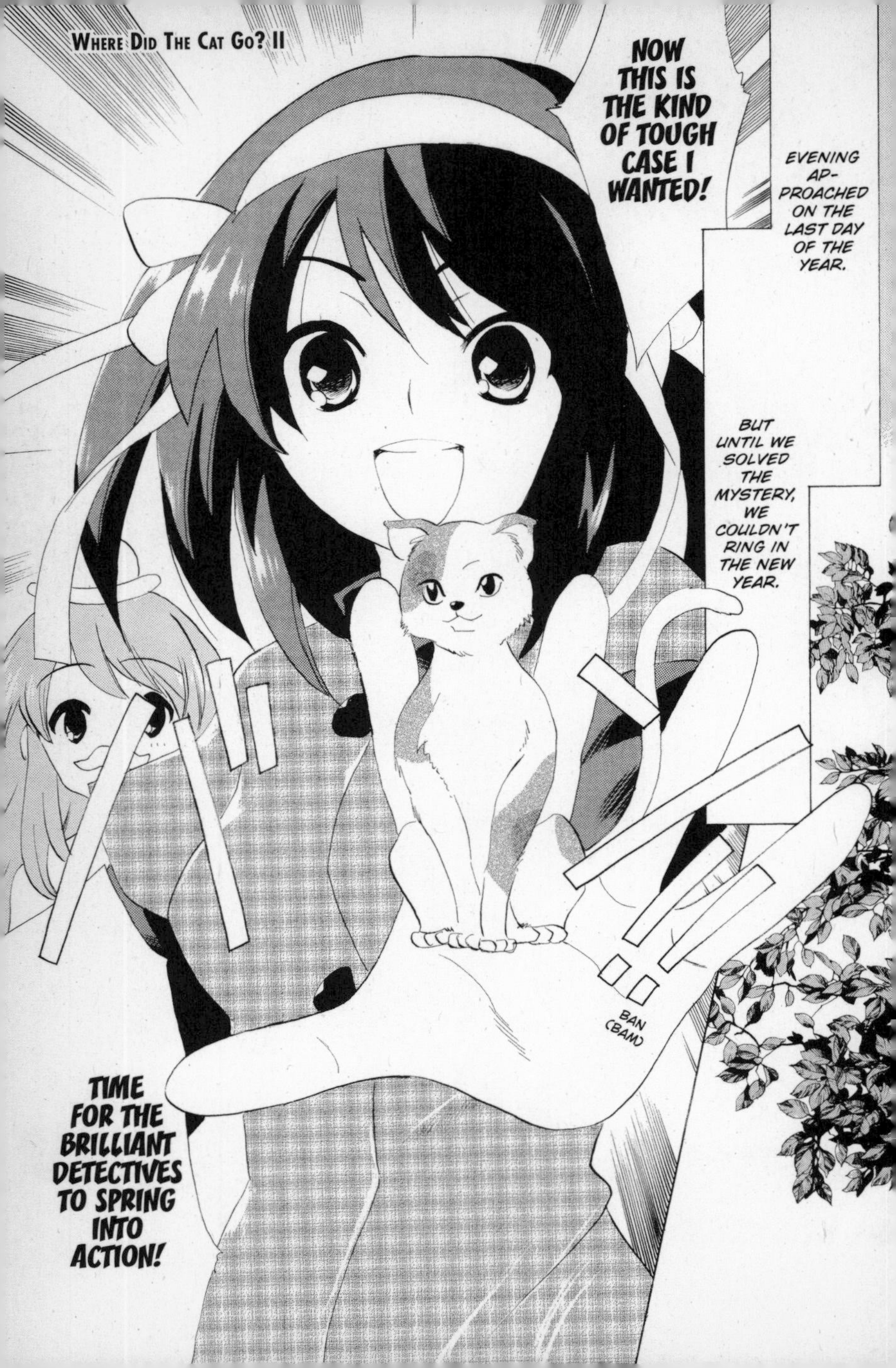
Evening ap-proached on the last day of the year.
Now this is the kind of tough case I wanted!
But until we solved the mystery, we couldn't ring in the new year.
BAN (BAM)
Time for the brilliant detectives to spring into action!

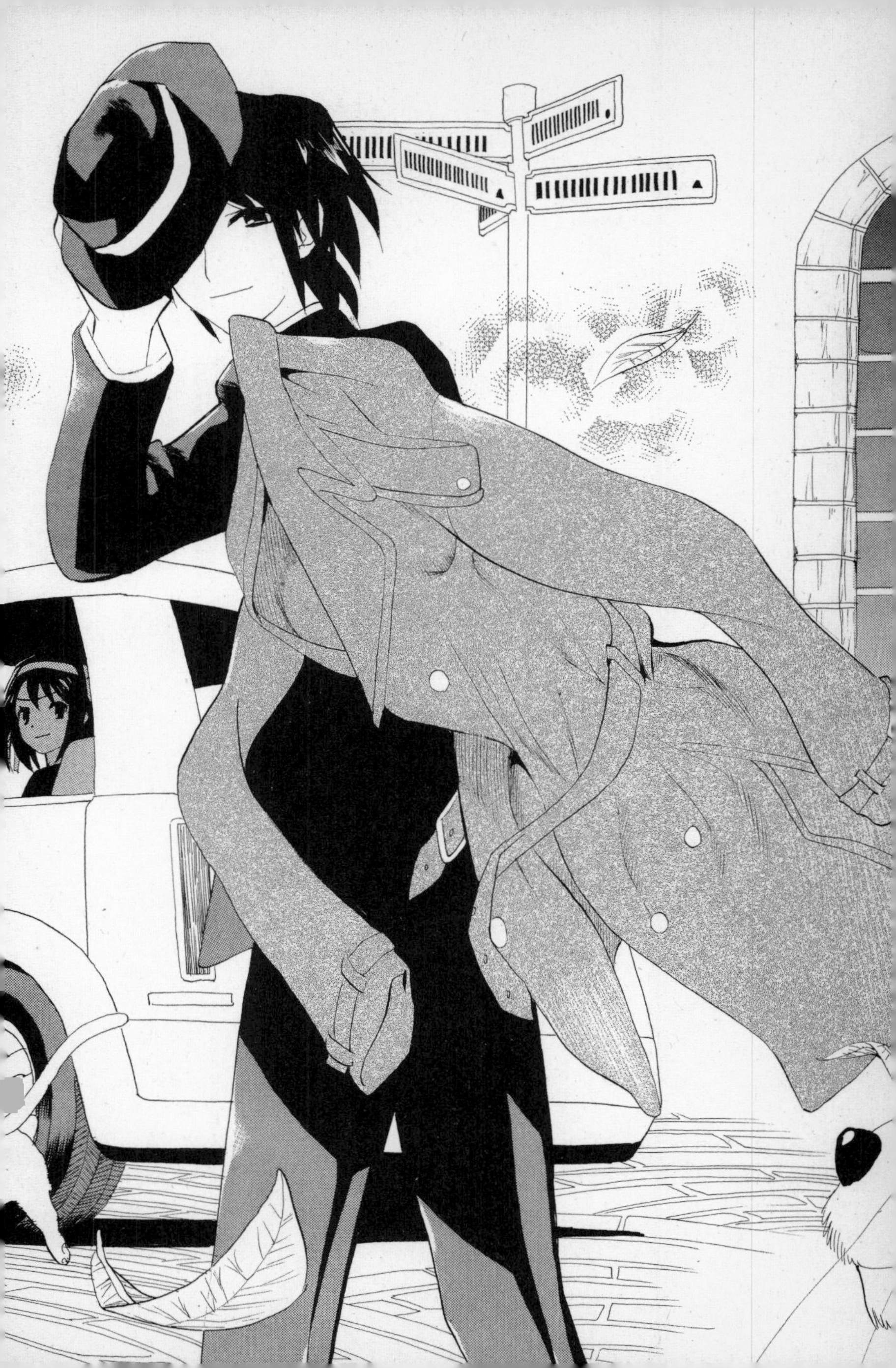

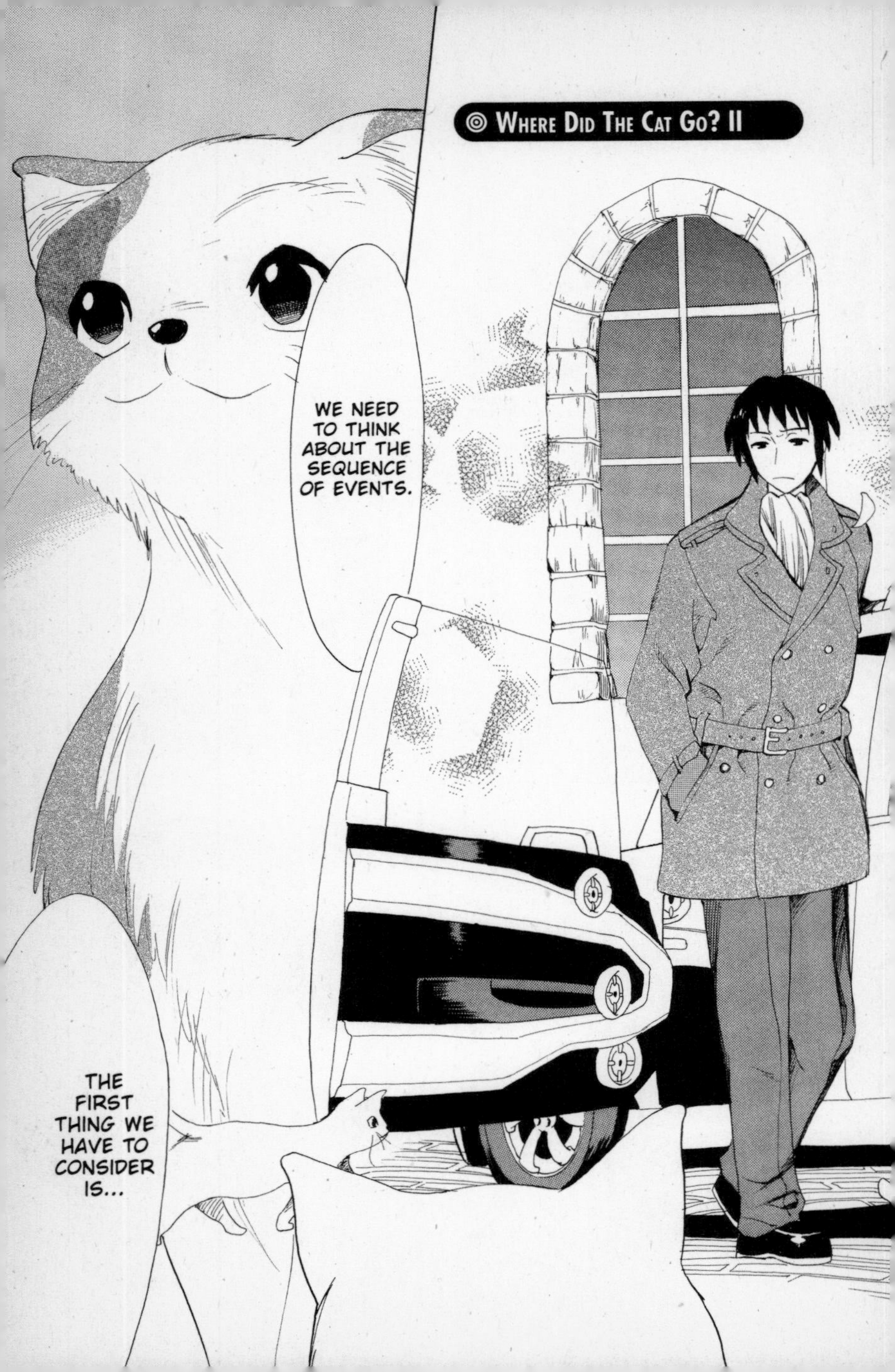
◎ WHERE DID THE CAT GO? II
WE NEED TO THINK ABOUT THE SEQUENCE OF EVENTS.
THE FIRST THING WE HAVE TO CONSIDER IS...

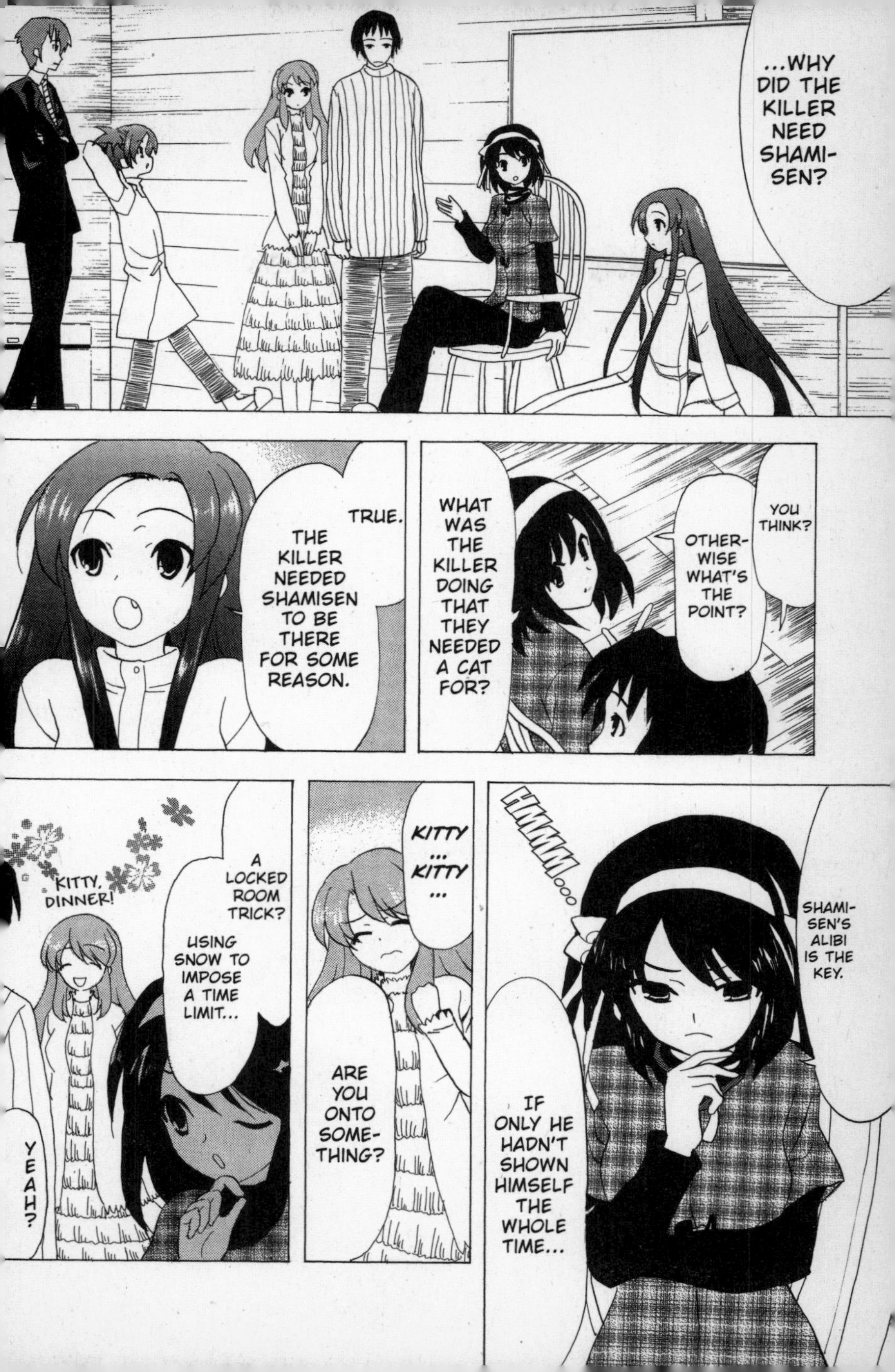
...WHY DID THE KILLER NEED SHAMISEN?
YOU THINK?
OTHERWISE WHAT'S THE POINT?
WHAT WAS THE KILLER DOING THAT THEY NEEDED A CAT FOR?
TRUE.
THE KILLER NEEDED SHAMISEN TO BE THERE FOR SOME REASON.
HMMMM...
SHAMISEN'S ALIBI IS THE KEY.
IF ONLY HE HADN'T SHOWN HIMSELF THE WHOLE TIME...
KITTY ... KITTY ...
ARE YOU ONTO SOMETHING?
A LOCKED ROOM TRICK?
USING SNOW TO IMPOSE A TIME LIMIT...
KITTY, DINNER!
YEAH?

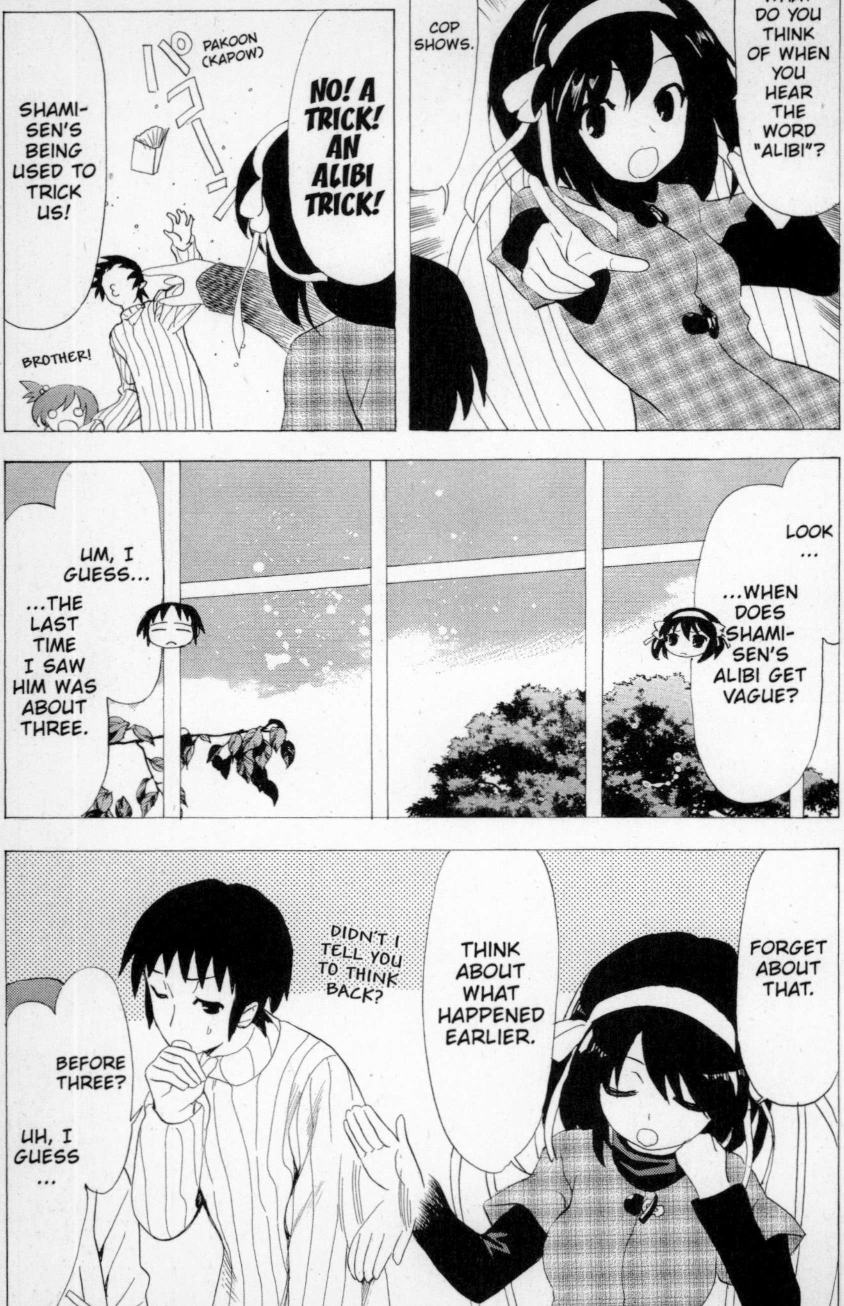
KYON, WHAT DO YOU THINK OF WHEN YOU HEAR THE WORD "ALIBI"?
COP SHOWS.
NO! A TRICK! AN ALIBI TRICK!
PAKOON (KAPOW)
SHAMI-SEN'S BEING USED TO TRICK US!
BROTHER!
LOOK ...
...WHEN DOES SHAMI-SEN'S ALIBI GET VAGUE?
UM, I GUESS...
...THE LAST TIME I SAW HIM WAS ABOUT THREE.
FORGET ABOUT THAT.
THINK ABOUT WHAT HAPPENED EARLIER.
DIDN'T I TELL YOU TO THINK BACK?
BEFORE THREE?
UH, I GUESS ...

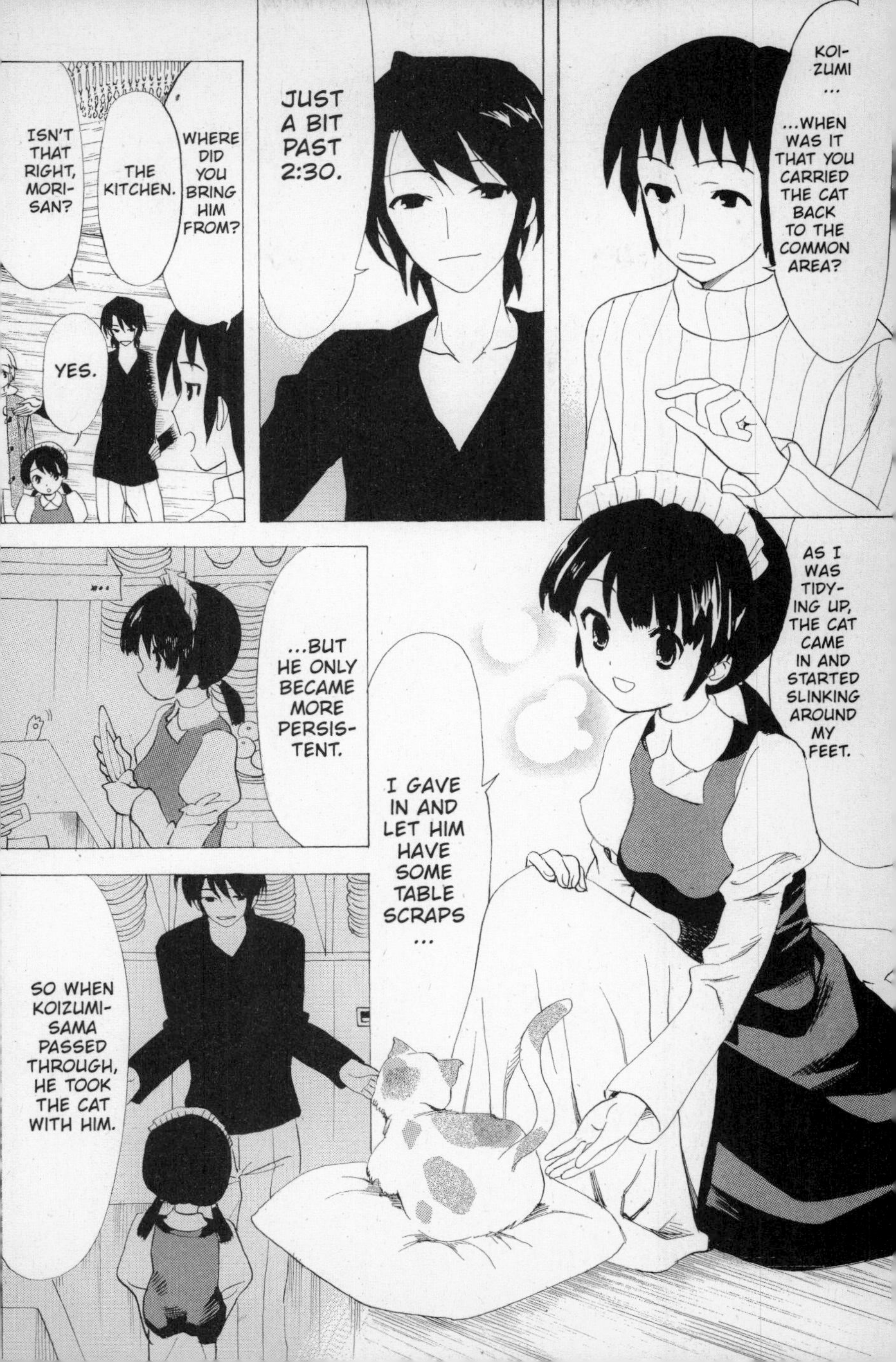
KOI-ZUMI ...
...WHEN WAS IT THAT YOU CARRIED THE CAT BACK TO THE COMMON AREA?
JUST A BIT PAST 2:30.
WHERE DID YOU BRING HIM FROM?
THE KITCHEN.
ISN'T THAT RIGHT, MORI-SAN?
YES.
AS I WAS TIDY-ING UP, THE CAT CAME IN AND STARTED SLINKING AROUND MY FEET.
I GAVE IN AND LET HIM HAVE SOME TABLE SCRAPS ...
...
...BUT HE ONLY BECAME MORE PERSIST-TENT.
SO WHEN KOIZUMI-SAMA PASSED THROUGH, HE TOOK THE CAT WITH HIM.

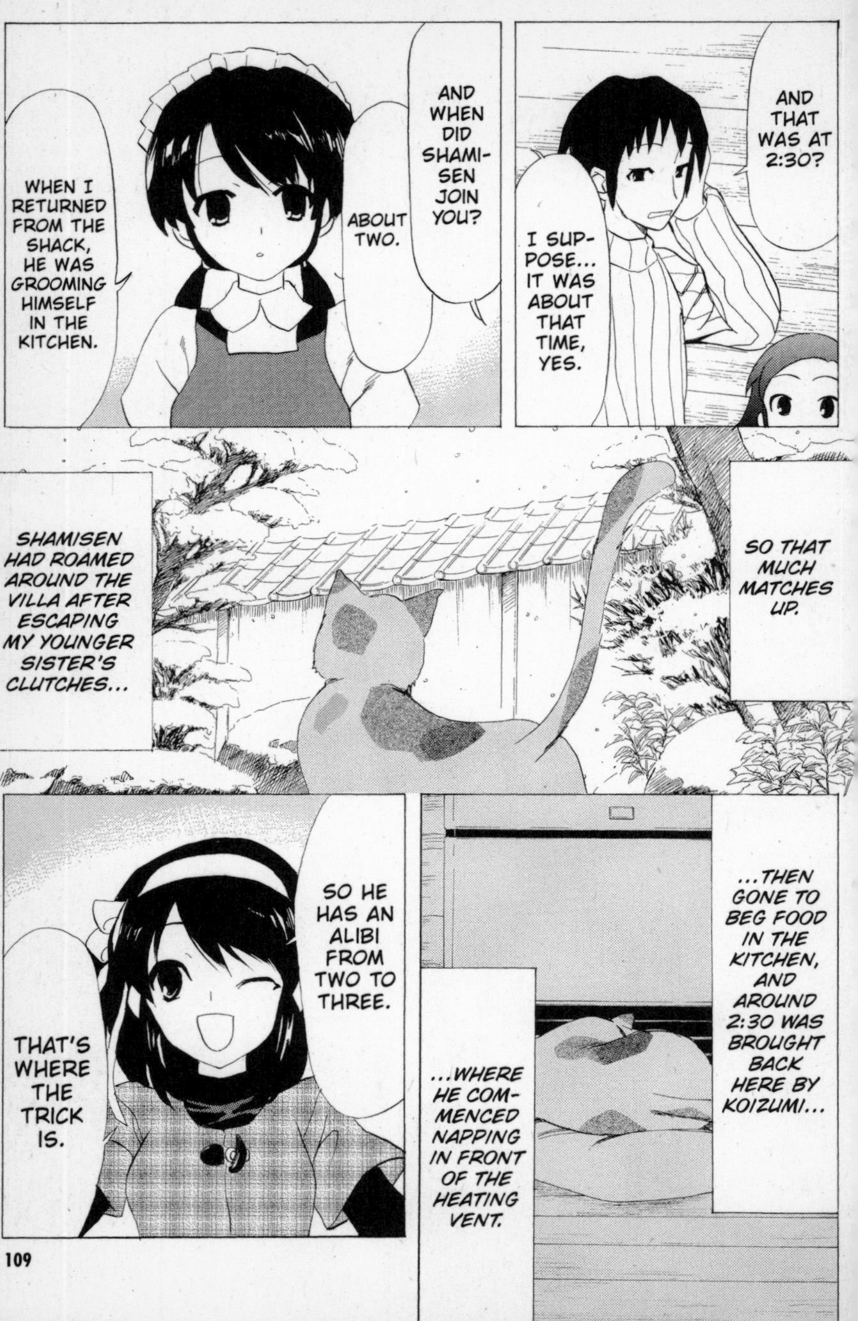
AND THAT WAS AT 2:30?
I SUPPOSE... IT WAS ABOUT THAT TIME, YES.
AND WHEN DID SHAMISEN JOIN YOU?
ABOUT TWO.
WHEN I RETURNED FROM THE SHACK, HE WAS GROOMING HIMSELF IN THE KITCHEN.
SO THAT MUCH MATCHES UP.
SHAMISEN HAD ROAMED AROUND THE VILLA AFTER ESCAPING MY YOUNGER SISTER'S CLUTCHES...
...THEN GONE TO BEG FOOD IN THE KITCHEN, AND AROUND 2:30 WAS BROUGHT BACK HERE BY KOIZUMI...
...WHERE HE COMMENCED NAPPING IN FRONT OF THE HEATING VENT.
SO HE HAS AN ALIBI FROM TWO TO THREE.
THAT'S WHERE THE TRICK IS.

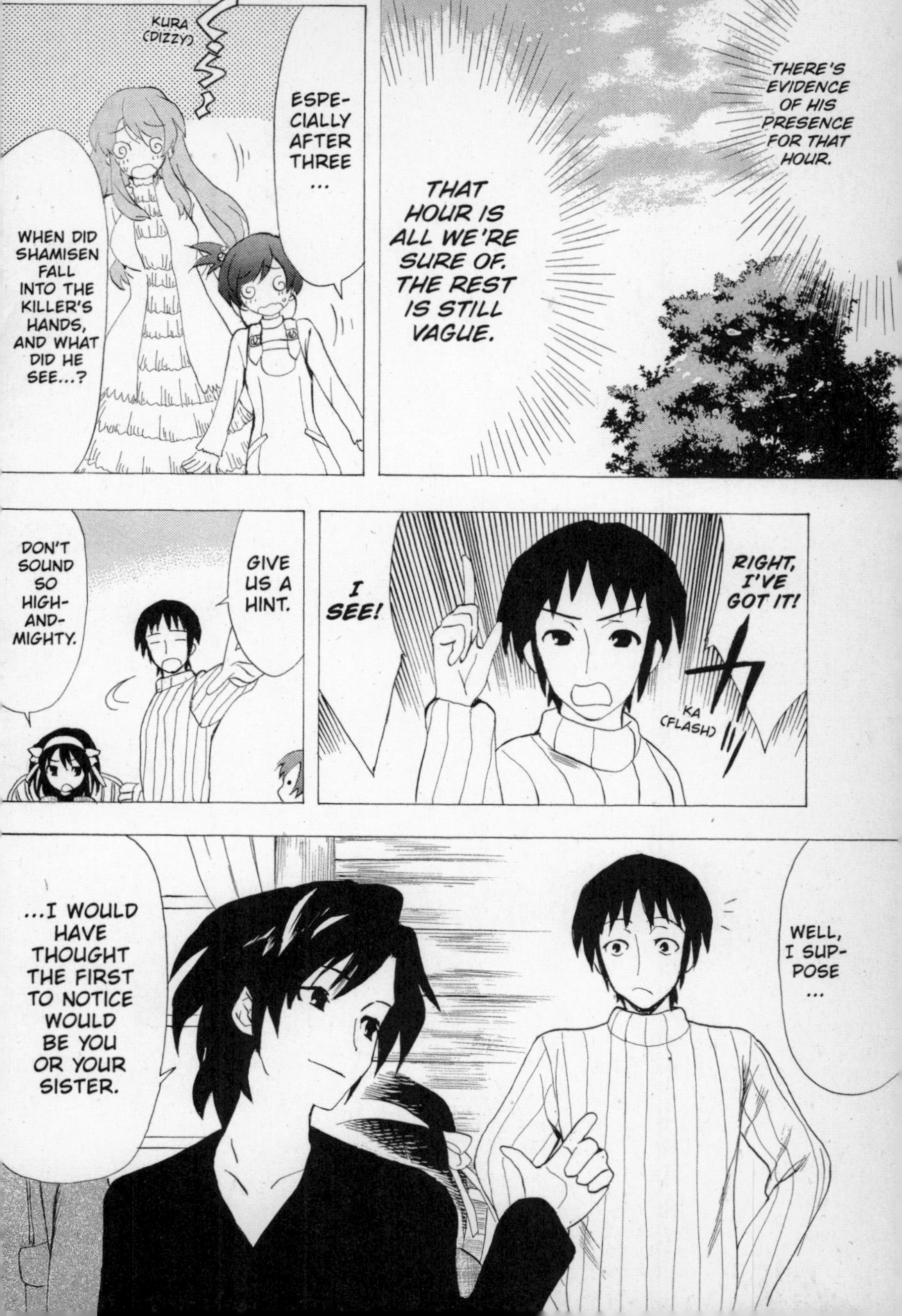
THERE'S EVIDENCE OF HIS PRESENCE FOR THAT HOUR.
THAT HOUR IS ALL WE'RE SURE OF. THE REST IS STILL VAGUE.
ESPE- CIALLY AFTER THREE ...
KURA (DIZZY)
WHEN DID SHAMISEN FALL INTO THE KILLER'S HANDS, AND WHAT DID HE SEE...?
RIGHT, I'VE GOT IT!
KA (FLASH)
I SEE!
GIVE US A HINT.
DON'T SOUND SO HIGH- AND- MIGHTY.
WELL, I SUP- POSE ...
...I WOULD HAVE THOUGHT THE FIRST TO NOTICE WOULD BE YOU OR YOUR SISTER.

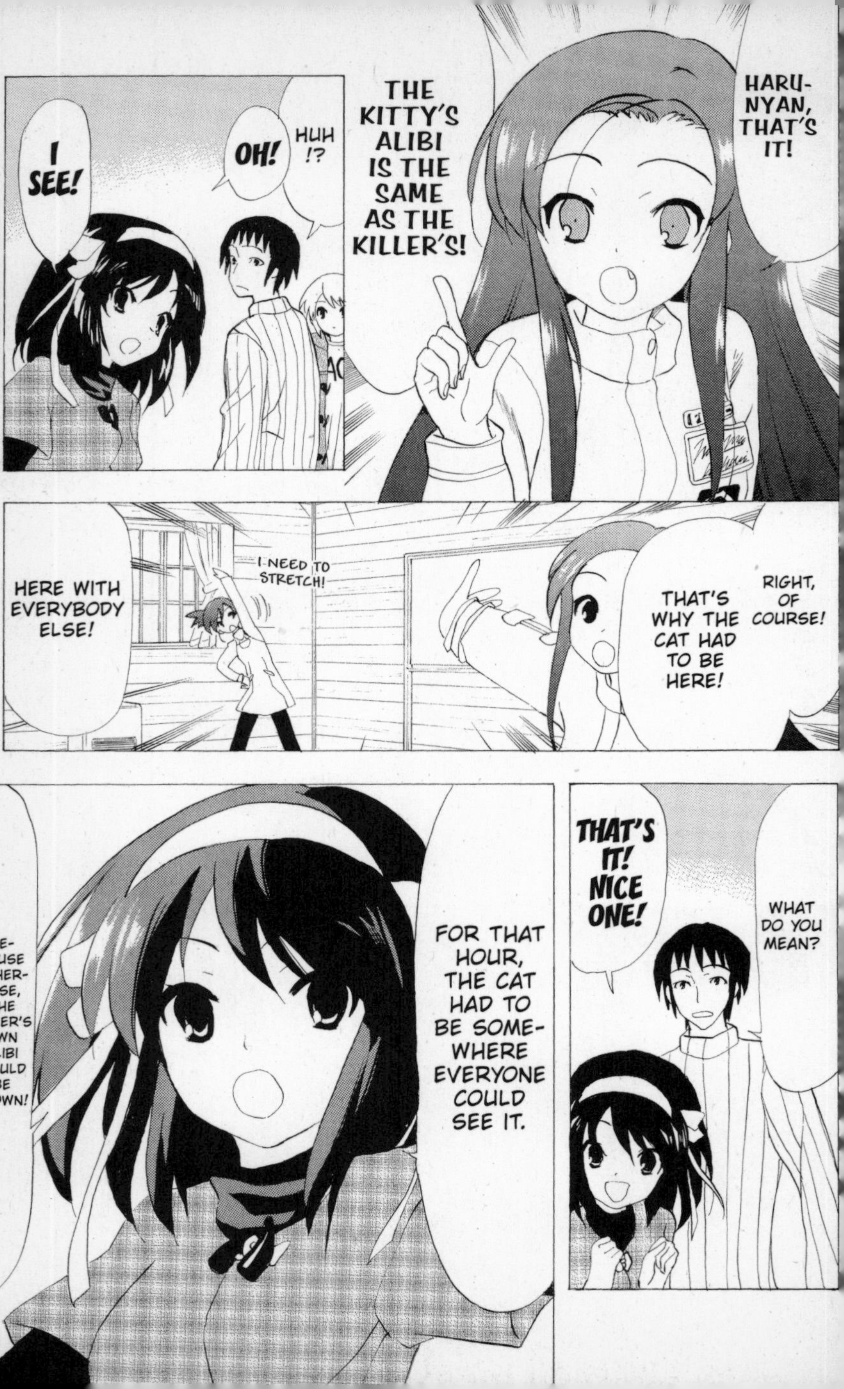
HARU-NYAN, THAT'S IT!
THE KITTY'S ALIBI IS THE SAME AS THE KILLER'S!
HUH!?
OH!
I SEE!
RIGHT, OF COURSE!
THAT'S WHY THE CAT HAD TO BE HERE!
I NEED TO STRETCH!
HERE WITH EVERYBODY ELSE!
WHAT DO YOU MEAN?
THAT'S IT! NICE ONE!
FOR THAT HOUR, THE CAT HAD TO BE SOME-WHERE EVERYONE COULD SEE IT.
BE-CAUSE OTHER-WISE, THE KILLER'S OWN ALIBI WOULD BE BLOWN!

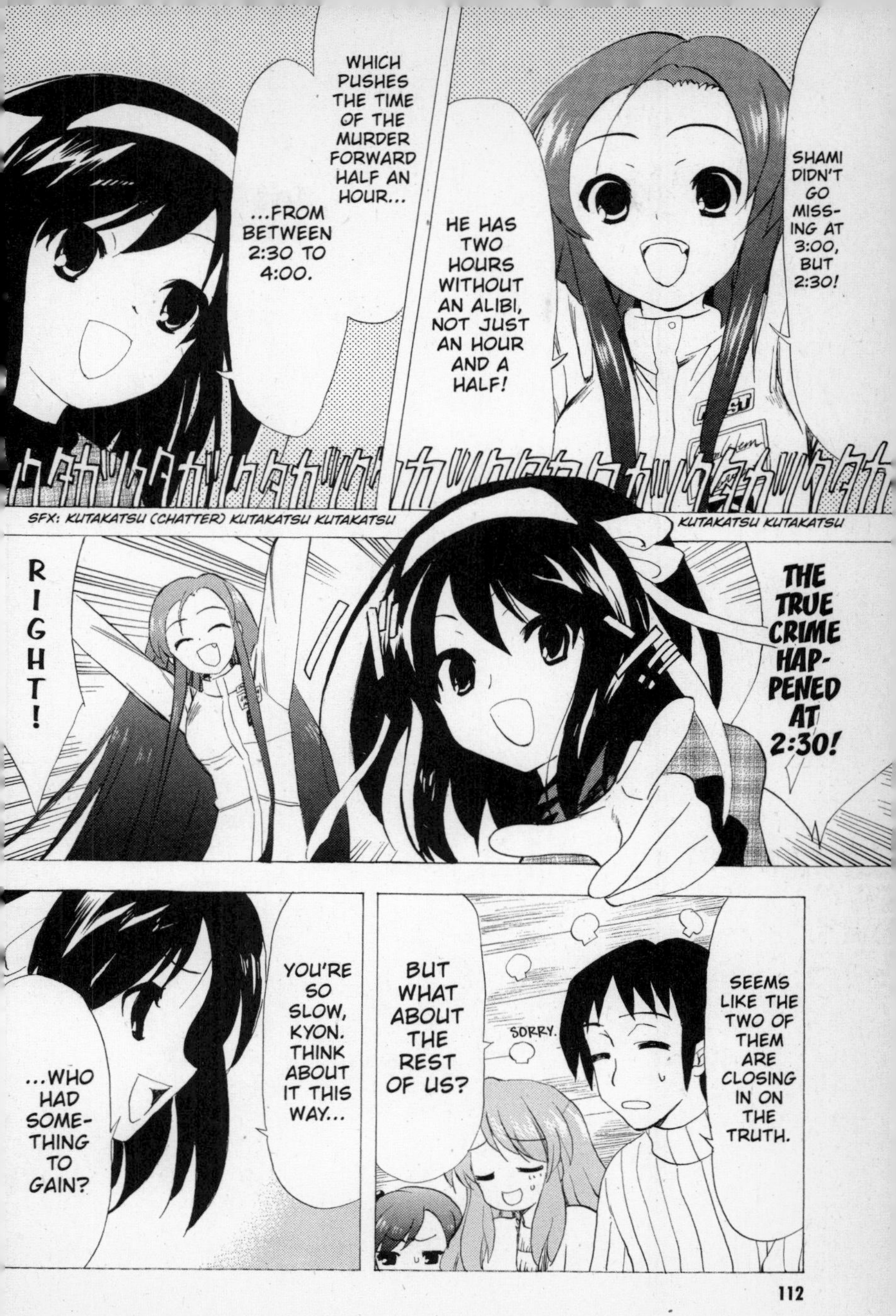
SHAMI DIDN'T GO MISS-ING AT 3:00, BUT 2:30!
HE HAS TWO HOURS WITHOUT AN ALIBI, NOT JUST AN HOUR AND A HALF!
WHICH PUSHES THE TIME OF THE MURDER FORWARD HALF AN HOUR...
...FROM BETWEEN 2:30 TO 4:00.
SFX: KUTAKATSU (CHATTER) KUTAKATSU KUTAKATSU
KUTAKATSU KUTAKATSU
THE TRUE CRIME HAP-PENED AT 2:30!
RIGHT!
SEEMS LIKE THE TWO OF THEM ARE CLOSING IN ON THE TRUTH.
BUT WHAT ABOUT THE REST OF US?
SORRY.
YOU'RE SO SLOW, KYON. THINK ABOUT IT THIS WAY...
...WHO HAD SOME-THING TO GAIN?

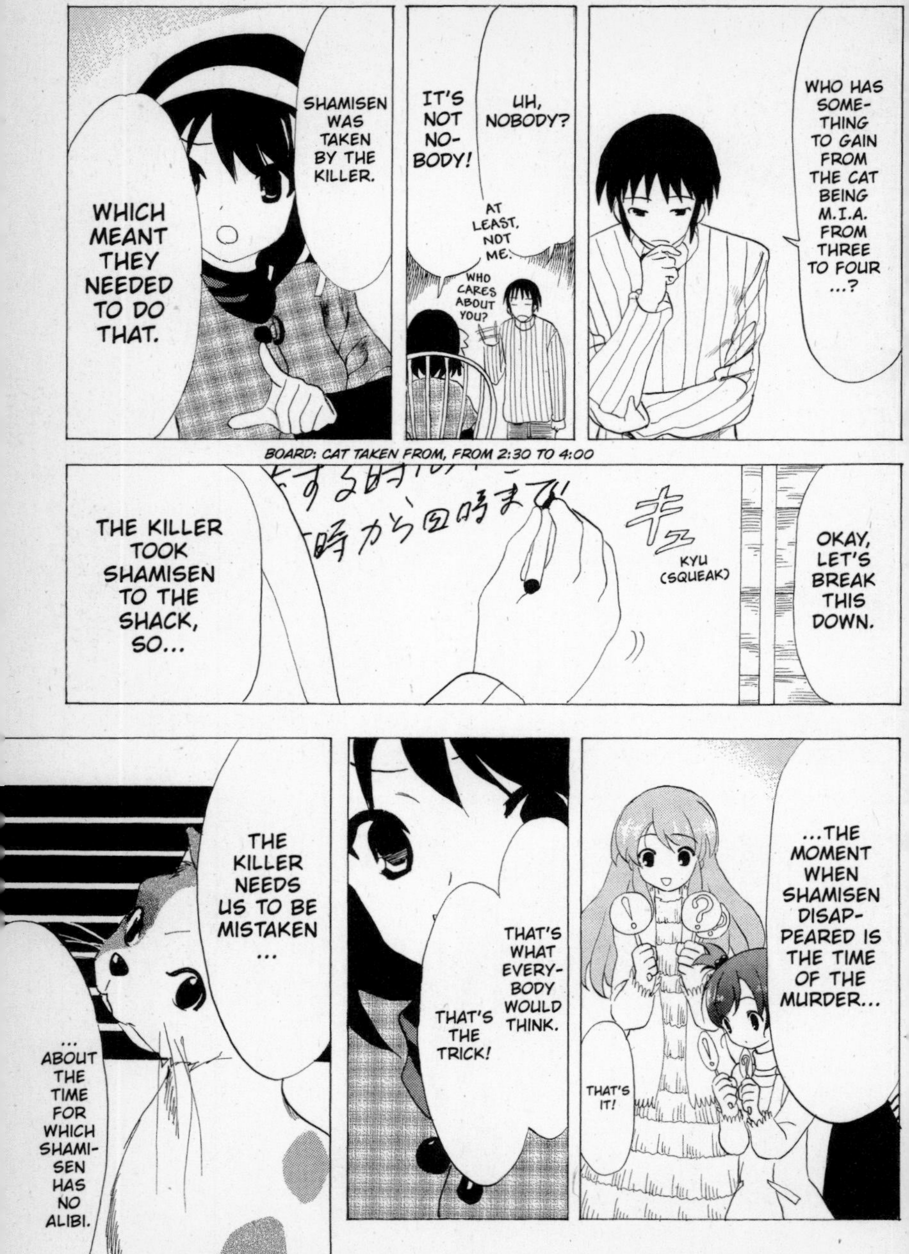
WHO HAS SOMETHING TO GAIN FROM THE CAT BEING M.I.A. FROM THREE TO FOUR ...?
UH, NOBODY?
IT'S NOT NOBODY!
AT LEAST, NOT ME.
WHO CARES ABOUT YOU?
SHAMISEN WAS TAKEN BY THE KILLER.
WHICH MEANT THEY NEEDED TO DO THAT.
BOARD: CAT TAKEN FROM, FROM 2:30 TO 4:00
OKAY, LET'S BREAK THIS DOWN.
KYU (SQUEAK)
THE KILLER TOOK SHAMISEN TO THE SHACK, SO...
...THE MOMENT WHEN SHAMISEN DISAPPEARED IS THE TIME OF THE MURDER...
THAT'S IT!
THAT'S WHAT EVERYBODY WOULD THINK.
THAT'S THE TRICK!
THE KILLER NEEDS US TO BE MISTAKEN...
...ABOUT THE TIME FOR WHICH SHAMISEN HAS NO ALIBI.

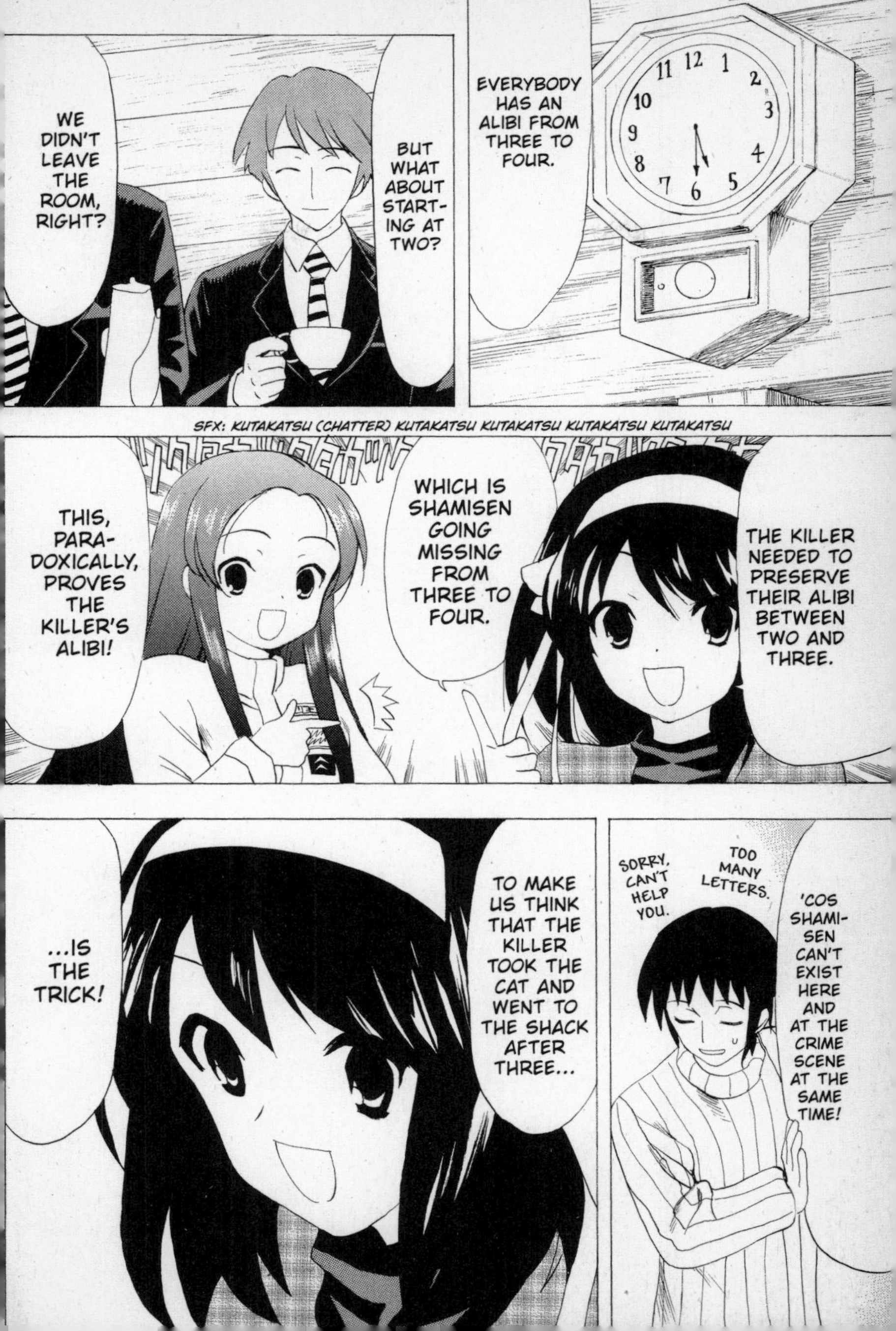
EVERYBODY HAS AN ALIBI FROM THREE TO FOUR.
BUT WHAT ABOUT STARTING AT TWO?
WE DIDN'T LEAVE THE ROOM, RIGHT?
SFX: KUTAKATSU (CHATTER) KUTAKATSU KUTAKATSU KUTAKATSU KUTAKATSU
THE KILLER NEEDED TO PRESERVE THEIR ALIBI BETWEEN TWO AND THREE.
WHICH IS SHAMISEN GOING MISSING FROM THREE TO FOUR.
THIS, PARADOXICALLY, PROVES THE KILLER'S ALIBI!
'COS SHAMISEN CAN'T EXIST HERE AND AT THE CRIME SCENE AT THE SAME TIME!
TOO MANY LETTERS.
SORRY, CAN'T HELP YOU.
TO MAKE US THINK THAT THE KILLER TOOK THE CAT AND WENT TO THE SHACK AFTER THREE...
...IS THE TRICK!

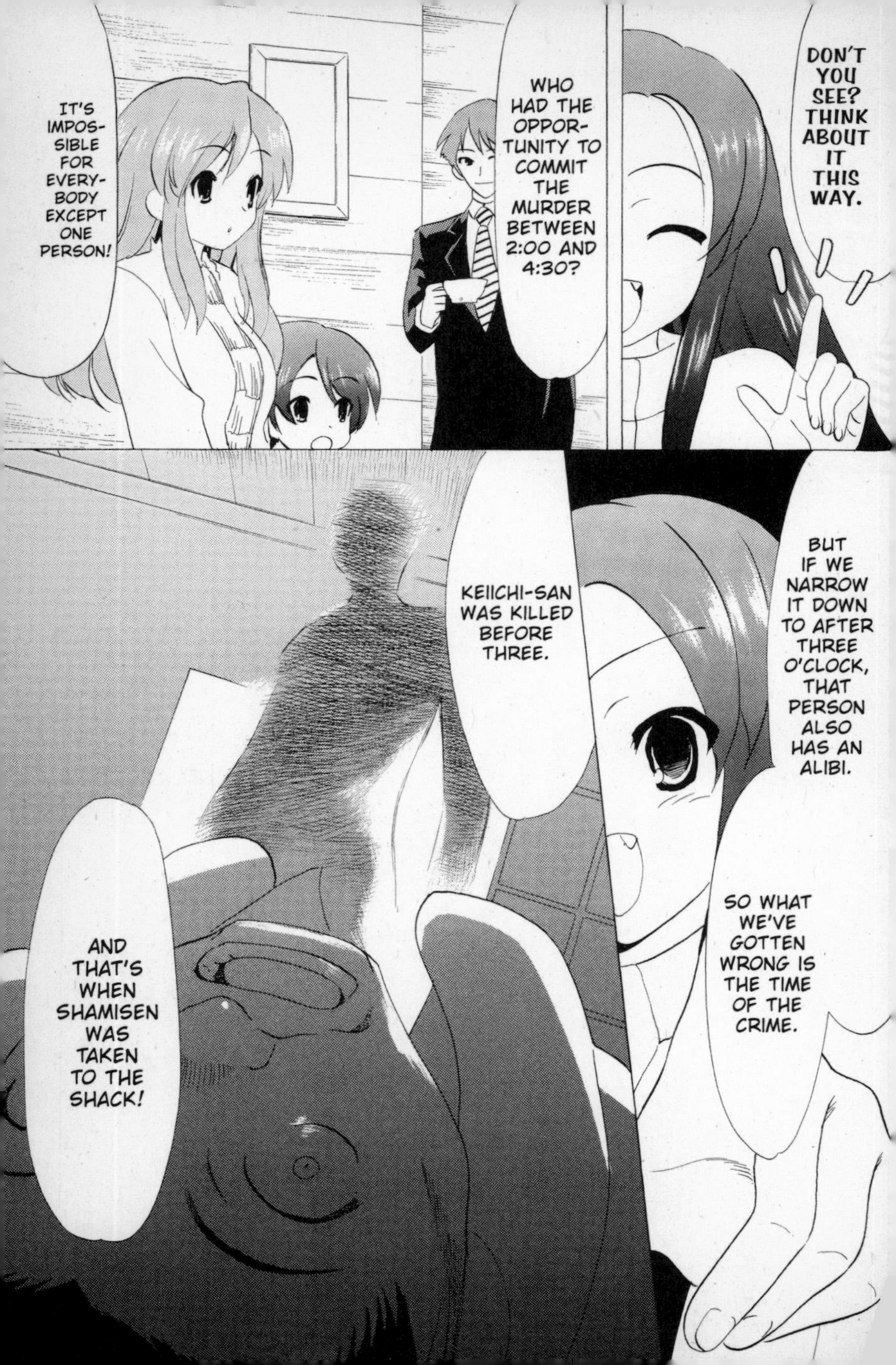
DON'T YOU SEE? THINK ABOUT IT THIS WAY.
WHO HAD THE OPPORTUNITY TO COMMIT THE MURDER BETWEEN 2:00 AND 4:30?
IT'S IMPOSSIBLE FOR EVERYBODY EXCEPT ONE PERSON!
BUT IF WE NARROW IT DOWN TO AFTER THREE O'CLOCK, THAT PERSON ALSO HAS AN ALIBI.
SO WHAT WE'VE GOTTEN WRONG IS THE TIME OF THE CRIME.
KEIICHI-SAN WAS KILLED BEFORE THREE.
AND THAT'S WHEN SHAMISEN WAS TAKEN TO THE SHACK!

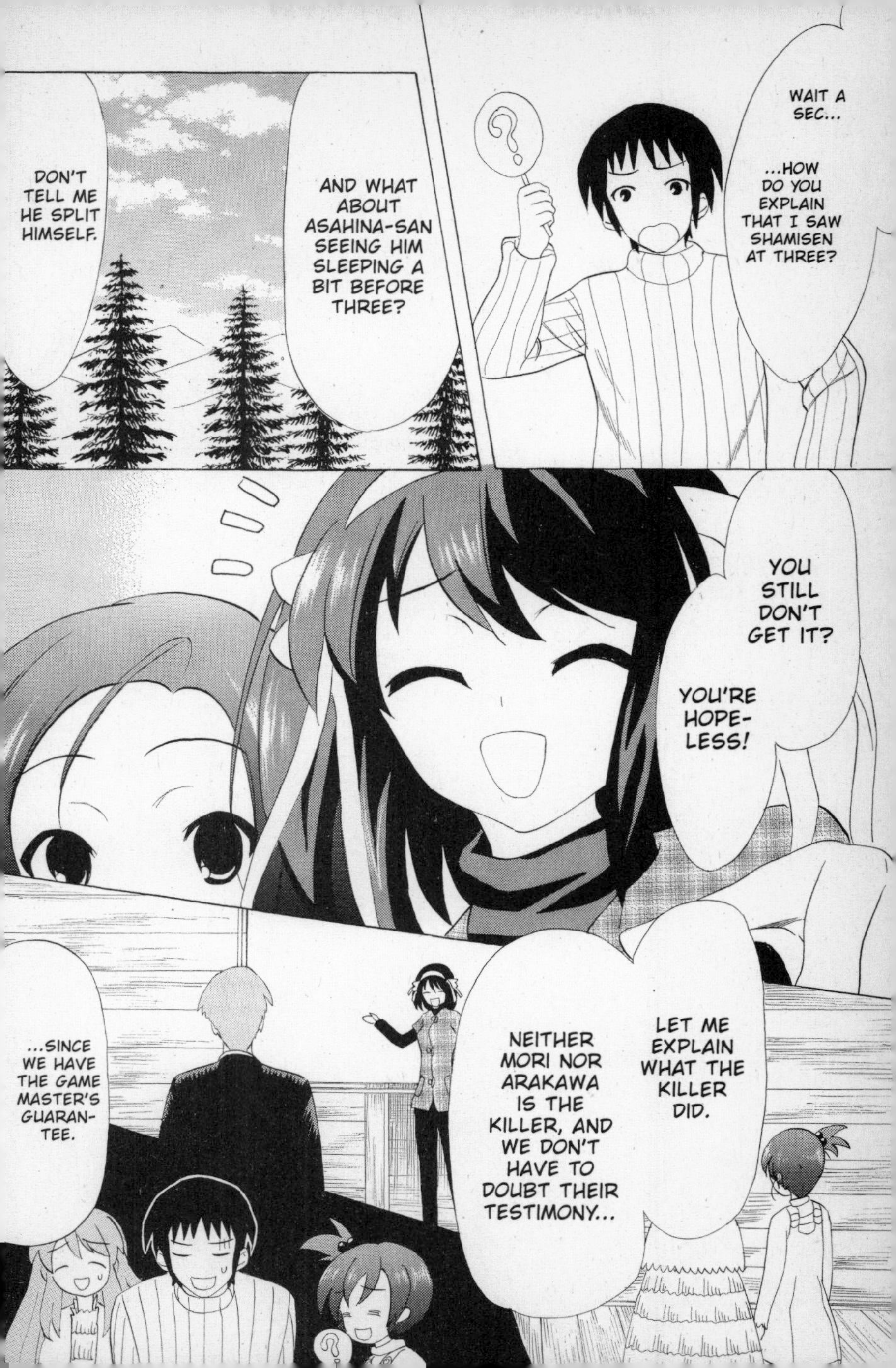
WAIT A SEC...
...HOW DO YOU EXPLAIN THAT I SAW SHAMISEN AT THREE?
AND WHAT ABOUT ASAHINA-SAN SEEING HIM SLEEPING A BIT BEFORE THREE?
DON'T TELL ME HE SPLIT HIMSELF.
YOU STILL DON'T GET IT?
YOU'RE HOPE-LESS!
LET ME EXPLAIN WHAT THE KILLER DID.
NEITHER MORI NOR ARAKAWA IS THE KILLER, AND WE DON'T HAVE TO DOUBT THEIR TESTIMONY...
...SINCE WE HAVE THE GAME MASTER'S GUARAN-TEE.

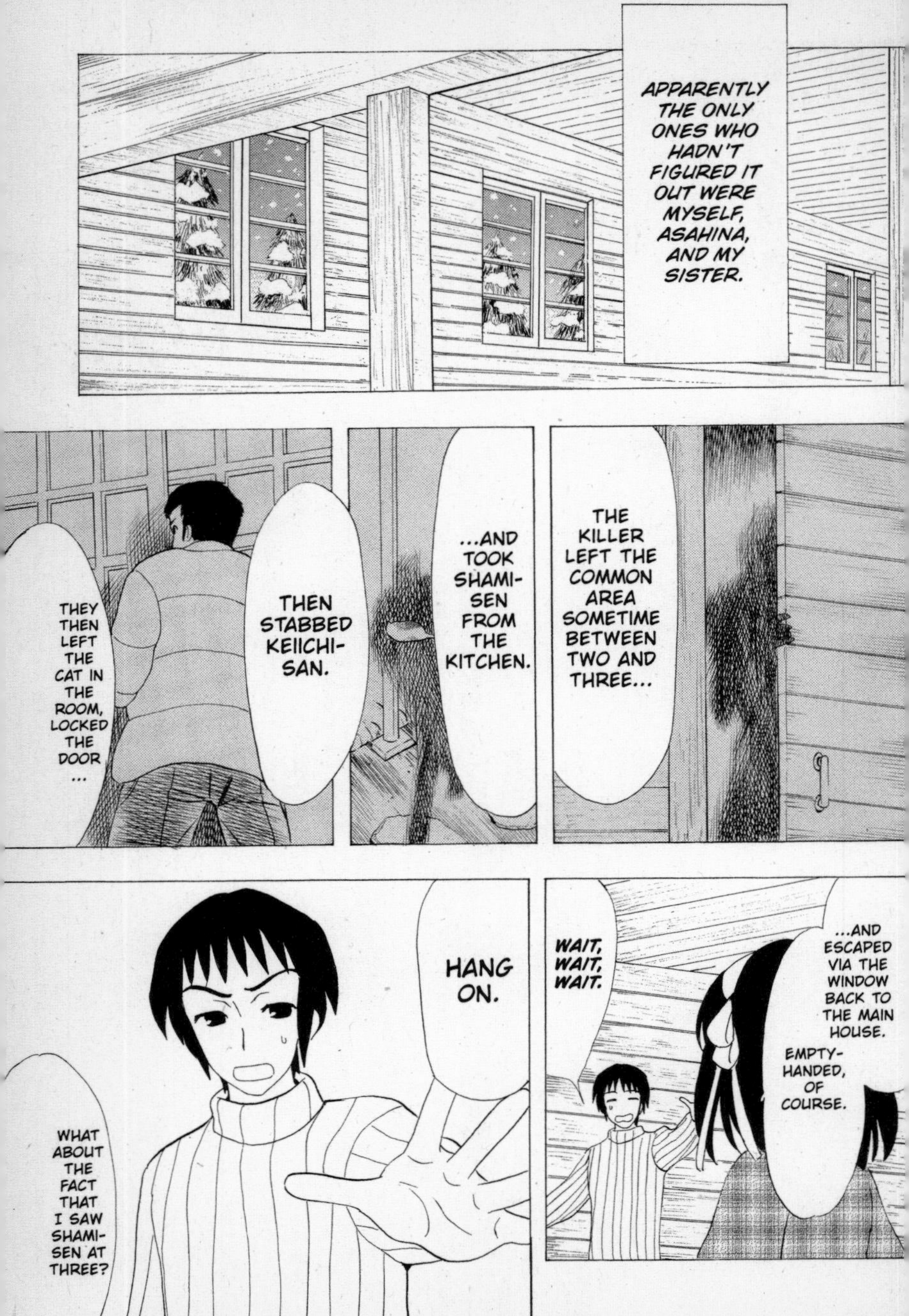
APPARENTLY THE ONLY ONES WHO HADN'T FIGURED IT OUT WERE MYSELF, ASAHINA, AND MY SISTER.
THE KILLER LEFT THE COMMON AREA SOMETIME BETWEEN TWO AND THREE...
...AND TOOK SHAMISEN FROM THE KITCHEN.
THEN STABBED KEIICHI-SAN.
THEY THEN LEFT THE CAT IN THE ROOM, LOCKED THE DOOR...
...AND ESCAPED VIA THE WINDOW BACK TO THE MAIN HOUSE.
EMPTY-HANDED, OF COURSE.
WAIT, WAIT, WAIT.
HANG ON.
WHAT ABOUT THE FACT THAT I SAW SHAMISEN AT THREE?

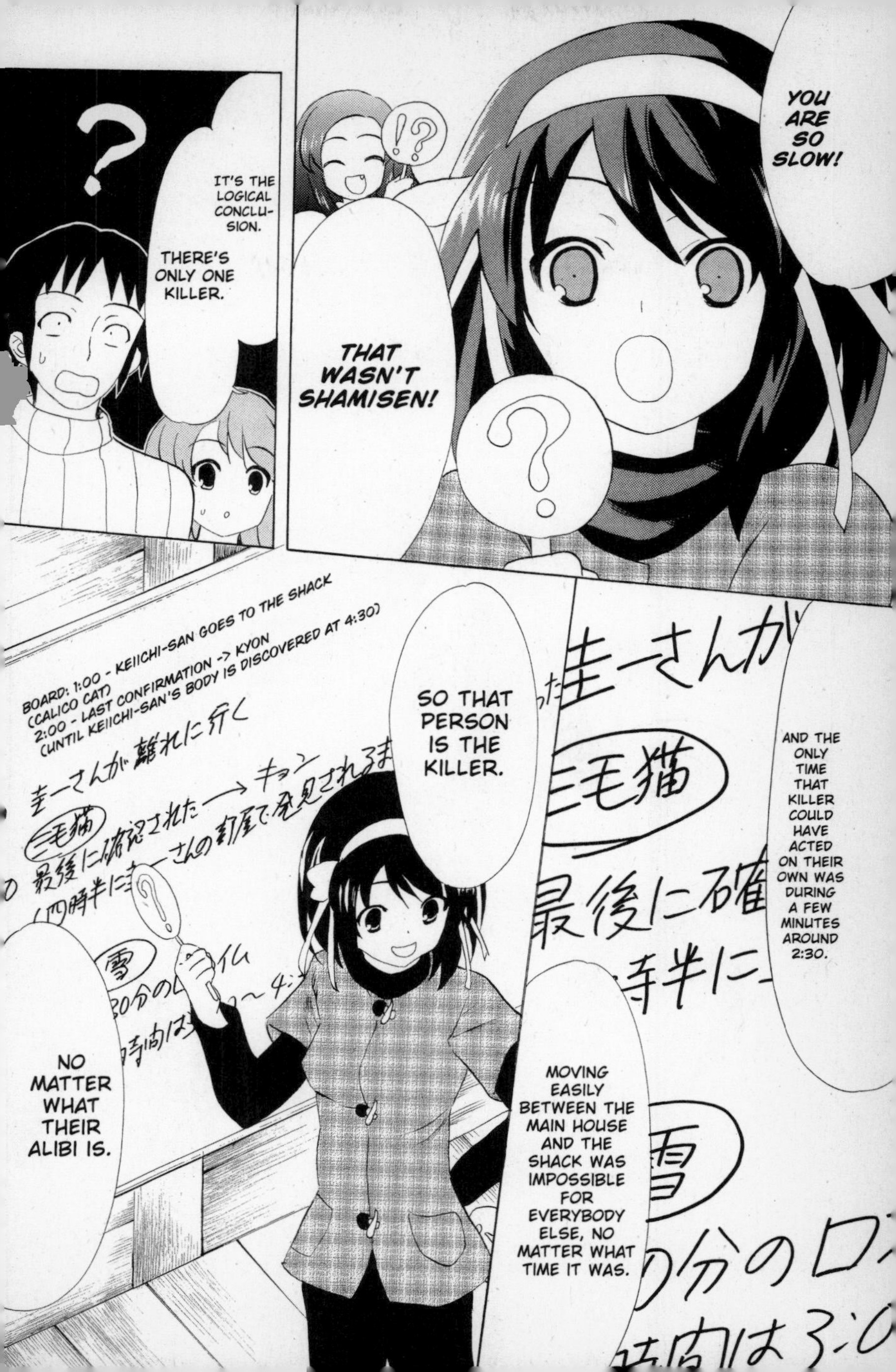
YOU ARE SO SLOW!
THAT WASN'T SHAMISEN!
IT'S THE LOGICAL CONCLUSION.
THERE'S ONLY ONE KILLER.
BOARD: 1:00 - KEIICHI-SAN GOES TO THE SHACK (CALICO CAT) 2:00 - LAST CONFIRMATION -> KYON (UNTIL KEIICHI-SAN'S BODY IS DISCOVERED AT 4:30)
AND THE ONLY TIME THAT KILLER COULD HAVE ACTED ON THEIR OWN WAS DURING A FEW MINUTES AROUND 2:30.
SO THAT PERSON IS THE KILLER.
MOVING EASILY BETWEEN THE MAIN HOUSE AND THE SHACK WAS IMPOSSIBLE FOR EVERYBODY ELSE, NO MATTER WHAT TIME IT WAS.
NO MATTER WHAT THEIR ALIBI IS.

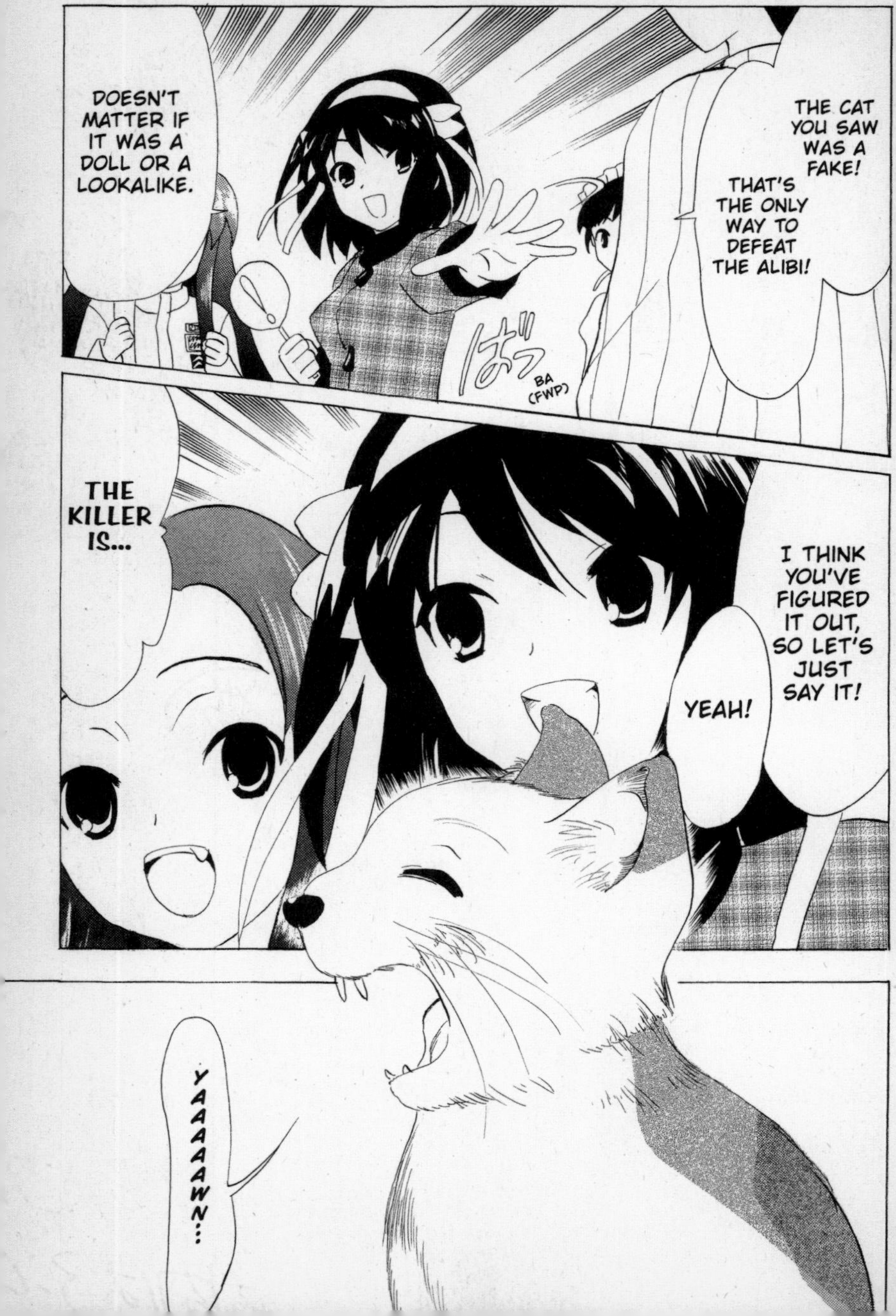
THE CAT YOU SAW WAS A FAKE!
THAT'S THE ONLY WAY TO DEFEAT THE ALIBI!
DOESN'T MATTER IF IT WAS A DOLL OR A LOOKALIKE.
ばっ
BA (FWP)
I THINK YOU'VE FIGURED IT OUT, SO LET'S JUST SAY IT!
YEAH!
THE KILLER IS...
YAAAAAAWN...

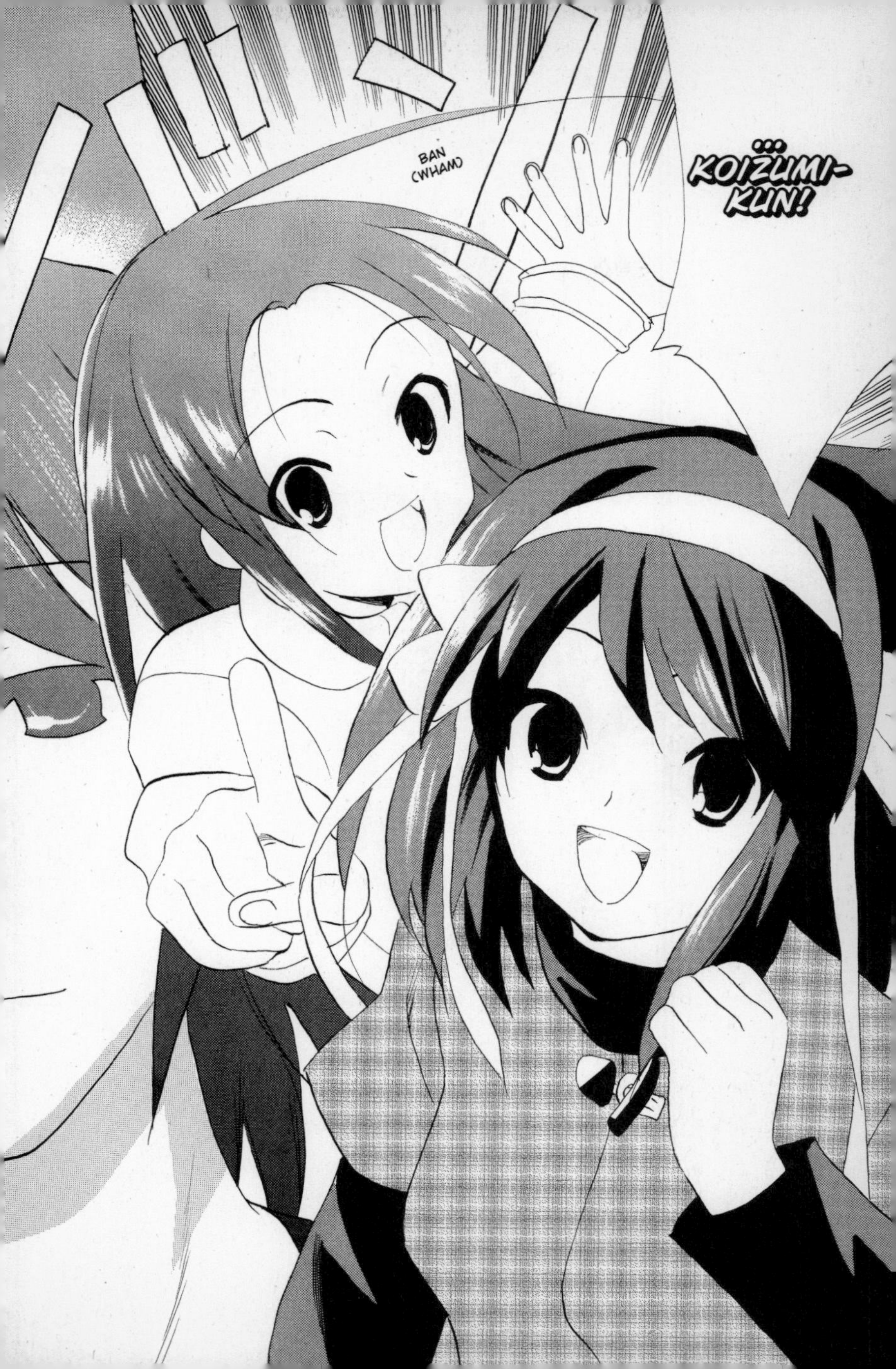
...KOIZUMI-KUN!
BAN (WHAM)

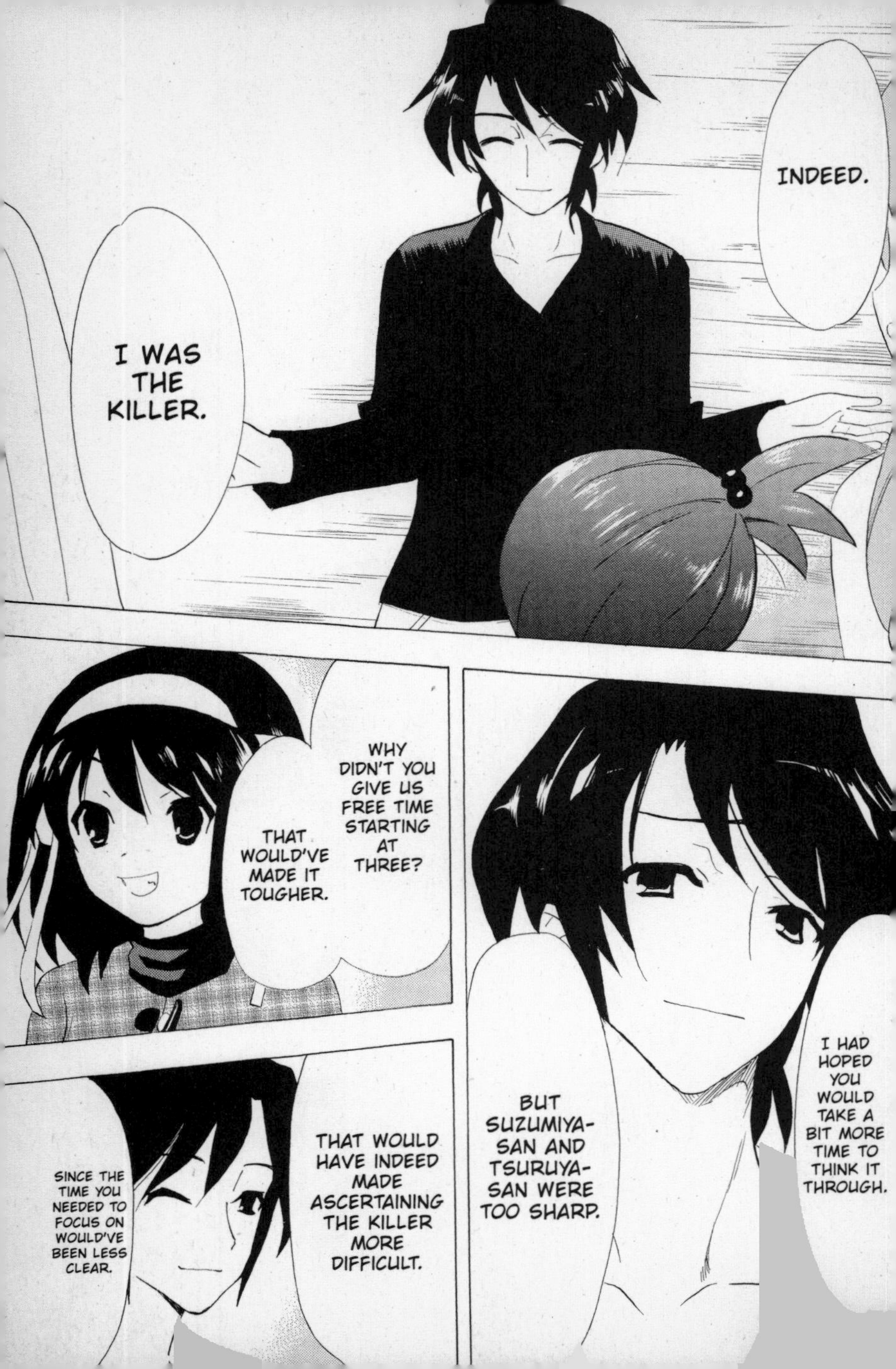
INDEED.
I WAS THE KILLER.
I HAD HOPED YOU WOULD TAKE A BIT MORE TIME TO THINK IT THROUGH.
BUT SUZUMIYA-SAN AND TSURUYA-SAN WERE TOO SHARP.
WHY DIDN'T YOU GIVE US FREE TIME STARTING AT THREE?
THAT WOULD'VE MADE IT TOUGHER.
THAT WOULD HAVE INDEED MADE ASCERTAINING THE KILLER MORE DIFFICULT.
SINCE THE TIME YOU NEEDED TO FOCUS ON WOULD'VE BEEN LESS CLEAR.

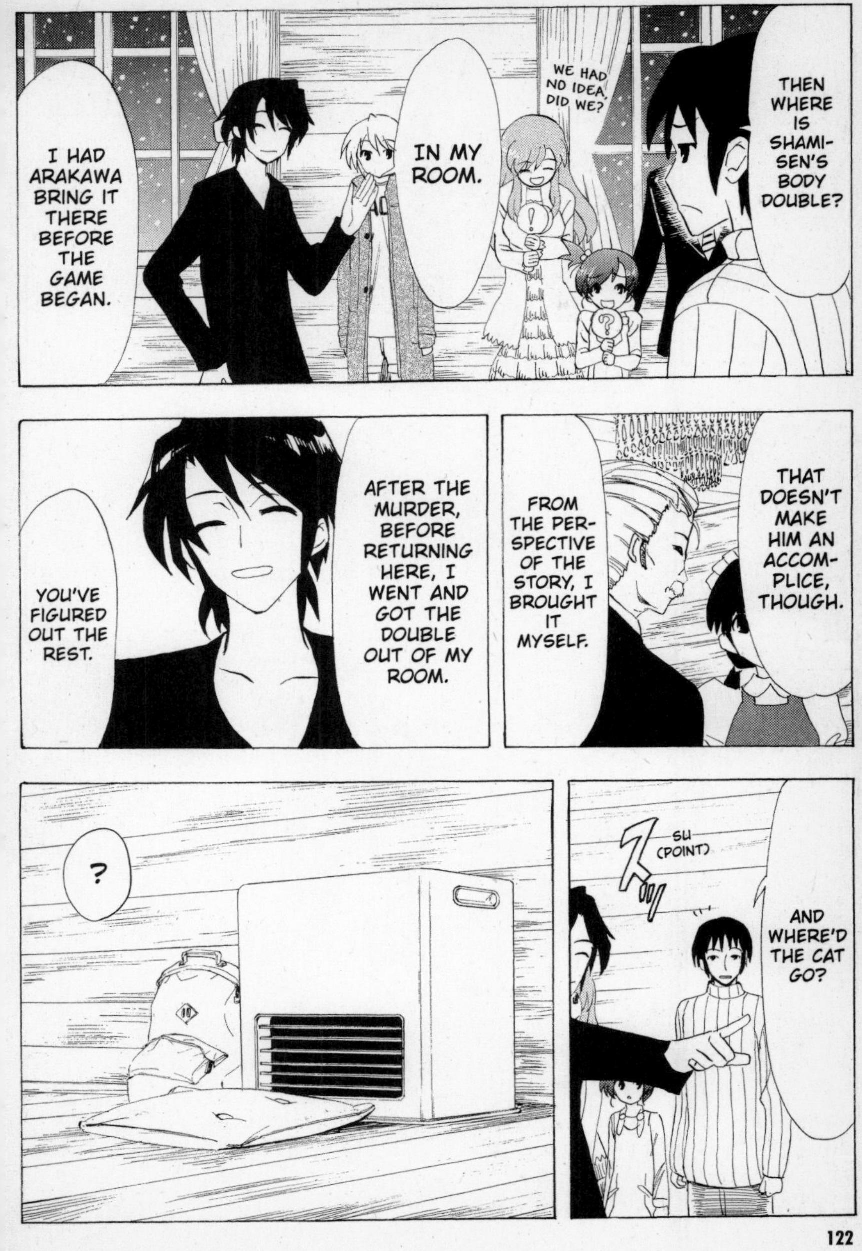

THEN WHERE IS SHAMISEN'S BODY DOUBLE?
WE HAD NO IDEA, DID WE?
IN MY ROOM.
I HAD ARAKAWA BRING IT THERE BEFORE THE GAME BEGAN.
THAT DOESN'T MAKE HIM AN ACCOMPLICE, THOUGH.
FROM THE PERSPECTIVE OF THE STORY, I BROUGHT IT MYSELF.
AFTER THE MURDER, BEFORE RETURNING HERE, I WENT AND GOT THE DOUBLE OUT OF MY ROOM.
YOU'VE FIGURED OUT THE REST.
AND WHERE'D THE CAT GO?
SU (POINT)
?

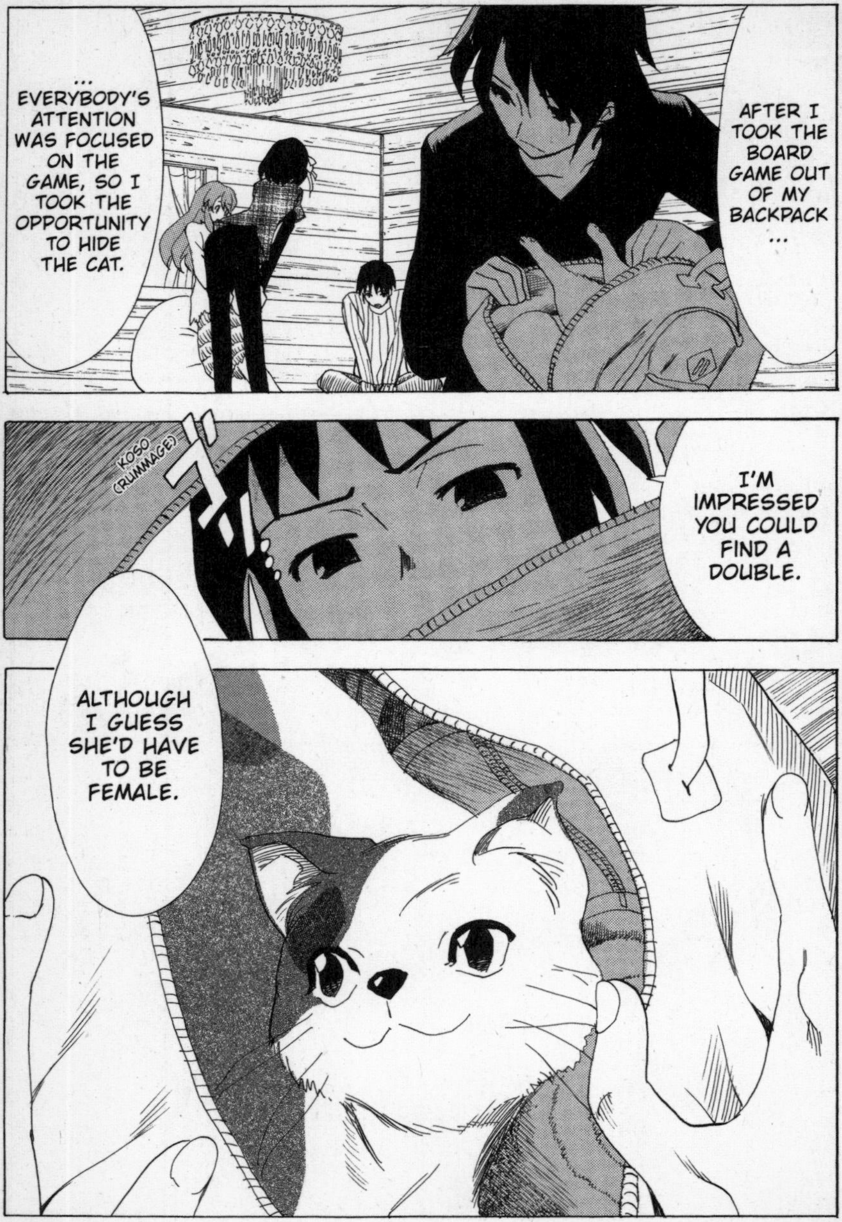
AFTER I TOOK THE BOARD GAME OUT OF MY BACKPACK...
...EVERYBODY'S ATTENTION WAS FOCUSED ON THE GAME, SO I TOOK THE OPPORTUNITY TO HIDE THE CAT.
I'M IMPRESSED YOU COULD FIND A DOUBLE.
KOSO (RUMMAGE)
ALTHOUGH I GUESS SHE'D HAVE TO BE FEMALE.

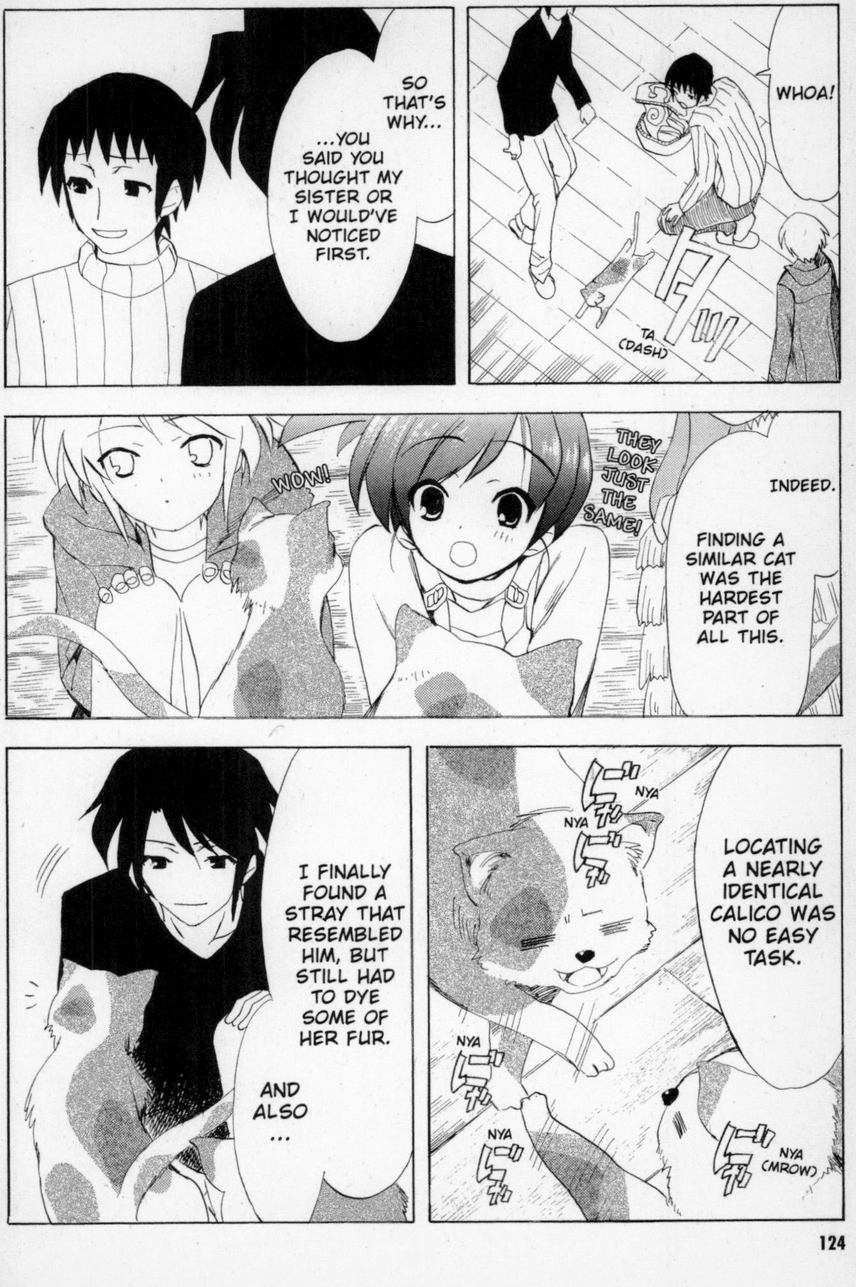
WHOA!
TA (DASH)
SO THAT'S WHY...
...YOU SAID YOU THOUGHT MY SISTER OR I WOULD'VE NOTICED FIRST.
INDEED.
FINDING A SIMILAR CAT WAS THE HARDEST PART OF ALL THIS.
THEY LOOK JUST THE SAME!
WOW!
LOCATING A NEARLY IDENTICAL CALICO WAS NO EASY TASK.
NYA
NYA
NYA
NYA (MROW)
NYA
I FINALLY FOUND A STRAY THAT RESEMBLED HIM, BUT STILL HAD TO DYE SOME OF HER FUR.
AND ALSO ...

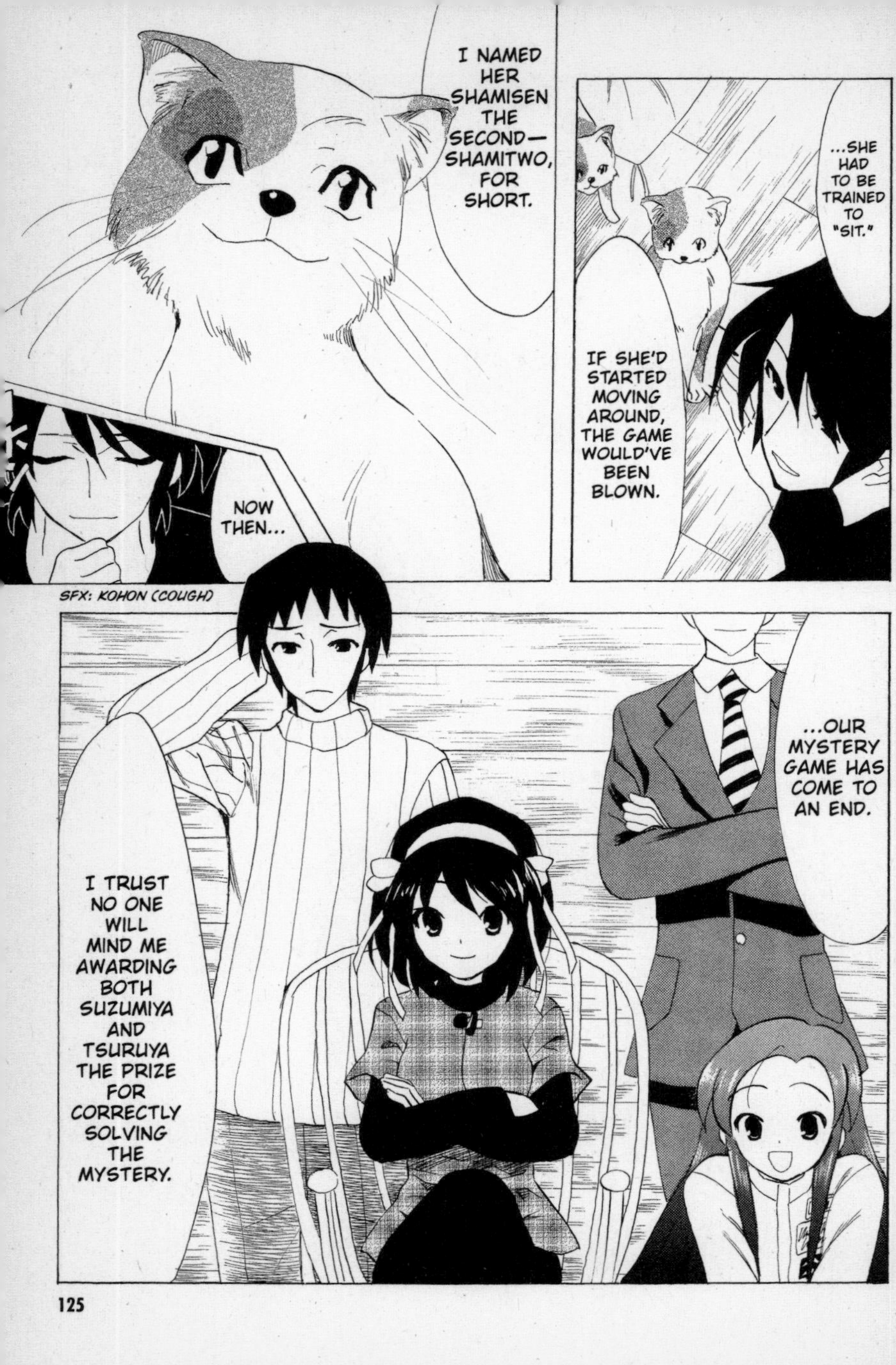
...SHE HAD TO BE TRAINED TO "SIT."
IF SHE'D STARTED MOVING AROUND, THE GAME WOULD'VE BEEN BLOWN.
I NAMED HER SHAMISEN THE SECOND—SHAMITWO, FOR SHORT.
NOW THEN...
SFX: KOHON (COUGH)
...OUR MYSTERY GAME HAS COME TO AN END.
I TRUST NO ONE WILL MIND ME AWARDING BOTH SUZUMIYA AND TSURUYA THE PRIZE FOR CORRECTLY SOLVING THE MYSTERY.

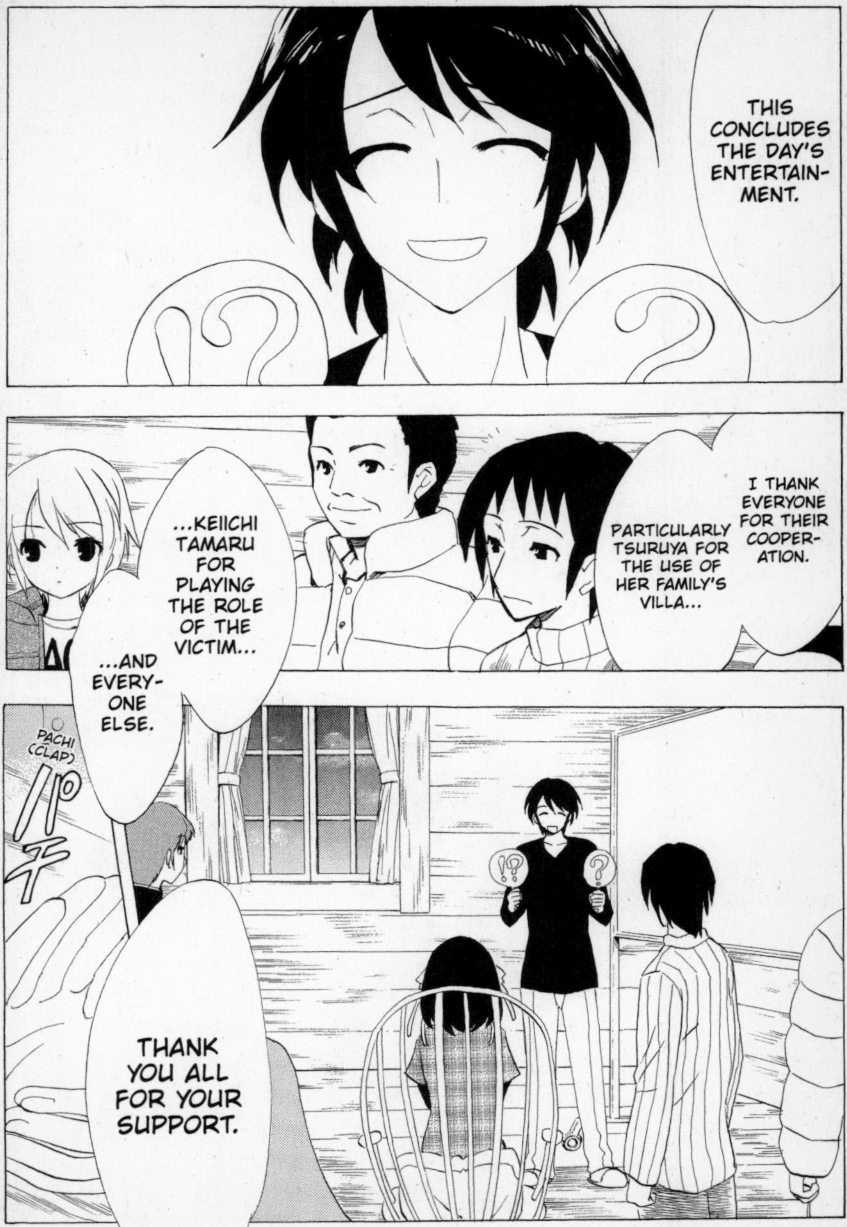
THIS CONCLUDES THE DAY'S ENTERTAIN-MENT.
I THANK EVERYONE FOR THEIR COOPER-ATION.
PARTICULARLY TSURUYA FOR THE USE OF HER FAMILY'S VILLA...
...KEIICHI TAMARU FOR PLAYING THE ROLE OF THE VICTIM...
...AND EVERY-ONE ELSE.
!?
?
PACHI (CLAP)
パチ
THANK YOU ALL FOR YOUR SUPPORT.

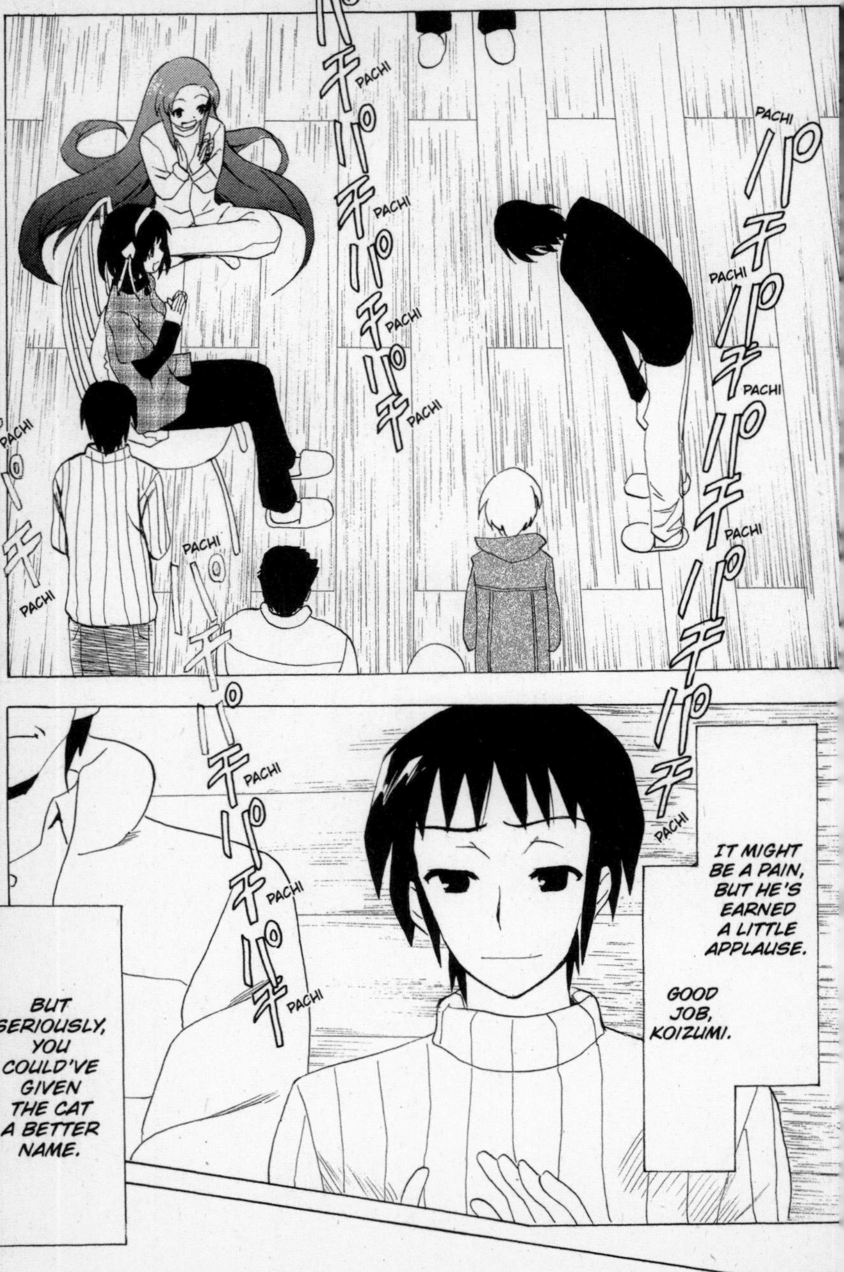
パチパチパチパチパチ
PACHI PACHI PACHI PACHI PACHI
パチパチパチパチ
PACHI PACHI PACHI PACHI
パチパチ
PACHI PACHI
パチパチパチパチ
PACHI PACHI PACHI PACHI
IT MIGHT BE A PAIN, BUT HE'S EARNED A LITTLE APPLAUSE.
GOOD JOB, KOIZUMI.
BUT SERIOUSLY, YOU COULD'VE GIVEN THE CAT A BETTER NAME.

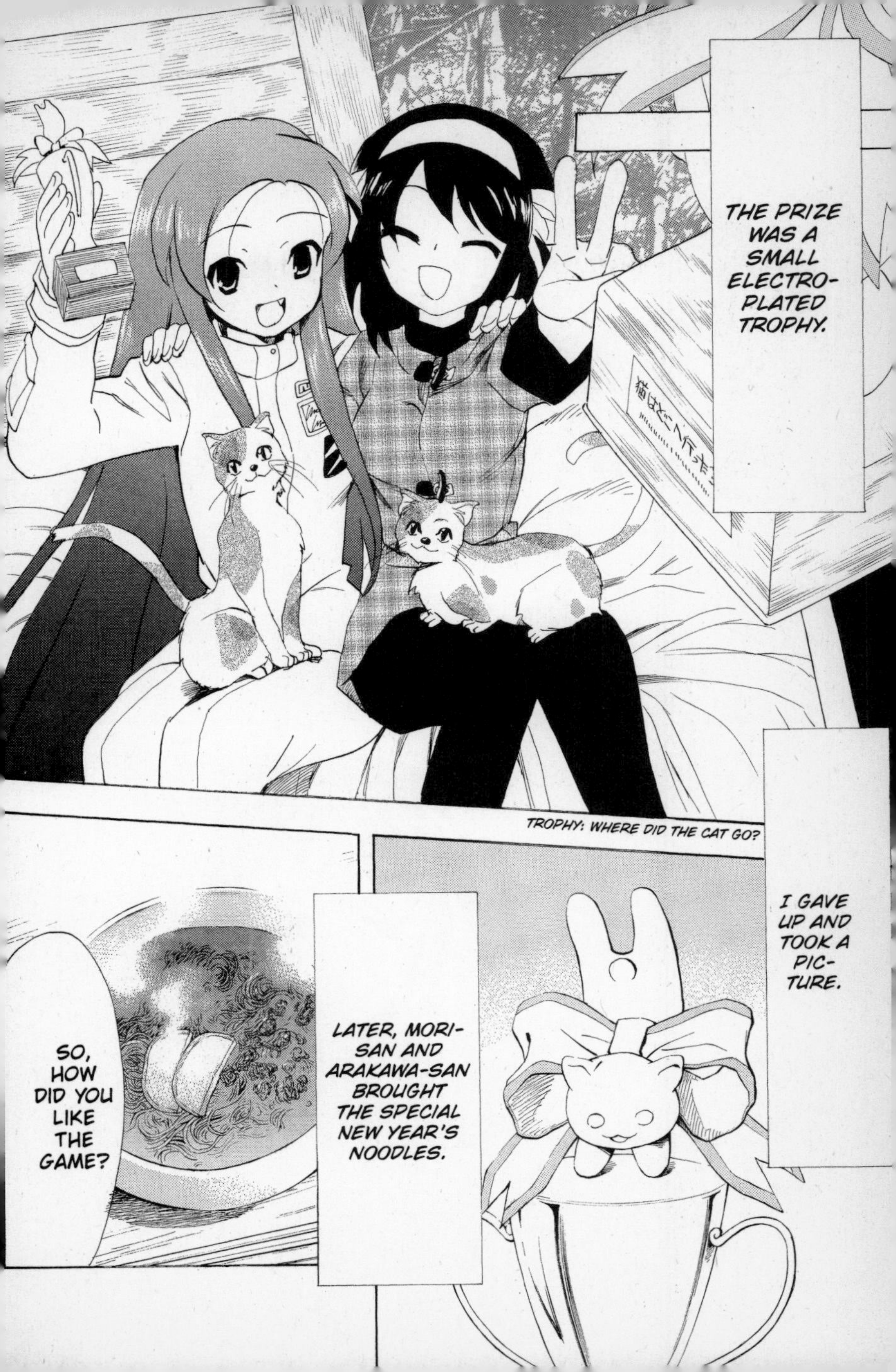
THE PRIZE WAS A SMALL ELECTRO-PLATED TROPHY.
TROPHY: WHERE DID THE CAT GO?
I GAVE UP AND TOOK A PIC-TURE.
LATER, MORI-SAN AND ARAKAWA-SAN BROUGHT THE SPECIAL NEW YEAR'S NOODLES.
SO, HOW DID YOU LIKE THE GAME?

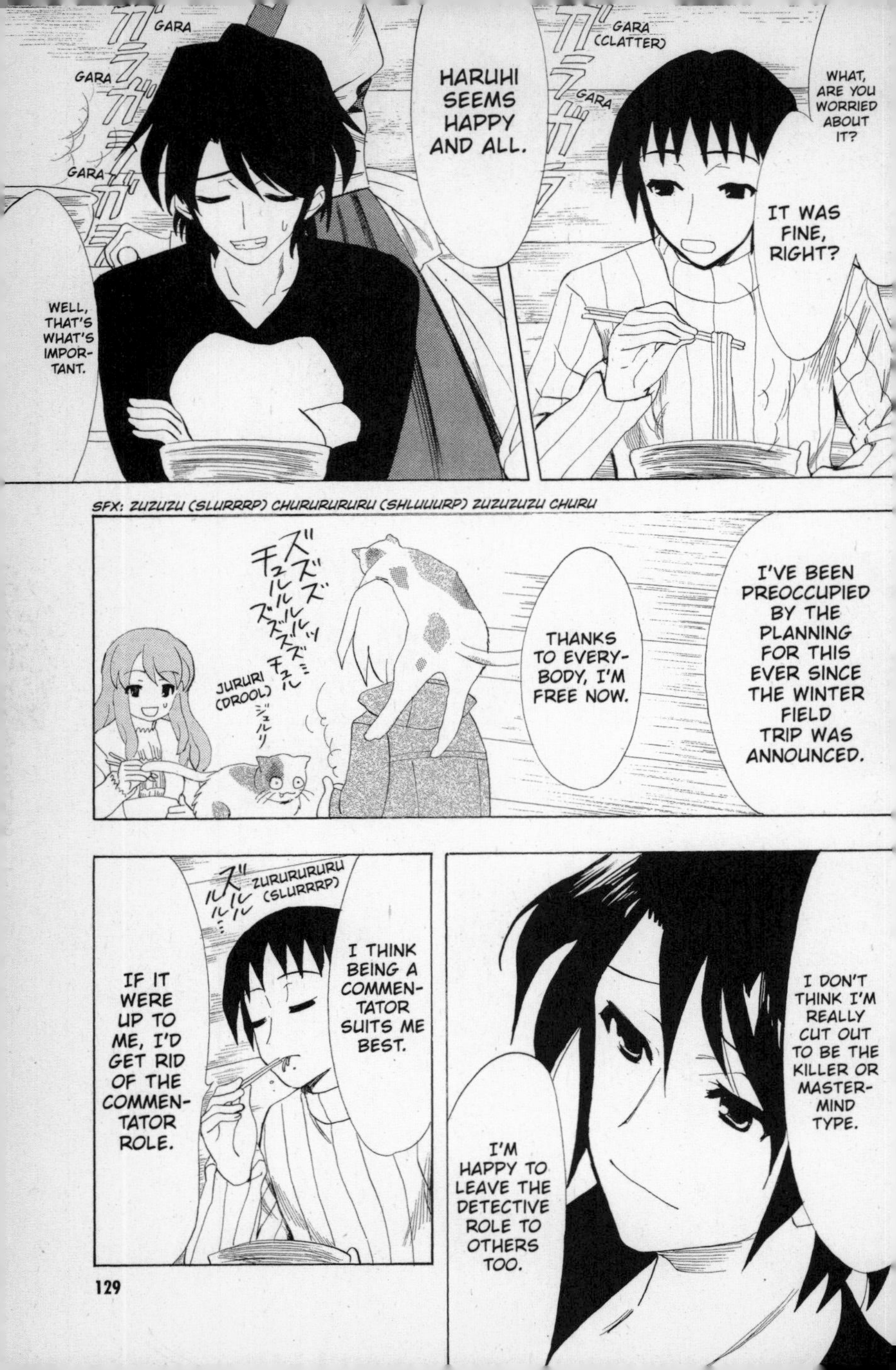
GARA (CLATTER)
GARA
WHAT, ARE YOU WORRIED ABOUT IT?
IT WAS FINE, RIGHT?
HARUHI SEEMS HAPPY AND ALL.
GARA
GARA
GARA
WELL, THAT'S WHAT'S IMPORTANT.
SFX: ZUZUZU (SLURRRP) CHURURURURU (SHLUUURP) ZUZUZUZU CHURU
I'VE BEEN PREOCCUPIED BY THE PLANNING FOR THIS EVER SINCE THE WINTER FIELD TRIP WAS ANNOUNCED.
THANKS TO EVERYBODY, I'M FREE NOW.
JURURI (DROOL)
I DON'T THINK I'M REALLY CUT OUT TO BE THE KILLER OR MASTERMIND TYPE.
I'M HAPPY TO LEAVE THE DETECTIVE ROLE TO OTHERS TOO.
ZURURURURU (SLURRRP)
I THINK BEING A COMMENTATOR SUITS ME BEST.
IF IT WERE UP TO ME, I'D GET RID OF THE COMMENTATOR ROLE.

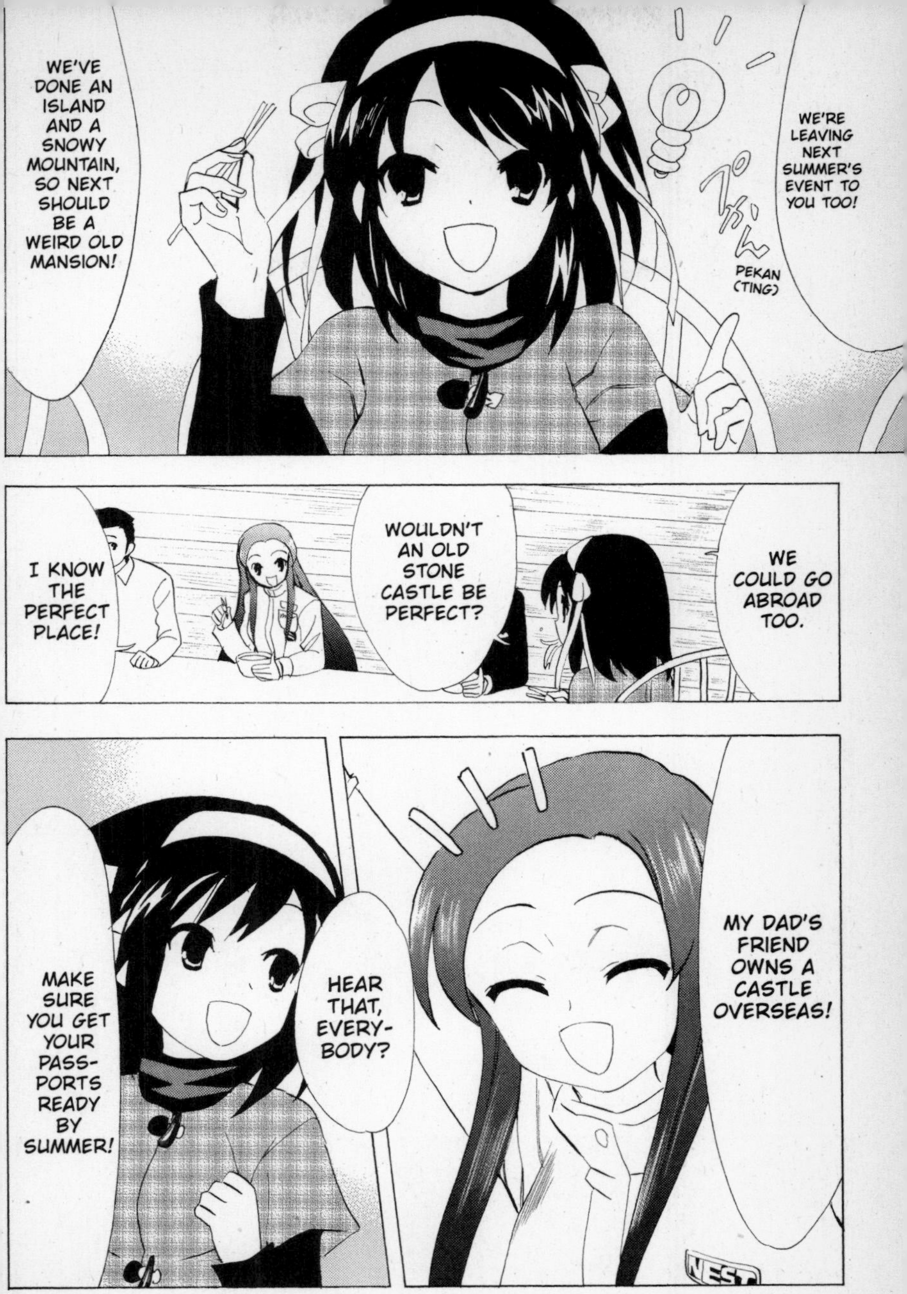
WE'RE LEAVING NEXT SUMMER'S EVENT TO YOU TOO!
PEKAN (TING)
WE'VE DONE AN ISLAND AND A SNOWY MOUNTAIN, SO NEXT SHOULD BE A WEIRD OLD MANSION!
WE COULD GO ABROAD TOO.
WOULDN'T AN OLD STONE CASTLE BE PERFECT?
I KNOW THE PERFECT PLACE!
MY DAD'S FRIEND OWNS A CASTLE OVERSEAS!
NEST
HEAR THAT, EVERY-BODY?
MAKE SURE YOU GET YOUR PASS-PORTS READY BY SUMMER!

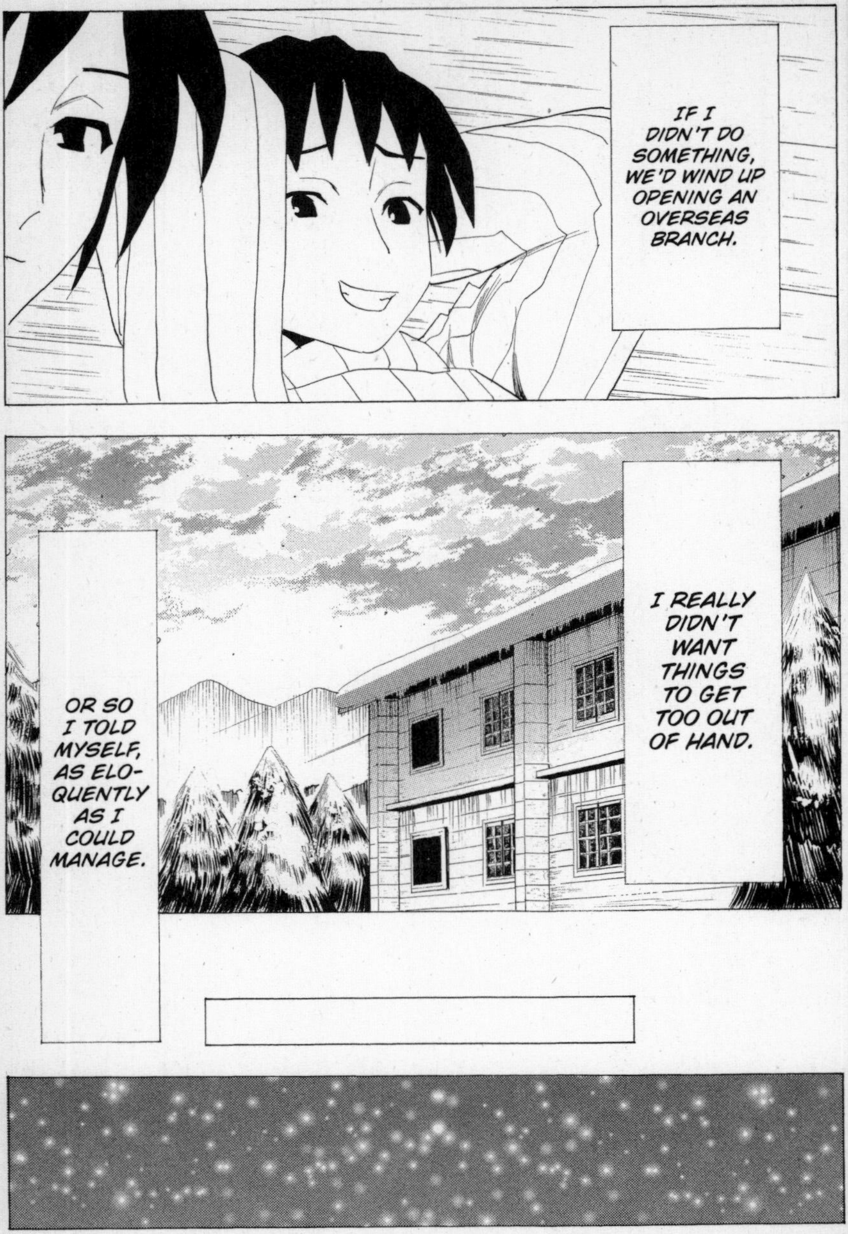
IF I DIDN'T DO SOMETHING, WE'D WIND UP OPENING AN OVERSEAS BRANCH.
I REALLY DIDN'T WANT THINGS TO GET TOO OUT OF HAND.
OR SO I TOLD MYSELF, AS ELO-QUENTLY AS I COULD MANAGE.

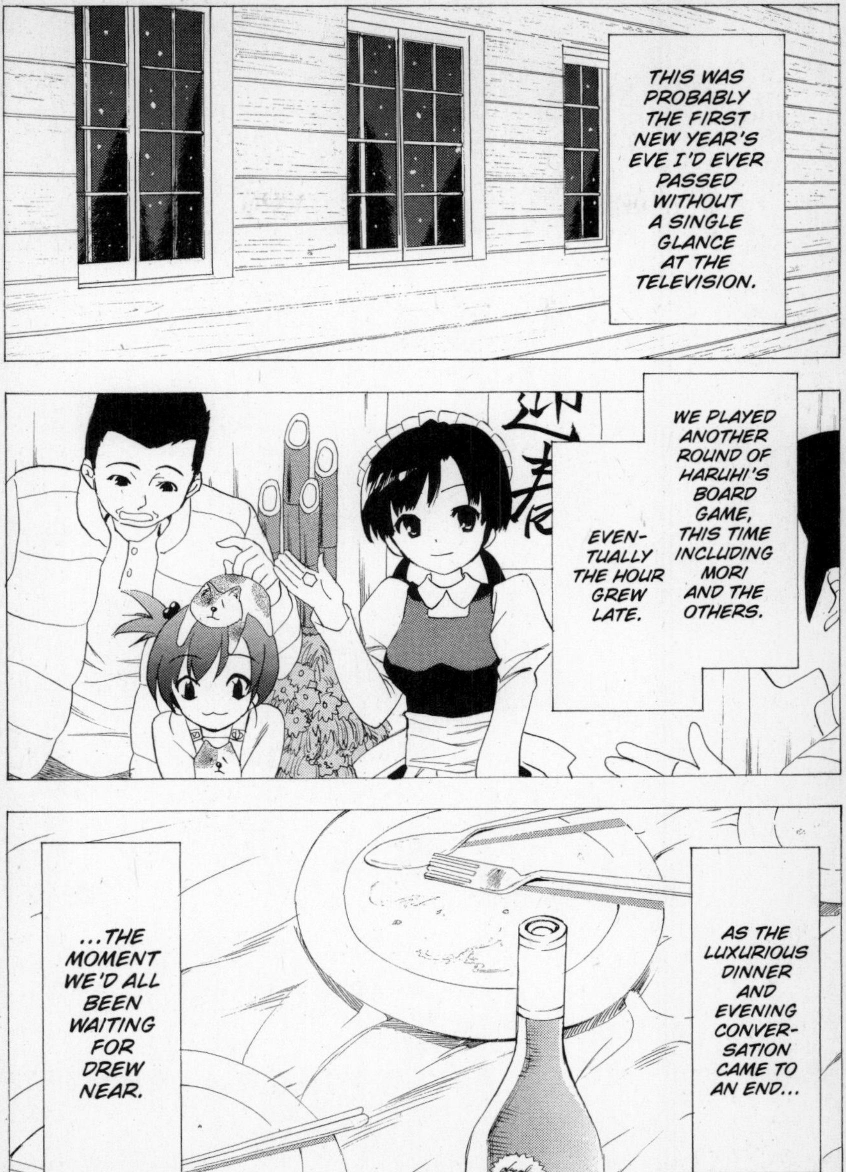
THIS WAS PROBABLY THE FIRST NEW YEAR'S EVE I'D EVER PASSED WITHOUT A SINGLE GLANCE AT THE TELEVISION.
WE PLAYED ANOTHER ROUND OF HARUHI'S BOARD GAME, THIS TIME INCLUDING MORI AND THE OTHERS.
EVEN-TUALLY THE HOUR GREW LATE.
AS THE LUXURIOUS DINNER AND EVENING CONVER-SATION CAME TO AN END...
...THE MOMENT WE'D ALL BEEN WAITING FOR DREW NEAR.

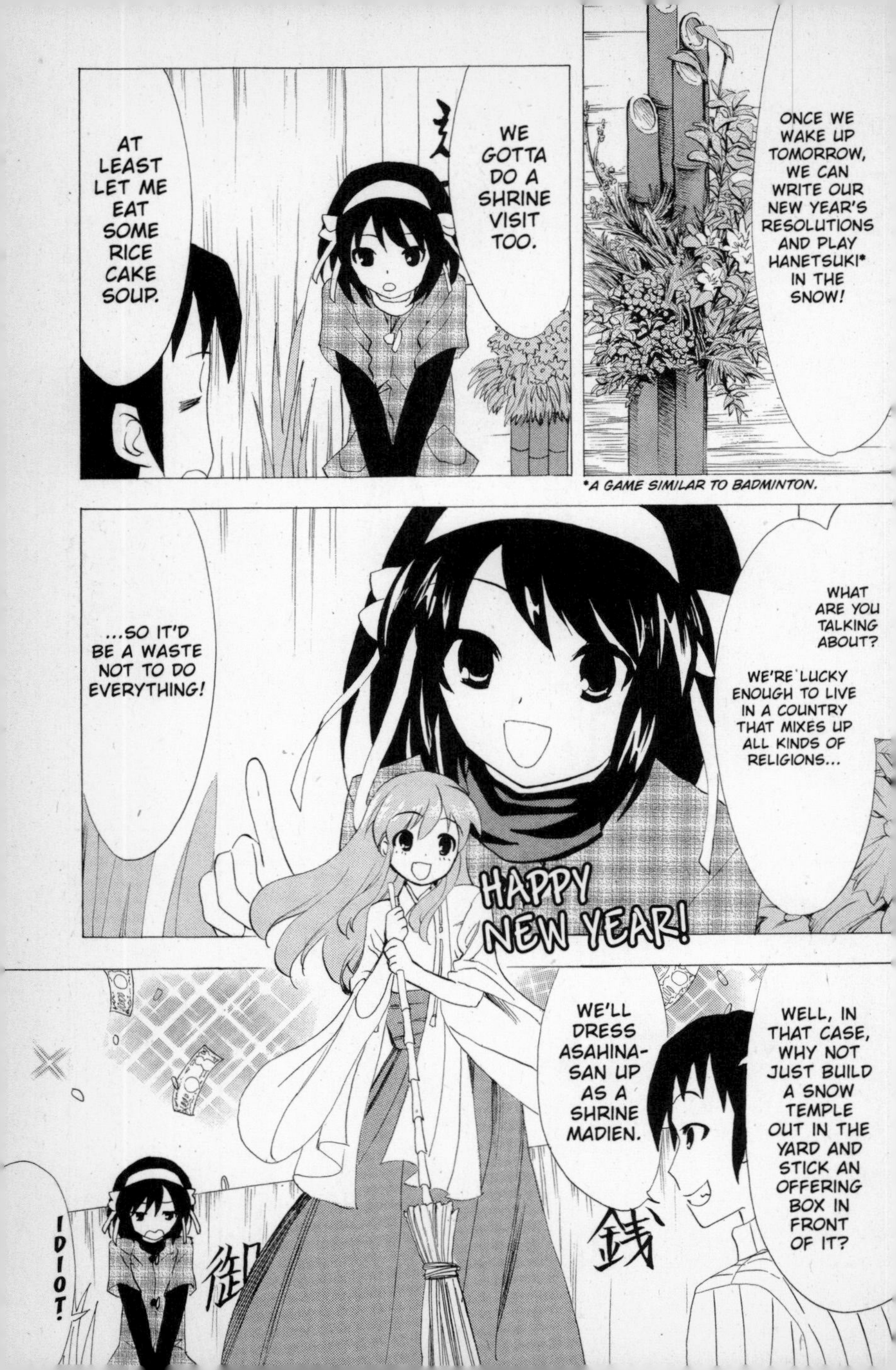
ONCE WE WAKE UP TOMORROW, WE CAN WRITE OUR NEW YEAR'S RESOLUTIONS AND PLAY HANETSUKI* IN THE SNOW!
WE GOTTA DO A SHRINE VISIT TOO.
AT LEAST LET ME EAT SOME RICE CAKE SOUP.
*A GAME SIMILAR TO BADMINTON.
WHAT ARE YOU TALKING ABOUT?
WE'RE LUCKY ENOUGH TO LIVE IN A COUNTRY THAT MIXES UP ALL KINDS OF RELIGIONS...
...SO IT'D BE A WASTE NOT TO DO EVERYTHING!
HAPPY NEW YEAR!
WELL, IN THAT CASE, WHY NOT JUST BUILD A SNOW TEMPLE OUT IN THE YARD AND STICK AN OFFERING BOX IN FRONT OF IT?
WE'LL DRESS ASAHINA-SAN UP AS A SHRINE MADIEN.
銭
御
IDIOT!

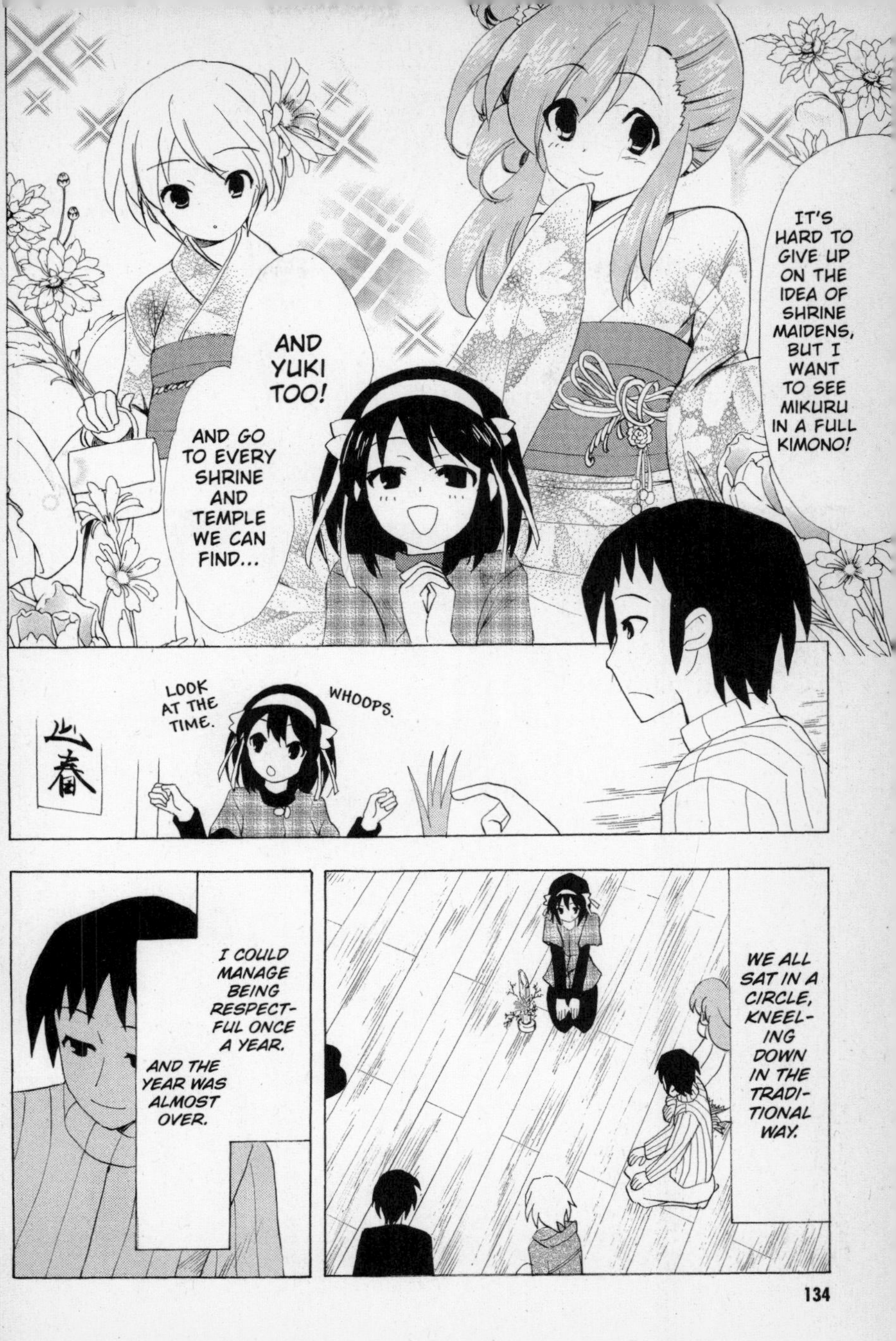
IT'S HARD TO GIVE UP ON THE IDEA OF SHRINE MAIDENS, BUT I WANT TO SEE MIKURU IN A FULL KIMONO!
AND YUKI TOO!
AND GO TO EVERY SHRINE AND TEMPLE WE CAN FIND...
WHOOPS.
LOOK AT THE TIME.
WE ALL SAT IN A CIRCLE, KNEELING DOWN IN THE TRADITIONAL WAY.
I COULD MANAGE BEING RESPECTFUL ONCE A YEAR.
AND THE YEAR WAS ALMOST OVER.

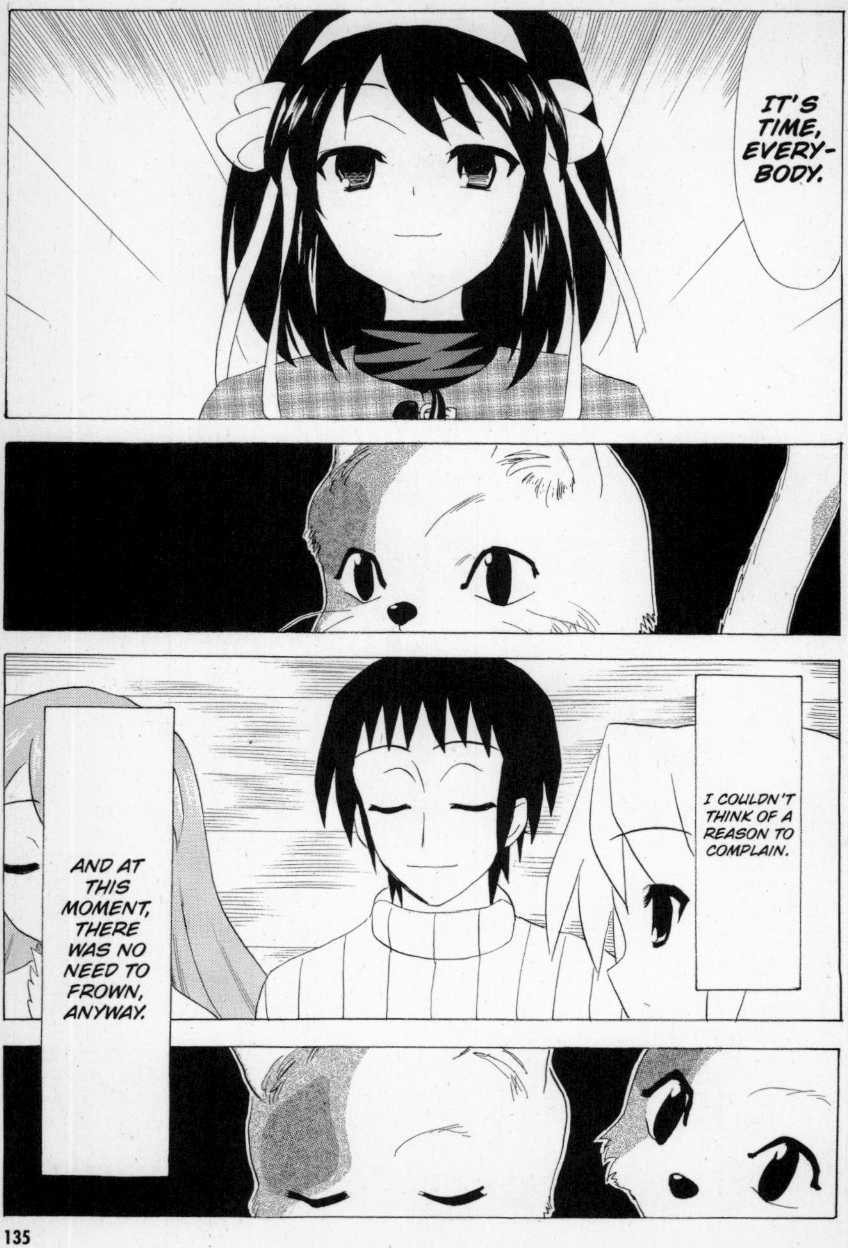
IT'S TIME, EVERYBODY.
I COULDN'T THINK OF A REASON TO COMPLAIN.
AND AT THIS MOMENT, THERE WAS NO NEED TO FROWN, ANYWAY.

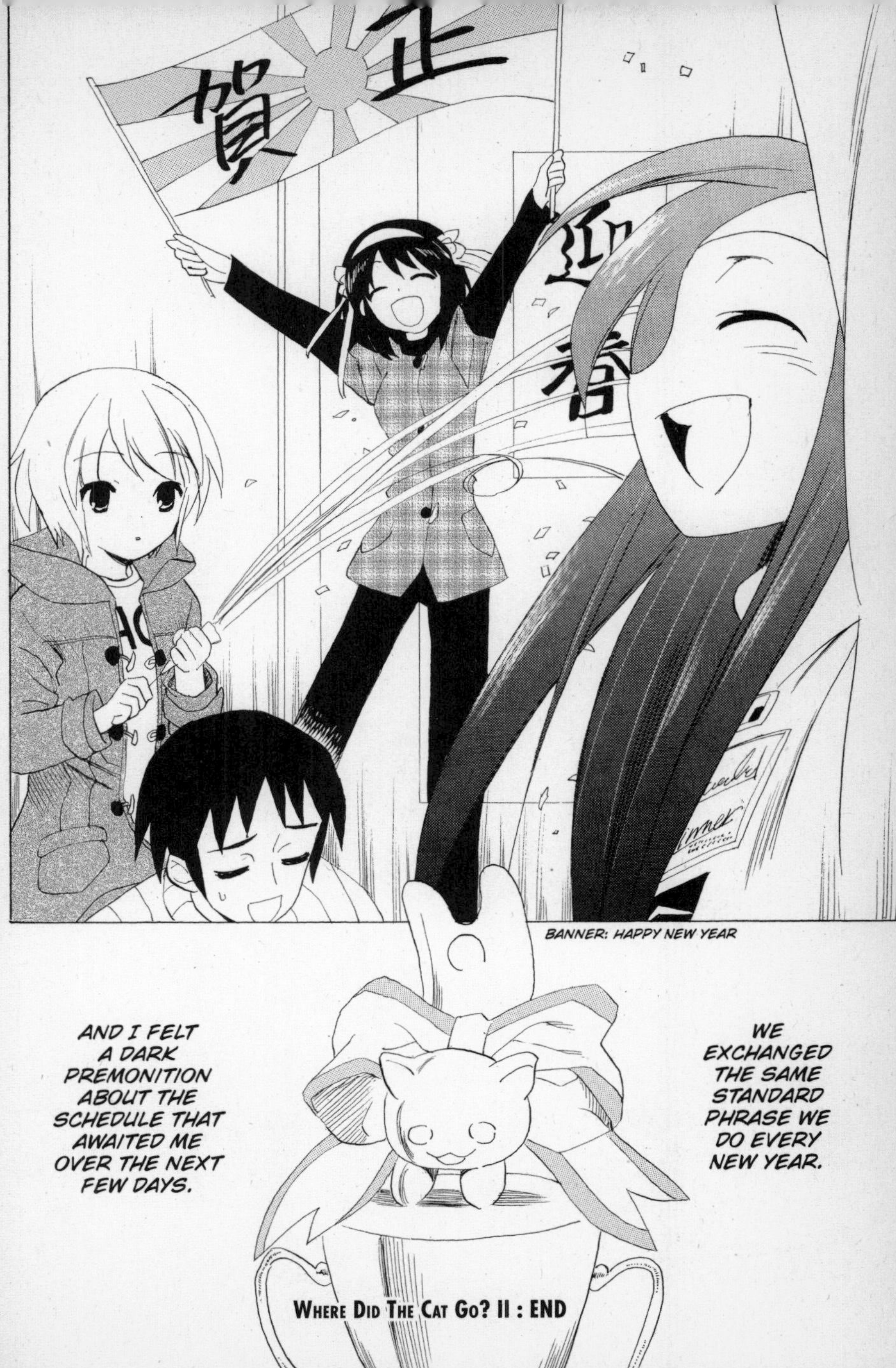
賀正
迎春
BANNER: HAPPY NEW YEAR
WE EXCHANGED THE SAME STANDARD PHRASE WE DO EVERY NEW YEAR.
AND I FELT A DARK PREMONITION ABOUT THE SCHEDULE THAT AWAITED ME OVER THE NEXT FEW DAYS.
WHERE DID THE CAT GO? II : END

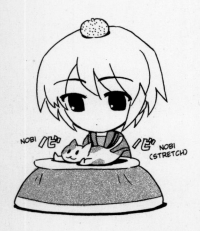
NOBI バビ バビ NOBI (STRETCH)

THE MELANCHOLY OF HARUHI SUZUMIYA

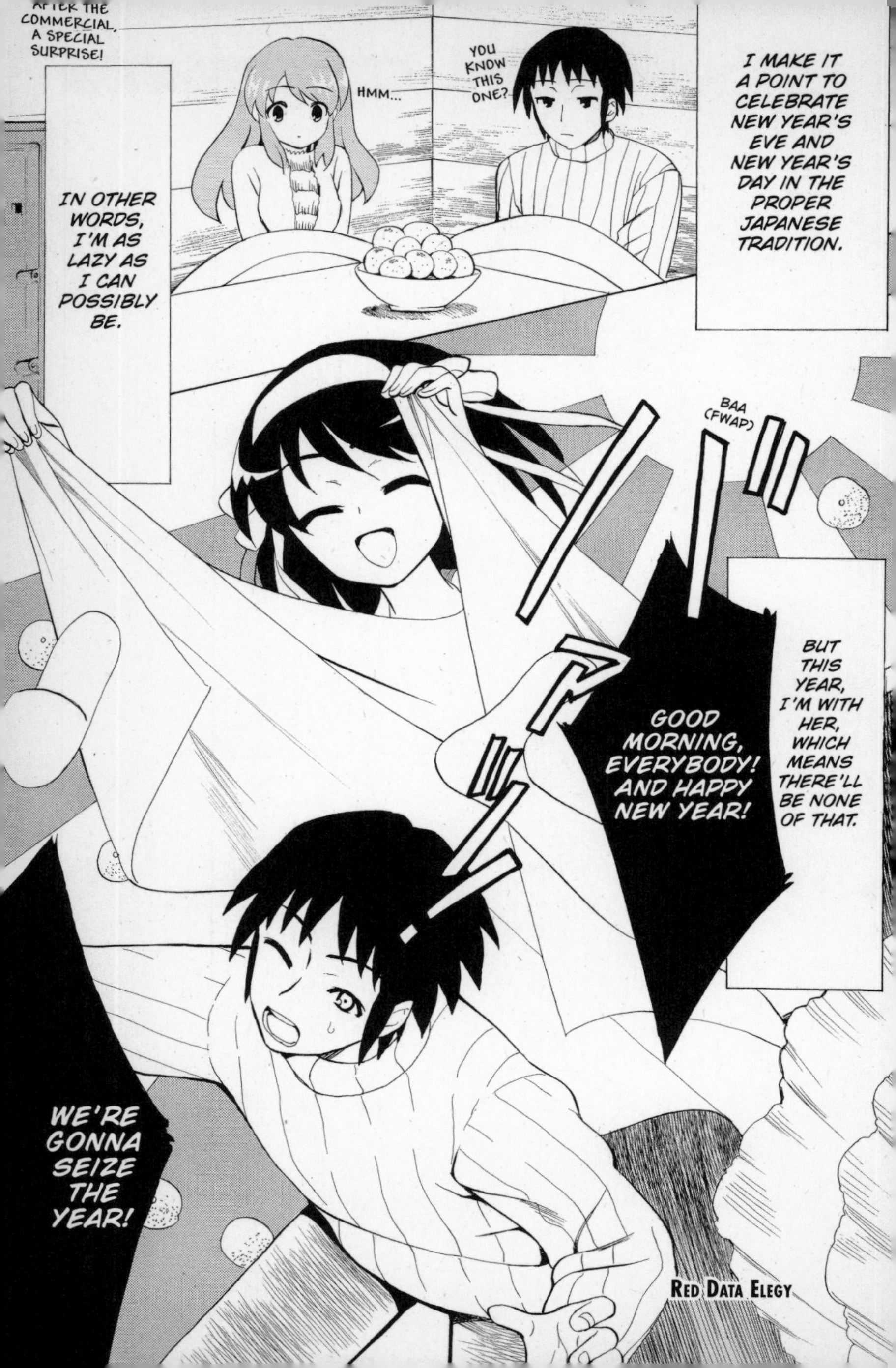
I MAKE IT A POINT TO CELEBRATE NEW YEAR'S EVE AND NEW YEAR'S DAY IN THE PROPER JAPANESE TRADITION.
YOU KNOW THIS ONE?
HMM...
AFTER THE COMMERCIAL, A SPECIAL SURPRISE!
IN OTHER WORDS, I'M AS LAZY AS I CAN POSSIBLY BE.
BAA (FWAP)
BUT THIS YEAR, I'M WITH HER, WHICH MEANS THERE'LL BE NONE OF THAT.
GOOD MORNING, EVERYBODY! AND HAPPY NEW YEAR!
WE'RE GONNA SEIZE THE YEAR!
RED DATA ELEGY

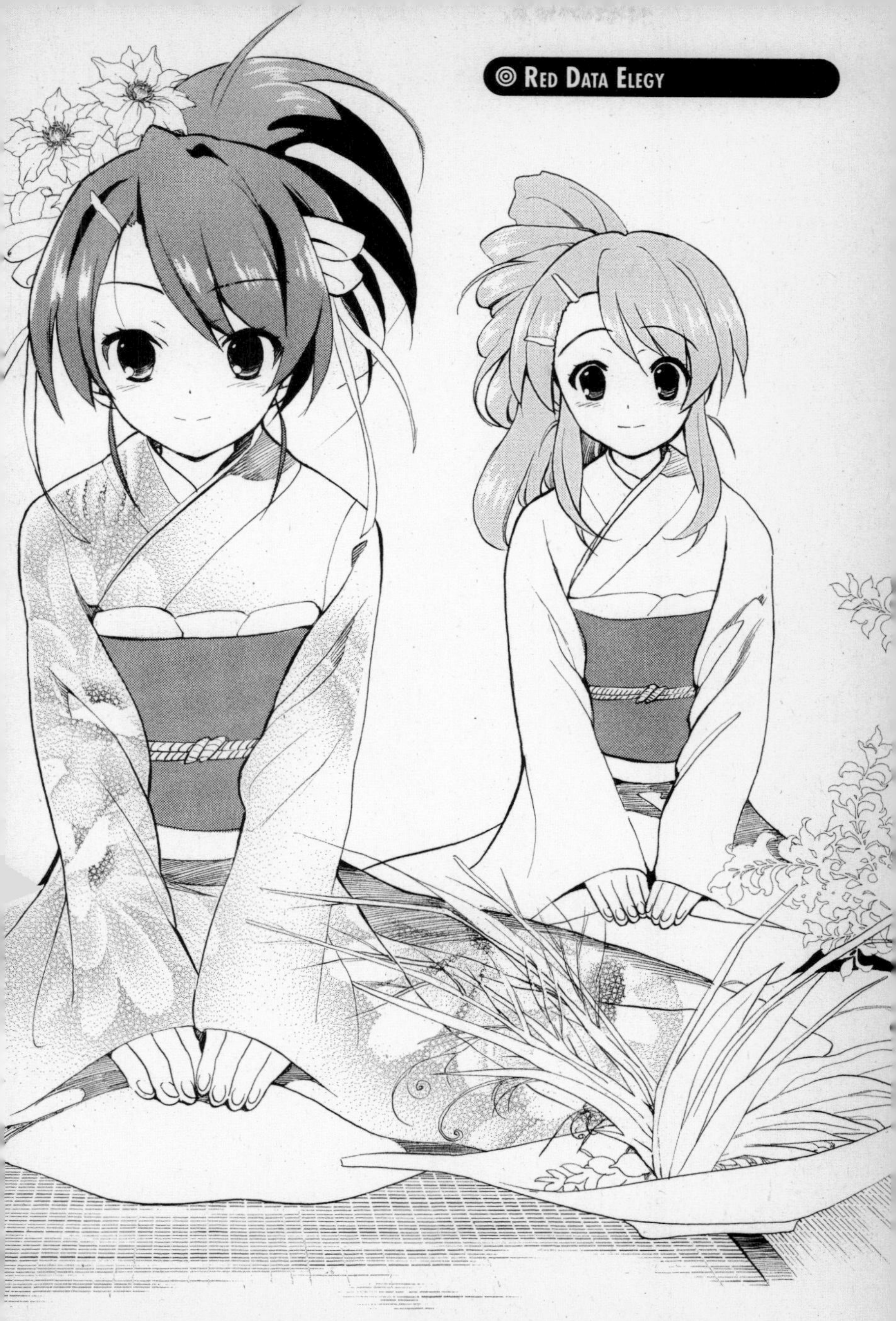

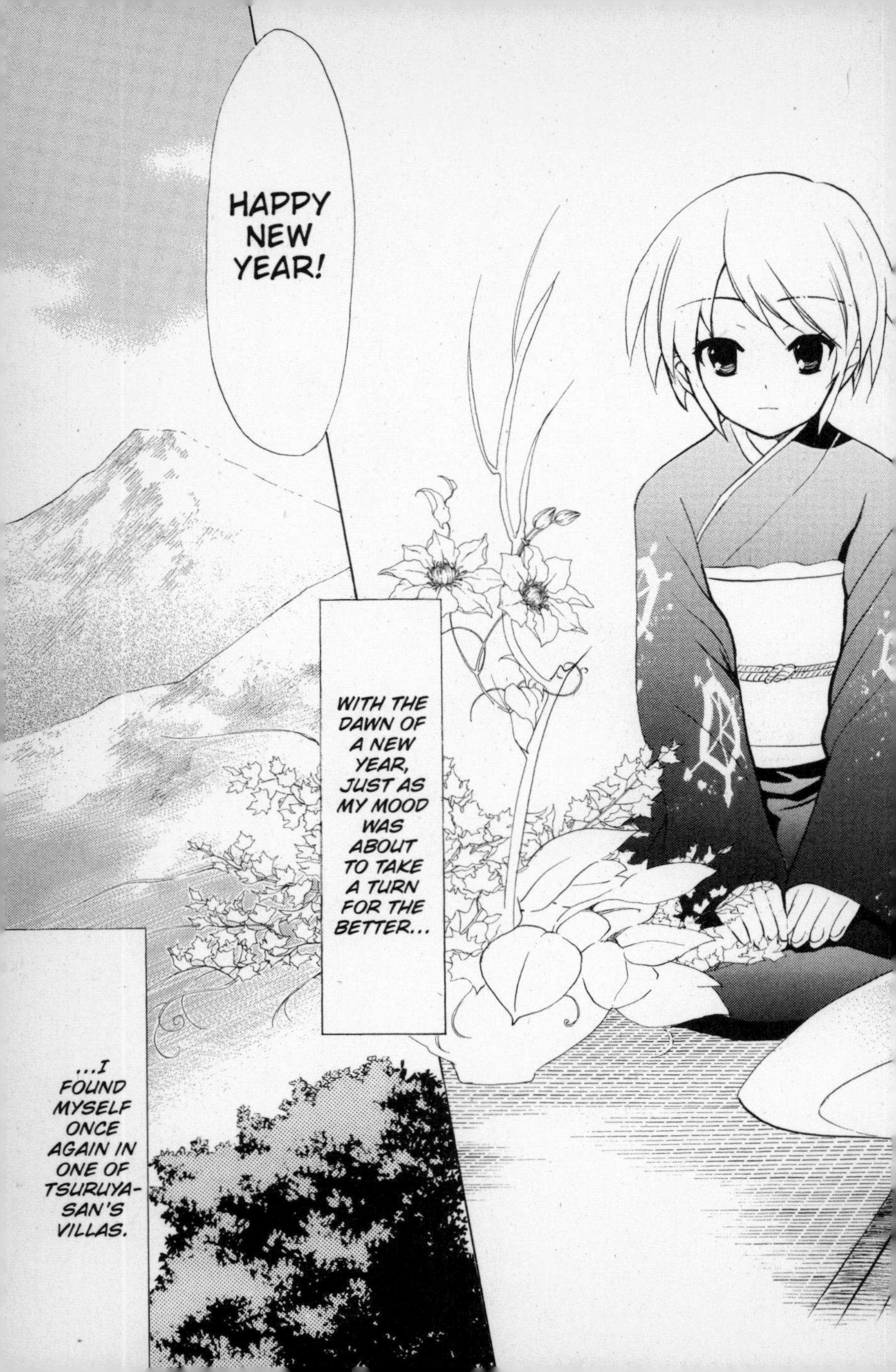
HAPPY NEW YEAR!
WITH THE DAWN OF A NEW YEAR, JUST AS MY MOOD WAS ABOUT TO TAKE A TURN FOR THE BETTER...
...I FOUND MYSELF ONCE AGAIN IN ONE OF TSURUYA-SAN'S VILLAS.

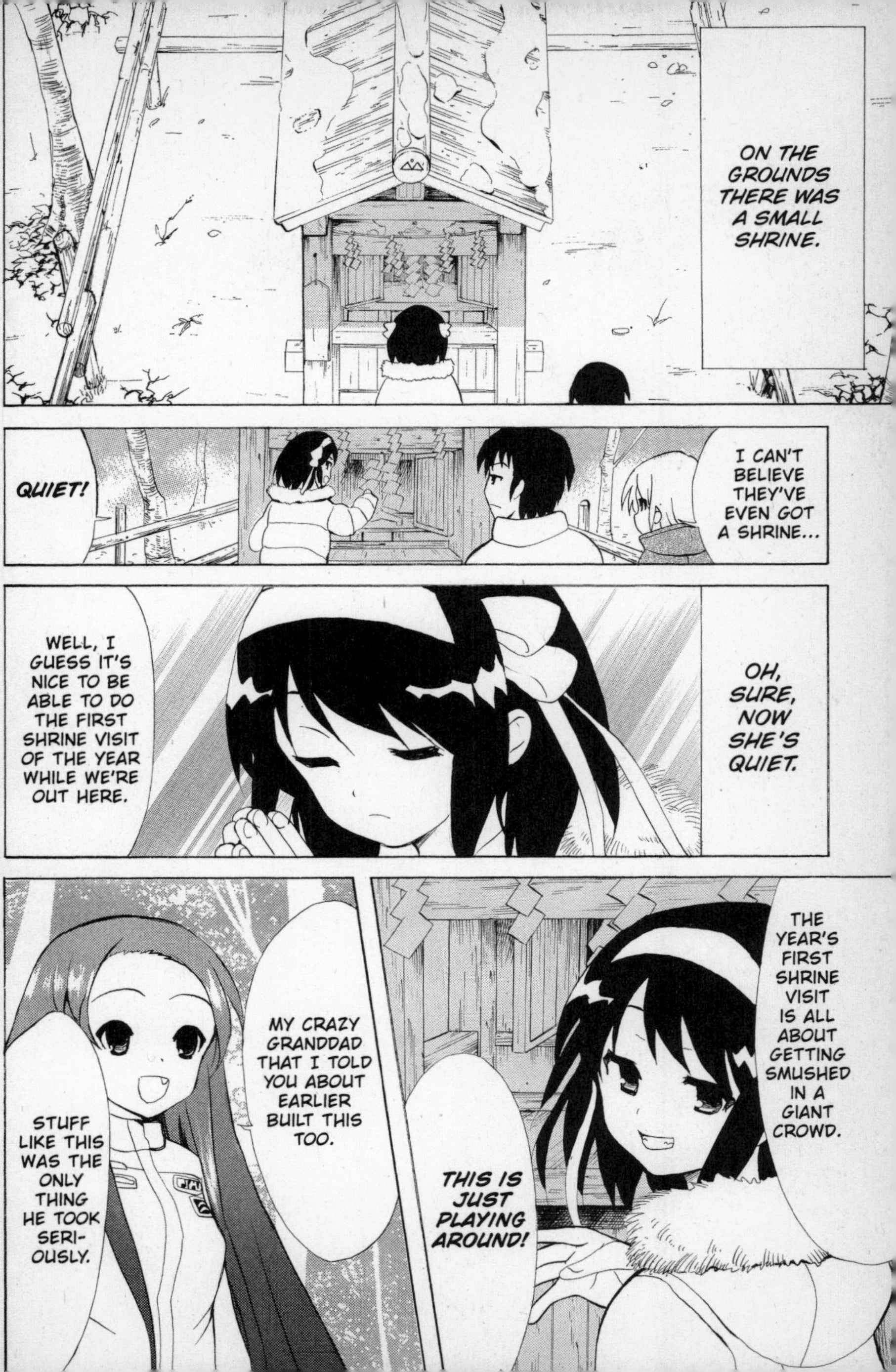
ON THE GROUNDS THERE WAS A SMALL SHRINE.
I CAN'T BELIEVE THEY'VE EVEN GOT A SHRINE...
QUIET!
OH, SURE, NOW SHE'S QUIET.
WELL, I GUESS IT'S NICE TO BE ABLE TO DO THE FIRST SHRINE VISIT OF THE YEAR WHILE WE'RE OUT HERE.
THE YEAR'S FIRST SHRINE VISIT IS ALL ABOUT GETTING SMUSHED IN A GIANT CROWD.
THIS IS JUST PLAYING AROUND!
MY CRAZY GRANDDAD THAT I TOLD YOU ABOUT EARLIER BUILT THIS TOO.
STUFF LIKE THIS WAS THE ONLY THING HE TOOK SERI-OUSLY.

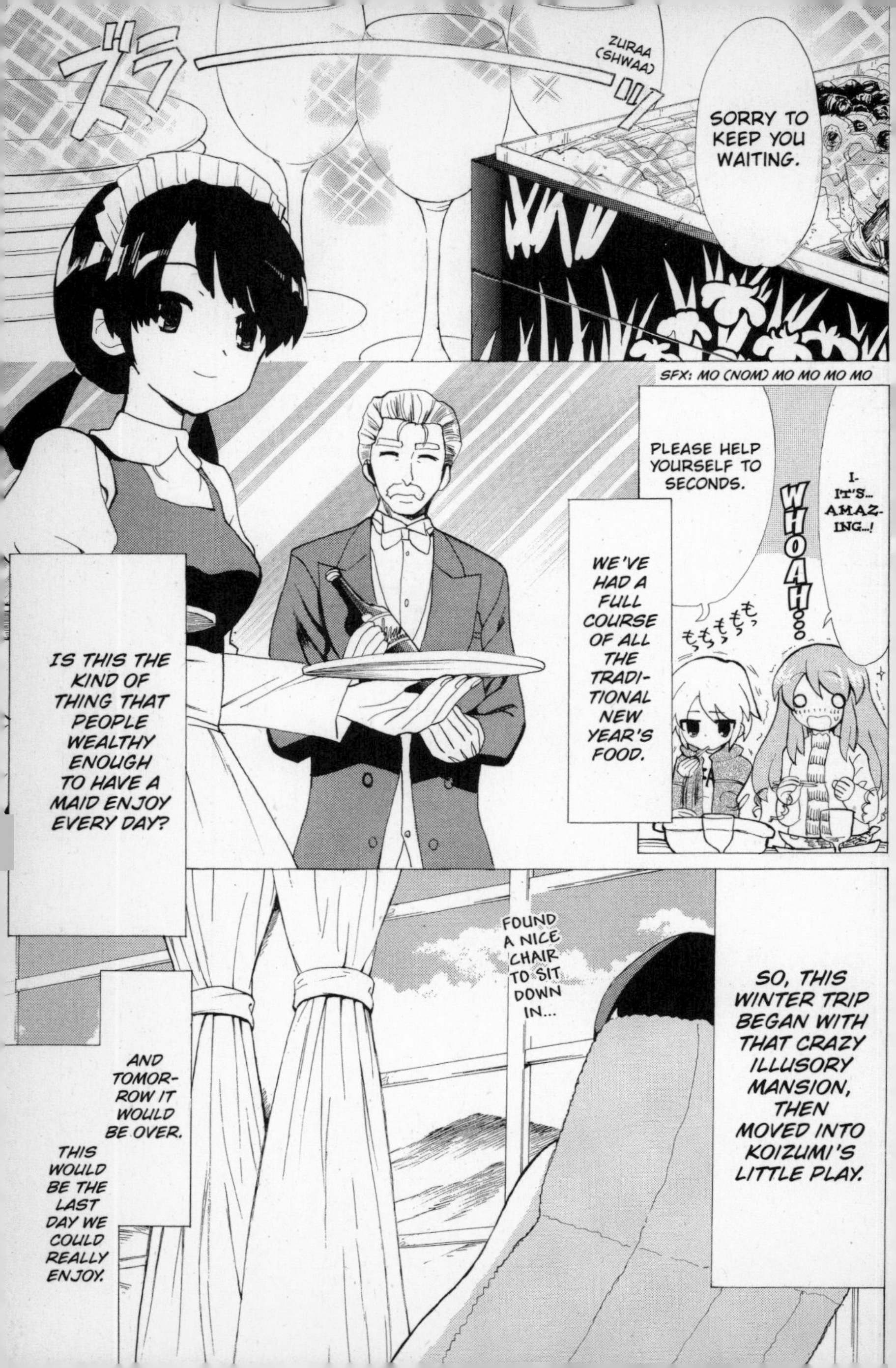
SORRY TO KEEP YOU WAITING.
ZURAA (SHWAA)
ズラ
SFX: MO (NOM) MO MO MO MO
PLEASE HELP YOURSELF TO SECONDS.
I- IT'S... AMAZ-ING...!
WHOAH...
もっもっもっもっ
WE'VE HAD A FULL COURSE OF ALL THE TRADITIONAL NEW YEAR'S FOOD.
IS THIS THE KIND OF THING THAT PEOPLE WEALTHY ENOUGH TO HAVE A MAID ENJOY EVERY DAY?
SO, THIS WINTER TRIP BEGAN WITH THAT CRAZY ILLUSORY MANSION, THEN MOVED INTO KOIZUMI'S LITTLE PLAY.
FOUND A NICE CHAIR TO SIT DOWN IN...
AND TOMORROW IT WOULD BE OVER.
THIS WOULD BE THE LAST DAY WE COULD REALLY ENJOY.

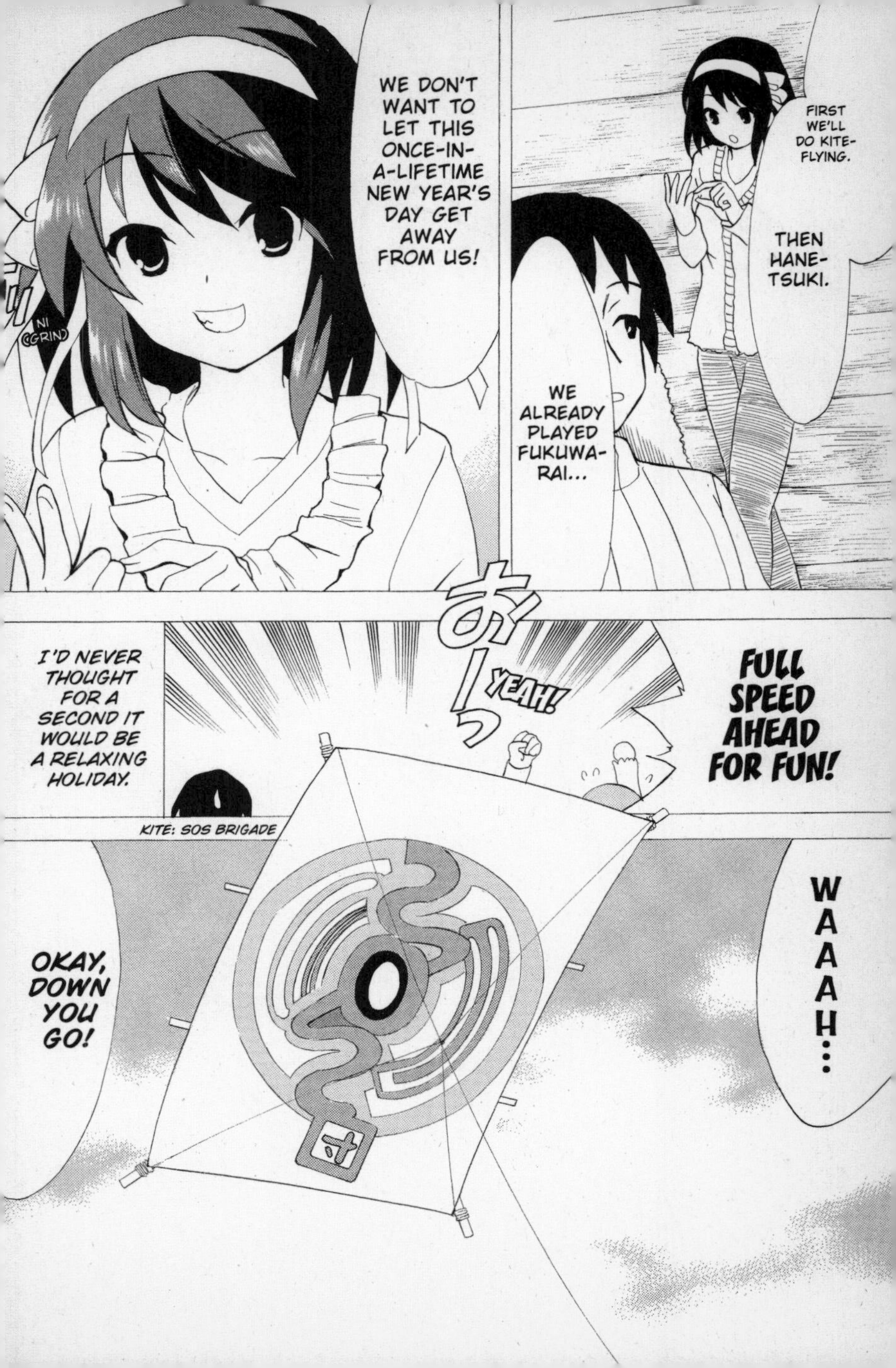
FIRST WE'LL DO KITE-FLYING.
THEN HANE-TSUKI.
WE ALREADY PLAYED FUKUWA-RAI...
WE DON'T WANT TO LET THIS ONCE-IN-A-LIFETIME NEW YEAR'S DAY GET AWAY FROM US!
NI (GRIN)
FULL SPEED AHEAD FOR FUN!
おーっ
YEAH!
I'D NEVER THOUGHT FOR A SECOND IT WOULD BE A RELAXING HOLIDAY.
KITE: SOS BRIGADE
WAAAAH...
OKAY, DOWN YOU GO!

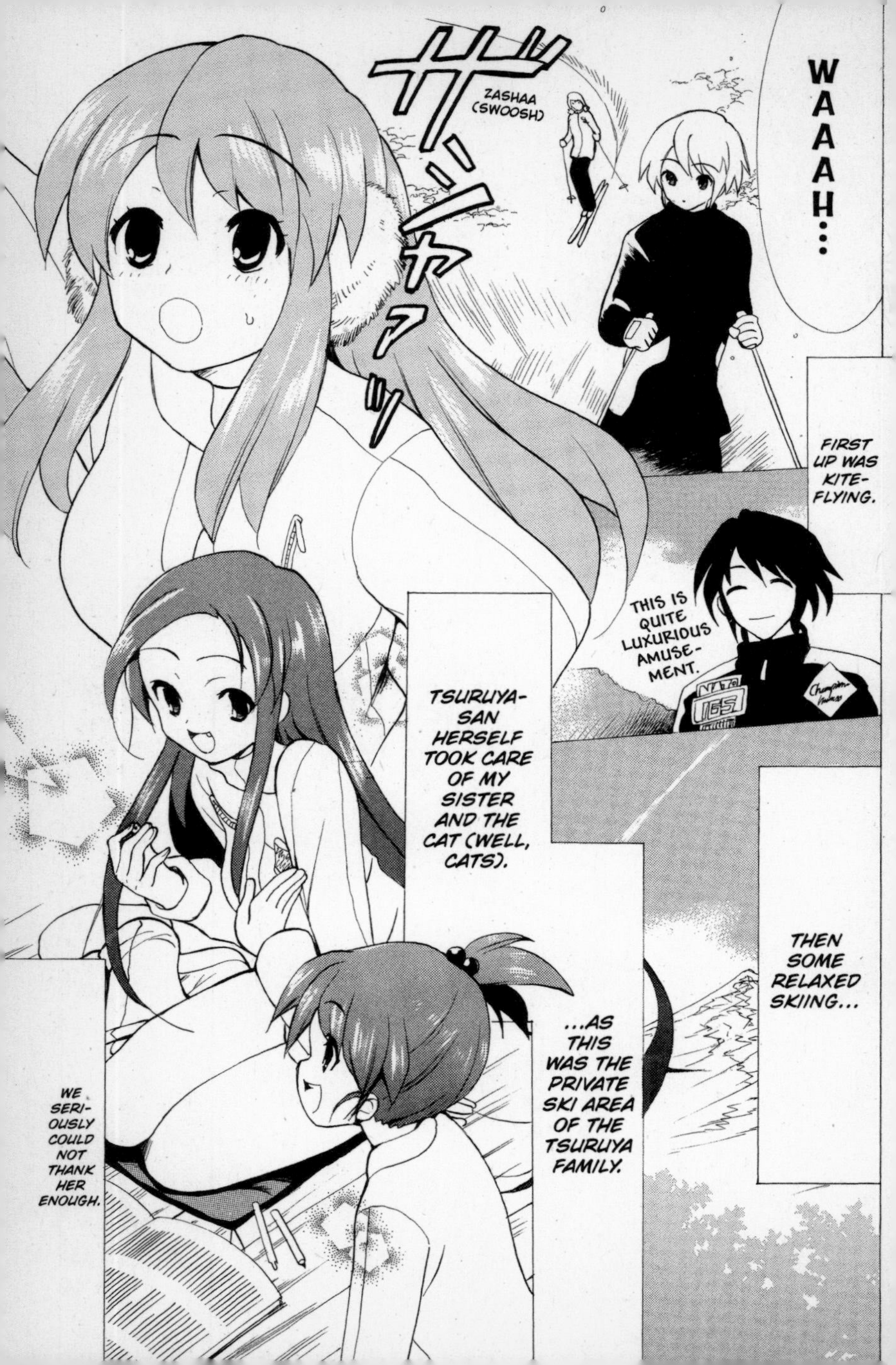
WAAAH...
ザシャァッ
ZASHAA (SWOOSH)
FIRST UP WAS KITE-FLYING.
THIS IS QUITE LUXURIOUS AMUSEMENT.
THEN SOME RELAXED SKIING...
...AS THIS WAS THE PRIVATE SKI AREA OF THE TSURUYA FAMILY.
TSURUYA-SAN HERSELF TOOK CARE OF MY SISTER AND THE CAT (WELL, CATS).
WE SERIOUSLY COULD NOT THANK HER ENOUGH.

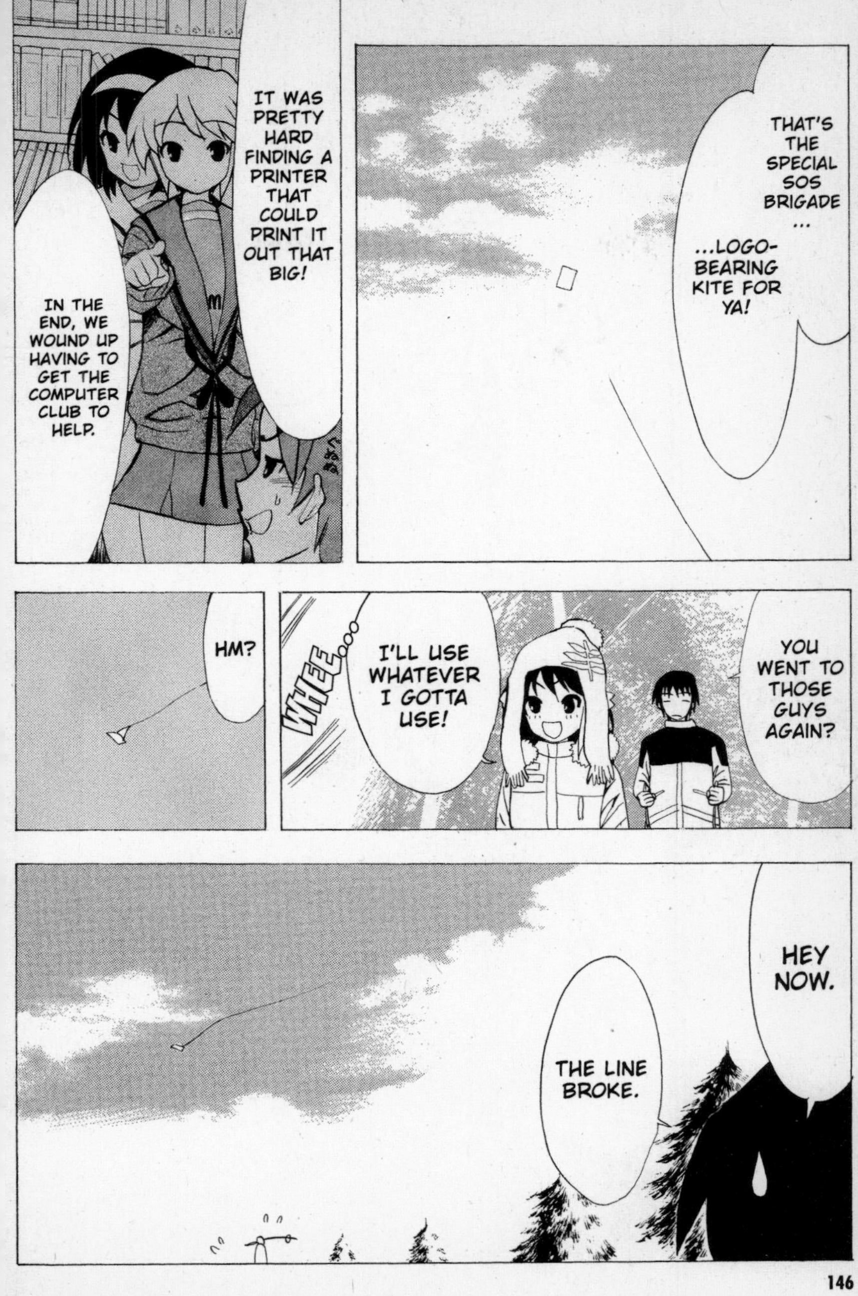
THAT'S THE SPECIAL SOS BRIGADE ...
...LOGO-BEARING KITE FOR YA!
IT WAS PRETTY HARD FINDING A PRINTER THAT COULD PRINT IT OUT THAT BIG!
IN THE END, WE WOUND UP HAVING TO GET THE COMPUTER CLUB TO HELP.
YOU WENT TO THOSE GUYS AGAIN?
I'LL USE WHATEVER I GOTTA USE!
WHEE
HM?
HEY NOW.
THE LINE BROKE.

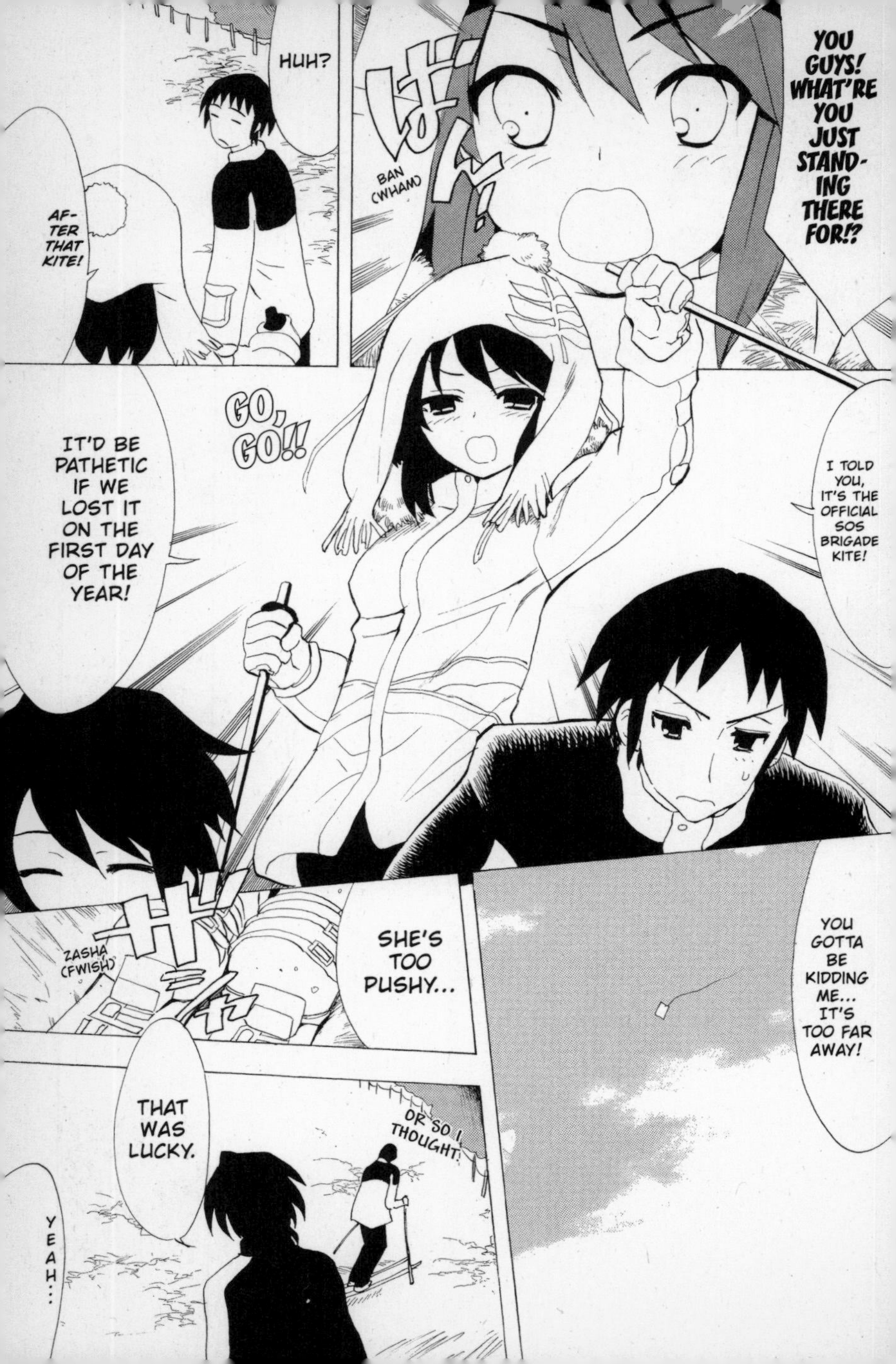
YOU GUYS! WHAT'RE YOU JUST STAND-ING THERE FOR!?
BAN (WHAM)
HUH?
AF-TER THAT KITE!
I TOLD YOU, IT'S THE OFFICIAL SOS BRIGADE KITE!
GO, GO!!
IT'D BE PATHETIC IF WE LOST IT ON THE FIRST DAY OF THE YEAR!
YOU GOTTA BE KIDDING ME... IT'S TOO FAR AWAY!
SHE'S TOO PUSHY...
ZASHA (FWISH)
OR SO I THOUGHT!
THAT WAS LUCKY.
YEAH...

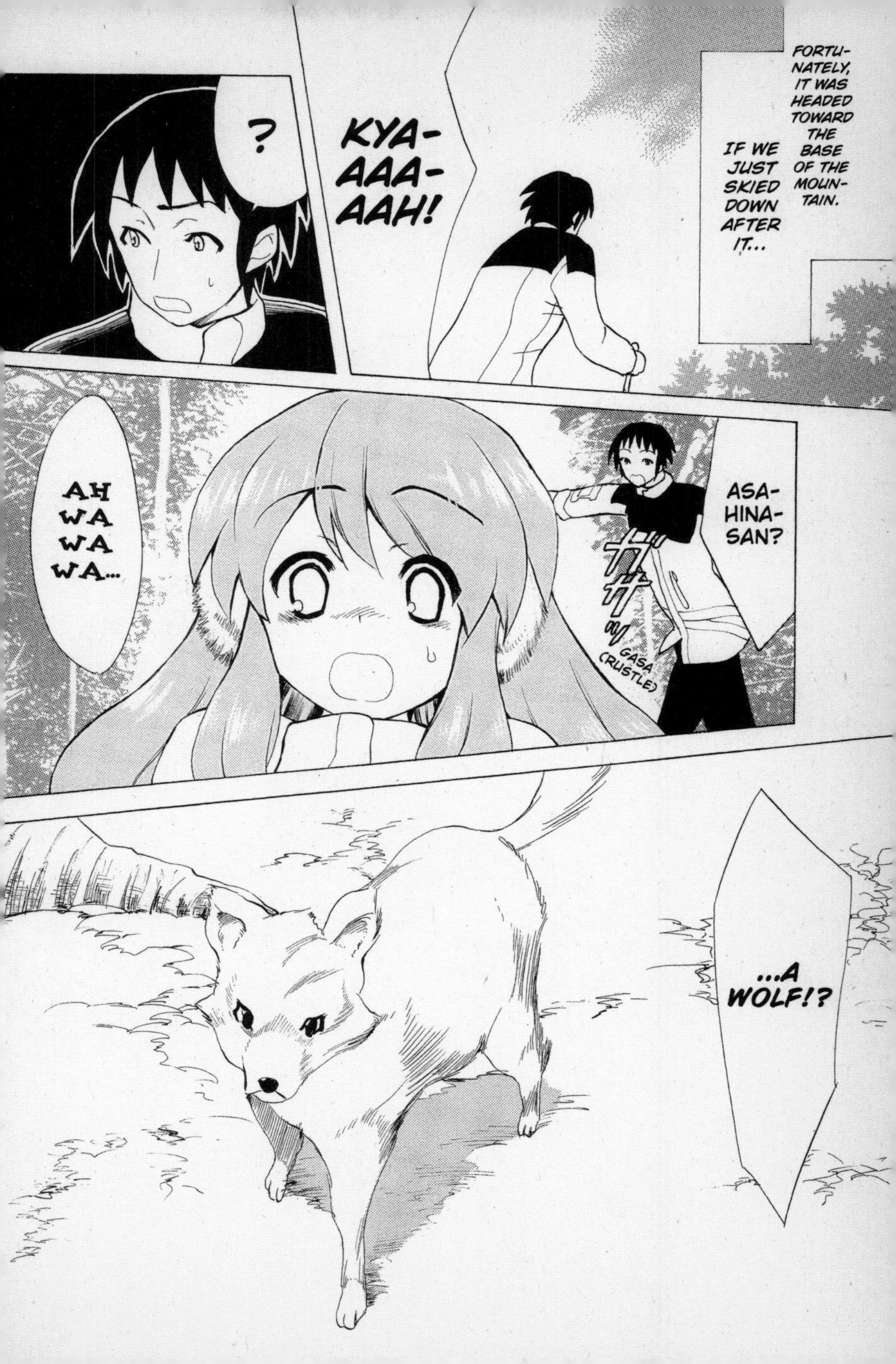
FORTUNATELY, IT WAS HEADED TOWARD THE BASE OF THE MOUNTAIN.
IF WE JUST SKIED DOWN AFTER IT...
KYA-AAA-AAH!
?
ASA-HINA-SAN?
GASA (RUSTLE)
AH WA WA WA WA...
...A WOLF!?

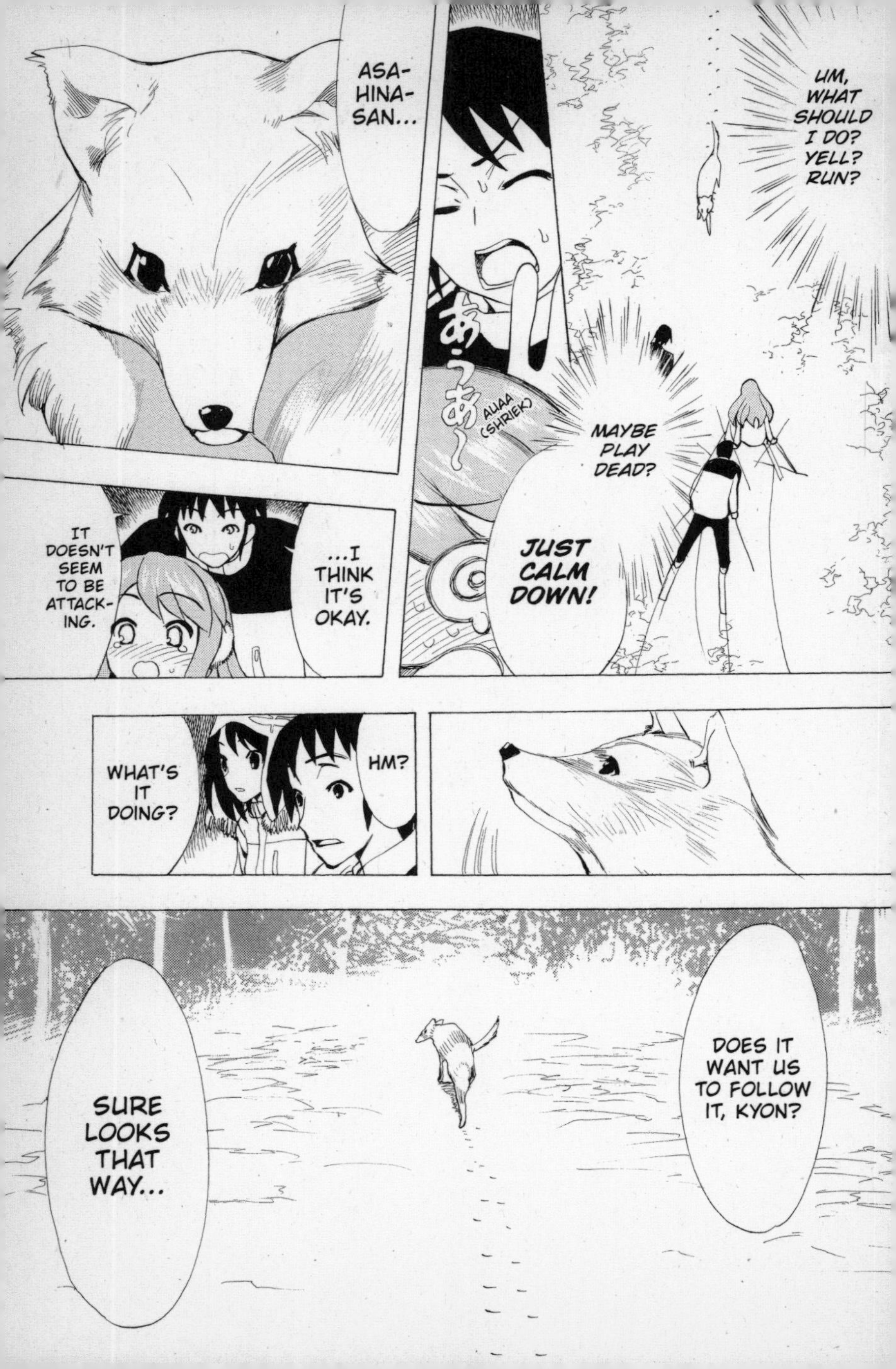
UM, WHAT SHOULD I DO? YELL? RUN?
MAYBE PLAY DEAD?
JUST CALM DOWN!
あうあ～
AUAA (SHRIEK)
ASA-HINA-SAN...
...I THINK IT'S OKAY.
IT DOESN'T SEEM TO BE ATTACK-ING.
HM?
WHAT'S IT DOING?
DOES IT WANT US TO FOLLOW IT, KYON?
SURE LOOKS THAT WAY...

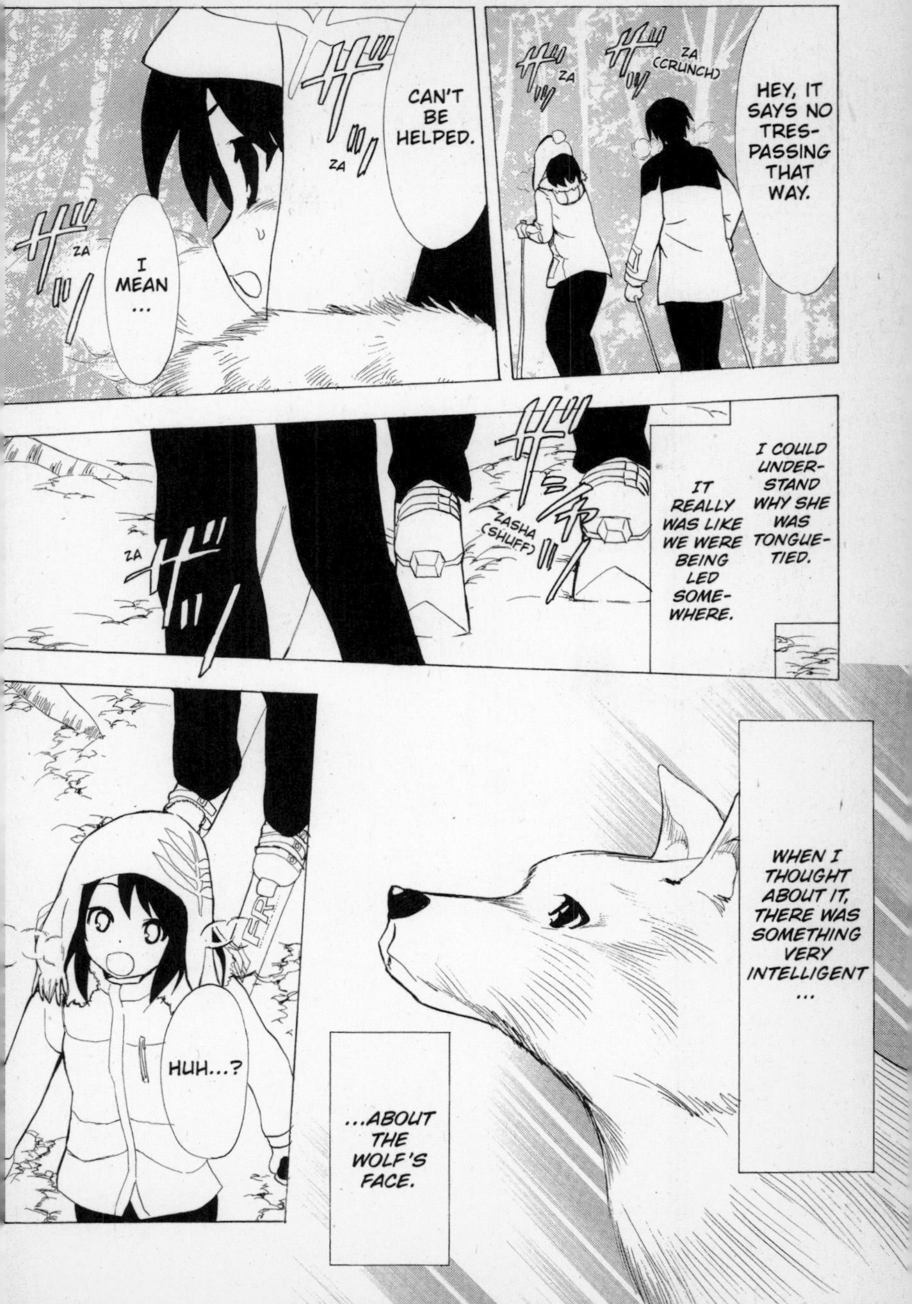
ZA (CRUNCH)
ZA
HEY, IT SAYS NO TRESPASSING THAT WAY.
ZA
CAN'T BE HELPED.
ZA
I MEAN ...
I COULD UNDERSTAND WHY SHE WAS TONGUE-TIED.
IT REALLY WAS LIKE WE WERE BEING LED SOMEWHERE.
ZASHA (SHUFF)
ZA
WHEN I THOUGHT ABOUT IT, THERE WAS SOMETHING VERY INTELLIGENT ...
...ABOUT THE WOLF'S FACE.
HUH...?

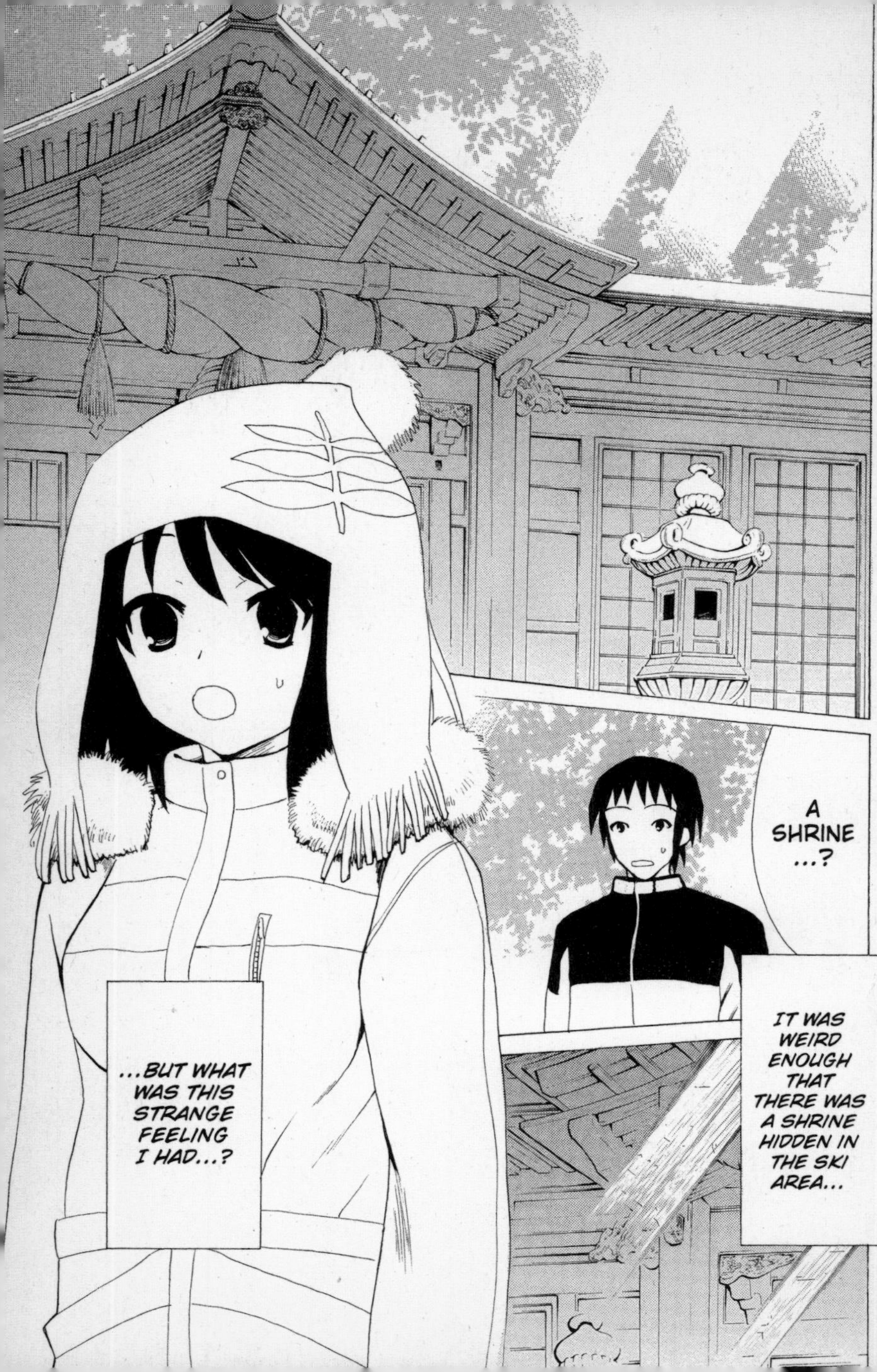
A SHRINE ...?
IT WAS WEIRD ENOUGH THAT THERE WAS A SHRINE HIDDEN IN THE SKI AREA...
...BUT WHAT WAS THIS STRANGE FEELING I HAD...?

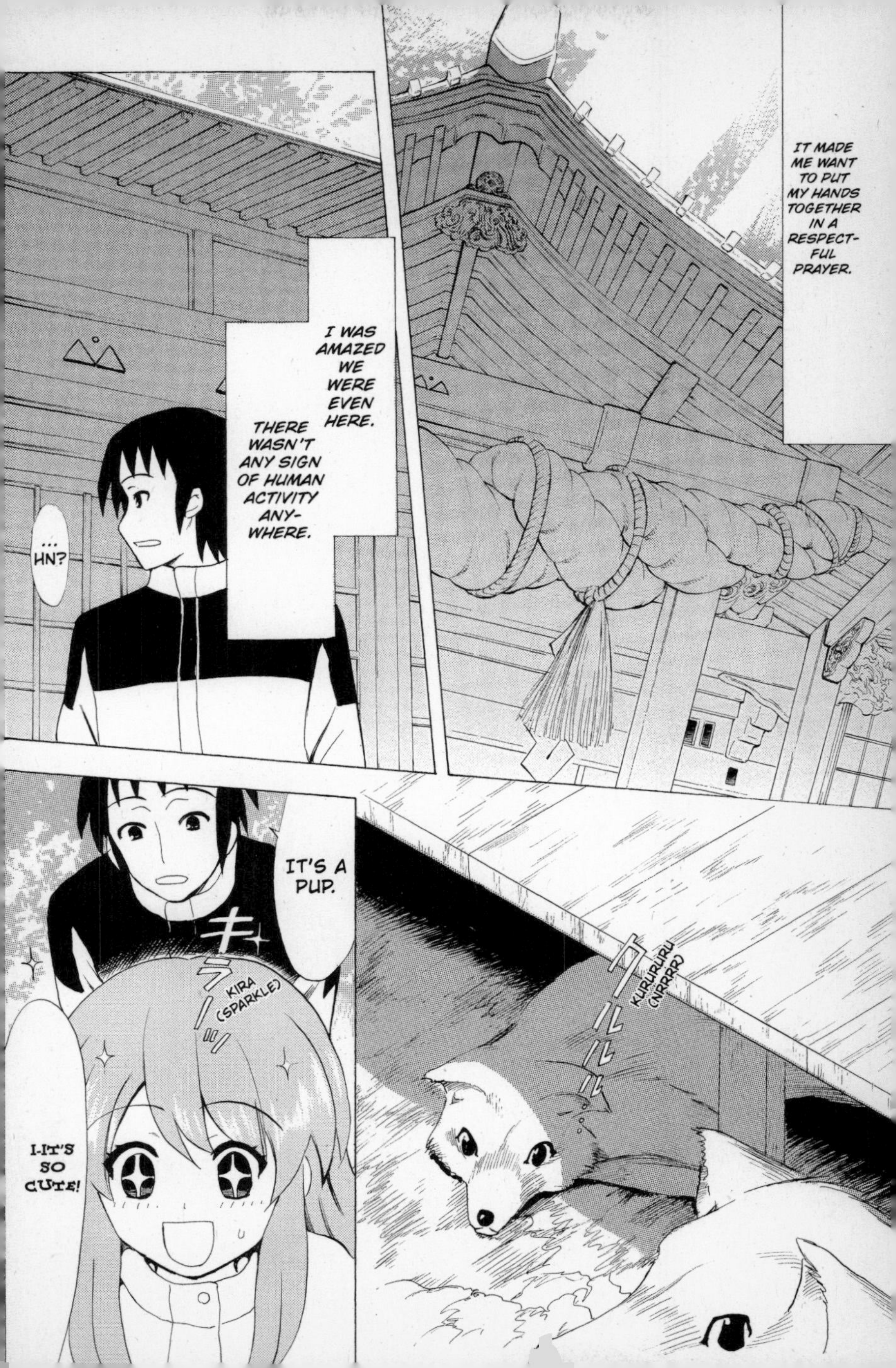
IT MADE ME WANT TO PUT MY HANDS TOGETHER IN A RESPECTFUL PRAYER.
I WAS AMAZED WE WERE EVEN HERE.
THERE WASN'T ANY SIGN OF HUMAN ACTIVITY ANYWHERE.
... HN?
KURURURU (NRRRR)
IT'S A PUP.
KIRA (SPARKLE)
I-IT'S SO CUTE!

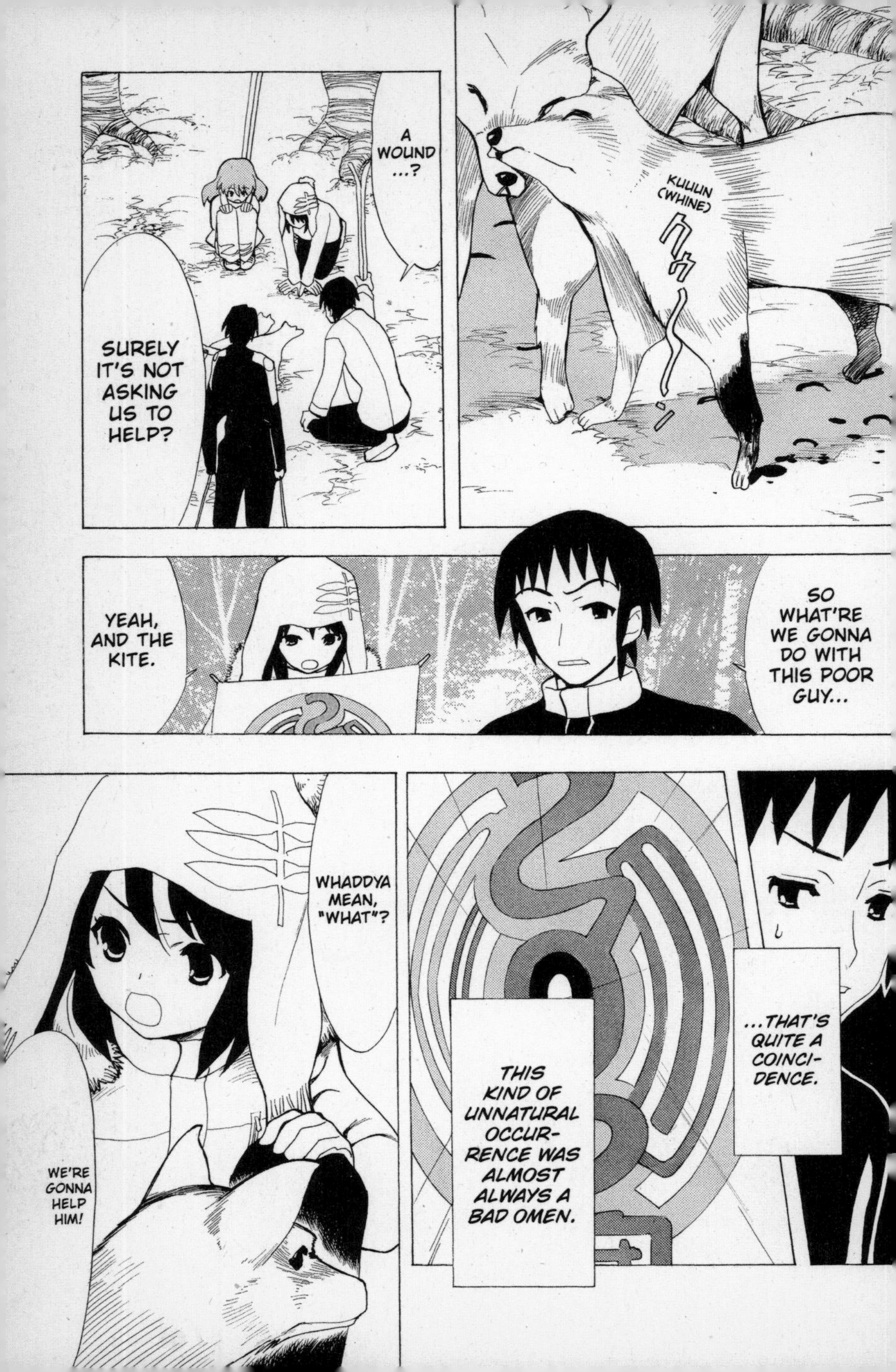
KUUUN (WHINE)
A WOUND ...?
SURELY IT'S NOT ASKING US TO HELP?
SO WHAT'RE WE GONNA DO WITH THIS POOR GUY...
YEAH, AND THE KITE.
...THAT'S QUITE A COINCI-DENCE.
THIS KIND OF UNNATURAL OCCUR-RENCE WAS ALMOST ALWAYS A BAD OMEN.
WHADDYA MEAN, "WHAT"?
WE'RE GONNA HELP HIM!

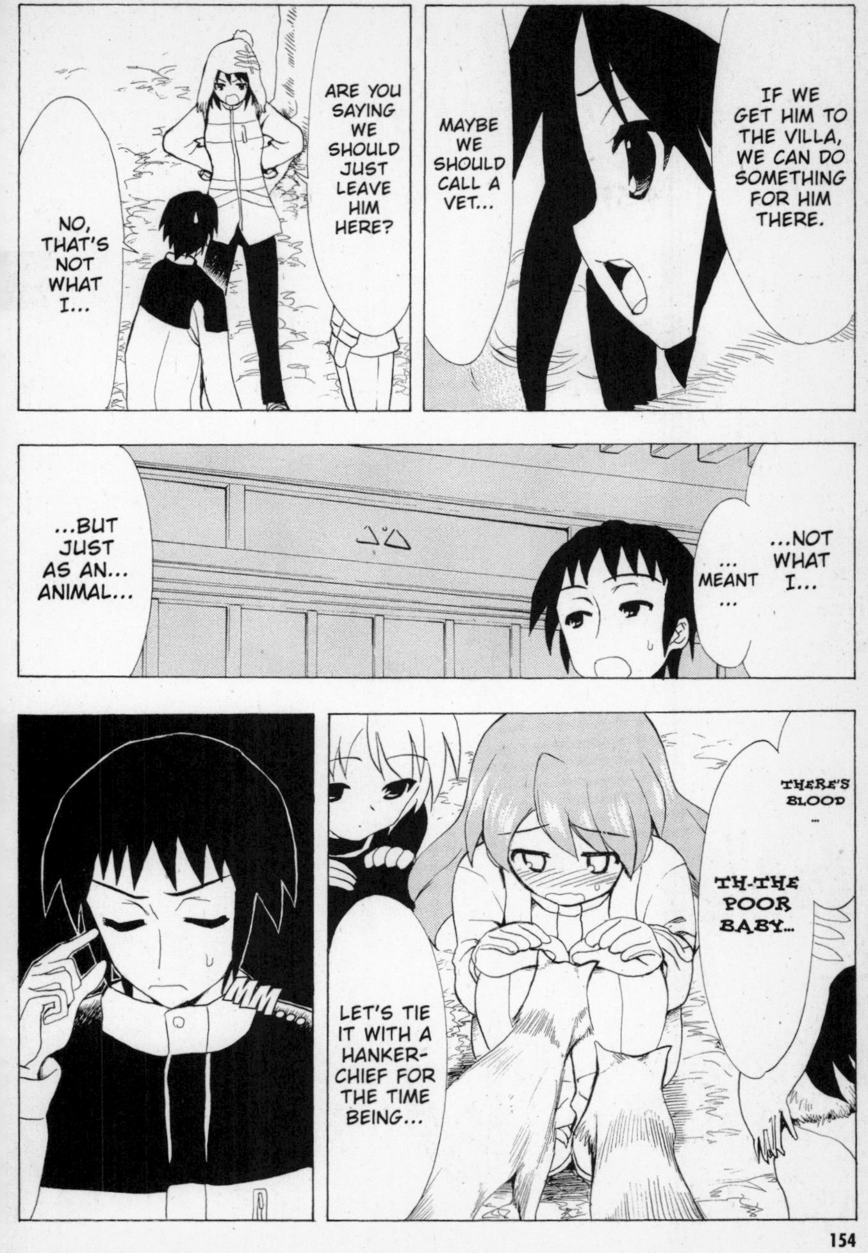
IF WE GET HIM TO THE VILLA, WE CAN DO SOMETHING FOR HIM THERE.
MAYBE WE SHOULD CALL A VET...
ARE YOU SAYING WE SHOULD JUST LEAVE HIM HERE?
NO, THAT'S NOT WHAT I...
...NOT WHAT I...
... MEANT ...
...BUT JUST AS AN... ANIMAL...
THERE'S BLOOD ...
TH-THE POOR BABY...
LET'S TIE IT WITH A HANKER-CHIEF FOR THE TIME BEING...
MM...

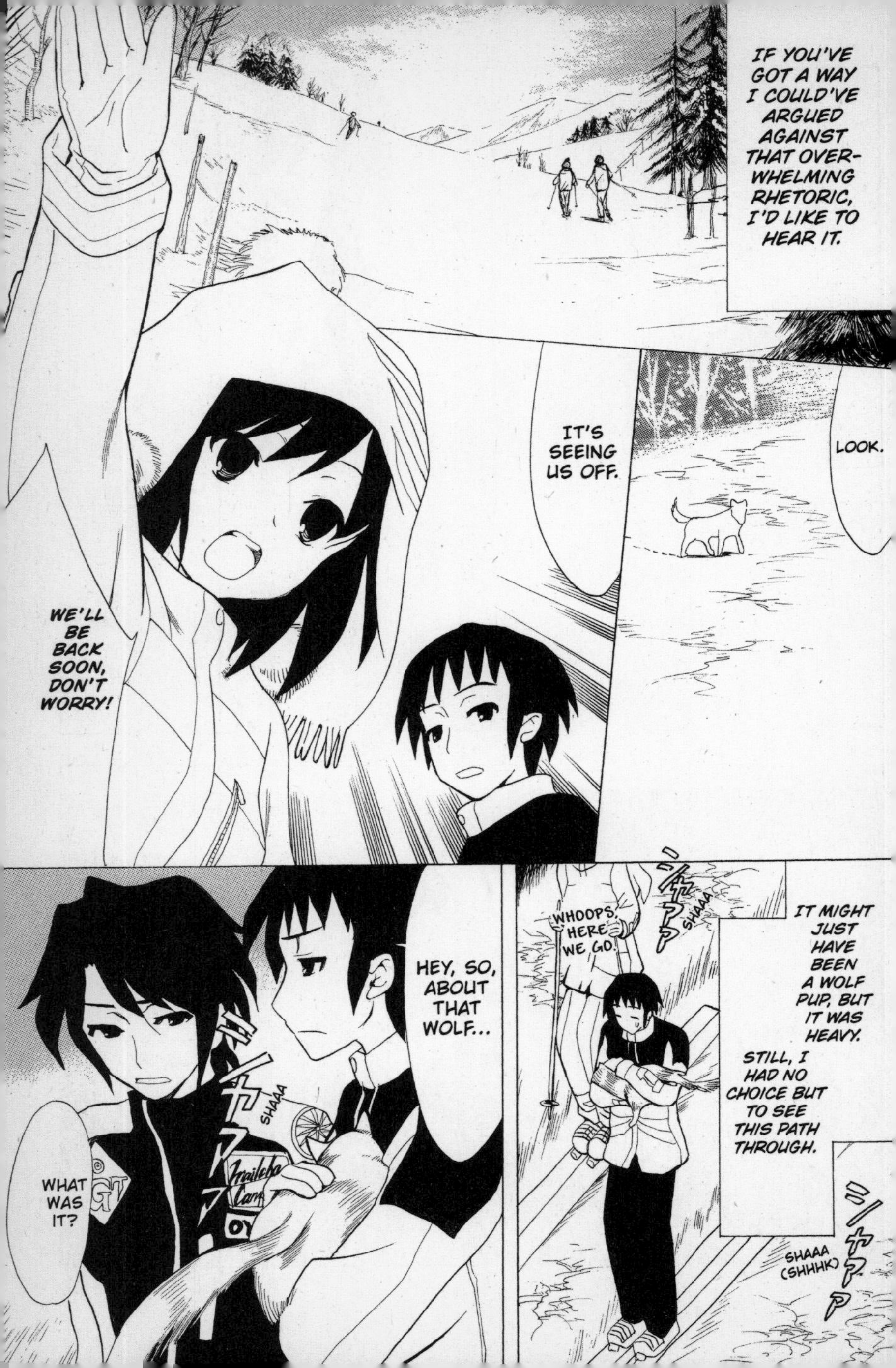
IF YOU'VE GOT A WAY I COULD'VE ARGUED AGAINST THAT OVER-WHELMING RHETORIC, I'D LIKE TO HEAR IT.
LOOK.
IT'S SEEING US OFF.
WE'LL BE BACK SOON, DON'T WORRY!
SHAAA
WHOOPS, HERE WE GO.
IT MIGHT JUST HAVE BEEN A WOLF PUP, BUT IT WAS HEAVY.
STILL, I HAD NO CHOICE BUT TO SEE THIS PATH THROUGH.
SHAAA (SHHHK)
HEY, SO, ABOUT THAT WOLF...
SHAAA
WHAT WAS IT?

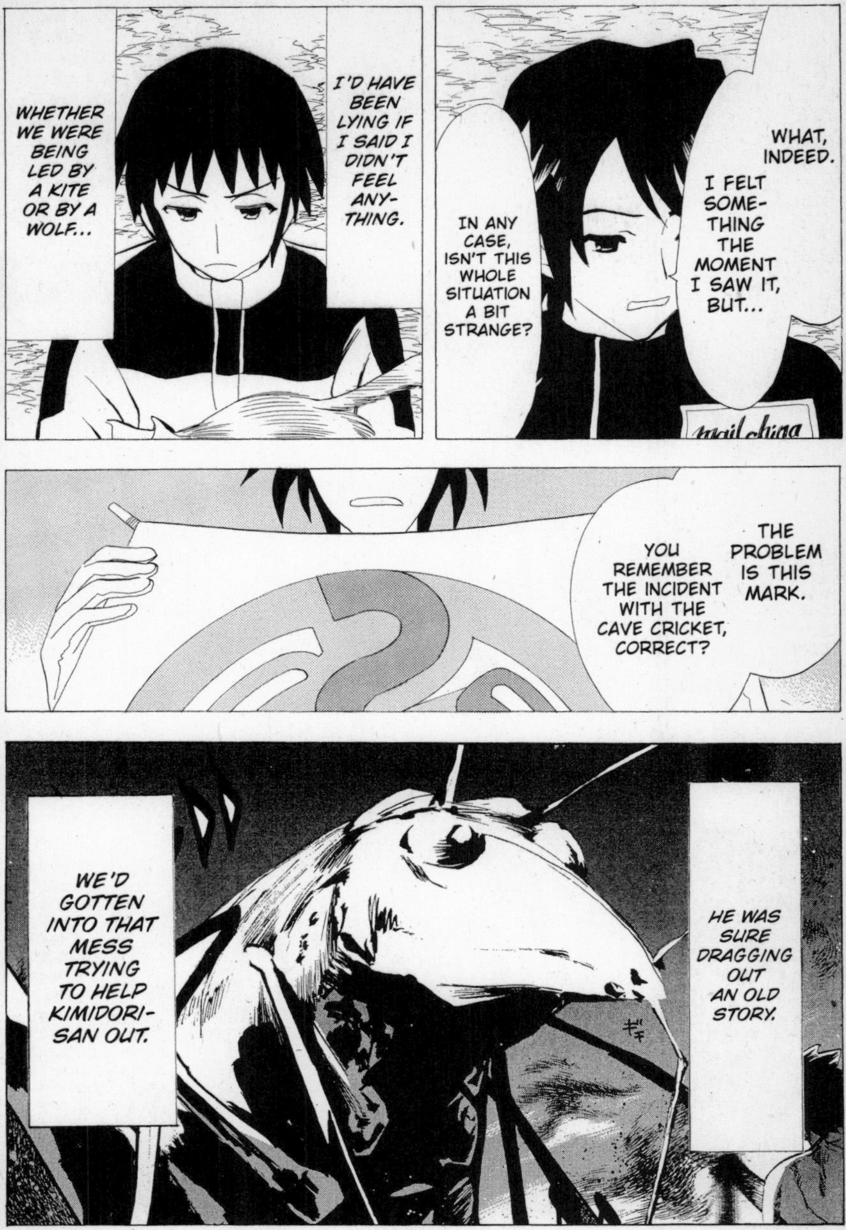
WHAT, INDEED.
I FELT SOMETHING THE MOMENT I SAW IT, BUT...
IN ANY CASE, ISN'T THIS WHOLE SITUATION A BIT STRANGE?
I'D HAVE BEEN LYING IF I SAID I DIDN'T FEEL ANYTHING.
WHETHER WE WERE BEING LED BY A KITE OR BY A WOLF...
THE PROBLEM IS THIS MARK.
YOU REMEMBER THE INCIDENT WITH THE CAVE CRICKET, CORRECT?
HE WAS SURE DRAGGING OUT AN OLD STORY.
ギチ
WE'D GOTTEN INTO THAT MESS TRYING TO HELP KIMIDORI-SAN OUT.

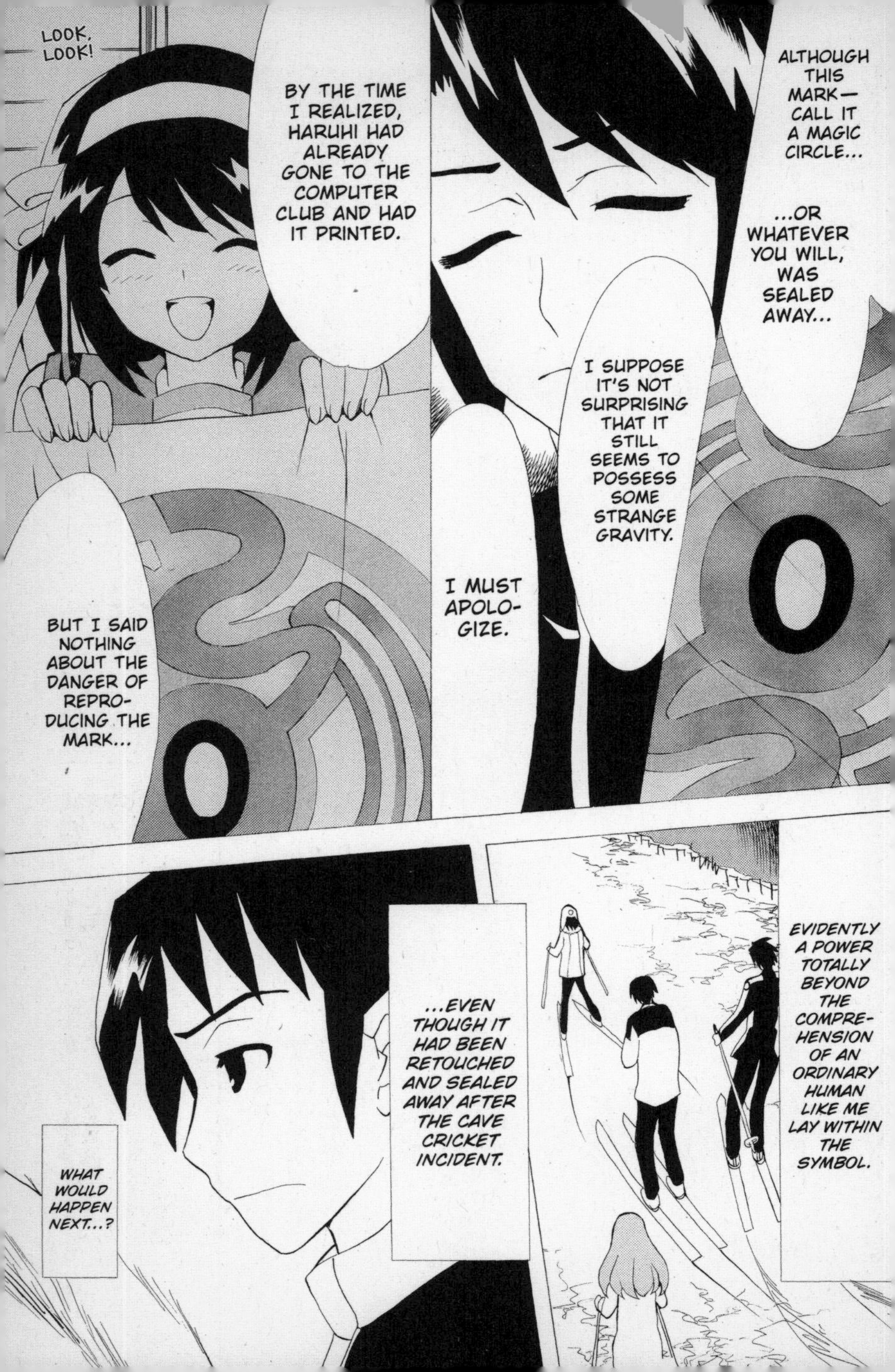
ALTHOUGH THIS MARK— CALL IT A MAGIC CIRCLE...
...OR WHATEVER YOU WILL, WAS SEALED AWAY...
I SUPPOSE IT'S NOT SURPRISING THAT IT STILL SEEMS TO POSSESS SOME STRANGE GRAVITY.
I MUST APOLO-GIZE.
BY THE TIME I REALIZED, HARUHI HAD ALREADY GONE TO THE COMPUTER CLUB AND HAD IT PRINTED.
LOOK, LOOK!
BUT I SAID NOTHING ABOUT THE DANGER OF REPRO-DUCING THE MARK...
EVIDENTLY A POWER TOTALLY BEYOND THE COMPRE-HENSION OF AN ORDINARY HUMAN LIKE ME LAY WITHIN THE SYMBOL.
...EVEN THOUGH IT HAD BEEN RETOUCHED AND SEALED AWAY AFTER THE CAVE CRICKET INCIDENT.
WHAT WOULD HAPPEN NEXT...?

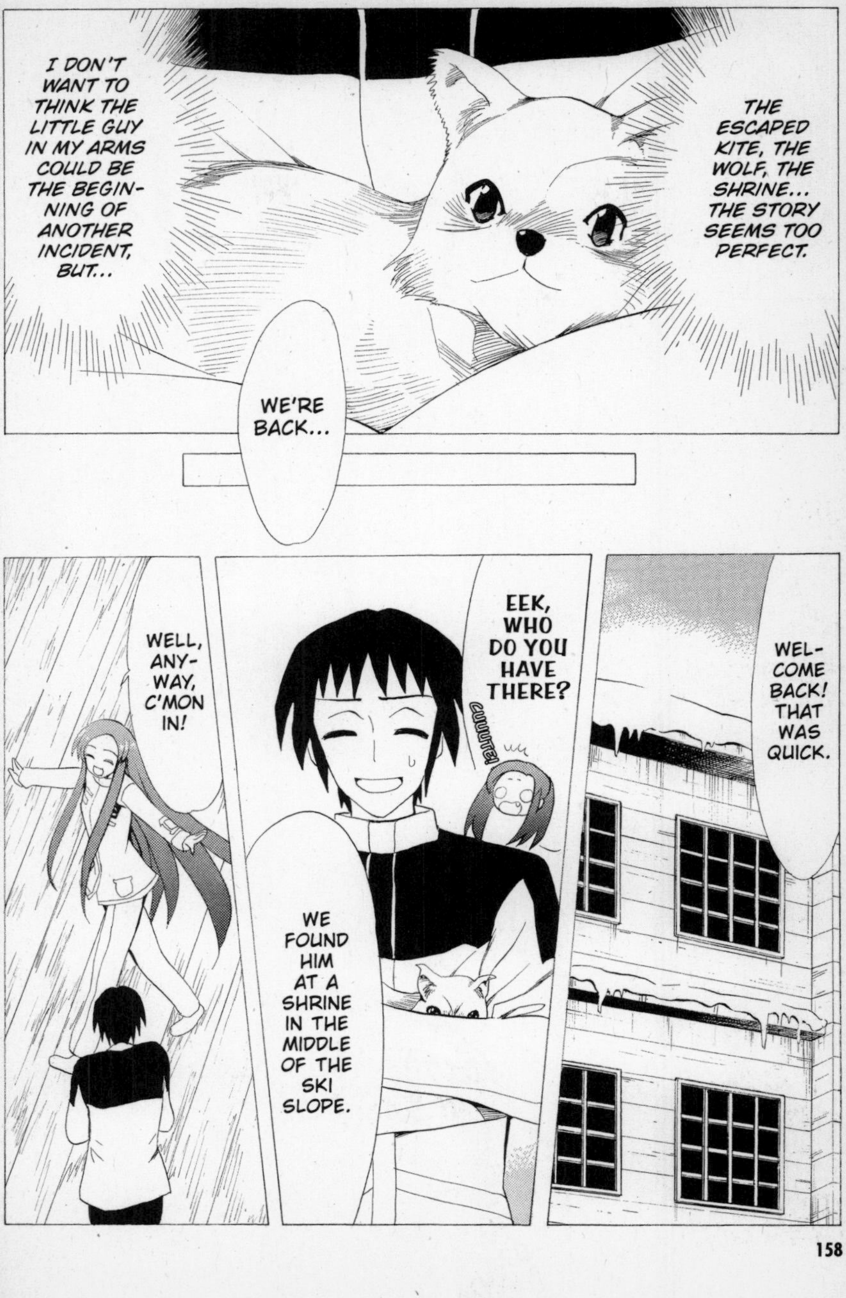
THE ESCAPED KITE, THE WOLF, THE SHRINE... THE STORY SEEMS TOO PERFECT.
I DON'T WANT TO THINK THE LITTLE GUY IN MY ARMS COULD BE THE BEGINNING OF ANOTHER INCIDENT, BUT...
WE'RE BACK...
WELCOME BACK! THAT WAS QUICK.
EEK, WHO DO YOU HAVE THERE?
CUUUTE!
WE FOUND HIM AT A SHRINE IN THE MIDDLE OF THE SKI SLOPE.
WELL, ANYWAY, C'MON IN!

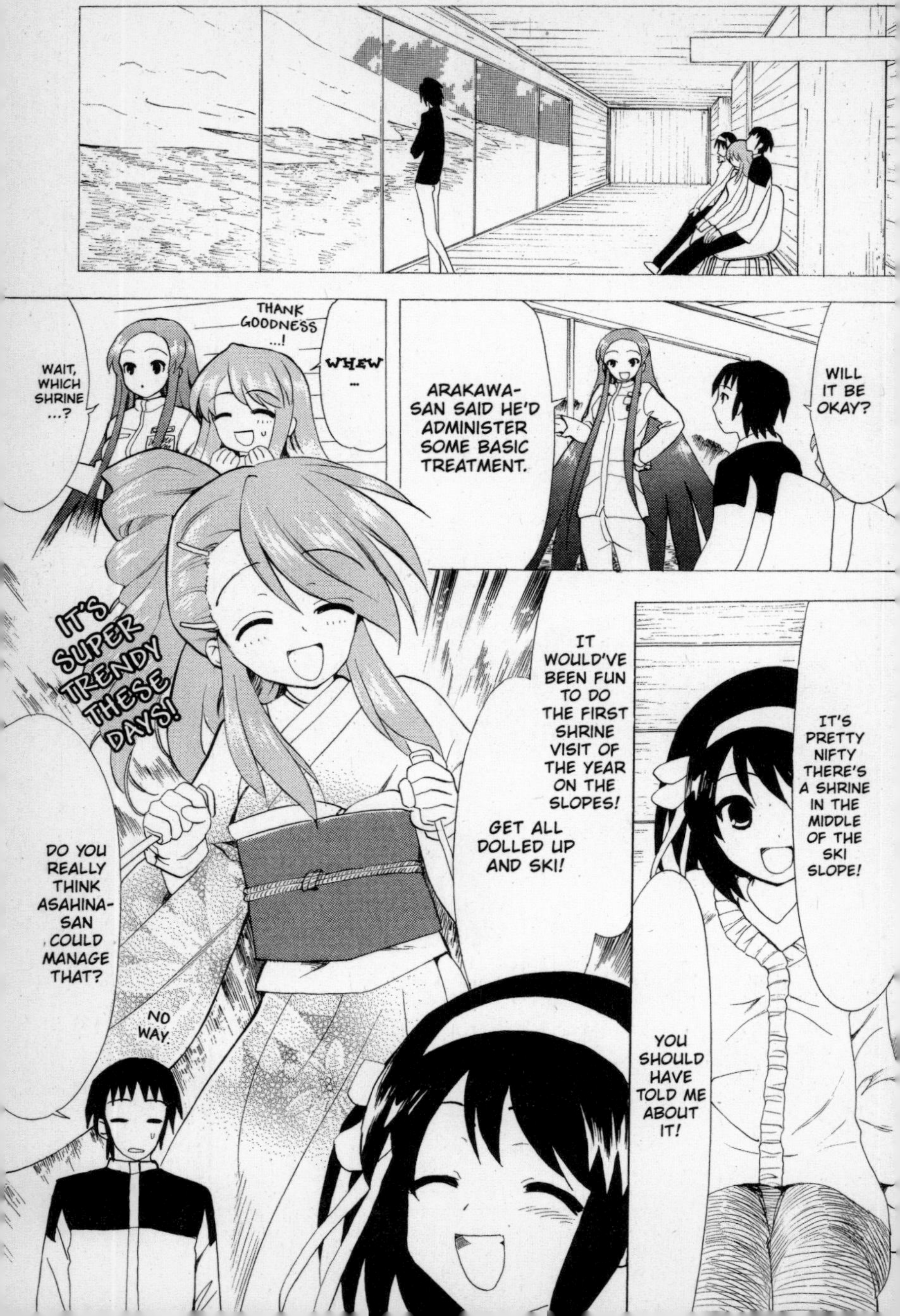
WILL IT BE OKAY?
ARAKAWA-SAN SAID HE'D ADMINISTER SOME BASIC TREATMENT.
THANK GOODNESS ...!
WHEW ...
WAIT, WHICH SHRINE ...?
IT'S PRETTY NIFTY THERE'S A SHRINE IN THE MIDDLE OF THE SKI SLOPE!
IT WOULD'VE BEEN FUN TO DO THE FIRST SHRINE VISIT OF THE YEAR ON THE SLOPES!
YOU SHOULD HAVE TOLD ME ABOUT IT!
GET ALL DOLLED UP AND SKI!
IT'S SUPER TRENDY THESE DAYS!
DO YOU REALLY THINK ASAHINA-SAN COULD MANAGE THAT?
NO WAY.

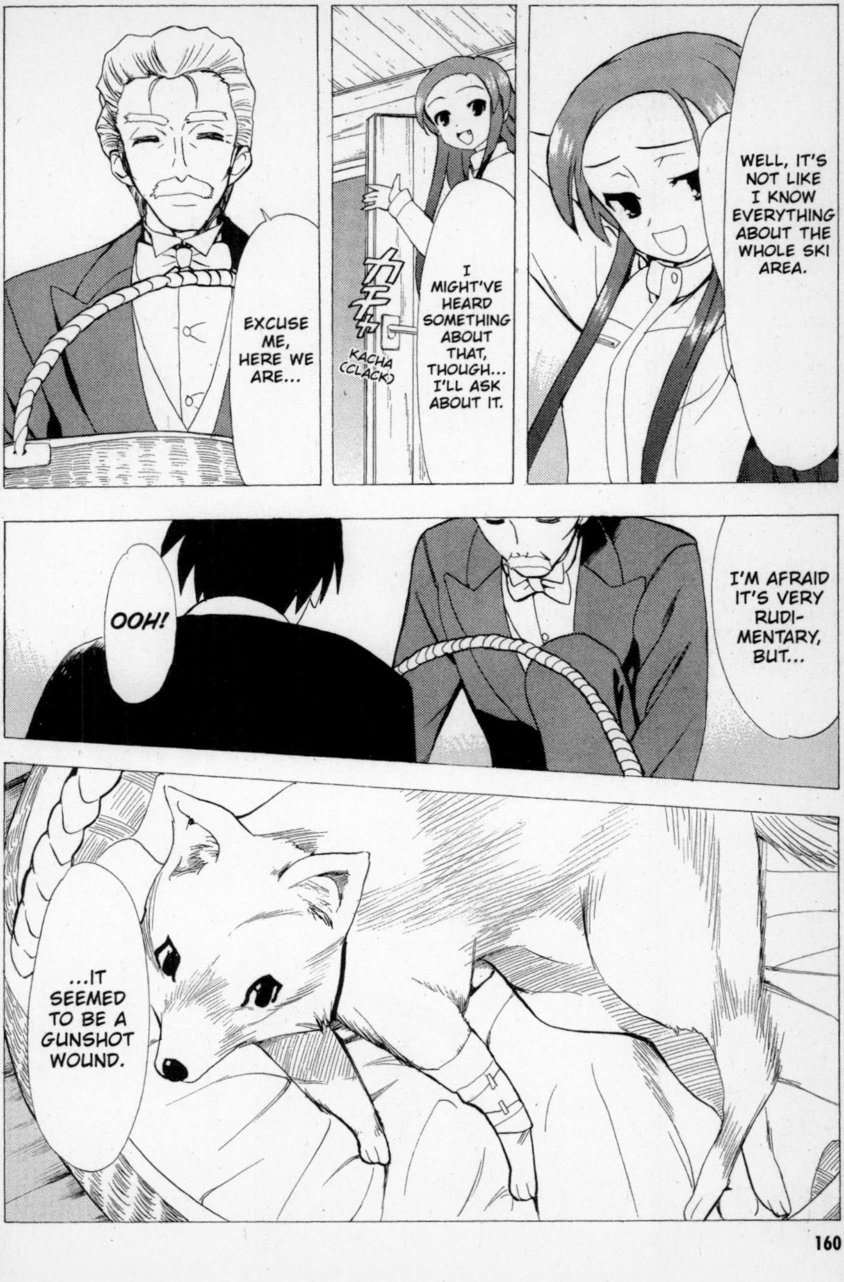

WELL, IT'S NOT LIKE I KNOW EVERYTHING ABOUT THE WHOLE SKI AREA.
I MIGHT'VE HEARD SOMETHING ABOUT THAT, THOUGH... I'LL ASK ABOUT IT.
カチャ
KACHA (CLACK)
EXCUSE ME, HERE WE ARE...
I'M AFRAID IT'S VERY RUDIMENTARY, BUT...
OOH!
...IT SEEMED TO BE A GUNSHOT WOUND.

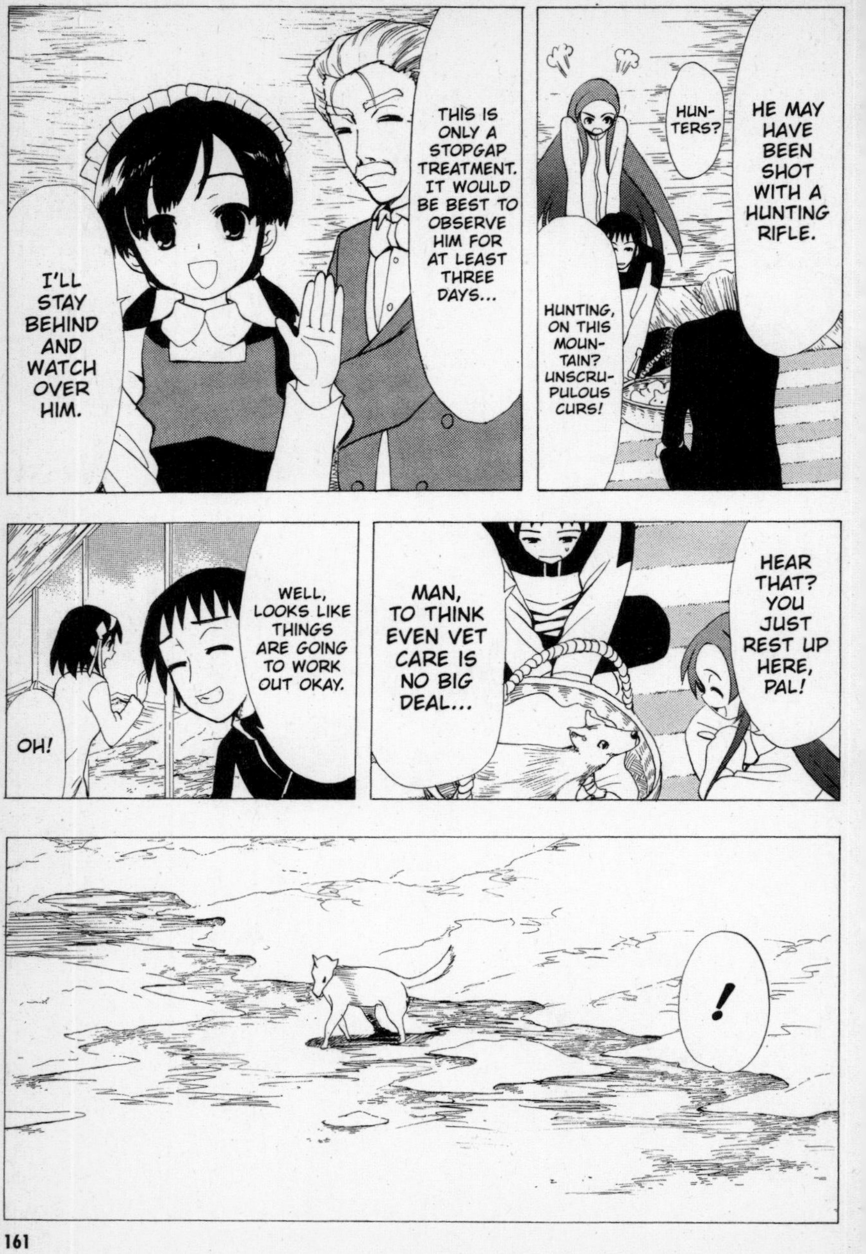
HE MAY HAVE BEEN SHOT WITH A HUNTING RIFLE.
HUNTERS?
HUNTING, ON THIS MOUNTAIN? UNSCRUPULOUS CURS!
THIS IS ONLY A STOPGAP TREATMENT. IT WOULD BE BEST TO OBSERVE HIM FOR AT LEAST THREE DAYS...
I'LL STAY BEHIND AND WATCH OVER HIM.
HEAR THAT? YOU JUST REST UP HERE, PAL!
MAN, TO THINK EVEN VET CARE IS NO BIG DEAL...
WELL, LOOKS LIKE THINGS ARE GOING TO WORK OUT OKAY.
OH!
!

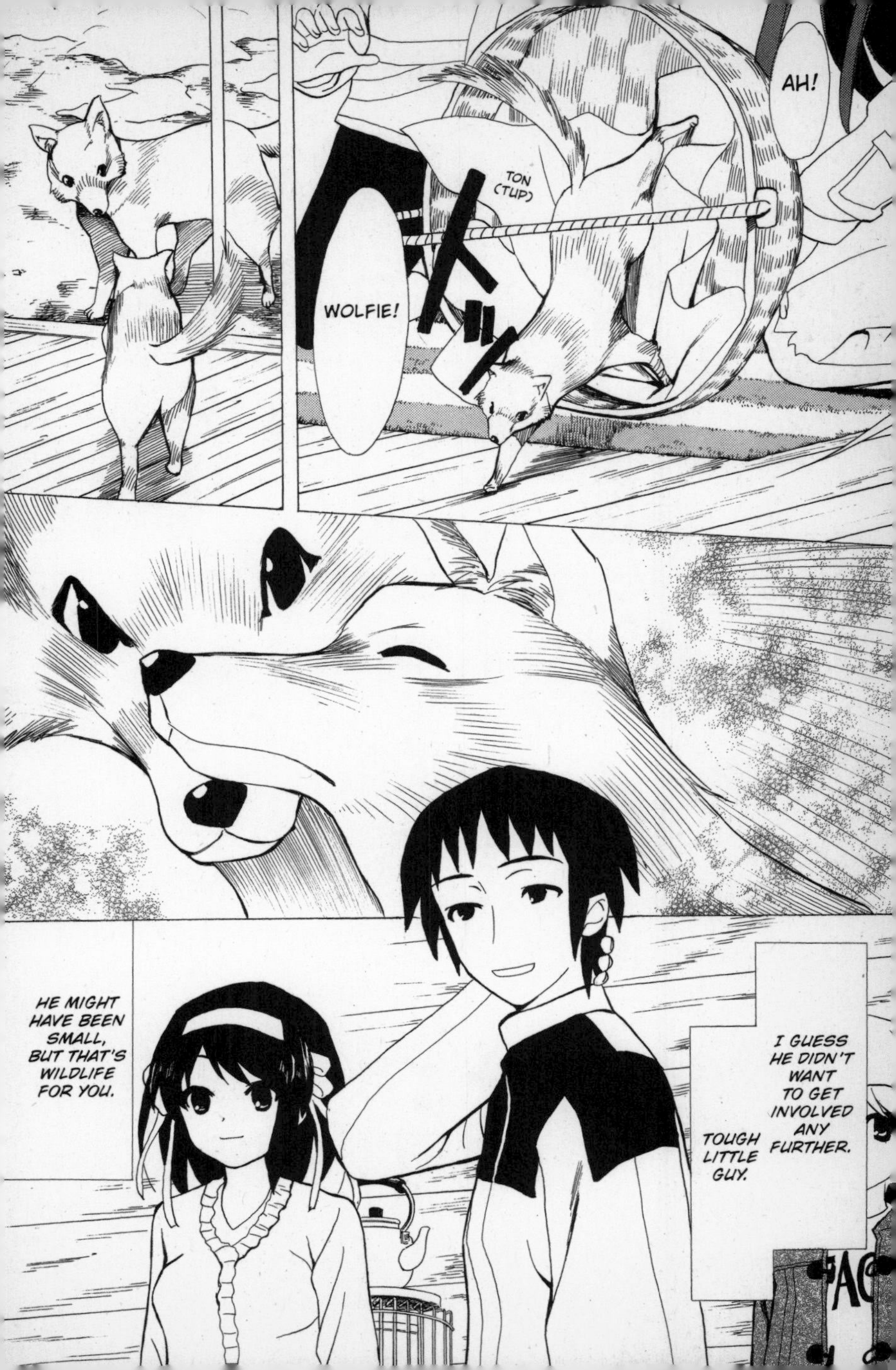
AH!
TON (TUP)
WOLFIE!
I GUESS HE DIDN'T WANT TO GET INVOLVED ANY FURTHER.
TOUGH LITTLE GUY.
HE MIGHT HAVE BEEN SMALL, BUT THAT'S WILDLIFE FOR YOU.

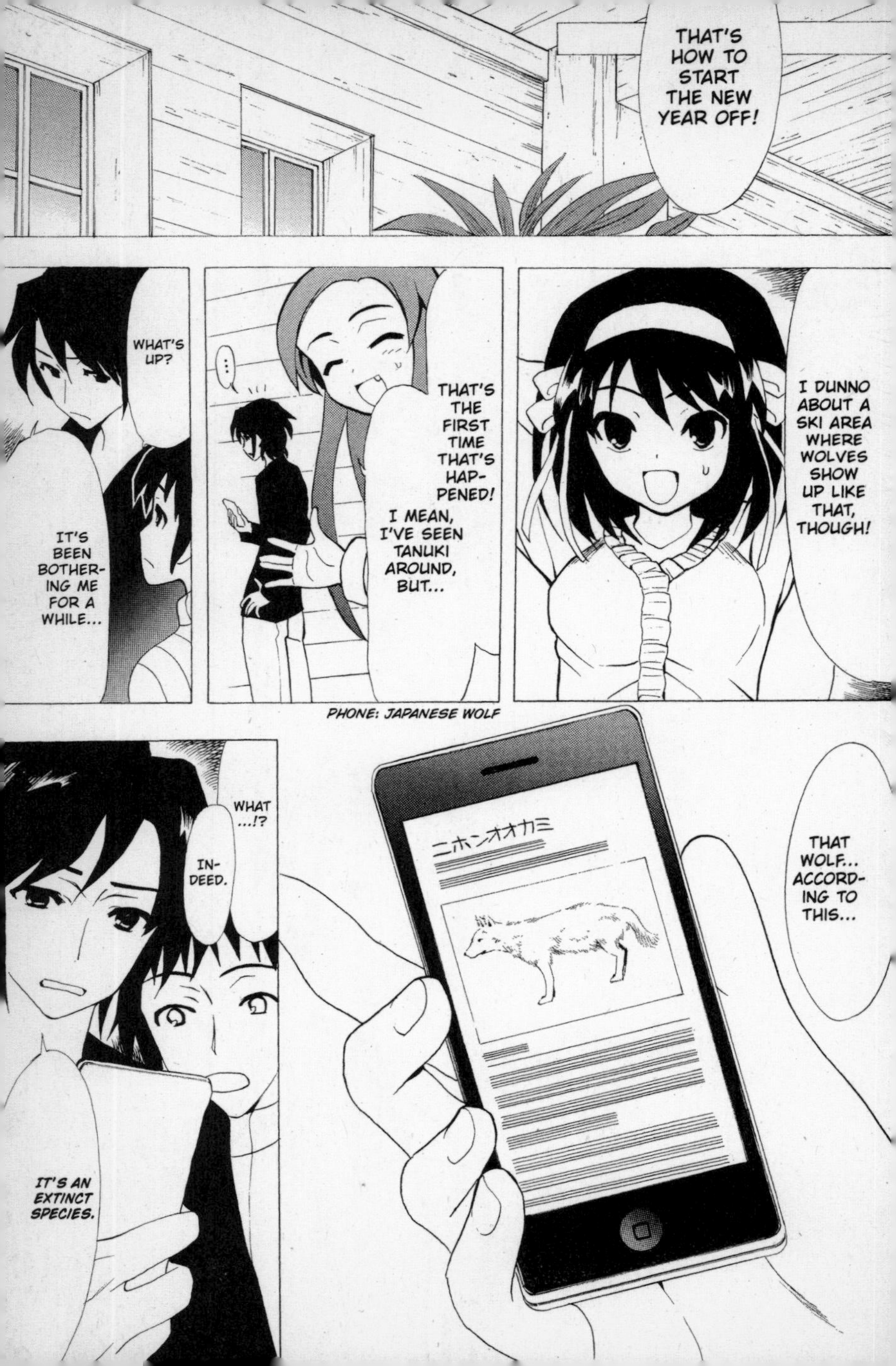
THAT'S HOW TO START THE NEW YEAR OFF!
I DUNNO ABOUT A SKI AREA WHERE WOLVES SHOW UP LIKE THAT, THOUGH!
THAT'S THE FIRST TIME THAT'S HAP-PENED!
I MEAN, I'VE SEEN TANUKI AROUND, BUT...
...
WHAT'S UP?
IT'S BEEN BOTHER-ING ME FOR A WHILE...
PHONE: JAPANESE WOLF
THAT WOLF... ACCORD-ING TO THIS...
ニホンオオカミ
WHAT ...!?
IN-DEED.
IT'S AN EXTINCT SPECIES.

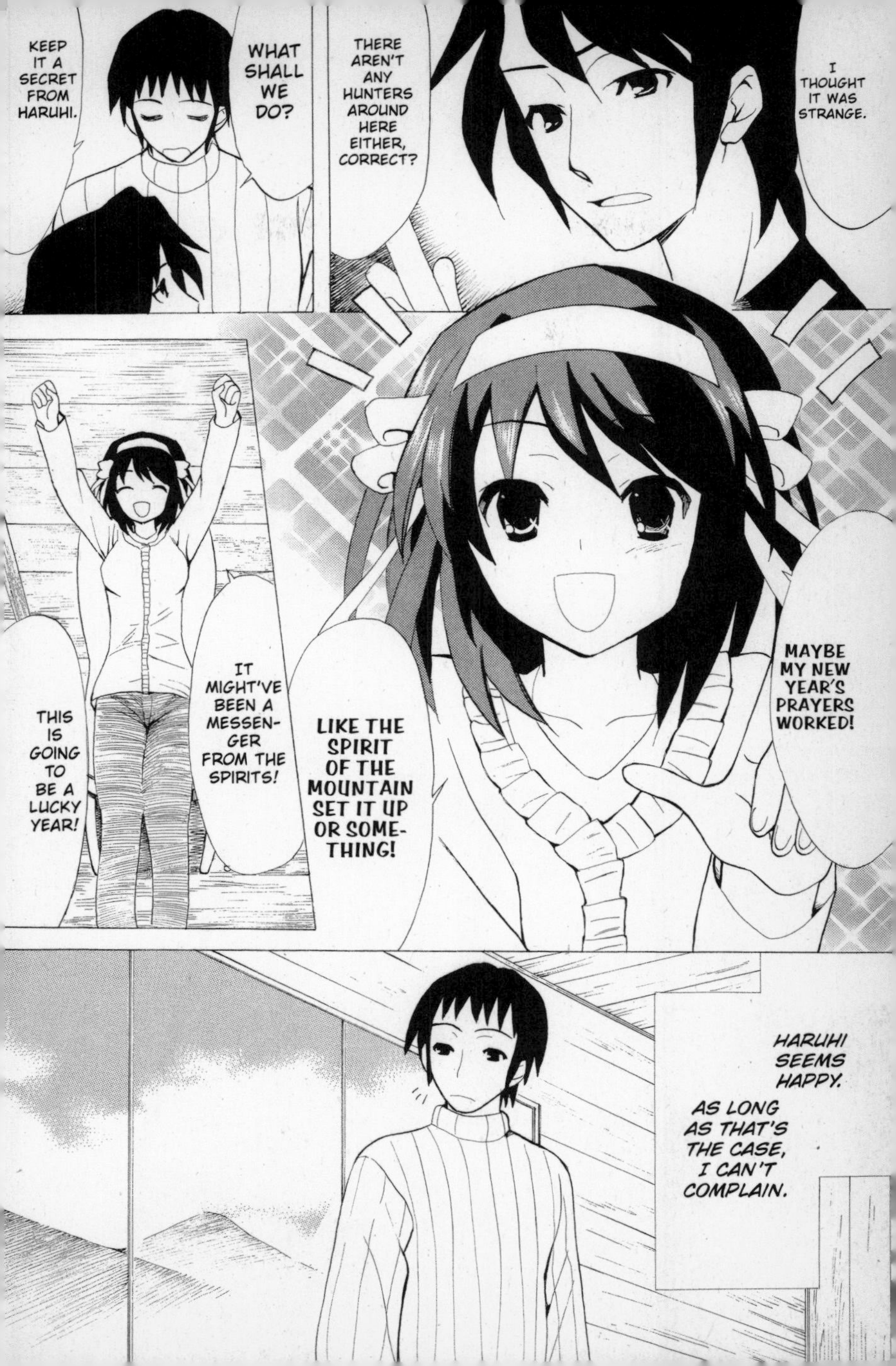
I THOUGHT IT WAS STRANGE.
THERE AREN'T ANY HUNTERS AROUND HERE EITHER, CORRECT?
WHAT SHALL WE DO?
KEEP IT A SECRET FROM HARUHI.
MAYBE MY NEW YEAR'S PRAYERS WORKED!
LIKE THE SPIRIT OF THE MOUNTAIN SET IT UP OR SOME-THING!
IT MIGHT'VE BEEN A MESSEN-GER FROM THE SPIRITS!
THIS IS GOING TO BE A LUCKY YEAR!
HARUHI SEEMS HAPPY.
AS LONG AS THAT'S THE CASE, I CAN'T COMPLAIN.

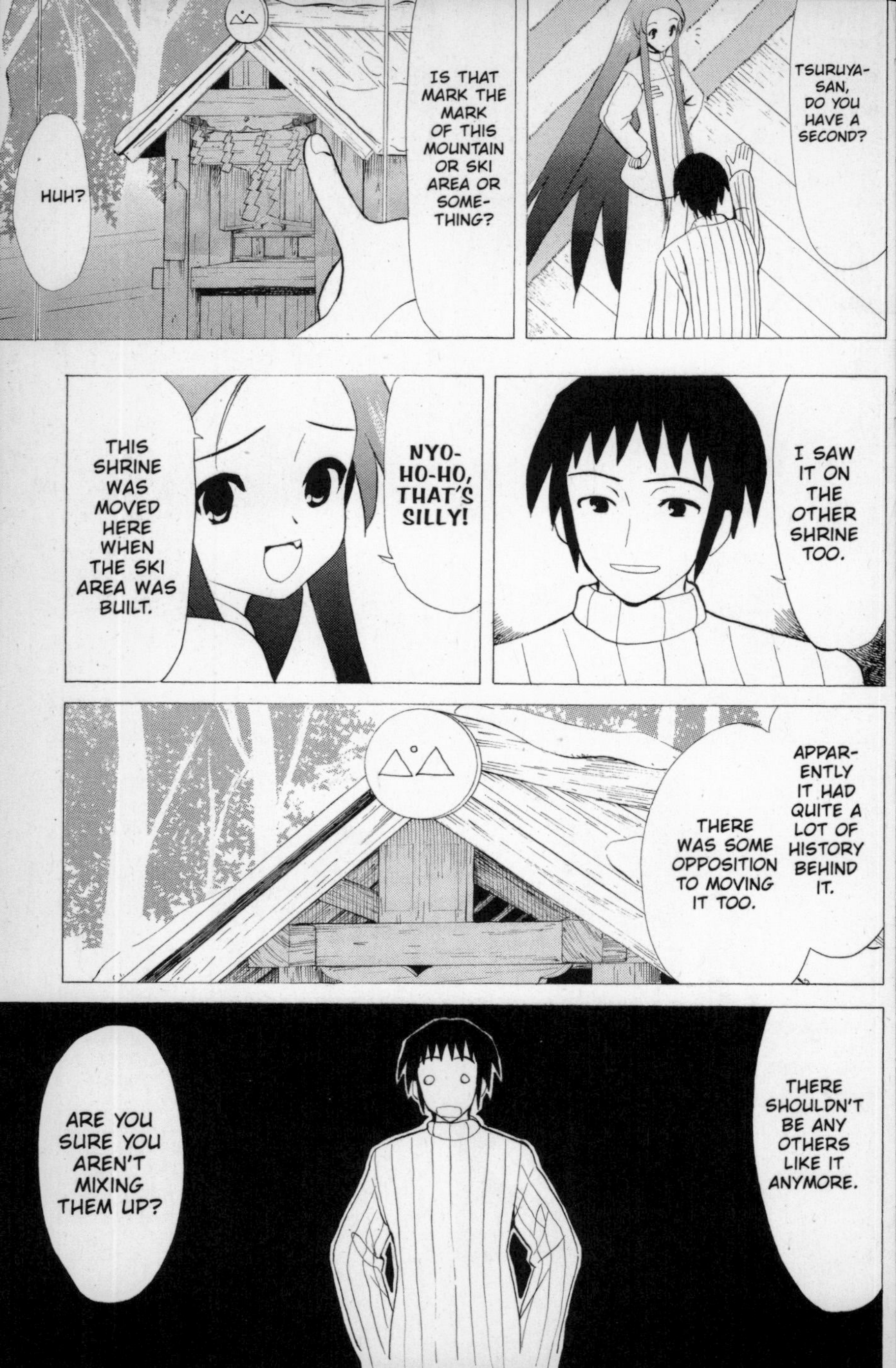
TSURUYA-SAN, DO YOU HAVE A SECOND?
IS THAT MARK THE MARK OF THIS MOUNTAIN OR SKI AREA OR SOME-THING?
HUH?
I SAW IT ON THE OTHER SHRINE TOO.
NYO-HO-HO, THAT'S SILLY!
THIS SHRINE WAS MOVED HERE WHEN THE SKI AREA WAS BUILT.
APPAR-ENTLY IT HAD QUITE A LOT OF HISTORY BEHIND IT.
THERE WAS SOME OPPOSITION TO MOVING IT TOO.
THERE SHOULDN'T BE ANY OTHERS LIKE IT ANYMORE.
ARE YOU SURE YOU AREN'T MIXING THEM UP?

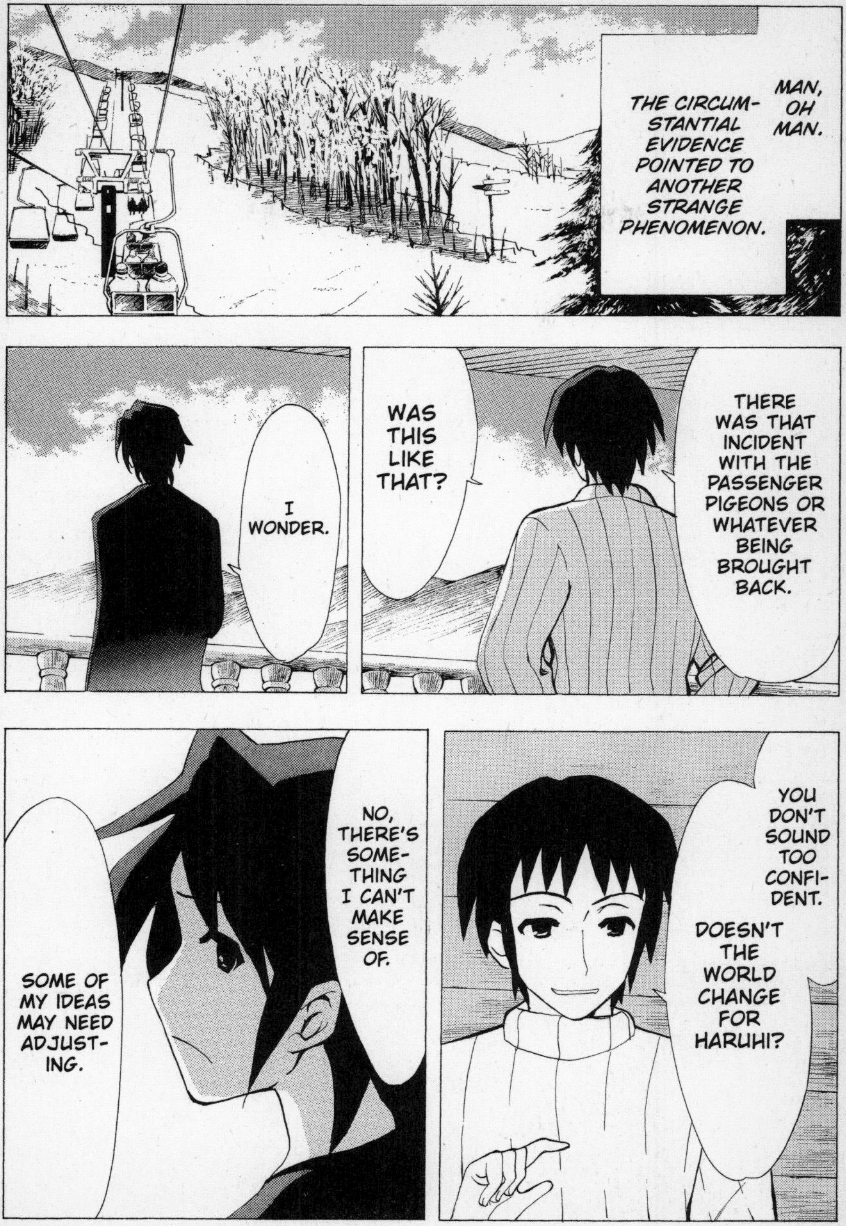
MAN, OH MAN.
THE CIRCUMSTANTIAL EVIDENCE POINTED TO ANOTHER STRANGE PHENOMENON.
THERE WAS THAT INCIDENT WITH THE PASSENGER PIGEONS OR WHATEVER BEING BROUGHT BACK.
WAS THIS LIKE THAT?
I WONDER.
YOU DON'T SOUND TOO CONFIDENT.
DOESN'T THE WORLD CHANGE FOR HARUHI?
NO, THERE'S SOMETHING I CAN'T MAKE SENSE OF.
SOME OF MY IDEAS MAY NEED ADJUSTING.

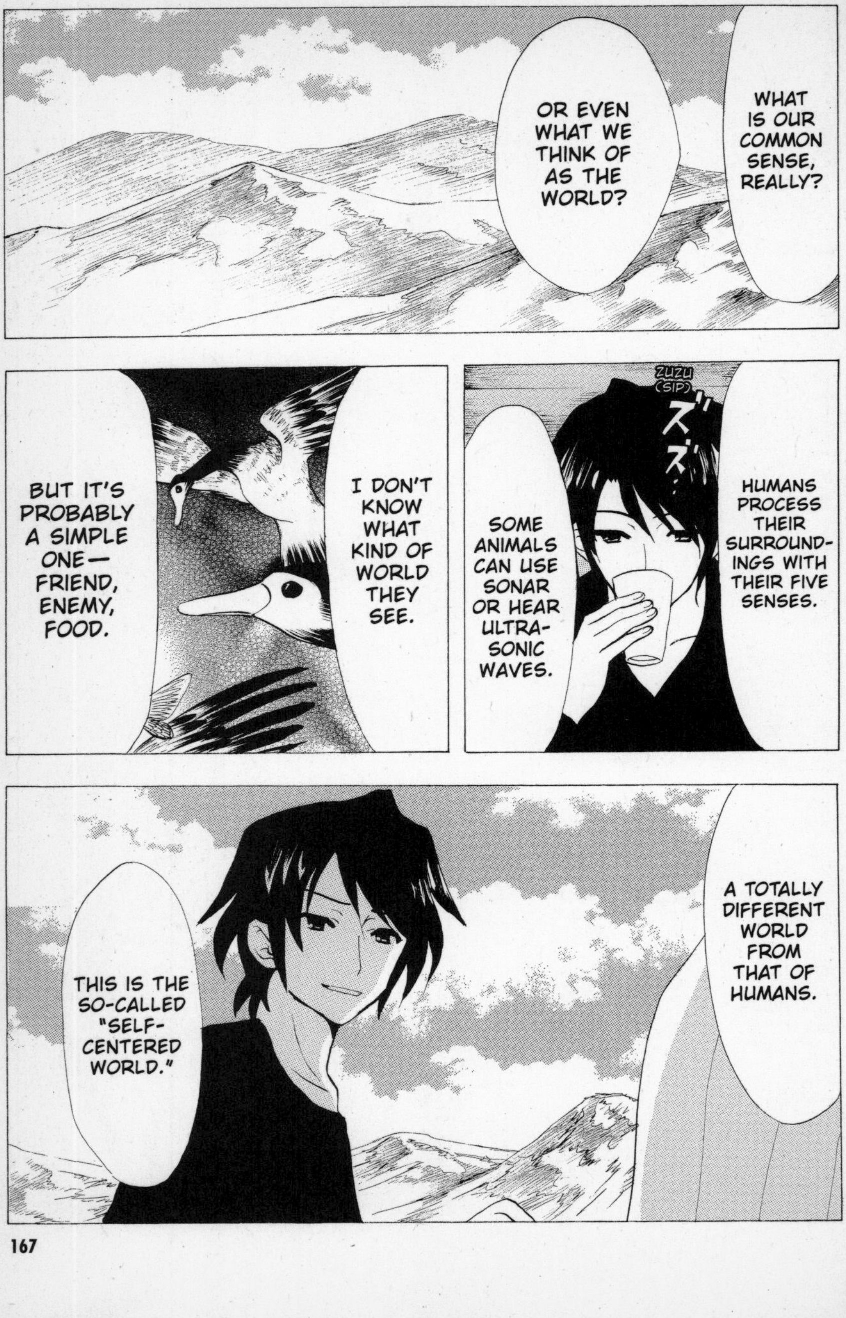
WHAT IS OUR COMMON SENSE, REALLY?
OR EVEN WHAT WE THINK OF AS THE WORLD?
HUMANS PROCESS THEIR SURROUND-INGS WITH THEIR FIVE SENSES.
ZUZU (SIP)
ズズ
SOME ANIMALS CAN USE SONAR OR HEAR ULTRA-SONIC WAVES.
I DON'T KNOW WHAT KIND OF WORLD THEY SEE.
BUT IT'S PROBABLY A SIMPLE ONE—FRIEND, ENEMY, FOOD.
A TOTALLY DIFFERENT WORLD FROM THAT OF HUMANS.
THIS IS THE SO-CALLED "SELF-CENTERED WORLD."

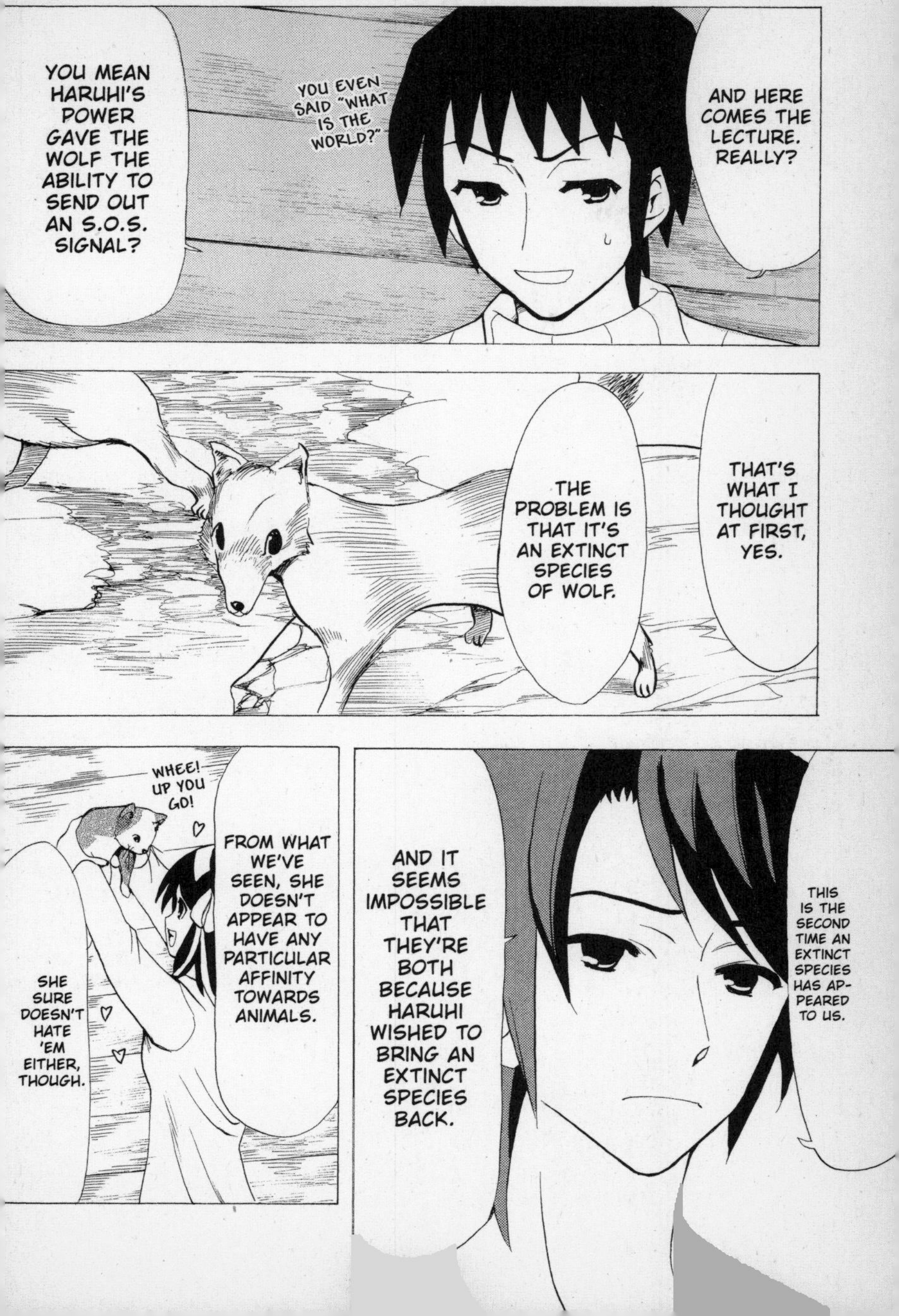
AND HERE COMES THE LECTURE. REALLY?
YOU EVEN SAID "WHAT IS THE WORLD?"
YOU MEAN HARUHI'S POWER GAVE THE WOLF THE ABILITY TO SEND OUT AN S.O.S. SIGNAL?
THAT'S WHAT I THOUGHT AT FIRST, YES.
THE PROBLEM IS THAT IT'S AN EXTINCT SPECIES OF WOLF.
THIS IS THE SECOND TIME AN EXTINCT SPECIES HAS AP-PEARED TO US.
AND IT SEEMS IMPOSSIBLE THAT THEY'RE BOTH BECAUSE HARUHI WISHED TO BRING AN EXTINCT SPECIES BACK.
FROM WHAT WE'VE SEEN, SHE DOESN'T APPEAR TO HAVE ANY PARTICULAR AFFINITY TOWARDS ANIMALS.
WHEE! UP YOU GO!
SHE SURE DOESN'T HATE 'EM EITHER, THOUGH.

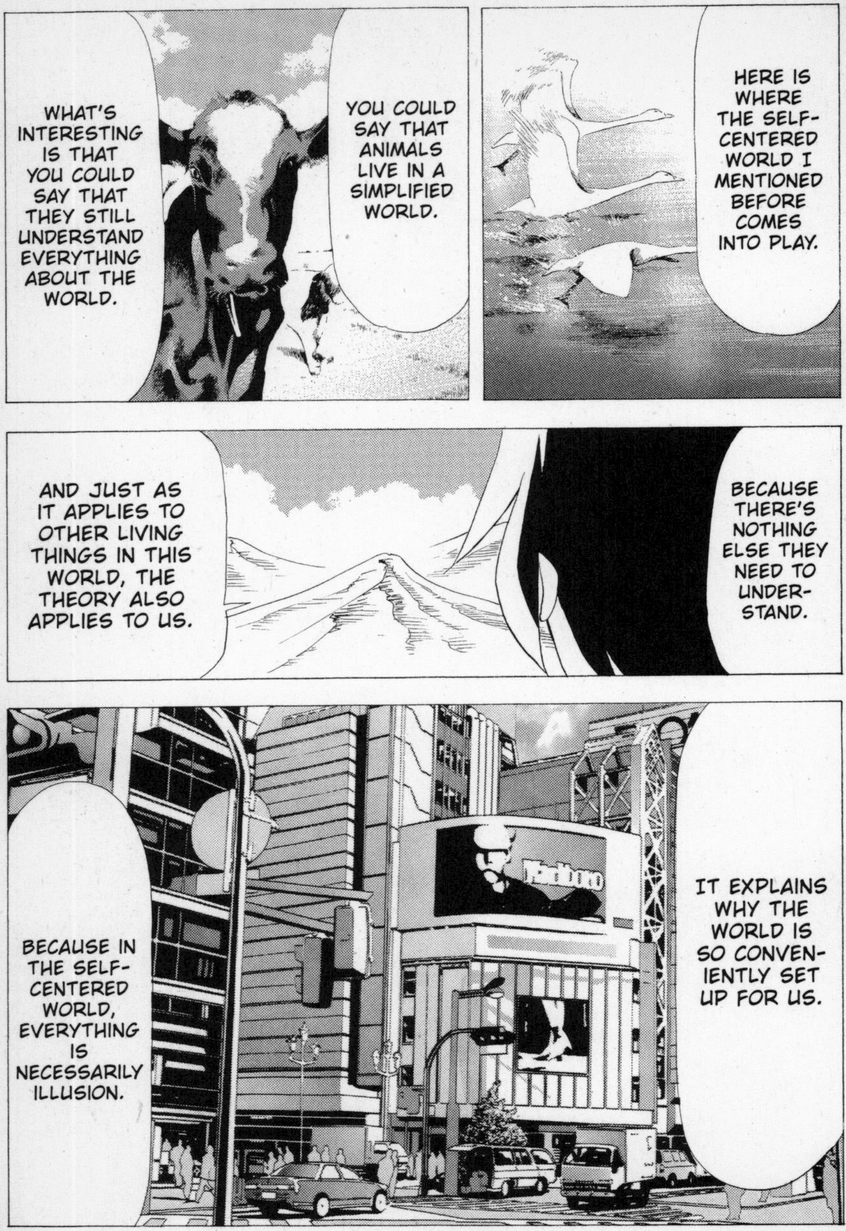
HERE IS WHERE THE SELF-CENTERED WORLD I MENTIONED BEFORE COMES INTO PLAY.
YOU COULD SAY THAT ANIMALS LIVE IN A SIMPLIFIED WORLD.
WHAT'S INTERESTING IS THAT YOU COULD SAY THAT THEY STILL UNDERSTAND EVERYTHING ABOUT THE WORLD.
BECAUSE THERE'S NOTHING ELSE THEY NEED TO UNDER-STAND.
AND JUST AS IT APPLIES TO OTHER LIVING THINGS IN THIS WORLD, THE THEORY ALSO APPLIES TO US.
IT EXPLAINS WHY THE WORLD IS SO CONVEN-IENTLY SET UP FOR US.
BECAUSE IN THE SELF-CENTERED WORLD, EVERYTHING IS NECESSARILY ILLUSION.

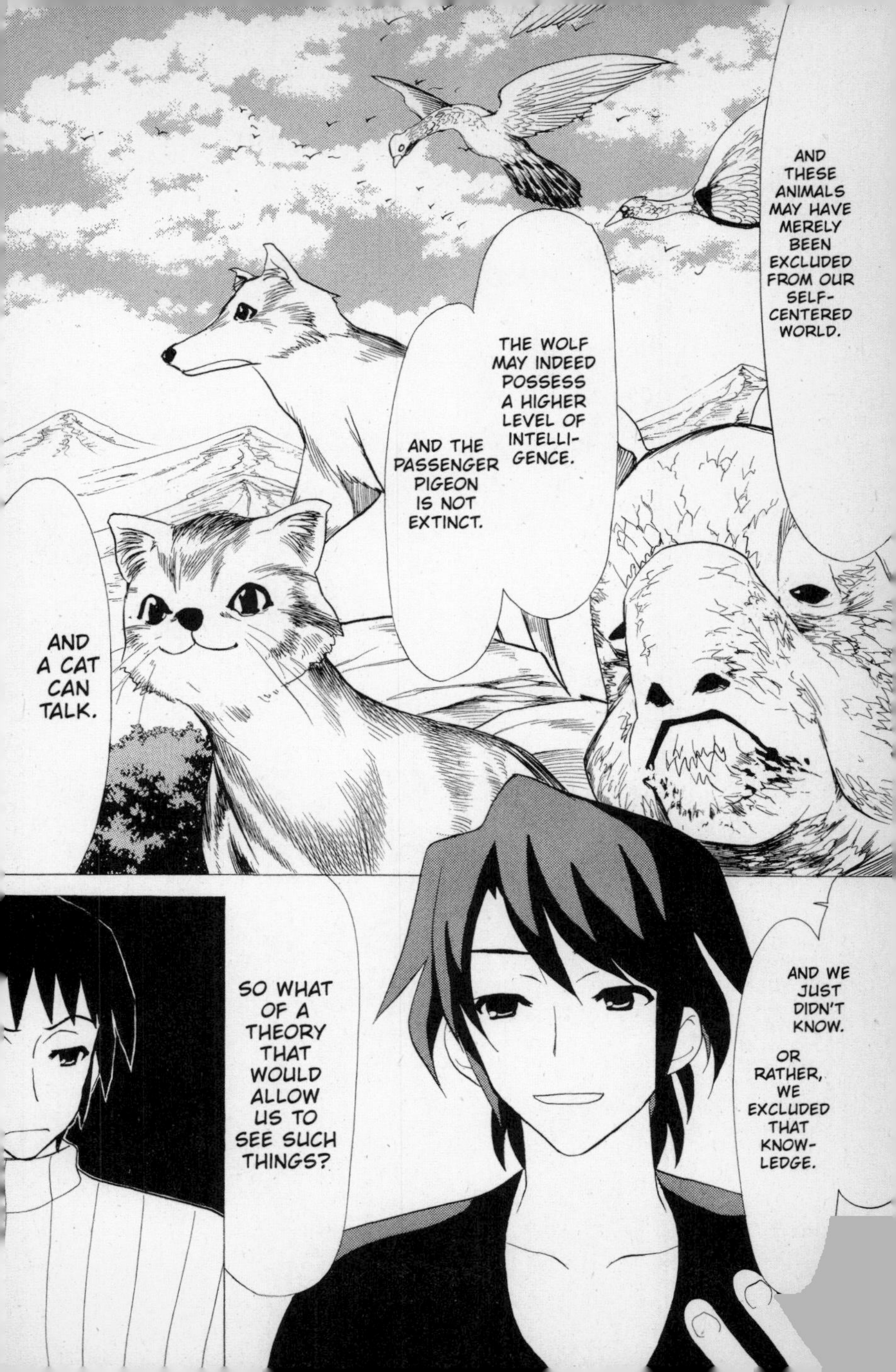
AND THESE ANIMALS MAY HAVE MERELY BEEN EXCLUDED FROM OUR SELF-CENTERED WORLD.
THE WOLF MAY INDEED POSSESS A HIGHER LEVEL OF INTELLIGENCE.
AND THE PASSENGER PIGEON IS NOT EXTINCT.
AND A CAT CAN TALK.
AND WE JUST DIDN'T KNOW.
OR RATHER, WE EXCLUDED THAT KNOWLEDGE.
SO WHAT OF A THEORY THAT WOULD ALLOW US TO SEE SUCH THINGS?

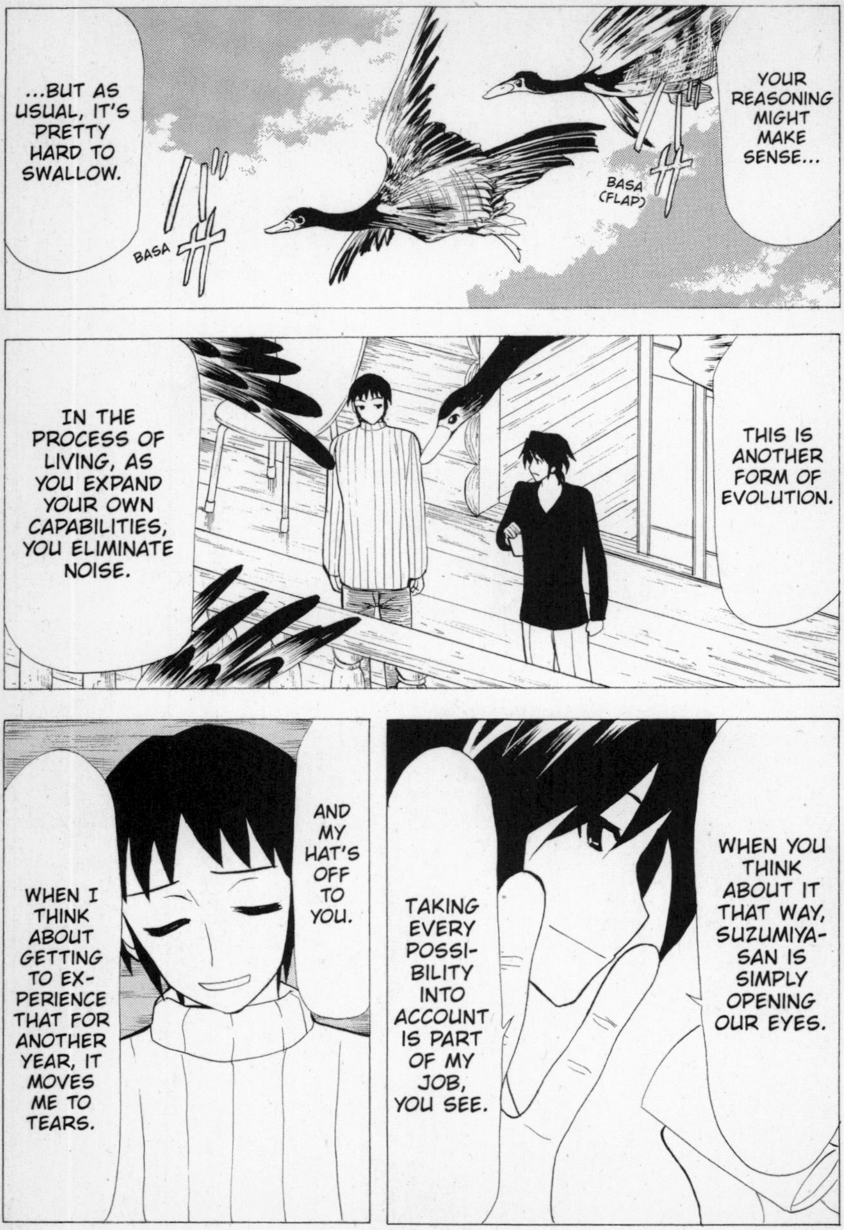
YOUR REASONING MIGHT MAKE SENSE...
BASA (FLAP)
BASA
...BUT AS USUAL, IT'S PRETTY HARD TO SWALLOW.
THIS IS ANOTHER FORM OF EVOLUTION.
IN THE PROCESS OF LIVING, AS YOU EXPAND YOUR OWN CAPABILITIES, YOU ELIMINATE NOISE.
WHEN YOU THINK ABOUT IT THAT WAY, SUZUMIYA-SAN IS SIMPLY OPENING OUR EYES.
TAKING EVERY POSSIBILITY INTO ACCOUNT IS PART OF MY JOB, YOU SEE.
AND MY HAT'S OFF TO YOU.
WHEN I THINK ABOUT GETTING TO EXPERIENCE THAT FOR ANOTHER YEAR, IT MOVES ME TO TEARS.

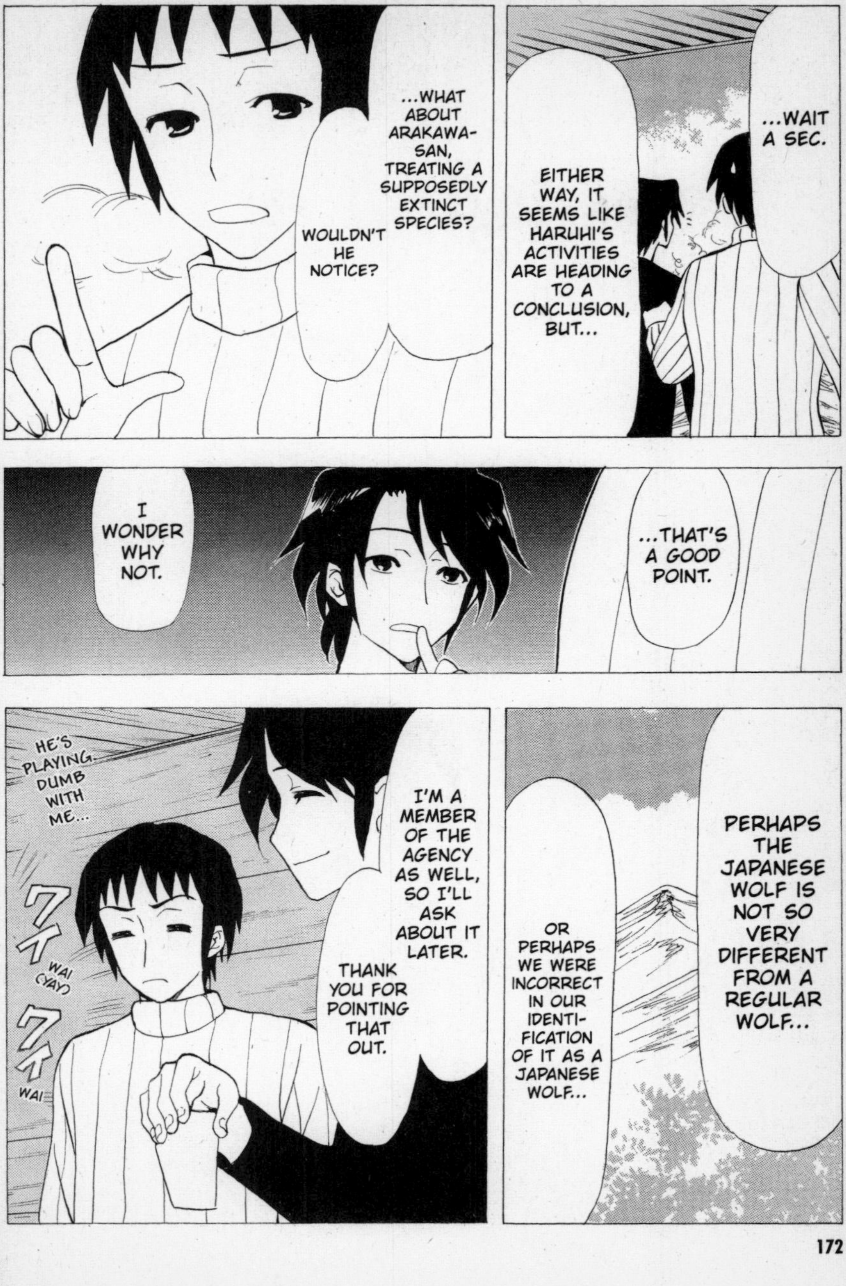
...WAIT A SEC.
EITHER WAY, IT SEEMS LIKE HARUHI'S ACTIVITIES ARE HEADING TO A CONCLUSION, BUT...
...WHAT ABOUT ARAKAWA-SAN, TREATING A SUPPOSEDLY EXTINCT SPECIES?
WOULDN'T HE NOTICE?
...THAT'S A GOOD POINT.
I WONDER WHY NOT.
PERHAPS THE JAPANESE WOLF IS NOT SO VERY DIFFERENT FROM A REGULAR WOLF...
OR PERHAPS WE WERE INCORRECT IN OUR IDENTIFICATION OF IT AS A JAPANESE WOLF...
I'M A MEMBER OF THE AGENCY AS WELL, SO I'LL ASK ABOUT IT LATER.
THANK YOU FOR POINTING THAT OUT.
HE'S PLAYING DUMB WITH ME...
ワイ
WAI (YAY)
ワイ
WAI

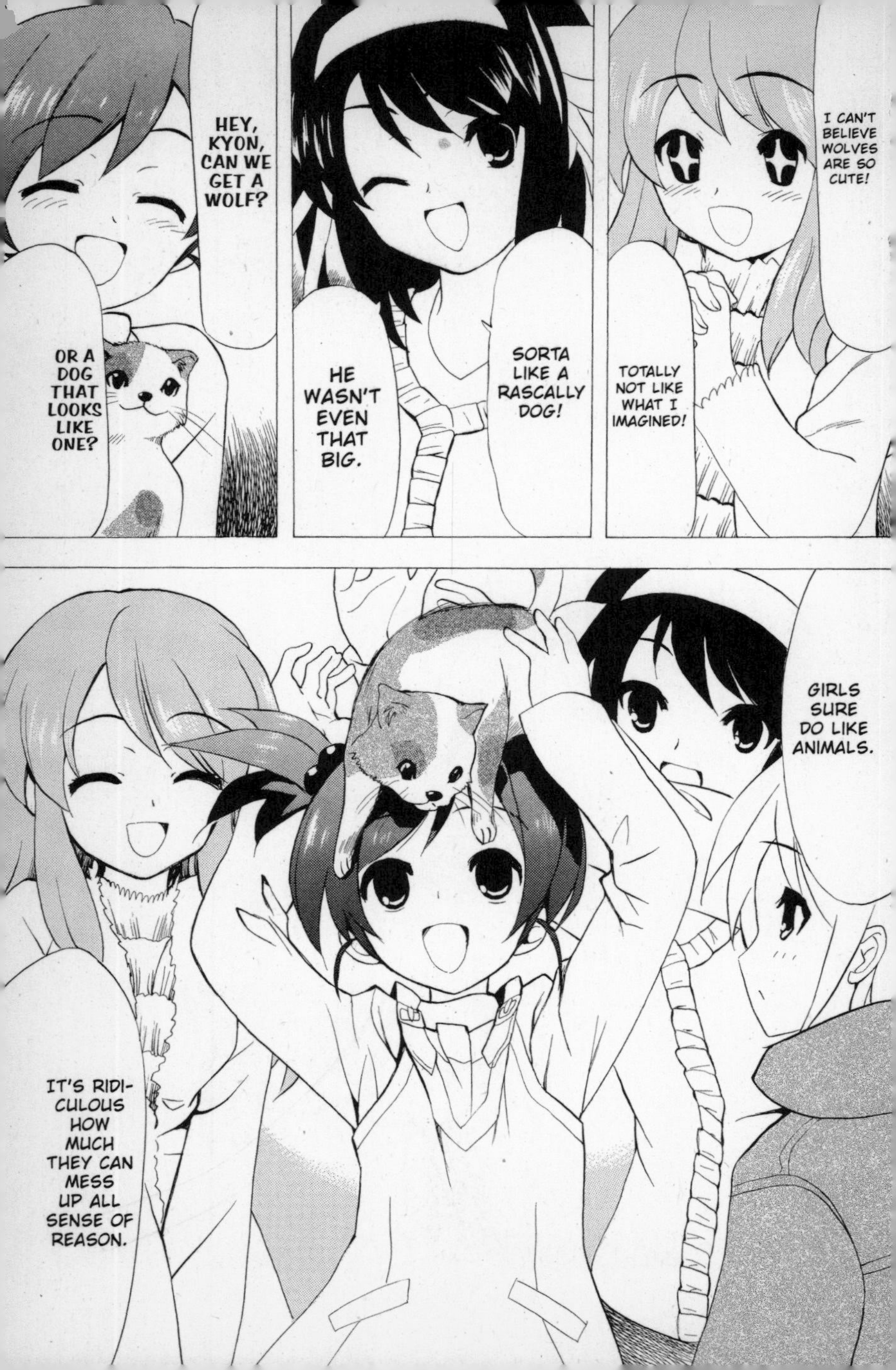
I CAN'T BELIEVE WOLVES ARE SO CUTE!
TOTALLY NOT LIKE WHAT I IMAGINED!
SORTA LIKE A RASCALLY DOG!
HE WASN'T EVEN THAT BIG.
HEY, KYON, CAN WE GET A WOLF?
OR A DOG THAT LOOKS LIKE ONE?
GIRLS SURE DO LIKE ANIMALS.
IT'S RIDICULOUS HOW MUCH THEY CAN MESS UP ALL SENSE OF REASON.

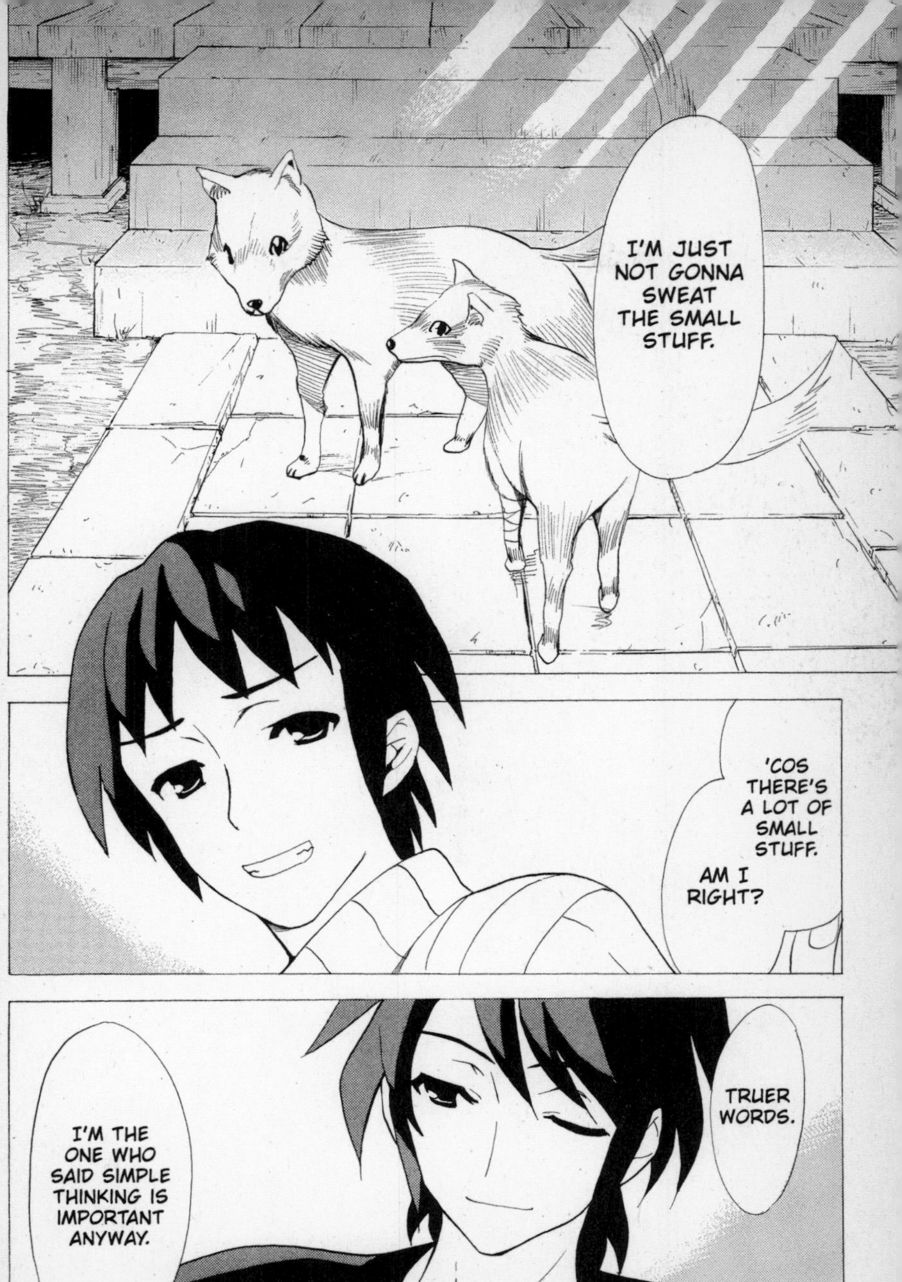
I'M JUST NOT GONNA SWEAT THE SMALL STUFF.
'COS THERE'S A LOT OF SMALL STUFF.
AM I RIGHT?
TRUER WORDS.
I'M THE ONE WHO SAID SIMPLE THINKING IS IMPORTANT ANYWAY.

Red Data Elegy : END

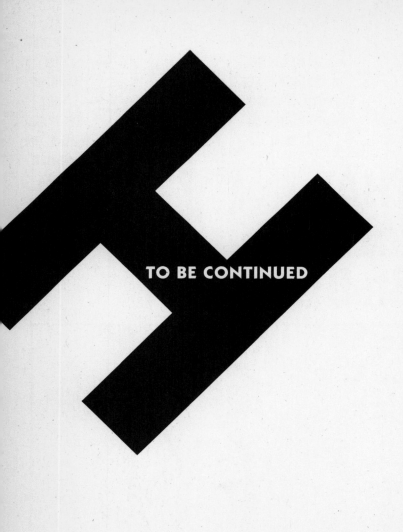

TO BE CONTINUED

It happened the evening they returned from the winter trip.

NOT JUST THAT— I WAS ORDERED TO GO WITH YOU AND NAGATO-SAN, AS A GROUP.
BUT WHEN I ASKED FOR DE-TAILS, THEY RE-FUSED TO SAY ANY-THING...

Kyon makes his decision and heads to a certain place with Nagato and Mikuru. It is...

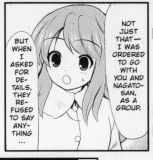

...THAT December 18th!!

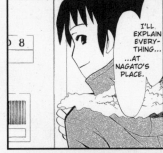

I'LL EXPLAIN EVERY-THING...
...AT NAGATO'S PLACE.

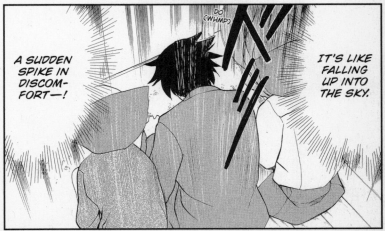

DO (WHMP)
IT'S LIKE FALLING UP INTO THE SKY.
A SUDDEN SPIKE IN DISCOM-FORT—!

OF ASAHINA MIKURU." AND "EDITOR IN CHIEF★FULL SPEED AHEAD!"

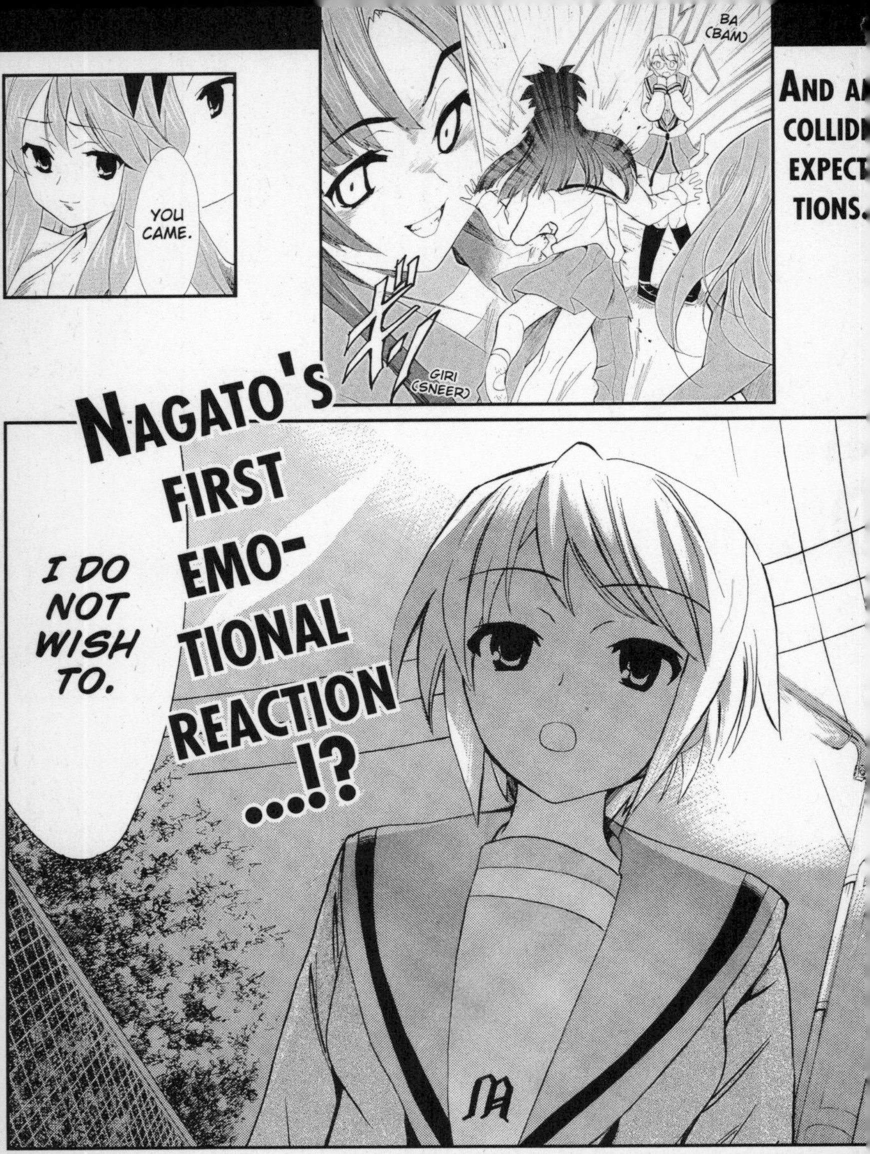
AND A
COLLIDI
EXPECT
TIONS.
BA (BAM)
GIRI (SNEER)
YOU CAME.
NAGATO'S FIRST EMO-TIONAL REACTION ...!?
I DO NOT WISH TO.

NEXT VOLUME:

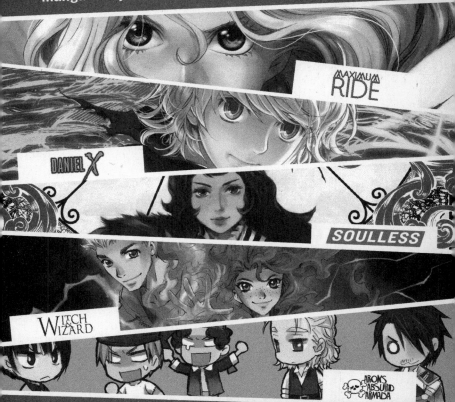

Can't wait for the next volume? You don't have to!

Keep up with the latest chapters of some of your favorite manga every month online in the pages of YEN PLUS!

MAXIMUM RIDE

DANIEL X

SOULLESS

WITCH & WIZARD

ARON'S ABSURD ARMADA

Visit us at www.yenplus.com for details!

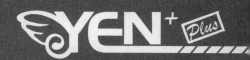

YEN⁺ Plus

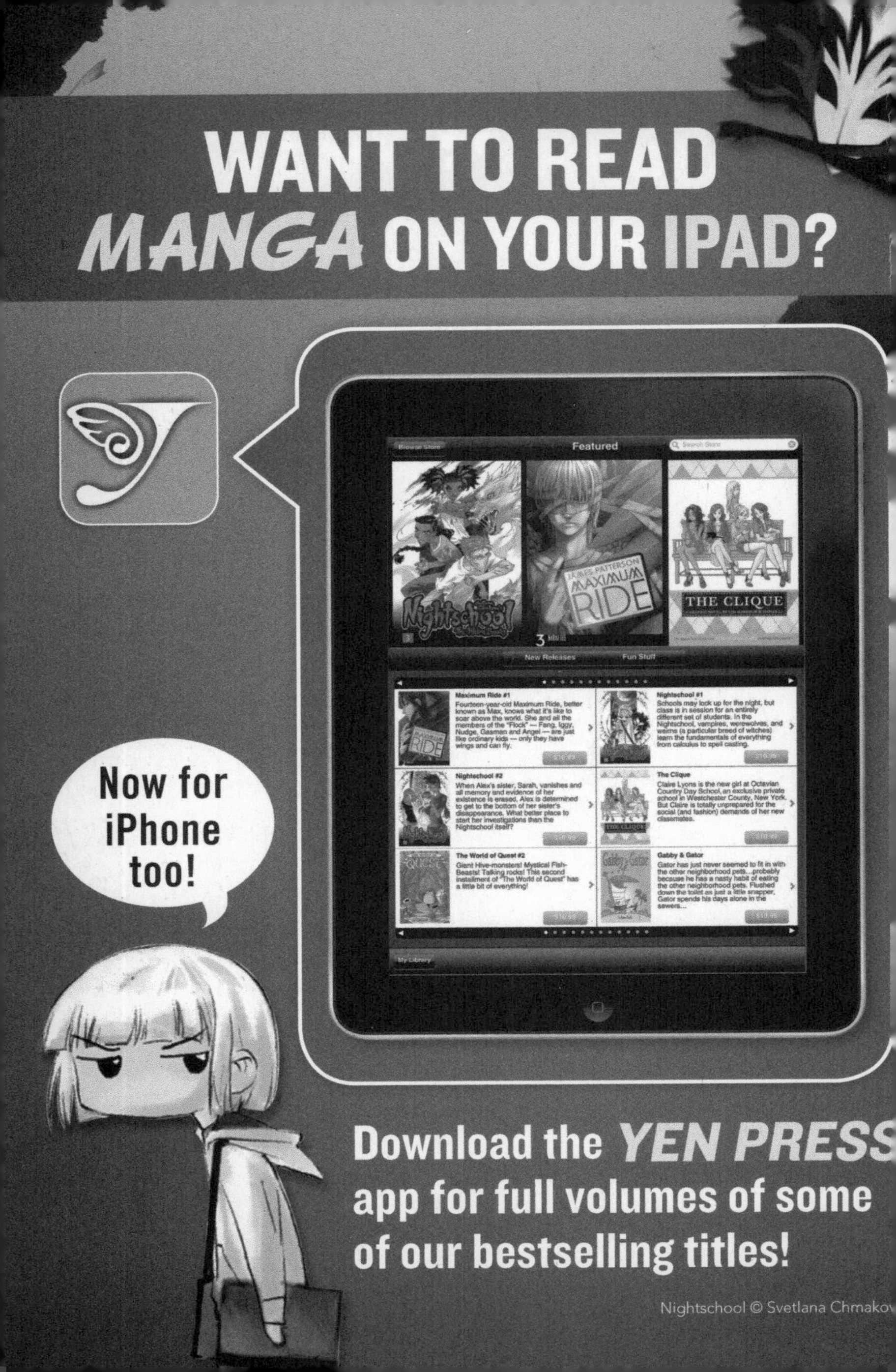
WANT TO READ
MANGA ON YOUR IPAD?
Now for iPhone too!
Download the YEN PRESS app for full volumes of some of our bestselling titles!
Nightschool © Svetlana Chmakova

THE MELANCHOLY OF HARUHI SUZUMIYA

P9-AEW-863

Original Story: Nagaru Tanigawa
Manga: Gaku Tsugano
Character Design: Noizi Ito

Translation: Paul Starr
Lettering: Alexis Eckerman

SUZUMIYA HARUHI NO YUUTSU Volume 11 © Nagaru TANIGAWA • Noizi ITO 2010 © Gaku TSUGANO 2010. First published in Japan in 2010 by KADOKAWA SHOTEN CO., LTD., Tokyo. English translation rights arranged with KADOKAWA SHOTEN CO., LTD., Tokyo through TUTTLE-MORI AGENCY, INC., Tokyo.

English translation © 2012 by Hachette Book Group, Inc.

Yen Press
Hachette Book Group
237 Park Avenue, New York, NY 10017

www.HachetteBookGroup.com
www.YenPress.com

Yen Press is an imprint of Hachette Book Group, Inc. The Yen Press name and logo are trademarks of Hachette Book Group, Inc.

First Yen Press Edition: February 2012

ISBN: 978-0-316-19576-8

10 9 8 7 6 5 4 3 2 1

BVG

Printed in the United States of America